The Universe behind Barbed Wire

Rochester Studies in East and Central Europe

Series Editor: Timothy Snyder, Yale University

Additional Titles of Interest

Witnessing Romania's Century of Turmoil:
Memoirs of a Political Prisoner
Nicolae Margineanu
Edited by Dennis Deletant

Plebeian Modernity:
Social Practices, Illegality, and the Urban Poor in Russia, 1906–1916
Ilya Gerasimov

Making Martyrs:
The Language of Sacrifice in Russian Culture from Stalin to Putin
Yuliya Minkova

The Balkans as Europe, 1821–1914
Edited by Timothy Snyder and Katherine Younger

An American in Warsaw:
Selected Writings of Hugh S. Gibson, US Minister to Poland, 1919–1924
Edited and annotated by Vivian Hux Reed
With M. B. B. Biskupski, Jochen Böhler, and Jan-Roman Potocki

Polish Literature and National Identity:
A Postcolonial Perspective
Dariusz Skórczewski
Translated by Agnieszka Polakowska

Beyond the Pale:
The Holocaust in the North Caucasus
Edited by Crispin Brooks and Kiril Feferman

Borders on the Move:
Territorial Change and Ethnic Cleansing
Leslie Waters

A complete list of titles in the Rochester Studies in East and Central Europe series may be found on our website, www.urpress.com.

The Universe behind Barbed Wire

Memoirs of a Ukrainian Soviet Dissident

Myroslav Marynovych

Translated by Zoya Hayuk

Edited by Katherine Younger

With a foreword by Timothy Snyder

University of Rochester Press

Published in cooperation with the Ukraine in European Dialogue program
of the Institute for Human Sciences (IWM) in Vienna.

Institut für die Wissenschaften vom Menschen
Institute for Human Sciences

First published 2021

Original Ukrainian edition: *Vsesvit za koli͡uchym drotom* by Myroslav Marynovych (Lviv: Ukrainian Catholic University Press, 2016).

University of Rochester Press
668 Mt. Hope Avenue, Rochester, NY 14620, USA
www.urpress.com
and Boydell & Brewer Limited
PO Box 9, Woodbridge, Suffolk IP12 3DF, UK
www.boydellandbrewer.com

ISBN-13: 978-1-58046-981-4; ISSN: 1528-4808

Library of Congress Cataloging-in-Publication Data

Names: Marynovych, Myroslav, 1949– author. | Hayuk, Zoya, translator. | Younger, Katherine, editor. | Snyder, Timothy, writer of foreword.
Title: The universe behind barbed wire : memoirs of a Soviet Ukrainian dissident / Myroslav Marynovych; translated by Zoya Hayuk ; edited by Katherine Younger ; with a foreword by Timothy Snyder
Other titles: Vsesvit za koli͡uchym drotom. English | Memoirs of a Soviet Ukrainian dissident
Description: Rochester, NY : University of Rochester Press, 2021. | Series: Rochester studies in East and Central Europe, 1528-4808 ; 26 | Includes bibliographical references and index.
Identifiers: LCCN 2020056171 (print) | LCCN 2020056172 (ebook) | ISBN 9781580469814 (hardback) | ISBN 9781787448322 (ebook)
Subjects: LCSH: Marynovych, Myroslav, 1949– | Dissenters—Ukraine—Biography. | Human rights workers—Ukraine—Biography. | Political prisoners—Ukraine—Biography. | Intellectuals—Ukraine—Biography. | Ukraïns′ka hromads′ka hrupa spryi͡anni͡a vykonanni͡u hel′sinks′kykh uhod (Kyïv, Ukraine)
Classification: LCC DK508.843.M37 A313 2021 (print) | LCC DK508.843.M37 (ebook) | DDC 365/.45092 [B]—dc23
LC record available at https://lccn.loc.gov/2020056171
LC ebook record available at https://lccn.loc.gov/2020056172

This publication is printed on acid-free paper. Printed in the United States of America.

To my dearest ones:

My mother, Liuba, my sister, Nadiika, and my wife, Liuba;
And to all those who had the courage
to love someone who was persecuted;
to not abandon someone deemed "articularly dangerous";
to shower a convict with gifts.

Contents

Foreword

Timothy Snyder

A young man named Myroslav Marynovych was arrested in 1977 for telling the truth about his country. The crime for which he was sentenced was the distribution of bulletins about human rights abuses in Soviet Ukraine. When he was arrested at twenty-eight, he was an agnostic. When he was released a decade later, he was a Christian ethicist and political thinker. This memoir is a humble, and a humbling, account of a man maturing in hell.

In the 1970s, human rights posed an unexpected challenge to Soviet power. Along with the United States, Canada, and every European state except Albania, the USSR signed the Helsinki Final Act in 1975. This treaty was a turning point in the Cold War. It confirmed existing boundaries, prepared the way for arms-control negotiations, and affirmed human rights. In the Soviet Union and its east European satellites, citizens seized upon the concept of human rights to define their own public activity. If human rights were now the law of the land, went their reasoning, it must be legal to document violations.

The Ukrainian Helsinki Group, which Marynovych joined in 1976, followed that logic. Its members published information about the harassment, arrests, trials, and sentences of Soviet citizens. This Ukrainian Helsinki Group's activity led directly to the persecution of its members, which was then recorded by those who remained. The milieu was loyal: some of those who were arrested refused to answer any questions at all; Marynovych claimed that he was personally responsible for all of the group's activities.

Myroslav Marynovych was arrested on April 23, 1977, interrogated for nearly a year, and tried on March 22, 1978. He was sentenced to seven years in the Gulag and to five more years in internal exile. The facility to which he was sent, Perm-36, was perhaps the most notorious camp of its time. In the 1970s and 1980s it was used for people deemed to have committed "especially dangerous crimes against the state": that is, prisoners of conscience.

In Perm-36 at this time, as throughout the Gulag during its entire history, a disproportionate number of the prisoners were Ukrainians.

Marynovych was released from Perm-36 on May 14, 1984, and sent to internal exile in Kazakhstan. The next year Mikhail Gorbachev became general secretary of the Communist Party of the Soviet Union. At a time of reform, the punishment of political prisoners became an embarrassment. Marynovych refused to petition for amnesty in early 1987 but was released later that year anyway, along with other dissidents. He returned from Kazakhstan to Ukraine, where he saw the Soviet Union come to an end in December 1991. He continued his civic engagement in independent Ukraine, culminating in his work as an instructor and administrator of the Ukrainian Catholic University in Lviv.

❧

Although this memoir begins with Marynovych's early life and concludes with his time in Kazakhstan, its center is the seven years that he spent as a prisoner of conscience in the Gulag. Its explicit theme is the meaning of incarceration for him. An implicit theme is how the national persecution of Ukrainians in the 1970s drew people such as Marynovych towards a form of dissidence that involved a universal ideal.

The concept of human rights can seem noble in its abstraction: certain obligations that every state must uphold with respect to everyone, flowing from an ethical ideal that no power can alter. Human rights could be a practical tool to use against Communist regimes, given the formal legal commitments they had made at Helsinki in 1975. Yet the nobility and the practicality do not quite explain the appeal. The dissidents of the time who are best remembered now, such as Václav Havel, spoke less of human rights as a concept or a tool, and more about their felt need to defend decency during the stale Communist 1970s. It had to do with the unperturbed living of an individual life, with all of its unpredictable commitments.

A concern with human rights, then, might or might not have to do with national questions. When it did, it was the sense that national expression and solidarity can make up part of a normal human life and might be inseparable from a personality. The idea was not that everyone must have a nationality—much less the same nationality—but rather that nationality was an element of the inner life of many individuals, such that suppression of nationality was also the suppression of the individual. A few snapshots from Marynovych's life before the Gulag reveal how the two issues are intertwined.

Marynovych, born to a Ukrainian family in western Ukraine in 1949, was educated in Ukrainian and Russian and spoke both languages. As an outstanding student in physics in high school, he was invited in 1967 to take a qualifying university exam in Kyiv, the capital of Soviet Ukraine. Knowing that he was taking a risk but wishing to be true to himself and his upbringing, he asked to take the (oral) examination in Ukrainian rather than Russian. In principle this was permitted, but in reality it was discouraged. He received a low mark, which prevented him from studying where and what he wanted and also amounted to a personal humiliation. Had he chosen to take the exam in Russian, everything might have been different. He studied instead at Lviv Polytechnic in western Ukraine.

Marynovych was drawn to Kyiv anyway, which he regarded as the center of everything Ukrainian and as the capital of some future independent Ukraine. This might have seemed a romantic idea in the 1970s when Kyiv was very much a Russian-speaking city. The Ukrainian language was associated with the provinces and the past. Few Soviet citizens, or indeed outside observers, imagined that the USSR might come to an end in their lifetimes. For Marynovych, the attraction of Kyiv was the presence of Ukrainians who chose to wear their culture on their sleeves, demonstrating who they were amidst the grayness around them. He was detained in May 1973 after he placed flowers at the foot of the monument to the Ukrainian national poet, Taras Shevchenko.

Russian colonialism emerges from within Soviet power in Marynovych's descriptions of life in Kyiv in the early 1970s. Marynovych recalls a Kyiv friend who was unable to summon an ambulance for his mother, who had just suffered a heart attack, because the dispatcher refused to take a call in Ukrainian. The distressed son was told to "speak a human language," which meant Russian. Later, when Marynovych was in the camp, he was required to speak Russian with his mother when she visited.

Yet what does it mean to be excluded from university admission and social advance by the use of one's native language, when in principle that language is officially endorsed? What does it mean to be arrested for laying flowers in front of a monument that is allowed to stand? This bespeaks a strange colonialism, one without a clear colonial mission. Ukrainians in the 1970s were expected to regard their own culture as backward but were given no grounds for seeing the Russian language as progressive—except in the purely personal sense that using it would make life easier. By that point, the basic idea was that Soviet culture was to be simplified for the pragmatic purposes of those who administered the state.

But what if some people found it easier to live by their own lights rather than for comfort and conformity? In the setting of the Soviet 1970s, the apparently abstract idea of human rights came down to the sense that a life ought to be lived for individual purposes rather than for the convenience of the powerful. In this situation, a dissident was someone who did not accept uniformity as an end in itself.

Ukraine was a challenge for the Soviet Union from the beginning to the end. Indeed, the national question always bedeviled Marxists. Was national loyalty an artifact of the feudal past, to disappear along with capitalist development, and thus irrelevant to the socialist future? Or might national identification actually arise with capitalism, making it a practical challenge for those wishing to make an international revolution? World War I had seen both workers and socialist leaders side with their own nations in a disastrous conflict that took tens of millions of lives. It was a demoralizing blow for the radical left. Lenin, however, drew from it the conclusion that capitalism had been pushed to the brink and that a revolt in the backward Russian Empire could push industrial nations into revolution and propel history forward to its next stage.

The Bolshevik Revolution of 1917 was meant to bring about a global conflagration, during which all national questions would collapse into nullity as the world turned socialist. It began in civil war and with wars against the nations on its borders. It ended roughly within the borders of the state where it had begun, having met national resistance on all sides. The USSR, established in 1922, was neither Russian nor global but something in between. It was an accumulation of national groups across Eurasia of which the Russians were the most numerous. The most important non-Russian territory of the old empire had been Ukraine, and it posed the greatest challenges for the Bolshevik experiment. Of all the national questions in the history of Communist politics, the Ukrainian-Russian proved to be the most important.

During the nineteenth century, the era of national movements, the lands of today's Ukraine were divided between the Russian Empire and the Habsburg monarchy. The Ukrainian national movement began in the 1820s in the Russian Empire, in eastern and central Ukraine. Taras Shevchenko (1814–1861), that national poet upon whose monument Marynovych laid flowers, exemplified European Romanticism. He defended a smaller language against a larger one and celebrated the past of the common people rather than the lineage of the powerful. For most of the nineteenth century, Ukrainian nation-building was a matter of collecting historical and ethnographic knowledge, an activity seen as a permissible part of a larger study of Russia. The Crimean War (1853–1856) and a Polish uprising (1863–1864) encouraged an attitude that identified the Russian language with the imperial state. In the 1860s and 1870s Russian imperial authorities suppressed the use of the Ukrainian language.

Ukrainian national activity shifted across the border to the Habsburg monarchy, known from 1867 as Austria-Hungary. Thanks to a free press and elections, national politics could flourish. Ukrainians in Austria-Hungary also had something like their own church. The Uniate Church, formed in 1596 with the ambition of merging Western- and Eastern-rite churches, was dissolved within the Russian Empire beginning in 1839. This church survived, however, under the Habsburg emperors, who renamed it "Greek Catholic," as it is still known today. One of Marynovych's grandfathers was a Greek Catholic priest. (Married men are permitted to become Greek Catholic priests.) The eastern part of the Habsburg crownland of Galicia became the center of the Ukrainian national movement, though it was always understood that the Ukrainian heartland lay across the border in the Russian Empire.

World War I brought national self-determination to much of eastern Europe but not to Ukraine. This was not for lack of effort. Ukrainians of the Habsburg monarchy established a West Ukrainian state, which was defeated by the Poles. Ukrainians in Kyiv founded another republic after the Russian Revolution of November 1917. Ukrainian territory was a major theater of the civil war between the Reds and the Whites, the armies of revolution and of restoration. In 1919, the Polish army intervened as an ally of the state based in Kyiv. After a brief conquest of Kyiv, the Poles (and their Ukrainian allies) were pushed back to the outskirts of Warsaw by the Red Army in summer 1920. A counterattack that August defeated the Red Army and brought the fighting to an end. The result was a peace treaty in 1921 and a Polish-Soviet border in which eastern Galicia (and some other territories inhabited chiefly by Ukrainians) was incorporated by Poland, whereas the majority of Ukrainian lands remained under Bolshevik rule.

The Red Army was meant to march through Warsaw and on to Berlin. The end of combat in Europe in 1920 was also the end of expectations that the Bolshevik Revolution was the beginning of a global transformation. Bolshevik Russia had to become a state, and the Ukrainian question influenced the form that this state took: a Soviet Union, a nominal federation of national republics. The experience of the revolution had taught that the national question was inevitable. Almost no one at the time doubted that Ukraine was a nation; the question was how to square that historical reality with the vision of a socialist future. The Soviet solution in the 1920s was "Ukrainization": the promotion of Ukrainians within the state and party apparatus and the support of Ukrainian culture, in the expectation that this would create political loyalty. The 1920s were thus a rich decade for Ukrainian art, literature, and scholarship, so much so that a number of activists who had earlier chosen Galicia (and after 1918 found themselves in Poland) moved east to Soviet Ukraine.

Ukrainization worked reasonably well so long as the Soviet revolution hung suspended between the seizure of political power in 1917 and the Communist mission to create a planned economy. Ukrainization coincided in time with the New Economic Policy, which legalized a certain amount of free enterprise and allowed farmers to own land and work it as they chose. This was important in Ukraine, where the struggle for private property had been intense (and sometimes violent) during the latter decades of the Russian Empire. In the late 1920s, however, Stalin was consolidating power; in 1928 he undertook the second great transformation: the economic revolution. Its central element was a forced industrialization campaign to be financed by extracting capital from agriculture. Stalin spoke of an internal colonization: richer agricultural regions such as Ukraine would be sacrificed in the name of development and progress.

In practice, this meant seizing farmland from peasants, forcing them to work in collective farms, exporting grain for hard currency, and exploiting the labor of those who resisted in concentration camps. As this collectivization of agriculture failed to improve crop yields, Stalin blamed Ukrainian officials and Ukrainians in general. Cultural policies that favored Ukrainians were halted, and the new generation of activists purged. Leading writers were executed or committed suicide. Because Stalin treated the problem in Ukraine as one of political resistance, collectivization was sharpened in 1932. The collective farms and villages that failed to meet production targets had their livestock seized and were cut off from the rest of the economy. Peasants were forbidden from traveling to cities to beg and locked in barracks to starve in the dark if they tried. Inhabitants of Soviet Ukraine were forbidden from leaving the republic. The result was death by hunger of nearly four million people. Marynovych refers to this atrocity as the *Holodomor*.

Such sharp alterations in Soviet policy towards Ukraine had little to do with actions taken by Ukrainians and much to do with larger demands of domestic or foreign policy. Given its agricultural potential, Western geographical location, and demographic weight, Ukraine was always in a sensitive position. It mattered greatly to the Soviet leadership but had no meaningful representation within the Soviet system, which was based upon central control by a small group of party leaders.

☙

The reversal in policy towards Ukrainians from the 1920s to the 1930s was characteristic. Although later shifts were never so drastic as that between affirmative action and mass starvation, the question as to whether Ukraine was to be treated as a threat or an asset was never firmly resolved. After Germany and its allies invaded the Soviet Union in 1941, Ukraine was suddenly important again, as the terrain of battles and as the Soviet republic (with the exception of Belarus) that suffered the most from German occupation. Stalin thus referred to wartime Ukraine as a heroic. Once Germany was defeated, however, a policy of cultural centralization followed in 1946. A certain relaxation followed Stalin's death in 1953. Under his successor, Nikita Khrushchev, Ukrainians protested for cultural autonomy and against Russification.

A diverse "1960s group" of writers, artists, and scientists, the *shistdesiatnyky*, led a cultural flowering comparable to that of the 1920s. Between 1963 and 1972 Petro Shelest was first secretary of the Ukrainian section of the party; he allowed these trends a certain space for development. These were the years when Marynovych was a teenager and a university student. This tendency was reversed by Leonid Brezhnev, who had Shelest replaced as the Ukrainian first secretary in 1972. Marynovych completed studies at Lviv Polytechnic in that year, worked for a while in Lviv, performed his army service, and arrived in Kyiv in 1974. He was coming to a Kyiv that was once again subject to intense Russification. This mattered a great deal. But it also mattered where he was coming from.

☙

Marynovych was born in 1949 in eastern Galicia. This territory had belonged to the Habsburgs until 1918 and then to Poland from 1918 until 1939. Although Ukrainians in Poland suffered various forms of discrimination, Ukrainian political and social life was far less hindered in the 1930s than in Soviet Ukraine. In interwar Poland, Ukrainians were harassed and discriminated against, but the basic shape of Ukrainian society remained intact. Traditions of religious practice, economic cooperatives, local media, and national politics continued. Ukrainian society in Poland was spared the mass starvation and terror of the 1930s.

The dominant trend in Ukrainian politics in interwar Poland was democratic and centrist. One minor strain of Ukrainian politics was the Organization of Ukrainian Nationalists, which directed violence against Polish moderates who sought to improve Polish-Ukrainian relations. In 1939, when Poland was destroyed, these nationalists took on a greater role. Nazi Germany and the Soviet Union, fighting then as de facto allies under the terms of the Molotov-Ribbentrop pact, invaded from the west and east. After Poland's defeat, its lands were divided between the conquerors, with the Soviet Union taking roughly the eastern half. In late 1939 eastern Galicia was annexed by the Soviet Union. In less than two years, these territories were subjected to the Soviet policies of the previous two decades: deportations, terror, nationalizations, collectivization. Ukrainian nationalists had opposed Polish rule; they had seen Germany as the agent that could destroy Poland. Now they hoped that Germany could destroy the USSR.

When Germany invaded the Soviet Union in 1941, the first lands the *Wehrmacht* reached were precisely those, such as eastern Galicia, which had just been incorporated into the Soviet Union. In eastern Galicia and indeed throughout Soviet Ukraine, much of the population expected that German rule would be preferable to Soviet collectivization and terror. Jews suffered first and most, as victims of a German campaign of mass shooting that brought in ever more local accomplices. The vast majority of Jews in Ukraine were murdered in 1941 and 1942, usually shot over pits close to where they had lived. Because Germans kept the hated collective farms, starved prisoners of war, and engaged in murderous terror, Ukrainian opinion turned against them.

After the Red Army defeated the Germans at Stalingrad in February 1943, turning the tide of the war, Ukrainian nationalists in western Ukraine formed a partisan army known as the UPA. Its plan was to allow the Soviets to defeat the Germans, and then to seize power from the Soviets. In 1943 it ethnically cleansed local Poles. It did indeed engage the Soviets in a bloody and doomed war, which was coming to an end when Marynovych was born. Soviet power continued the ethnic cleansing, forcing Ukrainians and Poles across the border established between Soviet Ukraine and a newly Communist Poland in 1945. Marynovych's family was expelled from its village by the new Polish Communist regime. These expulsions were presented in Polish Communist propaganda as a response to Ukrainian nationalism.

In the Gulag, Marynovych met Ukrainians of an older generation who were serving out very long sentences for resisting Soviet power by force.

Marynovych was thus a child of a displaced family in a territory that had been under Soviet rule for a very short time. Eastern Galicia had been drastically altered by the mass murder of Jews and the expulsion of Poles. It became Ukrainian in this negative demographic sense and Soviet in a political sense at the same time. Ukrainians in eastern Galicia found themselves, for the first time, a demographic majority in towns and cities such as Drohobych (where Marynovych was raised) and Lviv (where he studied). They were living within a larger unit called "Ukraine," but it was a Soviet republic without sovereignty. The institutions that had marked and supported Ukrainian civil society in eastern Galicia for decades, such as cooperatives and newspapers, were no longer possible. The Greek Catholic Church was forcibly merged into the Russian Orthodox Church, which was subordinate to Soviet power. Greek Catholic leaders, including Metropolitan Josyf Slipyj, were deported to the Gulag. Slipyj was held in the camps until 1963; Marynovych refers to his memoirs, which were published by the Ukrainian Catholic University.

Marynovych was thus raised in the 1950s and 1960s in western Soviet Ukraine in an environment where a special religious commitment hung in the background, although he regarded himself as an agnostic. He took Soviet power for granted as a young person and sympathized with Communism. In the late 1960s and early 1970s, so long as Shelest was first secretary in Ukraine, it was reasonable to think that some kind of secular Ukrainian identity would be permissible within the Soviet Union. Yet in Kyiv, Marynovych experienced new kinds of barriers. His arrest for laying flowers was symptomatic of larger changes. Beginning in 1972, Ukrainian writers and activists were systematically arrested and imprisoned. Brezhnev had consolidated power, Shelest lost his position, and a new calculation drove these repressions.

Brezhnev was less ideological than his forebears and less ambitious. He turned the official gaze from the future to the past, setting aside the dream of Communism in favor of a cult of World War II. The present was to be consumerist but without any of the political values of the West. The Soviet Union was therefore to become functional, served by educated classes with technical degrees who spoke Russian. Eventually the Soviet peoples would merge as a result of "real socialism," which Brezhnev claimed already existed. Ukrainians were expected to sacrifice their nationality but not in the service of any universal ideal. Ukrainian books would be removed from schools and the Ukrainian language would be marginalized in universities, but just why that should be was unclear.

Identity was to be sacrificed to efficiency. People were understood to be a means to an end, but there was in fact no end: except, perhaps, the self-preservation of an aging elite.

The Russification of the 1970s intruded into private lives. For a young Galician Ukrainian in the metropolis such as Marynovych, it felt like a restraint on normal camaraderie. In his account of the mid-1970s in Kyiv, social life blends into national life: his closest friend at the time is another committed Ukrainian. He speaks to his friends in his native language; he speaks his native language in public; he commemorates the Ukrainian past with his friends. As he puts it, his transgression was "trying to live a normal Ukrainian life" in the capital of Soviet Ukraine.

As his interrogators made clear to him in 1977, the problem was not his internal convictions but his public actions. This was no longer the 1930s, when Stalin famously said that Soviet citizens could be punished for their thoughts. That era of great terror was also a moment of grand vision, of a New Soviet Man who could be refashioned and repurposed. By the 1970s the Soviet secret police had no such ambitions. It made no sense to inflict pain in the name of a bright future that was no longer on offer. In Marynovych's account, his interrogators would have been perfectly content with hypocrisy. A good Soviet citizen was not a believer but someone who kept his disbelief to himself and behaved like everyone else. Power was no longer about changing the internal self but about quarantining it. What was normal was to conform.

Marynovych seemed to have other ideas about what was normal. It was normal for him to live as he pleased. When times got tough, as they did, it was normal to behave honorably, because that is what friends and family would expect. Normal was not what *was* but what *should be*. This kind of everyday idealism about the shape of an individual life fit the idea of human rights, which was just coming into currency.

Ironically, the Soviet Union had endorsed human rights in 1975 as part of an effort to keep things as they were. In the Helsinki Final Act, the signatories had endorsed the territorial status quo. This was what Brezhnev wanted: stasis. Yet the price he paid was the affirmation of a universal idea that generated demands for change. That created an implicit problem for Brezhnev's real socialism. In his version of history, everything was as good as it could be, all ideals had been fulfilled insofar as this was possible, and there was nothing more to be said. When ideology is insincere, it is difficult to challenge it with another ideology. Human rights offered not an alternative vision of the future but a different framing of the here and now.

If what mattered was the present, then what mattered in the present was the individual human life. A life could only be individual if a person was allowed to articulate and realize some of the values that seemed normal. The language of human rights communicated the desirability of a relationship between the inner life and the outer. It should be normal for a person to be able to act out at least a few preferences and convictions, rather than holding them all inside and lying all the time. It should be normal for people to have a certain freedom in life, to express their own views, to choose their own culture. Activity on behalf of human rights meant recording glaring violations by the state: arrests, repressions, deportations—very often for nothing more than speaking about human rights.

Human rights thus provided some Soviet citizens, such as Marynovych and his friends in the Ukrainian Helsinki Group, with a way to directly challenge the implicit Soviet value of conformity without directly challenging its explicit ideology of socialism. These dissidents emphasized their own lawfulness by declaring their activity openly and claiming that their only intention was to dignify the Soviet Union's own commitment to law. Soviet authorities recognized the implicit threat immediately and sought to break the human rights networks that emerged after 1975. Human rights activism was treated as the most dangerous form of political crime, and activists were sentenced accordingly.

During his work for the Ukrainian Helsinki Group, Marynovych was asked by a friend whether he was ready for prison. The question gave him pause. He knew that incarceration was coming, but he could hardly have known what it would be like. When he was arrested, he was a young man with some ethical commitments, good friends, and a mother and sister he regarded as models. During his interrogation he experienced an epiphany; by the time he was sentenced, he was a Christian believer. In the camp he became a philosopher: writing sentence by sentence on purloined scraps of paper, each of which had to be rolled up, hidden, and then eventually smuggled out of the camp in a way that will be familiar to those who know something of these matters.

The Gulag held tens of millions of prisoners and caused millions of deaths, and yet it has been all but forgotten by the official Russia of today. Perm-36, as it happens, was the very last worthy memorial to the Gulag on the site of a former camp. It served for a time as a humble but valuable museum of the Gulag as a whole, while hundreds of other camps were disassembled or allowed to return to wilderness. Then Perm-36 fell victim to Vladimir Putin's politics of memory. After Russia invaded Ukraine in 2014, the museum was labeled a foreign agent, on the logic that it glorified Ukrainian fascists. The old Soviet propaganda flourishes in Putin's Russia: prisoners of conscience and enemies of Russia merge. The museum has been altered to help the visitor identify with the camp guards.

What is left of the Gulag, then, are the state archives used by historians and the memories of survivors. The most famous of these is Aleksandr Solzhenitsyn, whose *Gulag Archipelago*, published in Russian in 1973 and in translation a year later, finally opened the discussion of Soviet concentration camps in the West. Earlier Gulag memoirs were written by people of Polish or Polish-Jewish background who could compare what they called "the land of the prisoners" (Julius Margolin, 1949), the "inhuman land" (Józef Czapski, 1949), or the "other world" (Gustaw Herling-Grudziński, 1951), with the world beyond the Soviet Union. The Ukrainian Danylo Shumuk, who spent three decades in the Gulag, published his recollections in 1984. Metropolitan Slipyj's memoirs, including his recollections of eighteen years in the Gulag, appeared in 2014.

Marynovych's descriptions of Perm-36, which he and other inmates called "the zone," must be read carefully because he evinces a certain manly tendency to describe the perils and the tortures indirectly, only as necessary for the development of an anecdote or a theme. This is a style he developed in his letters to his mother and sister.

Perm-36 was a "special regime" punishment facility, designed for people designated as dangers to the state. In 1978, when Marynovych began his sentence, about sixty prisoners were held behind its seven layers of barbed wire. Most of them, like Marynovych, were sentenced for words they had spoken, published, or distributed. A disproportionate number were Ukrainians. Some inmates were members of an earlier generation, punished for their armed resistance to Soviet power (in the UPA, for example). People of various nationalities had been sentenced as collaborators with the German occupation regime. It was characteristic of Soviet policy to confuse prisoners of conscience with Nazis. The association of Ukrainian political life with fascism has continued in Russia since the end of the Soviet Union, notably during the Russian invasion of Ukraine in 2014.

In Marynovych's account of prison, the reader will find several distinct kinds of cruelty above and beyond the inherent cruelty of years isolated from the world at hard labor. Perm-36 was located not in the city of Perm, which is about nine hundred miles east of Moscow, but about sixty miles further northeast—in the middle of nowhere. The climate was forbidding: not as lethal as other camps in the far north, but still below freezing all day and all night for five months of the year. The work itself was dangerous. Marynovych, who had fainting spells, was assigned work as a lathe operator. The prisoners were subject to rules that could not possibly all be followed. Not making a bed properly (in the eyes of a guard), failing to meet the dress code (in the eyes of a guard), or showing "disrespect" to guards could all result in punishment. Psychological abuse was the norm. Prisoners were told that their friends had betrayed them to the police and that their wives had betrayed them with their friends; guards and secret policemen went to great lengths to make the inmates believe that they were all alone.

Health problems led to medical torture. Prisoners who fell ill or who required surgery were told that they had to promise to improve their behavior (in other words, acknowledge their guilt) before they would receive medical treatment. Mykola Rudenko, a fellow inmate and member of the Ukrainian Helsinki Group, had been injured in World War II and classified as an invalid. That status was revoked inside Perm-36 in 1982 about four decades after he had been injured, when he was sixty-one years old. He was then assigned to labor he could not complete and punished for not fulfilling his quota. Prisoners responded to such outrages with sympathy hunger strikes for which they were sent to punishment cells. These were dark, cold chambers with water or ice on the floors and walls, uneven planks for beds, and no plumbing. It was routine for prisoners to be sent to the punishment cells for six-month terms. The careful reader will realize that much of Marynovych's seven-year sentence was spent in punishment cells, usually for such expressions of solidarity.

Marynovych, who was a young man serving his first term in the Gulag, makes a point of saying that he learned how to behave from other prisoners of conscience. In his account, the dissidents generally supported one another. Within the narrow confines of the camp, issues that might have been divisive outside, such as the national question, became topics of fruitful discussion. Marynovych notes that time in the camp "changed many things for the

Russian inmate," who was now in a minority and confronted with people whose national identifications were intermingled with their choice to suffer for human rights. He recalls debates about whether the Soviet system was to be understood as totalitarian or imperial. He records that a Ukrainian-Jewish dialogue about history began in the camp. This encounter among prisoners was continued by some of them, such as Joseph Zissels and Marynovych himself, after their release. Today, Jewish-Ukrainian history is a major subject of teaching and research at Marynovych's Ukrainian Catholic University.

Human rights activists recorded and published facts. The idea was that the regime should be held to the standard that it had formally accepted and that only the evidence of human lives disrupted by repression could serve this purpose. This work, incredibly, continued within Perm-36 itself. Prisoners continually wrote letters to higher authorities about their treatment, knowing that this could only redound to their personal disadvantage. As Marynovych recalls, "We never deviated from the truth, because the truth itself could be more condemning than any words. Likewise, reality itself could be more cynical than any description thereof." Prisoners who wrote such letters were punished inside the camp for "distorting Soviet reality." Speaking truthfully of personal experience in a punitive Soviet institution was the cause for more punishment in that institution.

The truthfulness of this memoir runs deep. Marynovych's personal honesty about his life blends into a rare and attractive humility. He writes openly about the foolishness of his own youth and that of his friends in Kyiv of the early 1970s. We see his immaturity because he is mature enough to reveal it. He accepts that his life might have gone entirely differently: if he had gotten a better job or had chosen a less morally demanding set of friends. He believes that his actions reflected the moral example of his mother and sister rather than any particular virtues of his own.

The moral risk, as he sees it, is taking pride in doing the right thing. He chose to go to prison in the defense of values and then had to resist what he calls "infectious bouts of glory." The prose runs along two tracks: the physical and the metaphysical. "One half [of me] was involved in the normal physical survival of a political prisoner, carving out my living space in daily resistance to the camp administration. My other half continued to hover in metaphysical space, accumulating more 'bumps' while experimenting and perfecting my religious mindfulness." He believes that there was "no better opportunity to test one's Christian devotion" than in the Gulag.

Perhaps the greatest challenge of this memoir to most readers will be its discussion of freedom. It will be tempting for people in the West to imagine that they were free in the 1970s and 1980s, and that the book that they hold in their hands is a description of Soviet unfreedom. This is not quite Marynovych's position. Of course he leaves a clear record of the horrors of the camp ("the zone") and of the Soviet Union itself ("the big zone"). And yet Marynovych speaks of himself and his companions as free people.

Freedom involves consistency between the inner life and the outer. This means that there must be some inner life, some set of commitments to religious, ethical, or aesthetic values that fix upon the world as it should be—as opposed to the world as it is. Freedom would also then require some ability to realize those values in the outside world or, failing that, taking risks or suffering for them. This is what Marynovych and his fellow prisoners of conscience had done.

Marynovych chose the values he wished to defend. Because he made a choice, he can characterize his own actions as a sacrifice, as suffering that was meaningful. The pain had a sense, because it closed the gap between a flawed outer world and the values held by people. In such a sacrifice, he writes, it is the sufferer who retains agency, whereas the torturer is pushed to the margins. As he recognizes, this ability to tell his own story puts him in a different position from people who are wrongly imprisoned but who did not choose the occasion.

Freedom, we have come to think, is about giving in to impulse, and complaining when that is not possible. Yet the more impulsive our actions are, the more they realize some transient emotion, the more likely they are to reflect the power of someone or something else. If we give in to impulse, then our interior life withers, and the outer world determines everything. This process is complete when we concede the word freedom itself, assigning it to our moments of unthinking rage and to our bestial selves. When we see no difference between freedom and instinct, the story of freedom ends.

It might not seem like freedom to stick your head in a latrine. We find offal physically revolting. We retch. Our senses and our nerves urge us to move away. In Perm-36, when a Russian poet had a birthday, his friends each composed poems for him and recited them the only way that he could hear them, which was through the tunnels dug for excrement. Hearing the poems brought the man joy. Only free people could have thought of such a gesture and carried it through. Marynovych realizes that the image will be puzzling for readers and stresses that doing this seemed natural at the time. He quotes Semen Gluzman's memoir: in Perm-36 "we created our own world, and we were free."

Marynovych faces down the most basic of instincts. He undertook several hunger strikes, an action that works directly against physical necessity. At one point he starved himself for twenty days in solidarity with a fellow inmate, the Russian Sergei Kovalev, who had undertaken a hunger strike. "Your self-preservation instinct," he writes, "cries out at the top of its voice when you are staring down the barrel of a machine gun, surrounded by vicious trained dogs, suffocating in overcrowded vehicles, so exhausted by malnutrition that your body swells up . . . But just as heroism is not eternal, neither is fear."

Marynovych believes that "the suffering that I endured provided me with the spiritual strength that gave my life its true meaning." That metaphysical meaning is an encounter with God. The earthly meaning arises in communion with others: with fellow inmates with whom and for whom he suffered, with fellow Ukrainians, with fellow Soviet citizens, with all those whose human rights were and are violated. Solidarity expresses a free choice.

Acknowledgments

I would like to express my great appreciation to the Rectorate of the Ukrainian Catholic University for providing me with the practical opportunity to work on my memoir and fulfill all other necessary duties connected with the publication of the book in Ukrainian at the Ukrainian Catholic University Press. I wish to acknowledge the help provided by the UCU Development Department and Ukrainian Catholic Education Foundation, in the United States, in searching for necessary funds.

I would like to offer my special thanks to the following for the financial and practical support during the process of writing, publication in Ukrainian, and translation into English: the Porticus Foundation, the Netherlands-Germany; the Wolodymyr and Stefania Lech Endowment Fund (WSLEF) within the Ukrainian Catholic Education Foundation, Canada; Roman Kozak, a benefactor from Moscow; and Onno Hansen from Amsterdam.

I express my gratitude to Ms. Zoya Hayuk for the translation of my text from Ukrainian into English, as well as Dr. Frances Forde Plude and Dr. Andriy Sorokowsky, both from the United States, for assistance in editing the English translation and providing me with valuable advice.

I am particularly grateful to Dr. Timothy Snyder, Richard C. Levin Professor of History at Yale University, and the editorial board of the University of Rochester Press as a whole for approving my book for publication in the Rochester Studies in East and Central Europe series. My special thanks are extended to Dr. Sonia Kane, editorial director of the University of Rochester Press, for solving many practical issues connected with the publication, and historian Dr. Katherine Younger for final editing of the manuscript.

Finally, I wish to thank my wife Liuba for her encouragement throughout my writing and invaluable support in editing the Ukrainian version of the book.

Note to the Reader

In the body of the text, a modified Library of Congress system is used for names: soft signs are omitted, and final "-yi" and "-ii" are rendered "y." Place and personal names with an established usage in the Latin alphabet are given in that form (e.g., Josyf Slipyj instead of Iosyf Slipy). Footnotes preserve standard Library of Congress transliteration. Footnotes also preserve the language of the document cited; names are therefore given in their Russian transliteration if the document itself is in Russian.

All biblical quotations use the New Revised Standard Version (NRSV).

Footnotes with the initials "M. M." are by the author; all others are contributed by Katherine Younger.

Introduction

And may Ararat, at least, remain beneath our feet—
A sliver of solace amidst a deluge of apprehension—
Sooner or later the water will recede, and the meadows will become green again.

—From a letter to my wife, Liuba, during my internal exile,
February 11, 1987

In my lifetime I have lived several lives, and they are separated from each other either by painful dramas or by radical transformations. And thus, the trunk of the tree of my life, as befits any tree, contains distinct rings. Two of those rings—the dissident and the inmate—are special, truly granted by God. It is a great blessing to have been instrumental in the demise of, as Yevhen Sverstiuk put it, an "empire of bent backs, humbly devoted faces, and raised arms."[1] For such a life, full of strife and challenges, you can only be grateful to Providence.

For the longest time I have had the feeling that every person is just one musical note on the heavenly keyboard, and once in a while that note is pressed by the finger of the Divine Pianist. It is a miracle indeed when you are the note that is required in His melody. But God will not hold his finger on your note forever. Inevitably there comes a time for you to humbly acknowledge that other notes are resonating nearby: your fervor declines, various health complaints begin to emerge, and then all grandiose plans go topsy-turvy.

Still, if one believes Ecclesiastes, both of these times have great meaning.

My description of the Ukrainian Helsinki Group, as indeed everything that I write in these memoirs, is obviously subjective. Will my account, however, be faithful to the truth? After all, so many years have gone by. . . .

1 Yevhen Sverstiuk (1928–2014): publicist, political prisoner, and fellow member of the Ukrainian Helsinki Group. Quote: Ievhen Sverstiuk, "30 zhovtnia – Den' politv'iazniv," October 30, 2007, http://khpg.org/index.php?id=1193709311.

Sometimes I catch myself thinking that some basic things might have fallen from my memory. Some mistakes may well be inevitable.

But I assure you that there are no deliberate fabrications. Once you begin to write something, it's important to do so with a sense of civic responsibility. My memoirs might differ from those of others. After all, each participant in those events carries with them their own mental recording of those turbulent years and their own "hologram" of the Ukrainian Helsinki Group.

My goal is not to produce a witness statement for a second Nuremberg trial, although I have no doubt that the Communist system certainly deserves such a trial. Indeed, the world cannot evolve if it does not condemn its Communist insanities. But I am writing a memoir—not the prosecution's closing arguments. Nevertheless, I write with the absolute conviction that my story would certainly be sufficient to find the Communist system guilty.

Far more important to me than any condemnatory testimony, however, is the love of those dear to me, the camaraderie of my friends, the nobility of sacrifice, and the spark of humanity in criminals. For surely the chronicle of Satan's deeds is not as majestic as the shining traces of God's light, which warmed my soul in bondage. His light can brighten the darkness of any prison.

Part One

In the Role of a Moth That Is Drawn to the Light

Chapter One

Establishing the Fundamentals of Fate

How I Became a "Homo Erectus"

My life as a dissident began in the office of a KGB officer. He was responsible for the so-called First Department of the Positron factory in the western Ukrainian city of Ivano-Frankivsk.[1] I had just returned from a business trip to Kyiv, where on May 22, 1973, I had been detained by the police, on KGB orders, for placing flowers at the Taras Shevchenko monument.[2] For a provincial KGB functionary this was an extraordinary event, one that left him vulnerable to being reprimanded. After all, one of his charges had transgressed—and before the very eyes of the capital's KGB at that! So, he harshly chastised me. But when he saw that his paternalistic exhortations were not having the desired effect, he warned me sternly: "Keep in mind, if you're not with us, you're against us!" I replied calmly: "Fine, then I'm against you."

I still marvel at how I found the courage to voice such a bold declaration. Today I would have been more cautious. At that time, however, I experienced an incredible sense of release—like a woman in childbirth, who upon

1 The Positron factory, opened in 1971, produced semiconductors, mainly for the defense industry. By the late 1980s, the factory employed approximately ten thousand workers.

2 Poet Taras Shevchenko (1814–1861) is often deemed the "bard of Ukraine." Because of his close association with the Ukrainian national movement, any celebration of Shevchenko was regarded with suspicion by Soviet authorities. The monument in Kyiv was erected in 1939 in a park opposite the national university.

hearing the baby's first cry understands that the prolonged agonies of labor have finally come to an end. Anyone who has ever experienced this sort of release from fear will understand how lucid the soul becomes when the burden of duplicity and doubt is finally shed. To be sure, to my dying days I won't be able to fully rid myself of all the characteristics of a *homo sovieticus*: this "birth trauma" stays with you forever. At the same time, I am grateful to God that on that momentous day, from within the ideological shell of a *homo sovieticus*, a dissident embarked on his conscious, active life.

My aforementioned visit to the Shevchenko monument was simultaneously an act of disobedience and the result of a compromise. After the wave of arrests of Ukrainian political dissidents in 1972–1973, the mass demonstrations at this monument that had been commonplace during the Khrushchev thaw were suddenly deemed objectionable.[3] Even though there was no official prohibition against honoring Shevchenko, it was certainly not encouraged. With the doctrine of the "merging of nations," the government expected its loyal citizens to willingly and enthusiastically abandon any rudimentary vestiges of nationalism.[4]

Placing flowers at the Shevchenko monument on May 22 meant violating this unspoken taboo. It was presumed that our socialist country had been subjected to the diversionary tactics of some diaspora "Banderites."[5] The authorities alleged that these Banderites, seeking to undermine the nationalities policy of the Communist Party of the Soviet Union, forced the Ukrainian community abroad to celebrate Taras Shevchenko not only on March 9 and 10 each year (the anniversaries of his birth and death,

3 These arrests were of the so-called *shistdesiatnyky*, or "Sixtiers," participants in a literary-cultural movement in Soviet Ukraine in the 1960s dedicated to universal moral and spiritual values, coupled with respect for the Ukrainian language, history, and traditions. The movement, led by a relative handful of creative (and courageous) individuals, defied the prevailing Soviet culture of fear, censorship, and conformity and is viewed as having laid the social-intellectual foundation for the dissident movement that followed in the 1970s and 1980s and independence, which came a generation later. –M. M.

4 Stemming from Lenin's writings, this doctrine maintained that nations were a vestige of an earlier phase of development and should fade away under Communism, being replaced by a single "Soviet people."

5 Refers to the supporters of Stepan Bandera (1909–1959), leader of the Organization of Ukrainian Nationalists. The official Soviet line maintained that many expressions of Ukrainian national sentiment were the result of foreign interference, specifically from the Ukrainian diaspora.

respectively) but also on May 22, the day when his remains had been transferred from St. Petersburg to the small town of Kaniv in central Ukraine so he could be buried on Ukrainian soil.[6] Any Ukrainian who tried to encourage this new commemoration in Soviet-controlled Ukraine automatically drew attention to his personal disloyalty to the Soviet government—and, much worse, to his nationalism.

During the Khrushchev thaw, the authorities more or less tolerated the massive celebrations organized by recalcitrant devotees at the Kyiv monument; in later years, however, they began to brutally disperse and persecute the participants in a variety of ways. Occasionally even non-Ukrainians were seized: I heard of a Georgian man who had come to honor Shevchenko being duly thrown in jail and accused of Ukrainian "bourgeois nationalism." So, in 1973 it was obvious to me and to my new friends Mykola Matusevych and Natalia Faustov (now Yakovenko)[7] that if we came to the monument on May 22 in the evening we would inevitably be seized. We still hoped, however, that if we brought our flowers that morning instead, it might not be perceived as a demonstration of defiance.

So that's what we did. We approached the monument slowly and laid down our flowers silently, almost physically sensing concealed, watchful eyes upon us. We bowed in silent meditation, and after a while we went our own ways—they went to work, and I headed for Zhuliany Airport for my return flight to Ivano-Frankivsk. It seemed that we had gotten away with it. But at Zhuliany I was apprehended by the police and taken for questioning to the nearest police station, where my things were searched, and then, finally, the crucial question was posed: "What was the purpose of your visit to the Shevchenko monument?" So, we had been watched. This year, apparently, Shevchenko was dangerous even in the morning.

I don't remember what my reply was, but it didn't much matter. The sticking point was the question itself. It encapsulated the anti-Ukrainian essence of the Communist Party's nationalities policy. It is this policy that I have to thank for my initial acquaintance with the KGB, although, as it turned out later, they had already had their eye on me for a long while. It seems

6 Shevchenko's burial site in Kaniv, where he was transferred two months after his death, became a sort of "sacred site" for the burgeoning Ukrainophile movement in the Russian Empire.

7 Natalia Yakovenko (née Faustov) (b. 1942): friend and colleague of M. M., involved in dissident circles in Kyiv in the 1970s; today a leading historian of early modern Ukraine.

that there were two main reasons for this: my "tainted" family history and my "anti-Soviet activities" at the Lviv Polytechnic Institute. I should explain what those things entailed.

Family as Destiny and Safe Harbor

Filling out any official forms always came with psychological hang-ups for my sister Nadiika and me. In the Soviet Union these forms had been formulated in such a way that officials could immediately flush out any "suspicious elements." We somehow always managed to raise suspicions: "Do you have any relatives abroad?" "Yes, Maria Mentsinska, my mother's sister, in Australia; our father's sister, Kateryna Senych, in the USA; and our father's other sisters, Maria and Sophia Deberre, in France." This list alone would make a Soviet bureaucrat's eyes pop out of his head.

The situation didn't get any better when it came to my father. His name was Franko—"Franyk" at home—derived from the Austrian "Franz," totally unconnected to the famous nineteenth-century Ukrainian poet Ivan Franko or the Spanish dictator Francisco Franco. But who knows, it might be worth looking into (I kid). My father's last name, "Dytsio," didn't arouse any suspicions because this region was full of similar Ukrainian names. I suspect, given that the family lived in a section of their native village called "Falkenberg," which had some German-speaking settlers, most likely my father descended from a Ukrainianized Austrian family named "Dietze." I didn't know my paternal grandfather Ivan Dytsio because he died in 1917, soon after my father's birth. My grandmother Hanna raised her four children by herself. Though "Dietze" had a nice Austrian ring to it, the name was not exactly mellifluous in Ukrainian. In our early youth, Nadiika and I suffered quite a bit over its constant mispronunciation: "Dy . . . what? Ditsa . . . ? Dits-i-u-o?" I suspected that I would not bear that name for long.

In fact, my first attempt to change my last name from my father's name to my mother's maiden name came soon after my father divorced my mother, when I turned sixteen years old. I went to the civil registrar with an application, but it was rejected, citing a law that allows you to change your name only once you reach eighteen. Back at home, I went into hysterics because my passport would be processed with the name "Dytsio."[8] But on January 5,

8 Refers to the internal passport, an identification document issued to Soviet citizens on their sixteenth birthday.

Figure 1.1. My mother, Liuba Yosypivna Marynovych, in her youth.

1967, the day after my eighteenth birthday, I returned to the registrar and was met by the same person. She smiled and said, "Now, since you've obviously made up your mind, I will change your name without any hesitation." So that's how I became Myroslav Marynovych.

After I changed my last name, things were easier for me psychologically, but not bureaucratically: from then on, I always had to note this change in all official documents. "Hmm, he's a man, not a woman, and yet he changed his name. Why did he do that?" Furthermore, this new name presented me with new problems: it might have been more melodious, but it was also less trustworthy.

Why less trustworthy? My maternal grandfather, Father Yosyf Marynovych, from whom I took my last name, was a Greek Catholic cleric, an archpriest,

Figure 1.2. My grandfather, Father Yosyf Marynovych, with the church in Stebnyk in the background

and in my time, the pastor of Stebnyk, a village in the Drohobych region of Lviv oblast.[9] Anyone who ever lived under the Soviet regime knows what it meant to come from a family of clerics: you immediately became suspect because of your connection to organized religion. My mother drew attention to her "untrustworthiness" every time she had to list in her documents that she was the daughter of a priest. Both she and her sister Evgeniia (called Nusia at home) were dragged through various offices in an attempt to sway them to take part in public antireligious propaganda—to no avail, thankfully.

Our untrustworthiness was compounded by a more recent event: my mother's brother Antin Marynovych had been arrested in 1944 as an "enemy of the people." Very soon after, in 1946, he died in one of the concentration camps in Magadan.[10] My mother recalled that one proof of his "criminal

9 Archpriest: supervisor of a number of parishes.

10 Magadan oblast, used interchangeably with the regional name Kolyma, housed a major Gulag cluster in the far northeast of Russia. During and immediately after the Second World War, large numbers of "suspect" populations, including Ukrainians, were sent to these camps.

activities" was the musical score to the Ukrainian national anthem, found during one of the raids on his home. For him—a respectable member of his village community, a loving husband and father of two—suddenly being relocated from the orderly world of pious family life to the hellish, tormented life of transfers from one concentration camp to another was the ultimate shock. In his second (and final) letter to his family he wrote: "I could never have even imagined that people could be such beasts."

My birthplace also aroused suspicions. Komarovychi, my native village in the Dobromyl region of Drohobych oblast, was close to the Polish border. Anyone who wanted to go to this region needed a special permit. But in comparison to my family I got off easily: Komarovychi was still relatively tolerable. It was worse for my mother, my father, and Nadiika because their passports listed their birthplace as the suspiciously named village of Viisko, which means "army," in Poland—on the other side of the border.

As a child I was bothered by this discrepancy in my biography. "Mama, why was I born in a different village than the rest of you?" But whereas for me my birthplace was merely a source of childish resentment, for my parents their birthplace was a source of additional difficulties. They had the status of displaced persons because right after the Second World War, as part of a so-called voluntary population exchange, they had been resettled from their native village of Viisko, near the pilgrimage site of Kalwaria Pacławska, where my grandfather had been the parish priest before the war, to the village of Komarovychi, near Dobromyl, which was now part of the USSR.[11] Resettlement brought both material and psychological losses. From that time on, this region had to endure the new Stalin-imposed border, like a fresh wound that festered in the living body and separated people into locals and "resettlers."

I became aware of myself as an individual in the city of Sambir, around fifty kilometers east of the Polish border. My parents moved there shortly after my birth and rented an apartment not too far from a bridge that spanned the railroad tracks. I can recall, in the mid-1950s, the residual effects of the 1947 famine: fried potatoes were for Sundays only.[12] Since then, eating them feels

11 As the result of a 1944 agreement between the government of the USSR and the Committee for the National Liberation of Poland, around five hundred thousand Ukrainians were relocated from Polish territory to the Ukrainian SSR.

12 After the war, extensive grain requisitions were mandated by Soviet authorities across the Ukrainian SSR, including the newly incorporated region of western Ukraine. These requisitions resulted in widespread famine.

Figure 1.3. With my mother at the May 1st demonstration, 1950s.

like a festive occasion. Once, together with several other men, my father somehow procured a calf and slaughtered it in our yard. This was my first experience of death, and it was like a bullet to my earliest childhood memories.

We didn't stay very long in Sambir because in 1955 we moved to the bigger city of Drohobych, where it was easier for my parents to find jobs and accommodations. Drohobych became "my city"—not by birth but by upbringing. I cherished my school, School #2, because it introduced me to my beloved teachers, as well as good friends, and of course my first love.

I grew up under the wings of the gentle love of my mother and my sister Nadiika. My mother's love stemmed from both her maternal feelings and her religious devotion. Well-versed in all religious rituals, my mother always amazed me with the purity of her piety, devoid of any fanaticism or hypocrisy.

Figure 1.4. In my father's arms.

Free from moralizing or maternal tyranny, my sister and I were grafted to the tree of faith less by customary duty than with our hearts and spirit.

As far back as I can remember, my mother always worked with books: first at the local book repository and later in various Drohobych bookstores. Then, just before her retirement, she worked in the subscriptions department of the Kameniar bookstore.[13] From earliest childhood I loved those neat bookshelves that hid so many fascinating things.

13 Kameniar ("stone cutter") is a reference to "Kameniari," a well-known political poem by Ivan Franko (1856–1916) that was ideologically embraced by Soviet authorities. Franko went to school and gymnasium in Drohobych.

Early in my childhood I discovered that while my father could be kind, he could also be extremely nasty, particularly when he drank. Then the house filled with his yelling, the furniture was smashed, and my mother was left moaning from my father's beatings. This earliest childhood fear gave me a mild stutter, which I didn't get rid of until much later in life. At the same time, a certain rebelliousness took root in my heart, and when my father routinely tested me by asking whom I loved more, my mother or him, I no longer wanted to respond with the answer I had been coached to give, fabricated for visitors: "both equally." My father had been raised in a rather traditional atmosphere, with a primitive notion of the family, which was proudly patriarchal and relegated the wife to an inferior role. If you were jealous of your wife it meant that you loved her. And beating her was how you educated her.

But the memories of his abusiveness are not the only ones I have of him because my father was a jovial person. In Drohobych we lived near a bus depot, and my father, who worked as a bus driver, would often bring home complete strangers who would have otherwise had to spend the night on the street. I loved those occasions because they always brought fascinating adventures: interesting conversations, but also—most importantly to my childhood self—getting to sleep on a mattress laid out on the floor.

It was rare for my father and me to talk one-on-one, although I do remember a period when we could well have become friends. At some point, he decided to teach me his vocation: driving. We went outside the city two or three times, and he would let me take the steering wheel. But either I was a rather incompetent pupil, or his patience just wore down, because those lessons did not last very long.

I will not go into any details about why and how my love for him died out—he is no longer alive: may he rest in peace. I will only say that I rejected all things paternal with the maximalism typical of youth. By the time I changed my last name, my father was already living with another family, and although my paternal grandmother Hanna loved me dearly, she decided to move in with him and his new family.

Thus, during my rebellious youth only two individuals remained with me as my blessed guardians: my mother, who protected me from evil every hour of the day with her love and prayers, and my devoted older sister, Nadiika, who stood in as loving father, guardian, and friend.

It is remarkable how my mother harbored both fear and courage. All her life, remembering the Soviet secret police raids of her youth, she would shudder when she heard any unexpected footsteps in the hallway. After I was arrested, however, she fearlessly brought me parcels and made the rounds of numerous KGB offices; she also came to visit me in camp and later in internal exile. In the years just prior to my arrest, when I wanted the whole world to stand up and fight against the Soviet system, I considered my mother to be weaker than she should be, and I often got angry with her. Today it is truly painful to recall this. The KGB was more clever than I was: they understood what role my mother had played in the development of my civic consciousness. That is undoubtedly why they didn't like her, and one of them told her so directly: "So there you have it—it's all your Uniate upbringing!" [14] They were actually right about that.

My mother taught me to love our heritage without hating that of others. She was familiar with all the ethnic idiosyncrasies of Poles, Russians, and Jews, and she didn't like all that these entailed. But she never harbored any animosities toward them because as a Christian she understood that we Ukrainians were not blameless either. Everyone was always welcome in our home.

My mother's challenging lot in life as a woman had consequences for my notion of human rights. My whiskers had not yet come in when, filled with a strong resolve, I began to intervene between my father and my mother to protect her from his drunken beatings. In my youth I could not tolerate it when a woman was mistreated in my presence—even today I find it pretty revolting. At some point I made a rule for myself that I would always dance with every girl at our school dances, and for the first dance I would ask the girl who had the least chance of attracting a boy. This in itself became a form of protest. I did not become a confirmed "feminist," because all ideologies turn me off. However, later on, with some light persuasion from the members of the Union of Ukrainian Women (*Soiuz ukrainok*) in Drohobych, I did become one of their associate members.[15]

My mother had a premonition that her son would have a difficult row to hoe in life. I had a birthmark on my right cheek, which they used to say portends an unusual path through life. When I was a child my mother comforted herself by saying, "Well, at least you will not become an intelligence agent." Indeed, I did not become a spook, but that birthmark didn't keep me from being labeled a "Canadian spy." (Why a Canadian spy and not an

---

14 Uniate: older term for Greek Catholic, considered derogatory by Greek Catholics.

15 Union of Ukrainian Women: influential women's organization in Polish-controlled western Ukraine. during the interwar period. Not in operation during the Soviet period, it was revived in 1989.

American one, for example, I honestly don't know, but that's the rumor the KGB spread about me in during my dissident days.)

This was not the only physical mark that singled me out. Toward the end of my studies, a noticeable spot emerged on my forehead. It appeared suddenly and unexpectedly, and Nadiika, my mother, and I were taken aback. I even considered going to a cosmetic clinic to have it removed. In a year or two, though, it just disappeared on its own. At some point I read somewhere that such marks appear when someone is slated for a challenging future.

When I grew up and my political preferences began to emerge, my mother used to beg me, "Son, just don't think of joining any underground movement!"[16] I promised her sincerely that I would not because I really had no desire to do so. When I later joined the Ukrainian Helsinki Group, my mother reproached me, "I did beg you not to join any underground groups, and you didn't listen to me." I answered her in earnest, "Sorry, Mama, but this group is not underground!"

Her motherly feelings fell in two baskets: one was a purely maternal dread that something bad might happen to her child. What mother doesn't know those fears! So, she felt she had to protect me from any danger. The second was pride for her son, and this was the one the KGB latched on to so effectively. Mykola Rudenko (a prominent dissident and one of the founding members of the Ukrainian Helsinki Group—more about him later) writes so eloquently in his memoirs about this motherly pride during my time in the Helsinki group:

> Myroslav invited some of his new friends from the Helsinki Group to celebrate his birthday. That is when I met his mother. I was most amazed that she thanked me for accepting her son into the Helsinki Group, thereby confirming our trust in him. Her gratitude was sincere, although in my view it would have been more natural for a mother to berate us for this, rather than thank us. But here I'm using the standards of another family entirely: Myroslav's mother was typical of the Galician intelligentsia, and that was a completely unfamiliar environment to me.[17]

Later, when my mother would get news from camp that I had declared a hunger strike, she would do the same and also go hungry. Not out of some political conviction but simply because she psychologically could not eat. She

16 Underground anti-Soviet activity persisted in western Ukraine throughout the postwar period.

17 Mykola Rudenko, *Naibil'she dyvo – zhyttia: Spohady* (Kyiv: Takson, 1998), 435.

told me later, "Just the thought that you were going hungry would wedge any food in my throat like a stone." At that time, my mother was no doubt thinking of the legacy passed down to her from the previous generation when her own mother, Maria Marynovych (née Mentsinska), would deliberately lie down on the cement so that she could feel what her son Antin might be feeling after he was thrown in an NKVD (The People's Commissariat for Internal Affairs) prison.

As for my sister Nadiika, she and I had a very special bond. When I was brought home from the maternity hospital and my mother started to change my diaper, four-year-old Nadiika cried out: "Be careful! You could smother my baby!" I was her property—and my mother had nothing to do with it.

If Nadiika was my first teacher, I was her first pupil: she could mold me like a piece of clay. To be sure, this clay would often fall out of her hands and cause mischief, like pulling his sister's hair or impishly hiding around a corner and startling her. Generally speaking, though, all the "delights" of our modest childhood were always shared by both of us. All we had to do was flip a stool over, cover its legs with one of my grandmother's scarves, and our two little heads would disappear beneath it: suddenly an enchanted princess and a brave prince on horseback would appear, with a favorite magical fairy tale to go along with it.

In her early youth Nadiika received a terrible blow. Physicians diagnosed her with scoliosis, a terrible illness that was common in our area. My parents sold the foundation of a house they had started to build to raise funds for her treatment, and my mother took Nadiika to Kyiv, where a course of physical therapy was prescribed for her. It seems that the physicians were mistaken, however, because her deformity progressed aggressively, and her spinal curvature finally reached the third and final stage. Thus, Nadiika's youth was shrouded in hopelessness and despair. Other women in her position would have surely broken down, but Nadiika's *joie de vivre* prevailed. Amazingly, after such a blow, she still managed to become the life and soul of her school, her student body, and later her teaching community.

Nadiika also shaped my life's philosophical credo. At some point, she shared a discovery she had made with her little brother: the concept of the "golden mean." It was duly imprinted on my consciousness, and ever since then I have automatically tried to find the golden mean between all opposing extremes.

A student of English philology at the Drohobych Pedagogical Institute, Nadiika was aware of my penchant for learning foreign languages. It is from her that I acquired proper English pronunciation. I also learned that Hemingway was a name, and there was no point looking it up in a dictionary,

Figure 1.5. My sister Nadiika in her youth.

as one of her schoolmates had done. Nadiika successfully finished her studies and went on to teach English in School #15 in Rivne, establishing roots in Volhynia for the rest of her life.[18]

It was my sister who convinced me not to study linguistics or history but to apply to Lviv Polytechnic Institute. In the 1960–1970s, studying the humanities doomed you to a constant barrage of indoctrination, whereas the

18 Volhynia: region in northwest Ukraine, part of the Russian Empire and interwar Poland before being incorporated into the Ukrainian SSR.

scientific track was a virtual oasis of freedom, comparatively speaking. After all, electrons move in a certain pattern not because the Communist Party deems it so but because of the laws of physics. Later I learned that this had also been the stance of another famous dissident, Leonid Pliushch: "Science was the antidote to 'Sovieticism', because there could be no ideological falsehood in the exact sciences."[19]

When I was arrested, Nadiika found it unthinkable to reject or denounce her brother. She had forewarned the KGB of this from the start. She communicated cautiously yet bravely with the other dissidents and their families. She was subjected to numerous humiliating measures, such as personal strip searches whenever she came with my mother to visit me in camp. I never heard any words of blame or reproach from her. On the contrary, her love, kindness and gentleness in fact seemed to have increased a hundred-fold. And, like a mantra, she repeated the phrase "Everything will be fine!"

Early on in prison, I realized that Nadiika and my mother were the most reliable pillars of my universe. They were the ones that had laid the foundation of my character and given me the fundaments of my worldview. The most fitting description of their role, however, was encapsulated by my dedication to them in my first essay, "The Gospel According to a Holy Fool," which I wrote while still in camp: "*I dedicate this to my Mama and my sister Nadiika, for being the first ones to teach me the power of Love.*"[20]

Though my mother and Nadiika played the two key roles, the story of the development of my worldview in childhood would not be complete without discussing my grandfather, who was a priest, first in the Greek Catholic Church, and then, by the time I was born, the Orthodox Church (I will return to the story of his confessional switch).[21] I didn't see him very often, usually just in the summer or for the holidays, but his influence on me was enormous. I still remember his vicarage in the village of Stebnyk outside of

19 Leonid Pliushch (1938–2015): Ukrainian mathematician and dissident, arrested in 1972 for anti-Soviet activity and subjected to punitive psychiatry. After his release and emigration from the Soviet Union, he joined the Ukrainian Helsinki Group from abroad in 1977. Gulnara Bekirova, "'My prosnulis' ot spiachki beznadezhnosti, ravnodushnogo priniatiia rabstva,'—Leonid Pliushch," *Krym.Realii,* April 26, 2015, http://ru.krymr.com/content/article/26978284.html.

20 See appendix.

21 The Ukrainian Greek Catholic Church is subject to a canonical Eastern Rite rule that allows seminarians to be married prior to being ordained as priests; my grandfather married Maria Mencinsky before his ordination. –M. M.

Drohobych; today it has been subdivided into several apartments. I warmly recall his dog, Karus, who would greet and nuzzle us in such a friendly manner; the smell of tomatoes from my grandfather's garden (today tomatoes no longer have such a divine aroma); and the five *karbovantsi* (an old monetary unit) that my grandfather would so proudly count out for every top grade on my end-of-year report card. I also remember how I enjoyed washing his dishes, to the joy of his maid, Hanna. Obviously, it wasn't the grease and dirt that I liked so much, I just relished the outcome—the clean dishes. Just a few swipes could produce such incredible results. Even today I enjoy this effect.

I also associate my grandfather with my early efforts to reach Herculean heights. At a very early age, I suddenly had an urgent desire to see my grandfather, who lived half an hour away by railroad. So, as a very small boy, without saying anything to anyone, I set out for the train station, which was some three kilometers away. Along the way, seeing a toy car in a shop window, I changed my mind and decided that going to grandpa's house by car would be much faster and not as tiring. In my pocket I had some pieces of paper with pencil tracings of coins, which to me meant that I had money. I stretched out my hand with the "money" toward the counter and asked the salesperson to sell me the car. For some reason she refused to sell it to me, so, dejected, I dragged myself to the train station. Once there, I attempted to board the train, but an angry stationmaster gave me such a talking-to when he heard me say "I want to go see my grandpa!" that, despondent and in tears, I was compelled to trudge back home.

At home I was met by a despairing but now overjoyed mother and also by my father, who asked me in jest, "So how many spankings do you think you deserve?" to which I replied in all fairness: "one." Later my mother commented that I got more than a double helping of them.

The memory of my grandfather, even later in life, frequently had the power of altering my behavior toward good. Perhaps my readers might not find this assertion very convincing because in my youth I had a certain degree of atheistic skepticism. My grandfather had instilled reverence for the clergy in me, but that did not prevent me from experiencing the full gamut of Soviet indoctrination: the Octobrists, Pioneers, and eventually the Komsomol.[22] My grandfather's memory had ethical significance, rather than ideological. I understood that some of my negative actions would not meet

22 Octobrists, Pioneers, Komsomol: standard Soviet youth organizations, for children between seven and nine, nine and fifteen, and fifteen and twenty-eight years old, respectively.

his approval, and I wanted to be worthy of his memory (although obviously this was not always possible). For me, my grandfather was a symbol of great nobility, a worthy spiritual persona who spoke to me with every word and gesture. I don't remember him explaining this to me, but his example was sufficient.

In the social environment of the 1920s and 1930s, during interwar Polish rule in Western Ukraine, being a Ukrainian Greek Catholic priest almost inevitably led to conflict with the Polish administration, or at the very least competition from the Roman Catholic clergy.[23] And indeed, as parish priest for the village of Viisko, he was imprisoned more than once—first in 1919–20 in the notorious Polish prison of Brygidki, and then in 1922 in the prison of the Przemyśl regional court.[24]

Historians have written that my grandfather was a devout Greek Catholic priest and active community leader, highly regarded by the clergy of the Przemyśl eparchy (the Eastern Christian equivalent of a diocese).[25] But fate presented him with a challenging role. Soon after the Second World War, a reign of terror began across the territories newly acquired by the Soviet Union that had previously been part of Poland. A large segment of the local population was arrested as "enemies of the state" and sent to Siberia. One of the victims of this terror was my grandfather's older son, Antin Marynovych.

At the same time, my grandfather became suspect as well. In their attempt to subjugate the Ukrainian populace, Stalin's regime decided to destroy its spiritual pillar, the Ukrainian Greek Catholic Church. The church was to disappear, and the clergy and the faithful were to "voluntarily convert" to Russian Orthodoxy. Historically, the Russian Orthodox Church had always considered the "Uniate" (Ukrainian Greek Catholic) Church to be heretical and had constantly tried to destroy it. To achieve this, the KGB engaged all sorts of lies and terroristic methods. The Ukrainian Greek Catholic Church

---

23 The Christian population of western Ukraine was historically divided between Roman Catholics (usually Polish-speaking) and Greek Catholics (usually Ukrainian-speaking). Most villages and towns had a parish of each denomination, and the two clergies often clashed.

24 Brygidki: a prison in Lviv established by the Habsburg administration housed in a former Bridgettine convent; one of the largest prisons in interwar Poland. During the Second World War it was a mass killing site for both Soviet and Nazi forces.

25 Bohdan Prakh, *Dukhovenstvo Peremys'koi ieparkhii ta Apostols'koi administratsii Lemkivshchyny*, vol. 1 (Lviv: Ukrainian Catholic University, 2015), 291.

was labeled as a "Nazi collaborator," and the bishops and clergy were given a choice: either convert to Russian Orthodoxy or expand the ranks of the Siberian Gulags.

Most Greek Catholic bishops, led by the prelate of the church, Metropolitan Josyf Slipyj, categorically refused to break their vows, and they were all arrested.[26] Thousands of priests followed their example and were also arrested. But there were some who did convert to Orthodoxy, and my grandfather was one of them. Even in my early youth, I always sought to understand why he did that. The fact that he was coerced was obvious. He made his decision while in jail, where most Ukrainian priests found themselves at that time. All the prisoners were brutally tortured. The KGB promised to release my grandfather's son Antin, who had been arrested in November 1944, and this was most certainly a deciding factor in my grandfather's decision. This promise was never kept, and Antin died in prison in Magadan.

Back in my youth, I once saw a Soviet documentary film about the "pseudo-Synod" held in Lviv in 1946. This gathering declared the "self-liquidation" of the Ukrainian Church and its "return to the bosom of the Russian Orthodox Church."[27] At one point, the camera scanned all those present, and I suddenly saw my grandfather's face, tense, full of pain, tragic. Generally speaking, everyone in the film looked tortured and doomed. They all looked like frozen masks of people who had been terrorized. These faces told me more about the depressing atmosphere of this event than any historical research ever could. They planted the first seeds of my decision in the 1990s, remembering the intimidation that had been perpetrated against my grandfather, to renew historic justice and return from Orthodoxy, the faith that I was baptized in, to the bosom of the Ukrainian Greek Catholic Church.

In the 1990s, while I was visiting Philadelphia, some of the local Ukrainians there told me that my grandfather, along with several other priests, converted to Orthodoxy at the directive of anti-Soviet underground

---

26 Metropolitan Josyf Slipyj (1892–1984): head of the Ukrainian Greek Catholic Church from 1944 until his death. He was arrested in 1945 and served an eighteen-year sentence in various Soviet prison camps until his release was negotiated in 1963. He then emigrated to Rome, which served as the seat of the Greek Catholic Church while it was outlawed in the Soviet Union.

27 "Pseudo-Synod" (*psevdosobor*): ceremonial dissolution of the Greek Catholic Church, organized by the KGB and convened by fraudulently appointed "hierarchs." At the synod, the hierarchs annulled the Union of Brest, which had created the church in 1596.

partisans, who called for "saving what was still salvageable."[28] This may be true, but my soul does not need this sort of justification. I simply cannot and refuse to judge my grandfather's behavior. I bow my head before all those priests who remained Greek Catholic even in their Siberian Golgothas and did not succumb to the incredible pressures exerted on them. At the same time, I will not throw stones at the apostates. During that satanic time, the Greek Catholic clergy were victims of brutal proselytizing—that is, forced conversion to another confession by means of state-directed terror. Throughout the world, it is not those who succumb and convert to this sort of terror who should be condemned but rather the system that resorts to it.

I was six when Father Mykhail Melnyk visited my grandfather's vicarage in Stebnyk. He was a former Greek Catholic priest whom the Moscow Patriarchate had consecrated as an Orthodox bishop just prior to the 1946 Lviv pseudo-Synod. Soon thereafter, a tragic event occurred. In September 1955, to commemorate the tenth anniversary of the Lviv pseudo-Synod, a pilgrimage had been planned to visit all the prominent Russian Orthodox churches. It was to include Bishop Melnyk, Father Volodymyr Kunovsky, and my grandfather. Just prior to the trip, my grandfather fell ill and could not travel. On October 7, just before boarding their train from Lviv to Kyiv, the other two had breakfast with Archbishop Pankratiy, the Lviv and Ternopil prelate of the Russian Orthodox Church. Soon after, both men died: Father Volodymyr first, still on the train, and then Bishop Melnyk in his hotel room on October 9. Officially, their deaths were attributed to chronic heart ailments, but word had it that they had been poisoned. There is even evidence that confirms this: just prior to his own death, the attending pathologist told Father Volodymyr's widow that her husband had been poisoned.[29] I still remember the grand funeral that was held for them in Drohobych.

Later conversations with some prelates and priests of the "Catacomb church" taught me something surprising: hardly anyone blamed those who had converted to Orthodoxy in 1946.[30] They certainly did not approve of their choice, which had been made under duress and not by conviction,

28 That is, conversion would have allowed him to remain in Western Ukraine and continue to work for the Ukrainian cause, whereas refusal would have resulted in imprisonment or execution.

29 Prakh, *Dukhovenstvo,* 1:572.

30 Catacomb church (*katakombna tserkva*): Common name for the Soviet-era Greek Catholic Church as it continued to operate secretly after it was officially eliminated in 1946.

and they considered it a big mistake. Yet each of them, in his own way, acknowledged that that period was too frightful to rally enough courage to even think of condemning them. Their stance was not one of moral relativism but was based on their genuine feelings and instincts, rooted in one of God's commandments: "Do not judge, so that you may not be judged" (Matthew 7:1).

I received the principal response to these conversions—and my grandfather's in particular—from the Greek Catholic Church in 1996, when the Bishop of Sambir-Drohobych, Yulian Voronovsky, invited me to join the eparchy's delegation to the first session of the Patriarchal Synod of the Greek Catholic Church to be held since the church's re-legalization in 1989. Subsequently, Bishop Yulian Gbur, the secretary of the Synod, sent me an official invitation. The symbolism of this lofty gesture was amazing: the grandson of a participant of the Lviv 1946 pseudo-Synod, some fifty years later, becomes a member of the first session of the Synod of the reinstated church. The same last name, the same family, with the deep scars of an ancient drama.

My maternal grandfather's family was very patriotic (as was my father's side of the family, for that matter), so it is not surprising that I was raised in an atmosphere of love for Ukraine. From my mother I inherited the spiritual code of my Ukrainianness: Taras Shevchenko's poetry, which she would read to me in the evenings. It was from her that I also learned of the sadistic behavior of the NKVD in the postwar period and their favorite way of identifying the relatives of dead partisans: they would display the partisans' bodies in the town square and make the whole town, particularly the women, walk among the dead bodies. According to her, many mothers tried to stifle their cries when they saw their dead sons lying in front of them in order to save the remainder of their families. I also learned from my mother how the finest villagers would "go into the forest" (i.e., join the partisans) to fight against the occupying regime.[31]

Practically every western Ukrainian family had to deal with similar problems in their family history, and the families of priests even more so. Everyone's pre-Soviet biography contained something that later left a big fat ideological blemish on their paperwork. This placed them in the category of

31 Soviet forces retook the territory of western Ukraine in 1944 and sought to quell widespread resistance from anti-Soviet Ukrainian partisans. The dead partisans referred to here may have been killed in armed conflict with the NKVD's paramilitary units or executed following arrest.

"untrustworthy citizens," and they could only rid themselves of this label by betraying their family, their honor, or truth itself. Such vulnerability in the face of future persecution had both positive and negative results. On the one hand, families rallied together and tried to maintain close relationships, even with distant relatives. On the other hand, one family member's carelessness could jeopardize everyone's life.

I consider families from Galicia, the west Ukrainian region where I grew up, to be particularly noble. Here I have in mind the often elusive but easily recognizable quality of dignity and spiritual nobility, friendliness, and tacit understanding, without which a person from Galicia just seems to wither. It is sorely missed, no matter where they might find themselves. I am not oblivious to Galicians' shortcomings, but when comparing them with people of any other region in Ukraine, it is in Galicia where you might still be able to find the remnants of this unique phenomenon: the clan, or family nest.

Indeed, I think of the family as a large beehive where I was able to acquire, like honey, certain life-giving qualities and lessons that helped me find my way in life. For me, the family was the hub where all my early principles, values, and cultural positions took shape. This is where I picked up my family traditions, and I am still very comfortable and at home with them even today. For this reason, I am so proud to belong to such a large and friendly family, and I love all my Marynovych and Mencinsky relatives very much.

When my life as a dissident led to imprisonment, my family's reactions were diverse. Certain family members approved of my actions and were proud of me. This was true not only of my family abroad, particularly the Mencinsky family in Australia who actively fought for my release, but also of my family in Ukraine as well.

They all provided great support for my mother and sister. But there were also those who were displeased and criticized me. The inertia of fear was very strong, and there was great concern that if one member of the family was arrested as an "enemy of the people," then other members of the family would be in jeopardy. There was even one handwritten document in my criminal dossier from one of my relatives trying to save her own brother, who became suspect when the authorities found him with a copy of the Ukrainian Helsinki Group Declaration that I had given him. Her act was not very noble, but I put the blame for this less on her than on the system that consciously bred this fear of possible persecution.

During my incarceration, I had already begun to realize that my fate had been shaped by specific moments from my childhood and early youth. I was amazed not so much by the cause-and-effect relationship, which was

Figure 1.6 Yuri and Olya Mencinsky and family, a branch of the wider Mencinsky family in Australia.

Figure 1.7. My Aunt Catherine Senycz with her two sons, Joseph Yacyk and Eugene Senycz, and their families in the United States.

obvious, but rather by how seamless and logical one's fate seems to be when you evaluate it as if turning the pages of the Book of Life.

Pollination by the *Shistdesiatnyky*

School was the next "crucible" where the diverse qualities of my character miraculously and sometimes haphazardly blended together. I was impressed with Nadiika's achievements and was constantly trying to catch up with her and reach her level. Perhaps that's why practically every year I managed to finish the school year with top grades. We both attended School #2, and I considered this a special blessing.

Generally speaking, I didn't divide the teachers into "ours" and "not ours"—that is, from Galicia or from eastern Ukraine. I am grateful to all of them for sharing a bit of their soul with me. I am truly thankful that we had teachers from the East in our school: because of this, I grew up with a broad pan-Ukrainian mentality. For me, Kyiv is not just a golden-domed dreamland beyond the Zbruch River, as it had been for my parents, but *my land*, my natural gravitational center, and I cherish this pan-Ukrainian worldview.[32]

It is with fondness and much gratitude that I remember my first teacher, Iryna Stadnyk, who came from the Drohobych region, as well as Valentyna Butenko, my homeroom teacher, who hailed from Cherkasy oblast in central Ukraine. Every so often one could hear her unexpected "Oh, my crocodiles, you!" It was spoken with such love that there was no risk of our young hearts misinterpreting it. I will always remember the smile of Elizaveta Pasternak, our Russian language and literature teacher, as she would berate me for ending my essays in a brazen manner. In reality, she was pleased with my youthful efforts at creative writing and would always give me a top grade.

I certainly felt the love and kindness of many of my teachers. Apparently, when I was arrested, not all of them approved of my actions, but why bother digging up all the details of Soviet subservience that was typical of the time?

I should, however, mention the teacher who had the most profound influence on the development of my civic comportment. This was my singing

32 The Zbruch River was historically the boundary line between eastern Ukraine, governed by the Russian Empire and then the Soviet Union, and western Ukraine, formerly part of the Habsburg Empire and between the wars under Polish, Czechoslovak, Romanian, and Hungarian control.

teacher from 1964–1966, Ivan Mykhailovych Rafa, a Galician native with deep roots in the region. Anyone who is even slightly familiar with the history of the Ukrainian cultural renaissance would know how pure, creative, and intense the national spirit was at that time. At that time, the KGB no longer permitted Ivan Mykhailovych to work in his field, Ukrainian language and literature, so he sought to exert influence beyond the classroom walls, finding ways to come in close contact with pupils' minds. I still remember some fragments of the poems of Mykola Vinhranovsky, one of the *shistdesiatnyky*, that he would read to me on our way home from school:

> *Maria, my dream, my reverie,*
> *My disconcerted Maria.*[33]
>
> *My native land, how fortunate*
> *That you exist in my life,*
> *Not swept away? No, you will not be cleared,*
> *If there is a cradle, the children will be there!*[34]

This poetry intoxicated me; it resonated in my soul. Later I read my fellow dissident Mykola Horbal's account of how the Ukrainian composer Vadym Smohytel read the poetry of Mykola Vorobyov, one of the founders of the late 1960s group of poets known as the Kyiv School, and I was amazed how similar our interpretations were:

> Today I no longer remember the gist of those poems, but oh my God, what blissful poetry! Suddenly it seemed that there were no spies in Kyiv, and life became easy and good, as if angels were floating nearby. This heavenly sensation has stayed with me to this day.[35]

The same was true of Ivan Rafa's soul: it remained in the 1960s. He radiated these feelings and inevitably inspired everyone around him. I would eventually read of this same delight in the young Ivan in my fellow dissident Svitlana Kyrychenko's memoirs:

> He enchanted my mother with his singing and his beautiful voice; he would read poetry and talk. And all this was done with such enthusiasm and sincerity, as if a

33 *Marie, mrie, mriechko moia / Moia Mariechko tryvozhna (from "Kachky letiat'!").*

34 *Narode mii, iak dobre te, / Shcho ty u mene e na sviti. / Ne zamelo? Ne zamete! / Bula b kolyska – budut' dity! (from "Vzhe vse proshchal'no").*

35 Mykola Horbal, *Prezentatsiia zhyttia* (Kyiv: BAT "Polihrafknyha," 2006), 33.

> young highlander were standing high on a mountain crest, grass under his feet, his life's horizon before him, with wings behind his back; there was no limit to what he could do on this earth. His blazing heart could bring such music to the world, he could sing so many songs.[36]

Svitlana was clearly not the only one who had noticed these wings, as a force surfaced that desired to cut them down: the KGB considered his devotion to Ukrainian culture to be dangerous to the regime. In later years, when the Khrushchev thaw was over, the KGB mercilessly bent the twig of his life, and his nature was too poetic to be able to straighten out after each onslaught. Apparently, his wife also put pressure on him, fearing his arrest. His determination had weakened, and he yielded somewhat to the KGB. But his soul had lost all interest in life because the pure glistening flames in his heart were gone. He did live long enough to witness the beginnings of Gorbachev's perestroika in the mid-1980s, but he left this life very young—one more victim of the totalitarian regime, virtually forgotten.

Looking back on my school years, I can distinctly trace the formation of the characteristics and tendencies of my personality that ultimately determined my adult life. My love for books and the aesthetics of the written word, my love for the religious celebrations of Christmas and Easter, my eagerness to listen to "enemy voices" (i.e., radio transmissions from the "Free World"), and my readiness to stand up for my dignity, while also not backing away from compromise (perhaps not always dignified or warranted): all this emerged in my early school years.

I remember that once—I must have been in the seventh or eighth grade—an extraordinary event took place in Drohobych: a gathering of students from throughout the Soviet Union. All the young people converged on the stadium where the celebrations were taking place. I, however, stayed home, deeply engrossed in one of the volumes of Alexandre Dumas's novel *The Three Musketeers*, which had been very difficult to procure. Even my mother tried to chase me out of the house, wondering why I was not rushing off to the stadium. To me, however, it was more interesting to delve into the imaginary world of Athos, my favorite character.

My school essays were always among the best in the class, whether written in Ukrainian or in Russian. Even then I was fascinated by verbal experimentation and appreciated the way meaning could be altered through wordplay.

36 Svitlana Kyrychenko, *Liudy ne zi strakhu. Ukrains'ka saha: Spohady* (Kyiv: Smoloskyp, 2013), 173.

My teachers didn't have any problems with me in any other respects either: I sang in the school choir, participated in a dance ensemble, and for a while was a member of the orchestra. I also attended the Drohobych Music School—though unfortunately for me, my lessons were on the much-hated *baian,* a type of accordion, which was much less expensive than a piano. In School #2, I was in the middle of everything, and no holiday celebration or outing to the Carpathian Mountains ever happened without me. I will never forget my appearances in various citywide competitions, such as when I performed a duet of the song "My Kyiv" with Mariia Smetana, my first school crush. Actually, even here, my sister Nadiika was my inspiration: in my mind, I can still see her as a ninth grader, all decked out in a Ukrainian folk costume, mounting the stage of the city's House of Culture to sing an arrangement of Taras Shevchenko's poem "The Poplar" (*Topolia*) in her beautiful voice.

My love for religious holidays, particularly Christmas, was always strong and unwavering. Even as a small boy I would go to the window of my childhood friend and neighbor, Nadiia Mykhailivska, to sing carols and marvel at their Christmas tree, which was always more ornate than ours. I am still amazed that they managed to hear my frail child's voice through their window. Our parents took Nadiia and me to church for our first communion, dressed in the fancy outfits customary for the occasion. As we walked to church, we heard a passerby object in Russian: "They're so little and they are already marrying them off!"

Every year without fail, my school friends and I would gather in groups to go caroling. Soviet propaganda had no dissuasive influence on such matters. On the contrary, to my friends and me, it was a matter of honor to go caroling at our friends' and relatives' houses. Likewise, on Good Friday we would go to the Holy Shroud, knowing full well that the schools were required to send teachers to patrol all the churches in Drohobych to note down the names of their "disobedient" pupils who took part in the ritual.[37] Furthermore, each of us would employ amazing inventiveness to find a legitimate reason that we would not go to the *subotnyk* that would be invariably scheduled for Easter Sunday.[38]

---

37 Holy Shroud: In Eastern Christianity, there is a tradition of venerating an ornamental cloth (epitaphios, Ukr. *plashchanytsia*) meant to represent the dressings in which Jesus was buried.

38 *Subotnyk*: day of "voluntary-compulsive" unpaid labor organized on weekends to provide community services such as collecting litter or fixing public amenities.

School brought me not only my first pleasures but also my first adolescent trials. I certainly did not eschew the usual adolescent rebelliousness. I recall one time, when Sofia Karpinska, my mathematics teacher, made a brisk remark of one kind or another, I bolted like an unbridled and unrestrained colt and snapped at her, "I'm not a horse for you to plod me around!" I can still remember my tumultuous adolescent emotions.

I received my political education (as did many others) through the "enemy voices" of Radio Liberty, Voice of America, the BBC, and Deutsche Welle. Thanks to these programs, I listened to things that were forbidden in the Soviet Union, starting with Aleksandr Solzhenitsyn's *One Day in the Life of Ivan Denisovich*. I even participated in a BBC competition about knowledge of British life. In those years I had my ear glued to the radio, attempting to perfect my ability to distinguish the voice of the announcer amidst all the Soviet jamming that blocked and interfered with the broadcast. Amusingly, during political instruction classes in school I always stood out because I was able to sum up the news that I had heard on one of the abovementioned radio programs—having mentally applied the appropriate ideological modifications to make it suitable for our Soviet school setting, of course. The teachers were clueless and praised me for such comprehensive knowledge!

I also remember the moment when, during a gathering at the Drohobych House of Culture, Nadiika and I heard an announcement that US President John F. Kennedy had been assassinated on November 22, 1963. At that time, he was an idol for the young people of Galicia, and the circumstances of his death, as well as the names of his officially recognized assassin, Lee Harvey Oswald, and Oswald's killer, Jack Ruby, were vividly carved in my teenage memory.

As did everyone around me, I diligently monitored the space race between the Soviet Union and the United States, and I was astonished when the American U2 spy plane piloted by Francis Gary Powers was shot down near Yekaterinburg. I watched the events surrounding the Cuban Missile Crisis and the duels between Nikita Khrushchev and John F. Kennedy, not particularly concerned that the world was on the brink of a nuclear war. Along with everyone else, I looked with disdain at Khrushchev pounding his shoe on the podium at the UN in New York and energetically discussed the circumstances of his ouster in 1964, skeptical of Leonid Brezhnev's arrogant face.

At that time, I didn't take note of the Second Vatican Council, Greek Catholic Patriarch Josyf Slipyj's elevation to cardinal in 1965, the construction of the Berlin Wall in 1961, or the clampdown on the workers' demonstrations in Novocherkassk.[39] I did observe—with derision—how the official rhetoric of the eternal friendship between the Soviet and Chinese nations changed as relations between the two countries were severed. Together with the "grateful" population of Galicia, I regarded with irony the promises of the Twenty-Second Communist Party Congress in 1961, which assured us that "the current generation of Soviet people will live under Communism."[40]

At the same time, we were truly overjoyed when the campaign to dismantle Stalin's cult started in 1956 and when his remains were removed from the mausoleum on Red Square in 1961. I was also overjoyed when, on June 10, 1964, a Shevchenko monument was unveiled in Moscow: I didn't know at that time that the USSR was racing to beat the United States in this regard, as a Shevchenko monument was dedicated in Washington, DC on June 27, 1964. And I didn't quite know how to respond when the city of Stanislav was renamed Ivano-Frankivsk, in honor of the poet. I was always eager to criticize any governmental decision, but Ivan Franko was a sacred figure.

Youth, of course, held its own, and I enthusiastically listened to Elvis Presley, the Beatles, and the Rolling Stones, which evoked strong objections from my uncle. In his view, my musical predilections (no doubt along with my worldview as a whole) were completely spoiled. At that time, the Soviet movie screens were showing films like *My Fair Lady*, with Audrey Hepburn; *The Umbrellas of Cherbourg*, with Catherine Deneuve; and *The Magnificent Seven*, with Yul Brynner. But most importantly, in my early youth, I had a real treat: I saw two French series of the "Three Musketeers." Even today I can still remember the thrill I felt as I took in the first few scenes of the film, and the music from that film still electrifies me to the core.

My first steps toward coming of age revealed to me the secrets of fashion. I suffered when I had to wear wide-leg pants because the cool guys were all wearing ultra-modern slim straight-leg pants (*dudochky*). When my mother purchased a traditional suit for my graduation ceremony, I finally rebelled, and before the graduation ceremony, while she was at work, I pulled out her

---

39 Novocherkassk: a 1962 workers' strike in the southwest Russian city over production quotas and food prices developed into a mass protest; armed forces dispersed the protest, killing nearly thirty people. The incident was censored in Soviet media and remained an official secret throughout the Soviet period.

40 Quote from Nikita Khrushchev's speech to the Congress, in which he announced that according to "scientific calculations" (Rus. *nauchnye raschety*) a Communist society would be built within twenty years.

old Singer sewing machine and narrowed the pant legs so much that I actually had a difficult time squeezing into them. In school, when she saw how happy I was, she just clapped.

The picture of my school years that I have painted seems so rosy that I should bring it down to earth a bit. This is where I should say a few words about the beginning of my career as a Komsomol organizer. It was inevitable that my leadership skills would be channeled into a formal role somehow, and so I was appointed the class Komsomol organizer. This was not a big deal for me, and I delved into this task with all my youthful idealism. My embrace of the role was fostered by the pervasive atmosphere of propaganda that was, of course, diligently nurtured by the schools. While my close family ties managed to protect me from outside influences, they nevertheless could not fully protect me from the influence of the Soviet school. Our teachers' words embedded themselves in their pupils' completely receptive minds, and they brought not only good, but like a Trojan horse, their words also bore the seeds of ideological weeds. Thus, on my spiritual "lawn" they left duplicitous traces. On one day I might enthusiastically (although somewhat clandestinely) sing the Ukrainian anthem, which was strictly forbidden by the Soviets; then the next day, at the city Komsomol headquarters, I might try to convince the leadership that although the number of Komsomol members might be declining, we would improve. Both assertions were equally sincere, and both were idealistic.

I don't blame fate that it splashed some Communist red on the banner of my youth. Even the sacred sunshine contains this color. Nor do I hold it against fate that, despite my traditional religious upbringing, I succumbed to atheistic skepticism for a while. This gave me an understanding of opposites and contradictions, which is the basic prerequisite for objectivity. Therefore, at this point I can unequivocally and firmly call the Communist ideology criminal, no matter how humane some of its individual postulates might appear to some. What's more, I always relate this part of my biography to anyone who might be interested, to convince them that reaching your desired firmness of conviction might require traveling down some winding roads.

In some ways, however, these stories have come back to bite me. When the Kharkiv Human Rights Protection Group was readying the *Biographical Glossary of Dissidents* for publication, they asked one of their young apprentices to jot down my biographical background.[41] As he listened to me talk

41 Kharkiv Human Rights Protection Group (*Kharkivs'ka Pravozakhysna Hrupa*, KhPG): leading human rights organization in independent Ukraine that

about my youthful enthusiasm, which the Komsomol had contributed to nurturing, without any malice this young man wrote, "In his youth he defended Communist ideals." This is a bit too drastic. But these words were published, and they keep resurfacing to this day in various introductions prefacing interviews I give.

Avoiding Richelieu's Spy Service

It was decided that I would major in physics. The alluring students of Kyiv University stared out at me from promotional leaflets, and I dreamed of becoming one of them. While I was still in the tenth grade, I had written a letter to one professor there, and when he unexpectedly replied, I thought it was a sign of destiny. Full of hopes and dreams, my classmate Khryzanta Hlukha and I headed to Kyiv. We were both gold medalists, so all we had to do was take a test in our main subject, get a top score, and we would automatically be accepted to the university.[42]

I decided to take the physics exam in Ukrainian, and the examiner was not too pleased about this. He encouraged me to switch to Russian, but I stood my ground, even though I understood that it might cost me dearly. And indeed, the test didn't last very long, and I got a three out of five, the lowest passing grade. It was not just any three: for a gold medalist this three was devastating. Khryzanta took the test in Russian and got a five, so she was admitted automatically. I cannot prove that the outcome was based solely on the language. Khryzanta was indeed an excellent student and had a passion for physics. But all my life I have seen my failure as the product of the examiner's malice, prompted by my linguistic inflexibility.

Out of inertia, I also took a written exam in mathematics, even though I had not prepared for that particular exam, and I got a four. Realizing that I would not get in on a competitive basis, I withdrew my documents and returned to Drohobych with what I considered a humiliating failure. (Only

---

advocates for contemporary human rights and chronicles the history of human rights activity in Ukraine. Their three-volume *Biographical Glossary of Dissidents* was published in the 2000s. Entry on M. M.: Borys Zakharov, "Marynovych Myroslav Frankovych," in *Mizhnarodnyi biohrafichnyi slovnyk dysydentiv krain tsentral'noi ta skhidnoi Evropy i kolyshn'oho SRSR*, vol. 1.1 (Kharkiv: "Prava liudyny," 2006), 425–28.

42 Gold medalist: Upon completing secondary school, top students were given a gold medal.

after many years did I recognize that this seeming disaster would eventually turn out to be a blessing.) I diffidently accepted an offer to work as a Komsomol secretary at a chisel factory in Drohobych. Since my job involved frequent visits to city's main Komsomol office, I became closely familiar with the real state of affairs—the hidden corruption and duplicity of the functionaries, who lacked all integrity—and my Komsomol idealism began to fade accordingly.

The following year, 1967, I applied to the Lviv Polytechnic Institute and was admitted with no problems (without any connections or bribes) to the department of electrophysics. As an "experienced Komsomol ringleader," I was made a Komsomol organizer almost automatically, but I didn't hold this post for long. As far as I remember, the last Komsomol activity in which I participated was a general meeting during which, at the instruction of the leadership, we were required to censure Andrii Khoma, one of our colleagues. He and his wife had apparently had a church wedding, which was a serious transgression in the eyes of the party bosses, requiring that Andrii be ousted from the Komsomol. But our whole class, including me, wholeheartedly stood by our friend because getting kicked out would have inevitably ruined his professional career. Instead, it was my "career" in the Komsomol that finally came to an end. Officially I remained a member, but I didn't take part in the organization in any way. In particular, my days as a Komsomol organizer were definitively over.

The students in my cohort at Lviv Polytechnic were like a miniature Tower of Babel, a blend of races and languages. The department was prestigious, as it trained specialists in the relatively new field of semiconductor technology. Because of this prestige, the Russian-speaking elite of Lviv made up a substantial percentage of the student body. In the dormitory, by contrast, the majority of students were ethnic Ukrainians from across Lviv oblast, some from the Carpathian Mountains. There were some ethnic Poles and even one Georgian. At times relationships among this diverse group were complicated, and tensions often arose when it came to national, social, and cultural differences. I remember one Russian classmate, Masha Starikova, while browsing at a book stall, exclaiming with surprise, "Look, they even thought of publishing *The Jungle Book* in Ukrainian!" This reminded me that a large segment of the Soviet population was fanatically convinced that Karl Marx's *Das Kapital* had originally been written in Russian.

Youth, however, has its own rules, so the atmosphere in our department was amicable on the whole. Our camaraderie was bolstered by working together on a collective farm for about two weeks before the start of

Figure 1.8. Anna and Igor Marinovich, my relatives from another branch of Marynovych family, in New York (the 1990s).

each school year: during that time, we all became good friends.[43] We used to harvest hops, and since then, whenever I travel by train to the city of Rivne, I always look out at the familiar hops plantations near the town of Brody, where we were sent, with a certain nostalgia. It was indeed during our work on the collective farm that I got to know my closest friends at the Polytechnic: Halyna Levkova, Vira Andrukhiv, Roman Yurechko, and two friends from central Ukraine, Fedir Marushchak and Sashko Parkhomenko.

I had never felt a calling to become an engineer, so I was a rather average student. I was certainly aware that I would never reach the same heights as those who had a natural talent for mathematics and engineering. I could explain how the electric current traveled along a diagram of an electric circuit, but I was hopeless when it came to explaining how it traveled along the wiring in a room. So, I was always amazed that once in a while I managed to

43 Soviet practice required students to work on a farm before each academic year, harvesting hops, tomatoes, grapes, etc., because the Soviet collective farming system struggled to manage the harvests, and the students constituted a free labor force.

get top grades on our exams. One exam in thermodynamics has forever been carved in my memory. This subject was one of the most difficult ones, and the professor was extremely demanding, so my chances of passing were rather slim. So as not to prolong the agony, I decided to be one of the first ones to take the exam. I somehow managed to answer the theoretical questions. But the practical exercise, dealing with calculating the entropy of chemical reactions, was beyond my ability because I could not remember the super-complicated formula. So, I explained to my professor, "I don't remember the formula, but since we have a solid reacting with a liquid, resulting in the formation of a gas, I can only say that the entropy would increase accordingly." The professor looked at me, a bit puzzled, took my report card, and recorded a grade of five out of five. When I left and showed this to my friends, I was not surprised when they eyed me rather suspiciously, thinking I might have bribed the professor.

In general, I never regretted listening to my sister and going to the Polytechnic. Studying the hard sciences trained me to think in a disciplined manner, and it gave me the ability to take a different approach in analyzing various problems, even using a different lexicon. In later years, I was occasionally called out for my excessive use of technical terminology. Most importantly, I grew accustomed to seeing people and society as a dynamic system, which I tended to observe from the sidelines, and to which I would apply rules that normally pertained to other realms of existence. From the scientific point of view, this approach is obviously unacceptable, but for the longest time I was fascinated with the integral unity of the world, and there was nothing I could do about this fascination—and I still cannot.

At some point, my classmates Sashko and Fedir invited several of us to visit their parents' homes in the Cherkasy and Kyiv regions, respectively. This was my first venture into Shevchenko's homeland of central Ukraine, and I anxiously gazed out of the bus windows, as if expecting a miracle. While in Sashko's native village in the Cherkasy region, one evening I naively asked him if we would be going to the *vechornytsi*—an old-fashioned custom I had read about in which village youth would gather in the evenings for traditional singing and dancing. He couldn't even make sense of my question. For a long time his village neighbors had been glued to their TV screens, and the ancient "ethnic Ukraine" I was imagining was gone with the wind. This caught me completely by surprise.

A group of us also went to the Carpathian Mountains. Since we didn't have any spare cash, we decided to hitch a ride on a freight train. We headed in the general direction of the mountains, without any particular destination in mind—we were just winging it. We had a lot of fun, sitting in the rearmost car and enjoying the beautiful panorama without a care in the world; we waved to all the guards at the crossings and bridges. Suddenly we noticed that our train was pulling into a station where there were only Polish trains. "Well, we're in for it now!" we thought. At that point, the border patrol approached us and took us to the border control station. It turned out that we had reached the border town of Sianky, still on the Ukrainian side of the border. At the station we were interrogated and searched, and since it hadn't even occurred to us to bring any documents with us, the stationmaster reported us to his superiors. Clearly, he heard something so drastic on the other end of the telephone line that he furiously slammed down the receiver and raged at us, "Scram, I don't want to see head or tail of you!"

I continued to follow politics, and my first few years at the Polytechnic were marked by pain at America's self-discreditation. The findings of the Warren Commission, which was charged with investigating John F. Kennedy's assassination, failed to produce any credible results. This was followed by the unthinkable assassination of Martin Luther King on April 6, 1968, and then Robert Kennedy's assassination on June 5 of that same year. All this was a great shock to me. Eventually the picture got a bit rosier, thanks to American accomplishments in space: the Apollo program and the broadcast of the moon landing. The whole world was glued to their TV screens.

I also observed the various wars being waged around the world with great trepidation, like the infamous US military involvement in Vietnam, the Six-Day War in 1967, and then the Sino-Soviet border conflict on Zhenbao (Damansky) Island in 1969.[44] All these conflicts proved to me that the world was far more complex than I had ever imagined.

But it was the Prague Spring that had the most significant influence on my developing worldview. In September 1968 we witnessed an astonishing event in Lviv: Soviet tank divisions returning from Czechoslovakia after the Kremlin had crushed Prague's defiant love of freedom. Back in August, when five Soviet Bloc armies had occupied Czechoslovakia, I had diligently followed events as they unfolded, never taking my ear away from the radio receiver. I still remember how stunned I was by the voice of a Czech radio announcer broadcasting a live minute-by-minute account of events as they unfolded. He described Soviet soldiers' attack on the headquarters of

44 Zhenbao (Damansky) Island: March 1969 armed conflict between China and the Soviet Union, part of a string of border disputes prompted by the Sino-Soviet split.

Radio Prague and Czech Television: how they stormed through the hallways through the entire premises and finally how they broke into the studio. Then his voice was cut off, and it became eerily silent. My heart was completely on the side of the vanquished, and in my soul, I sadly and silently said farewell to Jan Palach, who had publicly immolated himself in January 1969 in protest of the Soviet occupation and the Czechoslovak adaptation to the new situation.

During those September days, along with thousands of other Lviv residents I looked into the faces of the soldiers peering out of their tanks. It was extremely distressing: the soldiers were downcast and looked around nervously, while Lviv residents were silent and morose. At least that's how I felt. One might have expected the standard ovations to be blasted over the loudspeakers, the way it usually was during May Day parades, but I don't remember anything of the sort (or perhaps I just didn't want to hear them). There was complete silence, other than the rumble of the tanks' treads. In light of this, the events of 1970, just two years later, seemed logical: Aleksandr Solzhenitsyn was awarded the Nobel Prize for Literature, the Human Rights Commission headed by Andrei Sakharov was established in Moscow, and the first unrest surfaced in the Gdańsk Shipyards in Poland.

Even as this swell of resistance began to build, students of the time didn't live by politics alone. During the first two years of my studies, I was getting used to Lviv, toward which I felt both excitement and skepticism. The exhilaration of my student days made me fall in love with the city, coupled with lively get-togethers and youthful adventures with my friends from the Polytechnic. My infatuation was virtually carved into the attractive building facades and the mysterious meanderings of narrow side streets. Youthful reveries penetrated every crevice of the buildings' architectural embellishments and were lodged there forever. Lviv became the city of my romantic youth, and I love its twisted narrow streets, the spontaneous mosaic of its vast variety of architectural styles, and the fantastic fact that I can always resurrect some wonderful long-forgotten dream of my younger years there.

But there was also a certain distance between Lviv and me, and today I understand that I simply never really got to know the Lviv that I could love in a civic sense. The city had been too repressed by its numerous persecutions at the hands of the Soviet regime, and it didn't readily open itself up to a newcomer. After all, in those days, resistance in Lviv did not take the form of open public action but rather of preserving its way of life despite it all. And when Christmas carolers filled the city's streets, including the likes of Iryna and Ihor Kalynets, Stefa Shabatura, Olena Antoniv, Olha and Mykhailo

Horyn, Liuba and Bohdan Soroka, Yaroslav Kendzior, and the Krypiakevych family, as well as a host of other Lviv families who had brought prominence to the city, I would go to Drohobych to celebrate Christmas with my own family. Thus, our paths never crossed, and even though we lived in the same city, we were in our own parallel worlds.

To me Lviv presented its gray conformist face—perhaps because I was myself gray and conformist—and the rebellious part of me existed alongside the Soviet. Still, I hoped for some sort of miracle. For example, when my friend Orysia Savchuk made an ornate Ukrainian peasant-style vest for me in the early 1970s, I wore it often, fully aware of the challenge to the regime that it posed. Once again, I walked the same streets as a whole host of others who wore similar peasant jackets and vests, but we never crossed paths. I used to get angry because people in Lviv who knew the "Strilets" (Sich Riflemen) songs also had an innate sense of where to sing them and where not to.[45] I remember once I started to sing a Strilets song at a wedding, and everyone around me fearfully urged me to pipe down. I did understand why things were like this, but my young soul subconsciously craved a bold, public spirit of resistance, like I found in Kyiv just a few years later.

In the meantime, however, I faced an important test: becoming better acquainted with those who were secretly monitoring the loyalty of the population. It all started with a few conversations in the dormitory. During one of my trips to Kyiv I was amazed to discover that the capital of Ukraine was mostly Russian speaking. So, for a certain time I loved this city, but I regarded its residents with a certain chilliness. (This impression eventually changed with the Orange Revolution of 2004–2005, when Kyiv residents opened their homes to out-of-town participants in the protests against the falsified presidential elections.) I also became aware of the destructive consequences of the Communist Party's nationalities policy, which was boasted about in all party propaganda materials. I shared my views openly with my friends at the dormitory. Trust is an invariable part of youth, and the strong white wine that was popular among students quickly loosened everyone's tongues. It's amazing that it took as long as it did for someone to report me to the KGB. Only in my third year was I summoned to the Polytechnic's

45 Sich Riflemen: Military detachments of the Ukrainian People's Republic (1917–1921), formed in 1917 primarily of Ukrainian soldiers in the Austro-Hungarian army. Mentions of their lore and legacy were considered an expression of nationalist sentiment and therefore punishable.

First Department.[46] The accusations were serious: a warped interpretation of the nationalities policy of the Communist Party, as well as spreading malicious fabrications that dishonor the party itself.

The latter accusation stemmed from one incident in particular: the only Communist in our class, Ivan Starchuk, had been caught pilfering a term paper from one of his classmates. It caused a big scandal, and all his fellow students gleefully pointed to his association with the Communist Party, given that the party professed to be a moral entity. In the end, the KGB was obliged to roll up its sleeves and fix the situation.

Psychologically speaking, I was completely unprepared for a KGB summons—more precisely, I was not prepared to hear my interviewer tell me, "For your persistent anti-Soviet talk in the dormitory, you will be expelled from the Polytechnic Institute." It wasn't until much later that I realized that many a naïve student "fish" had gotten caught on this typical hook. This pronouncement would be directly followed by a hint of how to remedy the situation: "We might reconsider this decision if you can tangibly prove that you are not an enemy of the Soviet authorities and if you can demonstrate that you will work with us to promptly uncover such enemies." That is, the KGB's strategy was to recruit me into the ranks of informant-spies.

The threat of being expelled from the Polytechnic was devastating, and at first I did not have the strength to definitively refuse to cooperate. I therefore chose the option that seemed the most prudent to me at the time. One of my relatives described it as "Pretend to agree, but play dumb and tell them that you have neither heard nor seen anything." How was I supposed to know back then that the KGB had seen this tactic a million times already?

But then Providence came to my aid. After my conversation with the KGB, I returned to the dormitory and saw several of my friends drinking wine and trading anecdotes about Leonid Brezhnev. "So, from now on will I be required to remember all this and then sit down and write a report denouncing them?" I thought to myself and was truly horrified. I made my decision at once. I cut their conversation short and told them where I had been. I assured them that I would do everything in my power to free myself

46 First Department (Rus. *Pervyi otdel*, Ukr. *Pershyi viddil*): KGB-run department within every Soviet institution that dealt with secret information of any kind (including scientific or technical) or had printing capabilities, charged with maintaining secrecy and political security and controlling the flow of information.

from this noose, but until I did, I asked them not to discuss anything politically compromising in my presence.

The guys listened to me with amazement and nodded their heads—and then continued to swap anecdotes about Brezhnev. I wouldn't be surprised if they hadn't given any heed to anything that I had said. But their spontaneous trust generated a certain feeling of gratitude within me. I didn't know when I might be able to get myself off the hook, but I was certain that I would never become an informant.

I was also fortunate that the classmate whom we suspected of squealing on me had not been there among my friends that day because that meant that for the time being the KGB was not aware that I intended to free myself from their yoke. But soon the cat was out of the bag, and my continued claims not to have seen or heard anything annoyed the KGB. For my disobedience, however mild, I was punished by being denied participation in military training. This meant that upon finishing my studies, I would not serve in the army as a second lieutenant, like all my classmates, but as a private.

Thus, from the very beginning, pressure from the KGB created a head-on collision of two instincts: on the one hand, self-preservation pushed me toward compromises with the government; on the other hand, my moral instinct, or conscience, required that I uphold the truth. I was neither the first nor the last person in whose soul this "clash of civilizations" played out.

But, as the future demonstrated, the KGB had not yet lost all hope where I was concerned. On the eve of my final state exams, I was called to a KGB-maintained apartment in Lviv and was offered a very enticing carrot in their game of carrot and stick. I was told that until now they hadn't handled me appropriately. In order to rectify the situation, the KGB offered me radically different conditions for our cooperation: postgraduate work at the Polytechnic Institute, accommodations in Lviv, and wonderful career opportunities. Only one thing was required of me: my unequivocal readiness to carry out all assignments my supervisors might give me.

Fortunately for me, the timing of these propositions was singularly inauspicious thanks to several important events: it was in my fifth and final year of study that I met Mykola Matusevych and a group of his Ukrainian friends in Kyiv, all congregated around the Homin choir led by Leopold Yashchenko.[47] Orysia Savchuk was the one who introduced us. She had just moved to Kyiv for a job and invited me to the capital in early May 1972 for *maiivky*,

47 Homin choir: amateur choir formed in 1969, promoting Ukrainian musical traditions. Officially banned in 1971.

traditional Ukrainian festivities to celebrate the arrival of spring. The square in front of the Bolshevik metro station, where the gathering was scheduled to take place, was filled with a sea of Ukrainian embroidered shirts and the evocative sounds of Ukrainian being spoken. This provincial boy from Galicia totally lost himself in the sparkling Ukrainian humor. That first picnic was truly magical for me. Another time, on the Dnipro cliffs, where we went to party, my soul was deeply moved by the fabulous songs and the vigorous steps of the Hutsul *Arkan* dance.[48] Returning to Lviv, I did not come down from my soaring state of sweet exultation, leaving my heart in Kyiv with my new friends, and with Mykola Matusevych.

The vigor with which Mykola Matusevych entered my life and soul can only be compared to the turbulent floods of a mountain stream. Fiery and enthusiastic, Mykola melted me down to the core; he made fun of my typical Galician conformism and swept away all my youthful complexes. In other words, he turned me into a complete ruin, and only then did he start rebuilding a new personality for me.

At that time Mykola had already had some experience with being persecuted by the KGB: in 1972 they had expelled him from the history faculty of the Kyiv Pedagogical Institute for alleged "unreliability." In reality, the *Chronicle of Current Events* would later confirm that the real reason for his expulsion was his "sympathy for the Ukrainian intellectuals who in that year had been arrested."[49] By that time, he had also survived numerous brutal interrogations by KGB agents, but all this only elevated him, my mentor, several notches higher in the eyes of his admiring "pupil."

At first, our "training" was conducted via tempestuous letters: we wanted to share everything with each other, even the most inconsequential events, observations, and emotions. We quickly established an identical system of values and a similar view of the world around us. My life became a hundred times more interesting and enjoyable. Take, for example, a hilarious telegram Mykola sent me one day: "Something white appeared in the bushes!" We

48 Arkan: popular dance in the round from the Hutsul region, performed at breakneck speed by men and boys.

49 The *Chronicle of Current Events* (Rus. *Khronika tekushchikh sobytii*) was the main source of information about the dissident movement and life in the camps, disseminated in the USSR as samizdat. Further in the text the abbreviation *Chronicle* or *CCE* will be used. English translations of many issues were published by Amnesty International in the United Kingdom: *A Chronicle of Current Events*, 30 vols. (Amnesty International: London, 1971–1984). On Matusevych's expulsion see *CCE*, 49:6.

Figure 1.9. With my student colleagues (1970).

Figure 1.10. Inseparable friends: Mykola Matusevych and me in the early 1970s

laughed ourselves silly, trying to imagine how the KGB agents would toil and sweat, trying to decode the secret that might be concealed by this absurdity.

Thanks to Mykola, my life was enriched by yet another acquaintance, which even today ranks as one of the brightest moments of my life. It occurred, probably also in 1972, on a square in front of the Museum of Ukrainian Art in Kyiv, where we stood in line to see an Impressionist exhibit from the private collection of Armand Hammer, the American billionaire that the Soviet Union was courting at that time. Mykola arranged for us to meet Valentyna Chornovil, the sister of the recently arrested Viacheslav Chornovil, who was one of the leaders of the Ukrainian cultural and political revival at the time. I also met Irynka Volytska, the daughter of poet Atena Pashko.

At that time, I had already heard about the romantic, albeit tormented, love affair between Atena and Viacheslav Chornovil. To us, the rebellious youth of the 1970s, their love had become a symbol described variously as poetic, heroic, anguished, haunted, and confined, according to the different periods of Viacheslav Chornovil's biography. Atena endured and bore everything and managed to carve out her own heroic biography, gallantly standing firm against the all-powerful KGB and the whole lawless system. Every time Viacheslav was arrested, she continued the work he had left unfinished to the best of her ability.

That sunny day in Kyiv, the girls' friendly looks, the pleasure of the shared experience of enjoying art, the realization that this acquaintance had made me a sort of participant in the great national resistance: all of it is carved indelibly into my memory, so hungry for a monumental accomplishment. This is why my KGB handler's proposition to join his organization's ranks was akin to Cardinal Richelieu's proposal to d'Artagnan to join the Cardinal's Guard. I could follow the Musketeer's example and tell my handler that all my friends belong to a circle of Ukrainian patriots, and all my foes, due to some unfathomable, fatal, and unpredictable circumstances, seem to belong to the KGB. Therefore, I would be poorly received here, and totally misunderstood there.

So, I rejected the tempting proposition without any qualms, claiming that I had other plans for my life. Later, all my life I thanked God for having selected the sort of friends in front of whom I would have been embarrassed to do shameful things.

Later, after I was arrested, the investigator in charge of my case, Oleksandr Bereza, told me that the KGB officer who had been entrusted with turning me into an informant got into some hot water over this. Knowing that my grandfather was a priest, and that I had family abroad, the KGB apparently had high hopes of using me as an agent. Instead, my recruiter's lame efforts had ruined everything. Well, even if there is a grain of truth to this, the KGB's ineptitude turned out to be a saving grace for me.

Soon thereafter, even if I had any qualms about choosing this direction for my fate, such reservations completely ceased to matter. April 12, 1973, was the first time I visited Atena Pashko's always-hospitable home on Nishchynsky Street, 14, Apartment 6, in the eastern part of Lviv. I went there inadvertently, with no presentiments, and it was only after entering the apartment that I realized why I had been so mysteriously drawn to that house: sitting at the table, in addition to the hosts, were Viacheslav Chornovil's parents. They had all just returned from a court hearing, where Viacheslav had received his unjust sentence: six years of incarceration and four years of internal exile.

I sat there, overwhelmed, feeling that at that moment my past, my present, and my future had converged. From that day on, the suffering of these people was sacred to me, they themselves were beyond suspicion, and the path they traveled on was my path. (To continue the analogy to my beloved Dumas novel, this was the moment when d'Artagnan decided to join the Musketeers in a fight against the guards.) It's at such moments that you make decisions that affect the rest of your life.

This acquaintance made me feel honored to be taking part in something monumental. Later it turned out that I was not the only one who had experienced such a feeling. This is how Mykhailyna Kotsiubynska described it:

> Any pressures, persecutions, material deprivation, hardships, and the unlikelihood of self-actualization within the generally acceptable "legal parameters" were made up for by the wealth and joy of communicating with People in the real sense of the word, being part of this legendary "little band" of such people, with a certain intuitive faith in the victory of "humanity" over "brutality" that reaches beyond rationality. . . . And the good fortune to witness such victories – large and small! I would never trade my fate for any other, because it has never betrayed me.[50]

From then on, for the four years prior to my arrest, I frequently visited this cozy Lviv apartment, where the three women resided: grandmother, daughter, and granddaughter. I came not as a guest but as a pilgrim, and I never left without feeling their heartfelt blessing.

---

50 Mykhailyna Kotsiubyns'ka, *Knyha spomyniv* (Kharkiv: Akta, 2006), 101.

It was in this apartment that I first heard Atena Pashko's poems, which were read by her daughter, Irynka. Her hushed voice sounded particularly meaningful in this apartment that had been so thoroughly bugged by the KGB:

Oh Woman, how can you
sleep on this prison cot . . .
You are not a thief,
nor a murderer.
You should be bathing
each morning
In waters fragrant with
the scent of chamomile. [51]

Like a duckling that latches on to the first moving object it sees, believing it to be its mother, from then on my soul was also drawn to this wonderful poem and to its author. Later I realized that this contrast between the KGB's attempts to humiliate female prisoners and their virtuous and dignified behavior was a widespread trope.

I also found out that after Viacheslav Chornovil's arrest the KGB had refused to grant the "rebellious" couple a marriage license. But this did not prevent the KGB from using their love for each other to exert psychological pressure on Viacheslav, who was sitting in an isolation cell in Lviv. One day, after a search that lasted many hours, Atena was detained and brought to the same isolation prison. Then, supposedly by accident, they met in the hallway, so that Viacheslav could see that his beloved had also been arrested. (His sister Valentyna was also detained for three days.) This unexpected meeting—and Viacheslav's robust cry of "Atena, be brave!"—made her knees buckle, and she slid down the wall. She was released on the third night and returned by taxi to her worried but brave family—her mother, with her "boundless love, understanding, unequivocal politeness, tact, and nobility of soul" (here I am quoting Atena herself), and her daughter, who was often a great source of support for her mother.

This is how Atena's turbulent relationship with Viacheslav unfolded. It wasn't until 1978, during his internal exile in Yakutia, that they were finally allowed to marry. The main features of Atena's life when I got to know her were interrogations, searches, spies, listening devices, provocations,

51 *Iak zhe Vam, Zhinko / na narakh spyt'sia . . . / Vy zh ne hrabizhnytsia, / ani ne vbyvtsia. / Vam by kupatys' / kozhnoho ranku / U vodakh, shcho pakhnut' / zilliam rum'ianku.*

psychological pressure, and a host of other difficulties. Whenever Atena and I wanted to discuss something that was not meant for the KGB's ears, we would go for a walk around the neighborhood. Interestingly enough, the KGB spread a rumor among Atena's dissident community: "Those two are so silly—Atena and Myroslav going around hiding and whispering outside her house, thinking that we cannot hear them." I expect it must have been infuriating for them that at least some of what we said was not audible to them.

Atena's duel with the KGB was lopsided but noble, and her poems from that time are like a cardiogram found in the archives, testifying to her pain.

Why bother thinking?
Do not dare to think!
Why not turn into a robot—a robot!
And walk in rhythm,
And walk to the beat
Just trampling on the flowers
With your boots, with your boots![52]

Experience Gained from Other Challenges

But let us return to 1972, when, having completed my studies, I moved to Ivano-Frankivsk in August. I was working at the Positron factory, which produced semiconductor devices. Obviously, I was being watched there as well because I was summoned to the factory's First Department. This factory was under strict control, so such a summons was not unusual. The KGB had not yet given up on me and was still trying to lure me in by resorting to traditional "carrot and stick" methods. I was working in the factory's Information Department as an English interpreter, and when an exhibition of our products in Vienna was organized, I was supposed to escort the exhibition as an English-speaking guide. But I was summoned to the KGB office, where they asked me: "So will you cooperate with us, or not?" Since I refused yet again, I was not allowed to go abroad.

I didn't work at this factory for long because in the autumn of the following year I was conscripted into the army. My rapport with my coworkers was very good, so my Russian supervisor, Nina Bragina, who had recently moved to Ivano-Frankivsk from the Moscow region, attempted to make a deal with

52 *Navishcho dumaty? / Ne smity dumaty! / O, iakby tak: robotom, robotom! / I ity u rytmi, / I ity u takti / Otak po kvitakh—chobotom, chobotom!*

Figure 1.11. Atena Pashko and her husband Viacheslav Chornovil in exile in Yakutia.

the military recruiters to get me a deferment. However, as she told me later, this was firmly denied, the recruiters citing a KGB directive.

My year of military service was yet another phase of my civic education. I was with the Anti-Aircraft Surveillance Division in Vologda, Russia. Absolute obedience did not come easily to me, but neither was I genetically predisposed to rebellion. There was the usual ruthlessness from the officers and brutality from the rank and file. Of course, I understand that the ferment of male youth creates an environment that is not suited for gentle souls—this phenomenon replicates itself in armies all over the world. In the Soviet army of the 1970s, however, there were no lofty ideals to motivate us, and instead of cultivating heroes, oftentimes this mixture produced moral invalids.

Once I was in the army, the KGB did not harass me too much; but, as one of my supervising officers warned me, I was being watched diligently. The dirty work of scrutinizing the soldiers was done by particular army units, and they clearly didn't like the KGB, whom they considered their competitors. Later on, when comparing my situation in the army with my life in prison, I always noted that from a psychological perspective, the former had been more difficult for me. At least in prison you could lodge a protest or write a petition to the procurator, while in the army that was not possible.

I do, nevertheless, remember one protest I waged in the army because it cursed me for the rest of my life. At some point my platoon was ordered to perform a task that was well beyond our capacity and without any time for rest. "So when can we rest?" I protested. My company commander glared at me and blurted out, "You will rest in your grave!" His words turned out to be prophetic: my life has left little time for rest.

The hazing that is customary to the army was subdued in our case, especially as all eight of us new recruits had higher education, putting us in a unique category. Early on, the sergeants realized that the service we could provide for them was more valuable than any thrill they might have gotten from tormenting us. For example, I became the platoon "scribe," composing many greetings and love letters on the sergeants' behalf or embellishing the farewell scrapbooks that each soldier took home as a memento. When we became the "old-timers," we did away with the hazing altogether (at least during our service there).

I have kept in contact with two of my friends from that time: Gennady Plotkin, a Jew from Leningrad, and Gurami Parulua, an Abkhazian from Sukhumi. I see Gennady almost every year when I go to the United States, where he emigrated in 1978. In July of 2007, the three of us even organized a nostalgic reunion in Sukhumi. Gurami unfortunately passed away in 2013.

It was in the army that I first ran into the classic problem of collective responsibility. I had started growing a mustache back in my early youth; as soon as fuzz began to appear under my nose, I began cultivating this new aspect of my self-image. As I was getting ready to go off to the army, I knew that in the Soviet Army, only Georgians were allowed to have a mustache. This privilege dated back to the Stalin era; the official explanation was that the mustache was an object of national pride for Georgians. Indeed, Stalin, an ethnic Georgian himself, knew this well. I remarked on this with irony: "So, in the Soviet Union, it's only the Georgians who are allowed to have national pride."

Clearly, I bristled at the thought that I should voluntarily shave off my mustache. So, I kept my mustache even after I was conscripted. For a while it was tolerated, but then my company commander decided to put an end to this capriciousness. This happened on a Saturday, when the company was headed to the bath house to take their showers. Once we were all in formation, the company commander announced, "We will not go to the showers until Private Marynovych shaves his mustache." I refused. The whole

Figure 1.12. With the Soviet Army in Vologda (1974).

Figure 1.13. With my army buddies, Gennady Plotkin and Gurumi Parulua, near Lake Ritsa (2007).

company stood there as ten minutes passed, then twenty minutes. . . . Finally, someone had had enough, and before you know it the entire company started yelling at me: "So, there should be separate rules for you? Look at the dandy! Go shave your mustache; it's time to take our showers!" That was how I lost my mustache, and since then, I detest the concept of collective responsibility.

Regardless of what happened in the army, the greatest credit for my burgeoning civic awareness most certainly goes to Mykola Matusevych, who was my closest friend at the time. He was the one who grabbed me by the scruff of my neck and hoisted me to heights of bravery and civic disobedience, the likes of which I would never have been able to reach myself. By his side I became fearless, and thanks to him I became a *homo erectus*. He had that effect on others as well.

My dissident education was supplemented by self-published literature—*samvydav* in Ukrainian, more commonly known by its Russian name of *samizdat*. I mainly listened to this literature being read over Radio Liberty or other "enemy voices," but occasionally Mykola and I got our hands on photocopies or tattered pages of handed-down typewritten copies. For example, this is how I managed to familiarize myself with Ivan Dziuba's book *Internationalism or Russification?*, which was hugely influential among Ukrainian dissidents.[53] Today this work is regarded with some skepticism, so I will cite a fragment from Mykhailyna Kotsiubynska's memoir to highlight its importance at the time:

> This work was very important to me. It was virtually a Ukrainian literary primer and was able to explain and formulate those things within me that had been dormant and not thought through. Today, some of those who do not have a sense for history might not recognize the subtext that was "revolutionary" for those days, because the ideas in the work were bolstered by quotations from Lenin. But therein lies the historical meaning of Dziuba's truth, specific to those days: dismantling the stereotypes from within, presenting new ideas, rocking mainstream dogmas within an ideological domain that was familiar to everyone, utilizing recognizable terminology and a system of concepts that had been ob-

53 Written in 1965, *Internationalism or Russification?* was a response to the arrests of the *shistdesiatnyky*. In it, Dziuba, a literary critic, offered a Marxist critique of Soviet nationalities policy, arguing that since the Stalin-era Russian chauvinism had dominated and that the Soviet Union needed to return to Lenin's principles. The work was immediately banned; Dziuba was fired, expelled from the Writers' Union, and later arrested.

tained with our mother's milk. After all, one cannot reach Mt. Everest without previously mastering more accessible heights.[54]

From the moment I met Mykola, I felt pulled toward my beloved Kyiv, although at first it was impossible to follow that longing. Just before my army conscription, in September 1973 I married Mariia Labovka, a childhood friend from Stebnyk, where my grandfather had been parish priest until 1957. The Labovkas were his neighbors. Of course, Mykola was my best man at the wedding. Soon thereafter, he became my confidant when, mainly through my own fault, the life I shared with Mariia hit a dead end. He also came to visit me at my military camp in Vologda and, together with other friends, to the Kyiv train station to welcome me back when I returned to Ukraine after my year of military service. Then, when my family hearth was ultimately extinguished before it had even had a chance to catch flame, it was Mykola who helped me deal with the psychological stress and feelings of guilt that followed my divorce.

Now everything lined up so that I could finally move to Kyiv. At the factory in Ivano-Frankivsk where I returned after my military service, they offered me a different position, knowing full well that I would reject it. I abandoned everything, and with the faintest of hopes that I might be able to get a residence permit and a job, in the autumn of 1974 I boarded a train for Kyiv.[55] My mother remained alone in her house because at that time Nadiika was already teaching in Rivne, at School #15, and now her son had flown off to Kyiv, like a moth drawn to the light.

---

54 Kotsiubyns'ka, *Knyha spomyniv*, 50.

55 During the Soviet period, a residence permit (Rus. *propiska*, Ukr. *propyska*) was a prerequisite for employment in a given city. Otherwise, you were considered an illegal worker and subject to arrest.

Chapter Two

Finally in Kyiv

It's Not Easy to Be a Vagabond

At that time, the Ukrainian national self-defense front in Kyiv had been totally devastated, fragmented, and practically demoralized by endless defeats. The Khrushchev thaw had ended, and Leonid Brezhnev was in charge in Moscow. Petro Shelest, the Secretary of the Communist Party of Ukraine, was accused of "Ukrainian nationalism" and dismissed.[1] In 1972, Ivan Dziuba, the author of the revolutionary *Internationalism or Russification?* was arrested and ousted from the Writers' Union of Ukraine. The new regime left its mark through the strong-arm tactics of Volodymyr Shcherbytsky, the new party boss in Ukraine, who was hell-bent on "establishing order." That dark year, 1972, witnessed mass arrests of Ukrainian intellectuals, and this resulted in despondency and hopelessness. A new wave of Russification was underway. Ukrainophobes rejoiced. As the arrested dissident Zynovy Antoniuk, a major distributor of *samizdat*, was told by his interrogator, "After this, we'll have about ten years of peace."[2]

Then we got word that Ivan Dziuba had signed a statement of repentance and was subsequently released from prison.[3] I remember discussing this with

---

1 Petro Shelest (1908–1996): First Secretary of the Communist Party of Ukraine from 1963–1972, Shelest was known for encouraging—or at least tolerating—limited Ukrainianization in the spheres of culture and education. It was during his time in office that the *shistdesiatnyk* movement emerged; his removal from office coincided with Moscow's broader crackdown on Ukrainian "national deviation" that led to the arrest of many *shistdesiatnyky*.

2 Horbal, *Prezentatsiia zhyttia*, 208.

3 Dziuba was sentenced to five years in prison in April 1973; in November 1973 he issued a public recantation of the views expressed in *Internationalism*

Mykola Matusevych while strolling down Khreshchatyk Boulevard in the center of Kyiv. We felt as if our flag had fallen. We were young and not particularly interested in knowing the circumstances that led Dziuba to take this step. Our verdict was unequivocal. We certainly understood that when the army unit's banner falls, its spirit goes with it. As Dziuba's fellow dissident Svitlana Kyrychenko later put it, "It wasn't just yourself that you shot, Ivan."[4]

I felt the consequences of all this personally as early as 1975. When I spoke Ukrainian, it shocked people in the personnel departments that I frequented in an attempt to find work and provoked aggression in public locations. Informants were everywhere, my friends were intimidated by the KGB, and absurd charges were leveled at them. Members of the newly disbanded Homin choir, including my good friend Anna Koval, had been accused by a party boss of performing "an anti-Soviet dance," for dancing a traditional Hutsul dance.

All we could do in the face of all of this was cry—or laugh. Mykola and I chose the latter. Actually, he took the lead, and without him, I no doubt would have returned to the carefully ordered world of a provincial Galician. Our laughter did not diminish the suffocation we felt under Brezhnev, obviously; however, armed with sarcasm and jokes, young people helped themselves survive.

So, a new phase of my life began, and I had to set up my life in this new city. For strictly practical reasons, I boarded with the Matusevych family. It would be difficult to quantify the kindnesses that this family bestowed upon me—not only Mykola, but first and foremost his mother, Nastia, who taught biology at the middle school in the town of Vasylkiv outside of Kyiv, and Tamila, his sister, who at that time worked as an engineer at an electro-computing factory. Nastia's apartment in Vasylkiv and Tamila's in Kyiv became "my own"; I shared their daily lives and their holidays, not to mention their refrigerator.

Both women, Nastia and Tamila, were totally fearless when it came to the KGB. In Nastia's case, this bravery can be explained by her inherited natural nobility and by the spiritual bond between her and her son. And the two formed a mutual support system for each other. That was why Mykola always tried to be so brave: so that his mother could be proud of him, and his mother was fearless so that she would not be diminished in her son's eyes.

---

or Russification?, which was published in the influential newspaper *Literaturna Ukraina* (Literary Ukraine). He was subsequently released.

4 Kyrychenko, *Liudy ne zi strakhu*, 100.

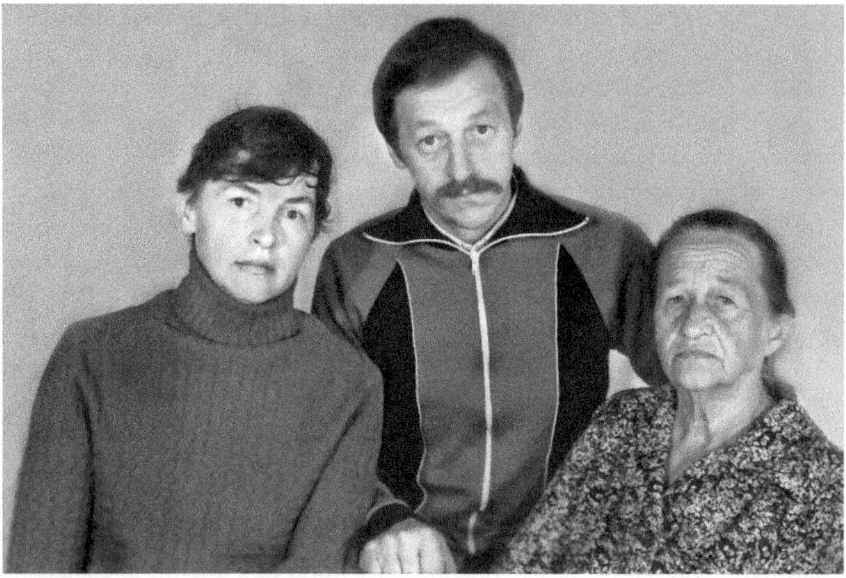

Figure 2.1. Mykola Matusevych with his mother, Nastia, and sister Tamila during his exile in the village of Kyra, Chita Region, 1984

Tamila's courage can be demonstrated by one incident: on March 6, 1977, Ukraine, and Kyiv in particular, experienced a small earthquake, the epicenter of which was in Bucharest. At that time, Mykola and I were already members of the Ukrainian Helsinki Group and anticipated that we would soon be arrested, without knowing when exactly it would happen. We had already endured surveillance, searches, and an official warning, and the KGB's constant attention was becoming exasperating. When the earthquake struck, Mykola and I were at Tamila's apartment. We were sitting in the living room, engrossed in something, when we heard the dishes rattling in the cupboard, and Tamila's voice rang out from the kitchen: "Those damned KGB—now they're even shaking the building!"

So, from the time I moved to the Kyiv region, for the most part I stayed in Vasylkiv at Nastia Matusevych's apartment or in Kyiv at Tamila's apartment. I'm still amazed that my hosts managed to tolerate this eternal vagabond who lacked any means of making a proper living. My income was only sporadic (as will presently become clear), and my mother's and Nadiika's ability to support me financially was limited at the time. Eventually, when I had been underfoot for long enough, Mykola and I rented an apartment in a small building in Kyiv, later moving to a similar building just across the street from the writers' house on Khmelnytsky Street, where the writer Borys Antonenko-Davydovych lived.[5]

Nastia tried to find me a job, introducing me to some people who might be able to help. Not only were Mykola and I grateful to her for this, but so were my mother and Nadiika. Our families got to know each other. Mykola and I still have a beautiful photo of both our mothers, most likely taken at Mykola's family's country house in the village of Shevchenkivka, outside Vasylkiv. Both of our mothers were holding a rake and a pitchfork. In this photo they both look so young—smiling and happy.

My relationship with the Matusevych family is an example of a shortcoming of mine that seems to hound me all my life: not only do I have a difficult time acknowledging and adequately appreciating those who assist me, sometimes I even cause them some grief. I have a difficult time tamping this down—it just rushes over me, beyond my control. A case in point is when Tamila was being courted.

Mykola and I often agonized over the fact the beautiful Tamila, a quintessential example of a Ukrainian woman, had remained single after her divorce. So, when we were invited to a party with a potential suitor, we were all delighted, and I was hoping to help things along in some way. When there was a lull in conversation during dinner, I tried to save the situation by starting a song. The first song that came to mind was a Transcarpathian folksong that included the lyrics "I was hoping for a young lad, but they gave me away to an old guy." When I got to that line, I turned bright red because the man was certainly not young, and the song could be interpreted as sending a message from the girl's friends. Unsurprisingly the tension at the table became even more pronounced, and I, red as a beet, had to finish the song all by myself. Soon thereafter the potential lovers went their separate ways, and I saw this incident as a symbol of how "graciously" I paid Tamila back for her assistance and kindness.

I ran into a similar situation with my friend Natalia Yakovenko's husband, Vasyl. I had met Natalia (then still Natalia Faustova) in 1973 in the Carpathians. At that time, she worked with Mykola Matusevych at the Central State Historical Archive of the Ukrainian SSR, so it was only natural that she soon joined the same group of Kyivites that I had recently become a part of. Our youthfulness and the Carpathian setting made for a wonderful atmosphere and, as was always the case, Mykola was the center of the

5 Writers' house: known as Rolit (*Robitnyk literatury*, "laborer of literature"), this building housed over one hundred authors and artists.

crowd: jovial, fiery, and sharp tongued. Discussions with him were not just idle conversations but also memorable intellectual jousting matches—cascades of brilliant polemical pronouncements. Natalia, with her quick-witted and sharp sarcasm, was the ideal match for him. I could never reach their level, but I suspect that they never really expected it of me. After all, every wordsmith wants not only worthy competitors but also admirers.

Natalia's apartment in Kyiv was always very hospitable and friendly. Many cups of coffee were drunk, and many laughs were shared in her narrow and crowded kitchen. An entire "Club of Coffee Drinkers" took up residence there. I considered every gathering with Mykola and our other friends in her apartment to be a festive occasion. I was rather proud that Natalia considered me a friend. But at the same time, I was in awe of her, recognizing the obvious superiority of her sharp intellect.

Once, a young psychology student was visiting Natalia's apartment, and having listened to our conversations, he rendered his professional verdict: "I don't know who you all are, but I can see that you certainly have some psychological issues with adapting to the social environment, and if you're not careful, sooner or later you will run into problems with the authorities." It was just a casual conversation, but it certainly made an impression on me. I was amazed that our defiant attitudes could be so easily recognized even in seemingly innocent conversations.

About that time, Natalia married Vasyl Yakovenko, and we all attended their wedding in Vasyl's home village. It was only at the wedding that Vasyl finally realized that he had married not only Natalia but also all of her friends, and they were not about to give her up. After the wedding, Vasyl moved in with Natalia, and soon thereafter (at her prodding), he temporarily offered me his one-room bachelor pad. This was a fantastic offer, and I was extremely grateful. The flashing red warning signal that I might inadvertently blurt out something inappropriate had not gone off yet in my head.

Two months later, knowing that Natalia would be stopping by the apartment, I decided to set up a gag for her before going to work. Today it is difficult to say why exactly I found this funny, but I planted footprints leading to the couch, where I left a note saying: "The steps to our happiness." I waited all day in vain for Natalia's laughing phone call, but when I returned home that evening, I found a sarcastic note—from Vasyl. This was classic. I immediately called Natalia and apologized, and she had to calm me down. After all, Vasyl understood that there was a big difference between betrayal and just a lame prank. I did, however, vacate Vasyl's apartment, and soon thereafter they traded in both their apartments for a larger one.

At some point, Mykola Matusevych, his friend Vasyl Shkliar (a young writer), and I decided to learn what our fates as bachelors would be. At that time, a well-known fortune teller from the Polissia region was popular in Kyiv, so we three guys decided that simply pulling petals off a daisy to predict if "she loves me, she loves me not" wasn't enough. With the impulsiveness characteristic of youth, soon the three of us were sitting on a bus, heading toward a remote village in Polissia.[6]

The grotesqueness of the situation became apparent as soon as we approached the fortune teller's house. The yard was full of women and girls, patiently lined up. I can only imagine how we three young men might have looked amidst this throng. Everyone maintained a solemn atmosphere, and we suppressed spasms of laughter, not daring to shatter the "hallowed" moment. We only allowed ourselves to crack up later.

I honestly do not remember what the old fortune-teller predicted for my friends, but for me she forecast that I would be married three times, and the third time would be a happy and long marriage. And eventually that's what happened. (I remain respectful of my two earlier spouses, but it remains true, even today, that my loving life partner appeared later—when I was in internal exile.) I do, however, take issue with the fortune-teller's other prediction: she told me that prison hovered around me. "It surrounds you, but you will not end up in it." Her pronouncement came flooding back to me when I was incarcerated in a KGB interrogation cell. I suppose I could sue the old con artist for misleading this young rebel!

Obviously, life in Kyiv was more than just these humorous episodes, and I will return to its other aspects later. Nevertheless, Mykola and I had an unfailing ability to find something amusing even in the most tragic events. My attempts to find a job can serve as an example. My first job in Kyiv was as technical editor of the journal *Pochatkova Shkola* (Elementary school), a maternity leave replacement position. It was Hanna Sushan, the mother of one of our new friends, Olia Heiko, who got me this job through her connections. She was well known in elite Kyiv circles because Volodymyr Semychasny, who had been KGB chief of the USSR from 1961–1967, was one of her friends. So, her recommendation was sufficient to get me the job. To us, however, she was just a friendly and pleasant lady, who regarded us—these unusual young boys who kept showing up at her apartment—with a certain amount of curiosity, and she didn't hesitate to help us.

6 Polissia: forested, marshy region straddling the Ukrainian-Belarusian border.

One can only imagine the shock the editor-in-chief, Alla Lukianets, must have experienced when the KGB revealed to her who it was she had hired for this position. Generally speaking, this woman was nice and good natured, but her concept of safety was based on unequivocal loyalty to the government. Once, when the artistic director suggested using yellow and blue colors to represent a flowery meadow and a blue sky, it caused a real scandal among the editors.[7]

At that time, Mykola and I were too young to fully understand the implications of the attention we were getting from the KGB. Somehow, Mykola talked me into leaving a package with a loudly ticking alarm clock on my desk overnight. I'm not sure if this prank had the desired effect, but soon thereafter, the editor reinstated the employee who had been on maternity leave (before the woman even had a chance to recover from giving birth), and this gave her legal grounds to fire me. Everyone at the editorial office understood what was happening. At my going-away party, the woman I had replaced even apologized to me because she realized how she had been used. She actually told me that she was being called back to work for just a few days to give them enough time to officially fire me. Still, in spite of my criticism of Alla Lukianets's behavior, I do nevertheless have pleasant memories of my work at the journal.

I should mention a moment of hesitation in my evolution as a dissident that happened before my time at *Pochatkova Shkola*. Initially, Hanna Sushan had hoped to set me up with the Ukrainian Soviet Encyclopedia (USE). I was well aware that at the time this was perhaps the most prestigious editorial office in Kyiv, and that it would be difficult to land a job there. So, as I walked to the interview, I contemplated an evil thought: should I get hired, I would suppress my rebellious streak and not visit the Shevchenko monument on May 22.

This was a significant moment! The "fish" had almost been hooked; I was virtually ready to swallow the lure. To my good fortune, the fisherman got distracted and didn't cast his line. We have so many treacherous thoughts in life that lure us to take the wrong turn, and if we let our guard drop, such thoughts might ultimately alter the direction of our entire life. Thankfully, my guardian "angels" were strong enough at that time, and such

7 The blue and yellow colors represented the pre-Soviet Ukrainian flag and were therefore anathema to the Soviet government, which viewed the flag as an expression of Ukrainian nationalism punishable by incarceration. The same flag was subsequently adopted by independent Ukraine.

psychological subtleties did not interest them. In the end, I was not hired for this job at the USE.

After the journal *Pochatkova Shkola*, my second job was with the Volunteer Society of Booklovers (*Dobrovil'ne tovarystvo liubiteliv knyhy URSR*), which was then located in the prestigious building that had been the German consulate before the war. Interestingly enough, on my first day at work, a young Party coordinator at this establishment invited me to lunch, and conspiratorially told me, "You still aren't a member of the Party? No way! You have to join right away! Once you become a Communist, you'll get an apartment; you will have everything! Don't you understand?" A few days later, he couldn't look me in the eye, having found out who I was, and having so carelessly and trustingly spilled the beans. I quit this job after a few months. It was unbearable to work on something so useless: the organization had evidently been formed to provide a home base for Vadym Sobko, a committed Soviet writer.[8]

I got my third job by compromising my soul. Previously, when looking for a job in Kyiv, I had scared away many potential employers by speaking Ukrainian. With fear in their eyes, they would inform me that an appropriate person had already been found. Consequently, when I got an interview at the publishing house Tekhnika (Technology), I wised up, and during my meeting with the personnel office I spoke Russian. I was immediately hired as a technical editor, and I duly waited the three days, a legal requirement for the hiring announcement to become legally valid. After that, to management's sheer astonishment, I started speaking Ukrainian with everyone.

My work there was pleasant overall, and I got along great with my colleagues. I didn't shirk additional menial duties that were assigned to me, so I was quickly accepted as one of them. But I had a feeling that this would not last long. Indeed, by the end of 1976 (by which time I had already become a member of the Ukrainian Helsinki Group), the director of the publishing house called me in and suggested that I write a memo requesting a promotion to a higher-level, higher-salaried position as a literary director. At the same time, I was told to write a parallel memo, asking to be discharged as a technical editor. Steadfastly, and with a smile, I looked at

8 Vadym Sobko (1912–1981): Ukrainian novelist whose work focused on military and labor themes. Awarded a Stalin Prize for literature in 1951.

the director to let him know that I was on to what he was doing. Without another word, I wrote both memos.[9]

I am fully aware that many dissidents would have fought to the last. But I follow a different rule: I prefer to leave people to face their own consciences. Unsurprisingly, no miracle took place, and the director did what was expected of him. Just after Christmas, he informed me in his office that the circumstances had changed, and due to some cutbacks, management had to eliminate the position for which I had been slated, but they did accept my resignation. He hid his eyes from me because he was fully aware of what he was doing. He behaved so awkwardly that I had to smooth things over, and with a smile, I told him that I was not surprised because I knew from the start what was going on.

The final straw came about a month later, when my colleagues at work told me that the director had awarded me a bonus for my excellent work. Everyone understood what had happened, and they all took my side.

A little further on, I will talk about the last job I had before my arrest, but for now I want to keep the chronology intact.

The Figures of "My Kyiv"

Our life in Kyiv was interesting. (I say "our," because once I moved to the capital, Mykola Matusevych and I became inseparable; people often even mixed up our names.) It basically boiled down to three elements: trying to keep the spirits of persecuted patriots and the families of those who had been incarcerated up, participating in the Ukrainian cultural life of Kyiv and frequently organizing our own events, and all the while living a life of youthful fun. Often it would even have been difficult to differentiate between these three activities. Our fellow dissident Vira Lisova gives a very clear description of our social life in Kyiv at that time:

> After many of the political prisoners had been arrested, sentenced, and sent to prison camps (1972–1974), their friends and families who were still free came together. In spite of KGB interference, we began to network more actively. We established contacts with the families of those who had been incarcerated from other towns and villages across Ukraine. We even created certain traditions:

---

9 The unspoken expectation was that he would collaborate with the KGB in return for a promotion; if he refused, not only would he not be promoted, he would be fired.

> sending birthday, New Year's, and other holiday greetings[. . .] Halyna Didkivska and her mother Hanna, as well as Svitlana Kyrychenko, Nadiia Svitlychna, Tamila Matusevych, and several others, were very good at that. Valentyna Berdnyk organized dressmaking classes, which were held at Vira Lisova's apartment. Being isolated in a society dominated by confusion, silence, and fear had brought us all closer together. This also allowed us to share the latest news from the camps and the prisoners' families.[10]

I suspect that many readers might ask, "OK, so what about all those anti-Soviet activities for which you were fired from your jobs, summoned to the KGB, and accused of public disturbances?" It is difficult to explain what exactly these activities consisted of: our public expressions of Ukrainianness, demonstrative solidarity with the political prisoners, refusal to denounce those who fell under KGB suspicion, preservation of our national and religious traditions, and refusal to succumb to fear, which was the glue that kept the powder keg together. We did what Lesia Ukrainka had said: "Through my tears I will go on laughing, sing songs through all my hardships."[11] Our major "transgression" was attempting to live a *normal* Ukrainian life. Indeed, the Soviet system saw this as a challenge worthy of punishment.

The pillar of the dissident movement was Borys Dmytrovych Antonenko-Davydovych, a Ukrainian writer who witnessed virtually the entire history of Ukraine under Soviet rule: he was born in the Russian Empire and lived until 1984. I met him just a few times—after all, one shouldn't go on pilgrimages too often. And indeed, I felt just like a pilgrim from the very first minutes of visiting his home. I don't remember anything from that first evening. Like a downpour flowing over a parched and cracked dry earth without ever soaking into it, his presence washed over me. It was Mykola Matusevych and one of the women, perhaps Atena Pashko or Mykhailyna Kotsiubynska, who kept the conversation going. My future visits did not differ much from the first one.

Without any coercion, Borys Dmytrovych immediately commanded the listener's attention and held on to it, never losing the thread of the conversation, even when it wandered. His words were honest and true, and the KGB's

10 Vira Lisova, "Zhinky v Rusi oporu simdesiatykh rokiv", Virtual'nyi muzei Dysydents'kyi Rukh v Ukraini, http://archive.khpg.org/index.php?id=1202337115.

11 Lesia Ukrainka (1871–1913): leading Ukrainian poet in the Russian Empire. Quote is from her poem "Contra Spem Spero!"

attempts to turn him into a "soul catcher" were utterly futile.[12] What was most striking about Borys Dmytrovych was his noble stature; his slimness, which he kept into deepest old age; his gallantry toward women; and his eternally youthful face—a true knight. He would always express his admiration for the heroes of the Battle of Kruty, which is the Ukrainian version of the Battle of Thermopylae.[13] In the 1970s, not a trace remained of the graves of those young boys in the Kyivan hills. Once, Mykola and I went and scattered some flowers on the grass there.

Borys Dmytrovych was a spiritual father to many. It took a great spiritual gift to burn so brightly and steadfastly and to be able to bestow one's light upon others in the midst of Soviet sociopolitical mayhem and relentless persecutions, despite the seeming absurdity and loftiness of such nobility. He played this role both for me and for my future wife, Liuba. She and Mykhailyna Kotsiubynska, as well as several other compassionate souls, stayed with him and witnessed his journey toward the end of his life.

I personally do not remember him as frail. For me, he will always be a tireless storyteller, sitting in his chair with his dog Palma on his knees, or else standing with the upright posture of a soldier when we came to sing carols, singing his favorite song at his request: "The Eternal Revolutionary," with words by the poet Ivan Franko. Our caroling always brought boundless joy to both sides. He would become emotional because of the consideration that had been shown to him, but he also served as a source of energy from which all the parched and powerless drew strength.

Mykhailyna Kotsiubynska was Borys Antonenko-Davydovych's neighbor, and one can only imagine how nervous I was when I went to see her for the first time. Her name was the pride and joy of the *shistdesiatnyky*. It legitimized the dissident movement in the eyes of the public because a movement that was supported by people like the niece of the great Mykhailo Kotsiubynsky could not be anything but morally and culturally valid.[14] Anyone who wanted to associate with Mykhailyna understood that she had

12 That is, to recruit him to, in turn, recruit and/or entrap his colleagues.

13 Battle of Kruty: fought on January 29, 1918, between Ukrainian and Bolshevik forces. Ukrainian forces, attempting to block the Bolshevik advance on Kyiv, were outnumbered approximately eight to one. Though around half the Ukrainian soldiers were killed, they were able to delay the Bolsheviks sufficiently to allow the government of the Ukrainian People's Republic to sign the treaty of Brest-Litovsk.

14 Mykhailo Kotsiubynsky (1864–1913) was a prominent Ukrainian ethnographer and writer who championed nothing but the truth. –M. M.

Figure 2.2. Mykhailyna Kotsiubynska as a young associate at the Ukrainian Institute of Literature, Kaniv, 1961.

entrusted her friends with her most precious possession—her renowned family name—and she always wanted to remain worthy of it. She trusted them to never dishonor that name.

As a twenty-five- or twenty-six-year-old young man, I considered my friendship with Mykhailyna to be a distinct honor. From the first days of our acquaintance, I will always remember her sparkling humor and her characteristic laughter, which demonstrated her ability to appreciate a good joke. Much later, while serving my prison term in Camp 36 in the Perm region, I received a postcard from Mykhailyna, in which she hilariously described the ongoing preparations for the celebration of the fifteen hundredth anniversary of Kyiv's founding. I still remember one ironic phrase she wrote at that time: "Kyiv washed its neck to go with the deep décolletage." But fate also brought her suffering, and at times her suffering was clear—like on her birthday, as she sang the sad song "*Tsvyntari*" (Cemeteries). She sang it warmly but with the pain of separation from its author, Mykola Horbal, who at that time was already a political prisoner.[15]

I will always be grateful to Mykhailyna for unveiling to us, her closest friends, the domestic and family world of famous Ukrainian poets and writers, concealed behind the ideological facades of official Soviet propaganda. Mykhailyna showed me the spiritual world of the real Pavlo Tychyna, who had been a brilliant Ukrainian poet in his youth but not strong enough to withstand the Bolshevik "tsunami" later in his life.[16]

Mykhailyna remained loyal to the noble spirit that unified all the *shistdesiatnyky*. The more friends of hers who left for Siberia (or for the hereafter), the more firmly and tenaciously she held on to the invisible flag of the dissident resistance movement. Later on, I will talk about the important influence she had in my own growth as a dissident.

It is virtually impossible to imagine the Ukrainian Kyiv of the 1970s without Oksana Yakivna Meshko.[17] She was the force behind all sorts of community events meant to reawaken Ukrainian national consciousness, spirited discussions, and vibrant emotions. She belonged to a special category of "reawakeners," those who would not let the average citizen sleep peacefully. She sparked countless ideas, which then resulted in many articles and books written under her direct influence, prodding, and urging. Many people who had promised her various things hid from her to

15 Horbal was arrested in 1970 for producing and distributing samizdat materials.

16 Pavlo Tychyna (1891–1967): prominent Ukrainian poet. His early works synthesized baroque and symbolist styles; in the early 1930s, he embraced the Soviet regime and switched to writing in a socialist realist style. He was a harsh critic of the *shistdesiatnyky*.

17 Oksana Meshko (1995–2001): longtime dissident and founding member of the Ukrainian Helsinki Group. She was arrested and imprisoned several times over her life and under constant KGB watch.

avoid her biting sarcasm, until works that went on to join the pantheon of Ukrainian culture finally saw daylight.

It is not easy to get too close to motivators like this. In her lifetime Oksana Yakivna was a legendary woman. Her willful, almost despotic character evoked fear and trepidation in our softhearted Ukrainian Cossack souls. Her son, Oles Serhiienko, explained: "People of strong character, and she was one of them, tend to be rather despotic toward their family."[18] Kyiv had its own "Iron Lady," long before the renowned Margaret Thatcher. But this sobriquet pales in comparison to other analogues: Vasyl Ovsiienko remembers that our fellow dissident Yury Lytvyn called her "our Joan of Arc." Vasyl himself had perhaps the best name for her: "our immortal and beloved Cossack mother."[19]

Oksana Meshko was intimately familiar with prison latrines. During Beria's time, she was tried by a proletarian "high court," the infamous "troika," a trio of judges, and one young arrogant member of this trio kept advising her, "You are young and beautiful, and in camp you will age and bend quickly."[20] These words resounded like a refrain in her soul for the rest of her life. When I met Meshko, the years had already taken their toll, and her once-slender girlish frame was bent. She told me how once in the 1970s she ran into her former judge on a street in Kyiv. She recognized him, even though he had also aged. But seeing him, she immediately stood tall: "No, I will never allow him to see me bent over!" Indeed, even though everyone saw the signs of her aging, no one ever saw her bent over—not even during the worst of times—during the new wave of persecutions—which she endured even after my arrest, particularly during her incarceration in a psychiatric hospital.[21] Here is a fitting testimony by Svitlana Kyrychenko:

> The day Oksana appeared on our doorstep, right after her release from the insane asylum, her look and walk, with a high updo and an erect spine, an elegant suit with lace over her shoulders that could have been from Belgium . . . no legiti-

---

18 V. V. Ovsiienko and O. F. Serhiienko, eds., *Ne vidstupliusia! Do 100-richchia Oksany Iakivny Meshko* (Kharkiv: Folio, 2005), 68.

19 Vasyl' Ovsiienko, "Kozats'ka Matir (Oksana Meshko)", Virtual'nyi muzei Dysydents'kyi Rukh v Ukraini, http://archive.khpg.org/index.php?id=1121792907.

20 Meshko was arrested in 1947 on charges of plotting to kill Nikita Khrushchev; she was sentenced to ten years in a labor camp.

21 Punitive psychiatry was prevalent in the USSR in the 1970s and 1980s: opposition figures were confined to psychiatric institutions and subjected to various "treatments." Meshko spent seventy-five days in a psychiatric hospital in 1980.

> mate queen would be a match for her, much less illegitimate concubines! She answered my inquisitive look with a victorious smile in her half-shuttered eyes: "So did you think that they would break this broad? That will never happen! My ancestors have strong genes!"[22]

It was difficult to be friends with Oksana Yakivna—she was the most demanding person I have ever known. Her ability to lift people up, propel them to daring deeds, and help them overcome fear was her creative forte; that's how her unique talents manifested themselves. But friendship with her was also rewarding because she would not shy away from praising others. She was always able to recognize the germ of someone's unique talent, which would invariably come to fruition. Other people's merited glory always brought her great joy.

I must mention some of the encounters she had with her invariable and undesirable companions from the KGB, who constantly persecuted and searched both her and her apartment, and how she, an older woman at that time, was arrested and dragged around the Khabarovsk region of Siberia.[23] It is an understatement to say that she was brave and uncompromising. After a conversation with her one could no longer claim, "I knew not what I was doing." Everything she thought and observed she said brazenly to your face, and this drove more than one person crazy. The KGB went mad from dealing with her, and they would do anything to get even.

I also met Oles Berdnyk, a fantasy fiction writer, who had recently been expelled from the Writers' Union.[24] His life was rather bleak at the time, as he himself later described: "living like a pauper, unable to be published, constantly persecuted by the security establishment, searches, surveillance, provocations, raiding of my literary archive, and no opportunities for creative expression" (from his letter to the then Leader of the Communist Party of Ukraine, Volodymyr Shcherbytsky, dated March 18, 1977).[25]

22 Kyrychenko, *Liudy ne zi strakhu*, 397.

23 After her stint in the psychiatric hospital, she was sentenced to five years of internal exile in the Khabarovsk region (southeast Russia), from 1980 to 1985.

24 Oleksandr (Oles) Pavlovych Berdnyk (1926–2003): writer and founding member of the Ukrainian Helsinki Group. Imprisoned in the 1950s for "counterrevolutionary propaganda." Expelled from the Writers' Union in 1972 for production and distribution of samizdat copies of Ivan Dziuba's *Internationalism or Russification?*

25 *Ukrains'ka Hromads'ka Hrupa spryiannia vykonanniu Hel'sins'kykh uhod*, ed. Vasyl' Ovsiienko, vol. 2, *Dokumenty i materialy 9 lystopada 1976–2 lypnia*

He was a tall, well-built, stately man with long blond hair, resembling a religious prophet, an image that he openly cultivated. Eventually I learned that he had indeed experienced a religious revelation, so his image as a prophet and a missionary was not accidental. He showed us his artwork, where this image was projected particularly clearly. At some point, Berdnyk came to visit Mykola and me in our rented apartment. It was clear that he found our fun-loving lifestyle at that time hollow and immature. Indeed, how else could a serious-minded person interpret a bottle of wine, with a handwritten label reading "Tears for Mao," sitting in the middle of the table among some snacks? (In September 1976, it was announced that Mao Zedong had died.) If only I had been thinking as I do now!

I was delighted to meet Halyna Didkivska in Kyiv that year. She was the wife of the arrested samizdat distributor Yevhen Proniuk. Today, I would describe her as a person with an exceptionally powerful evangelical grounding. She endured much grief and many provocations from the KGB, but she withstood everything with great stalwartness, not even for a minute considering that she might betray her husband for the sake of her own peace. Among friends, Halyna was the epicenter of peace and friendship.

Besides her, there were other wives and close friends of political prisoners that belonged to our circle. Leonida (nicknamed Liolia) Svitlychna opened the unique world of "the apartment on Umanska Street," which was mentioned in the memoirs of more than one *shistdesiatnyk*. At that time, the apartment still had the aura and warmth of its owner, Liolia's husband Ivan Svitlychny, who had been arrested, and Liolia did everything she could to maintain that spirit.[26] Ever-present in the apartment were not only his books but more importantly, upon entering this home, one could immediately feel the magical spirit of the owners' hospitality. A simple get-together always turned into a banquet. Like Mykhailyna Kotsiubynska, Liolia also had a sense of humor that made her stand out. I remember one anecdote in particular, now well known, related to some Soviet anniversary celebration. The propaganda megaphones were blaring about it incessantly, to the point that no matter what you plugged in, whether the TV or a radio, everywhere they

---

1977 (self-pub), 61, http://library.khpg.org/files/docs/Part2.pdf (henceforth *Dokumenty*).

26 Ivan Svitlychny (1929–1992): Poet and literary critic, cofounder of the Club of Creative Youth in the early 1960s. Arrested in 1971 in conjunction with the case against Yaroslav Dobosh, a Belgian of Ukrainian heritage involved in distributing anti-Communist literature in Ukraine.

were talking about nothing but this jubilee. So, the anecdote ended with its hero arriving at work in wrinkled slacks, and he tried to excuse himself by saying that now he was afraid to even plug in an iron. I can still hear the characteristic intonation of Liolia's voice, swelling with enjoyment at this scathing humor.

Vira Lisova, wife of the arrested philosopher Vasyl Lisovy, always impressed me with her firm dignity as well as with her erect posture.[27] When Mykola and I, by then members of the Ukrainian Helsinki Group, visited her at her home, her behavior never betrayed a single trace of fear. Later I will return to her dignified appearance at my trial. This woman endured all her suffering and persecutions with great dignity, without ever seeking fame or praise for her actions. Everything she did was out of conviction and not for fame.

I have already described my meeting with Vyacheslav Chornovil's sister Valentyna. She waged a tireless and endless battle with the KGB for the right to work as a teacher and love her illustrious brother at the same time. Her temper would flare up when she got annoyed, and the KGB was always very good at annoying people. Valentyna suffered greatly from her lack of comfort at home, and she always dreamed of having hot water in her kitchen. Eventually Valentyna married Mykola Plakhotniuk, a doctor and member of the Club of Creative Youth who was a victim of punitive psychiatry, and once again her life was filled with profound self-sacrifice.

At some point, I met Svitlana Kyrychenko and her husband, Yury Badzio, at Borys Antonenko-Davydovych's home. Rumors were circulating about a major analytical book, *The Right to Live*, which Badzio was allegedly writing, and I have no doubt that the KGB had heard those rumors as well because many near-fantastic stories were spread about this book.[28] One day, the manuscript "accidentally disappeared." Once Yury rewrote it, it was confiscated during a search of his house, and then finally the author was arrested as well.

Over time, this couple had to endure a lot of difficulties, and Svitlana was occasionally compelled to resort to some bold measures:

27 Vasyl Lisovy (1937–2012): participant in the samizdat scene and public critic of the crackdown on the *shistdesiatnyky*. His open letter defending the *shistdesiatnyky* led to his arrest in July 1972.

28 *The Right to Live* (*Pravo zhyty*) argued that the Ukrainian nation was discriminated against within the Soviet Union and that the foundations of "real socialism" were in fact totalitarian. The first draft, around fourteen-hundred pages long, was taken from Badzio's apartment in 1977, and the second was confiscated in 1979.

Figure 2.3. Mykola Rudenko; Vira Lisova; Vasyl Lisovy's son, Oksen; Yevhen Sverstiuk; and Vasyl Lisovy, at Pyrohovo, an open-air museum near Kyiv, May 1985.

> In a drug store I purchased a three-liter bottle of distilled water and started a hunger strike. I wrote a telegram: "I'm declaring a hunger strike, protesting the persecution of my son, and the moral tyranny over the whole family. Svitlana Kyrychenko." Under "moral tyranny" I had in mind the fact that for three years Yury had been forbidden to see his family; I was constantly getting fired from any job I managed to get, even as a mail carrier or nanny; and we were being blackmailed by phone.[29]

At Borys Antonenko-Davydovych's home I also met his stepdaughter, Yaryna Tymoshenko, who was the daughter of Borys's wife Hanna; she treated him like her own father. I also met Valentyna Popeliukh, wife of the incarcerated Vasyl Stus, but I was not close to her. As I understand it, she had a very difficult time coping with the constant persecutions she faced. I was on friendly terms with Lilia (Valeria) Andrievska, the wife of Yevhen Sverstiuk, a poet and literary critic who was also incarcerated at that time, though I did not see her very often. Once, Mykola Matusevych introduced me to Tetiana

29 Kyrychenko, *Liudy ne zi strakhu*, 551.

Figure 2.4. A group of Kyiv and Lviv political dissidents saying farewell to Nadiia Svitlychna as she leaves to go abroad, (left to right): Oksana Meshko, Vira Lisova, Mykhailyna Kotsiubynska, Nadiia Svitlychna, Odarka Husiak, Mykhailo Horyn, Atena Pashko, Valentyna Chornovil, Kyiv, October 12, 1978.

Zhytnikova, the wife of the mathematician Leonid Pliushch, who had been arrested and thrown into an insane asylum. Today I only remember the large apartment building on the left bank of the Dnipro River where she lived. I still remember how steadfastly she worked to rescue her husband from the clutches of that punitive machine.

Once Mykola Matusevych and I went to visit Nina Marchenko, the mother of Valery Marchenko. At that time, Valery was already serving a prison term for his journalism, which had been deemed overly independent and pro-Ukrainian. I had no way of knowing then that I would soon meet Valery personally in the camps. In those days, his mother had only one goal: to protect her son from injustice and evil. We still had many years of strong friendship and mutual respect for each other ahead of us, up until her death at a ripe old age. Mykola and I saw her sister Alla more frequently, and we were overjoyed when we heard that she and Mykola Horbal were married upon his release from prison.

I never met the legendary Alla Horska prior to her death. Initially, I heard about her from Mykola Matusevych, when one day we were walking past her father-in-law's house in the town of Vasylkiv, where Alla had been killed on November 28, 1970. We stood by the house in great sorrow, feeling like pilgrims. Eventually, Nadiia Svitlychna, Ivan's sister who had returned from her own stint in prison, told us more about her. One story stayed in my mind, a very characteristic one: Nadiia remembered that once she and Alla had joined several friends in a restaurant to celebrate some event. Suddenly, a rather inebriated man, who seemed to be restless and upset, walked into the restaurant. When the waiters refused to serve him, he grabbed an empty bottle, smashed it against a pillar, and glared menacingly at everyone. The waiters demanded that he gather the shattered glass, but the drunk refused. Everyone just stared. Suddenly, Alla walked up to the pillar and started gathering the glass shards. She radiated such understanding and compassion for the inebriated man, whom she perceived to have experienced some great trauma, that he himself felt diminished and unsettled and quietly left the premises. This story told me more about Alla than any formal biographical sketch ever could. Now, when I am asked to describe what it means to be "made of dissident stock," this amazing story inevitably flashes into my mind.

I also cherish a very pleasant memory of my acquaintance with Olena Yanovska, a Jewish woman from Kyiv. By her own words, she was a "child of Ukrainization," speaking Ukrainian and sometimes also Russian; but by nature, she was a typical Kyivite, to the core.[30] She was a very brave woman, taking the bold step of going through a fake marriage with Danylo Shumuk[31] so that after his release from prison he could live in Kyiv.[32] As a newcomer, I sat there quietly in her apartment, while Mykola joked around with her,

30 Ukrainization: Soviet policy in the 1920s promoting Ukrainian language in education and culture, which led some former citizens of the Russian Empire, now living in the Ukrainian SSR, to adopt Ukrainian.

31 Danylo Shumuk (1914–2004) was a communist in interwar Poland, a combatant against the Germans in a Soviet penal battalion, then a soldier of the Ukrainian Insurgent Army (UPA). For this he was sentenced to death by Soviet authorities, commuted to twenty years. He had served terms in Polish prison and was held in a German POW camp. All in all he spent more than forty years in captivity.

32 Former prisoners were never granted residency permits on their own, as they were deemed politically unreliable. If married to a resident, however, a permit could be obtained.

since he knew her well and liked her very much. When she noticed that we were very timid in helping ourselves to the food that she had placed for us on the table, she teased us, "Eat, don't be shy, once I've placed the food on the table, I've already given up on it!" Mykola and I burst out laughing because we were not particularly familiar with this breed of pure Jewish humor, so to us it was twice as funny. Since then, this phrase has been one of my favorites.

Once I took a trip to the city of Uman, in central Ukraine, with Mykola and Mykhailyna Kotsiubynska to visit Nadiia Surovtseva, but unfortunately my memory of it is rather foggy. Like Borys Antonenko-Davydovych, this woman was a relic of an older era that was totally unfamiliar to us. On the way to Uman, my friends told me that Nadiia had been enamored with Marxism in the 1920s, without abandoning her Ukrainianness. She therefore represented the Ukrainian Communist movement, and under the Soviets she had paid for her pro-Ukrainian position with a lengthy prison term. Since Nadiia Surovtseva's name is unfortunately little known, I will cite Mykhailyna's account of our visit with her:

> The door is opened by a medium-height, neatly dressed older woman, with wavy grey hair, wearing a vest and a necklace. Her unwavering friendly smile and eyes sparkle with the joy of meeting you. . . . We sit at the table with hot coffee, and the conversation flows freely and endlessly, without having to choose words—here they know how to listen, and they know how and what to answer. Before me stood a wise person with an amazingly young spirit. . . . Everyone felt at ease and festive here, having partaken in the communion of the most valuable pleasure of one person engaging with another.[33]

In addition to Mykola's sister Tamila and Natalia Yakovenko, Mykola's and my friend group consisted of those with whom we got together the most often. First and foremost, this meant the members of the Homin Choir, such as Alla Koval, Liudmyla Savchenko, and Ivan Debeliuk. Ivan was in love with Alla, and the two of them were constantly together; eventually they got married. At one point, I also had my eye on her because she was always so cheerful and liked to sing. It is difficult to count the occasions that brought us together; it all remains in my memory as one tender and warm blur of pure, unblemished friendship.

There was one evening get-together at Liudmyla Savchenko's house that unfortunately left a painful memory. My sister Nadiika was visiting me at that time, and she came along. Generally speaking, Mykola got along well

33 Kotsiubyns'ka, *Knyha spomyniv*, 74–75.

with Nadiika, but once in a while his explosive character flared up, and once that happened no one could calm him down. Among Liudmyla's guests were some of her Russian-speaking neighbors, and my sister was sitting next to them. At some point, wanting to make them feel included in the general festivities, Nadiika sang a romantic Russian song. When Mykola heard it, he burst out in anger toward Nadiika and smashed a bottle on the table. The party broke up; Nadiika and I left, and this was perhaps the most difficult moment in my relationship with Mykola. I was on the verge of a full-blown nervous breakdown, and it took a while for me to get over the shock. In time, similar outbursts of "Dostoevskian" behavior came to poison my memories of Mykola and distanced me from him psychologically.

Nina and Yevhen Obertas were also good friends to me at that time. Their hospitable apartment was always open to me, and often I would spend the night there. They were a mixed Kyiv-Galician couple: Nina came from the Kyiv region, and Ivan was from the Ivano-Frankivsk region. As I will return to later, they both appeared as witnesses at Mykola's and my trial, and they did so with great dignity.

The home of the Stokotelny siblings, Olia and Pavlo, which they shared with their mother, was also always open and hospitable to us. This family's bravery in defending their right to remain Ukrainians was paired with their watchfulness against possible KGB threats. It was in this apartment that our group gathered in 1976 to rehearse for our upcoming caroling. We celebrated the 1977 New Year with this family, and then the holiday suddenly became clouded: at that time, I was married to one of Mykola Matusevych's acquaintances, and we lived in the village of Kalinivka near Kyiv. Even though she was not inclined to the dissident life, she nevertheless helped me a great deal at that time. Notwithstanding the tremendous pressure she endured from the KGB, not only toward her but also toward her daughter, she courageously bore all subsequent persecutions. Even after she divorced me, our relations remained amicable.[34] That day, we agreed that she would join us for the celebration at the Stokotelny apartment when we finished caroling. However, when we returned, the Stokotelnys' frightened mother told us that some strange woman had been knocking at the door demanding to be let in but that she had refused to let her in. I understood immediately that this had been my wife, and that on New Year's Eve she had to return home

34 After the first edition of my memoirs came out, she requested that her name not be mentioned. I have respected her wish.

all by herself. This made it absolutely clear to me how difficult people found it to endure the persistent pressure from the KGB.

Earlier, when Nadiia Svitlychna had returned to Kyiv from the camps in 1976, Pavlo Stokotelny took particular care of her. I must not have picked up on the signals because the news that Nadiia and Pavlo had subsequently gotten married was rather unexpected. I am not certain that Pavlo was psychologically ready to take on the role of an emigrant, which eventually happened when he moved Nadiia and their children to the United States. As we will see later, emigration was the only viable solution for Nadiia and her son, Yarema, and Pavlo courageously accepted his fate.

Pavlo's sister Olia Stokotelna also acted with great dignity. Her commitment to the Ukrainian dissident movement meant that she had to endure harassment at work. Later, when Mykola Horbal wound up behind bars for a second time (by this point he had already divorced his first wife, Alla Marchenko), Olia came to visit him, and they got married there.

Orysia Savchuk, my old friend from the Lviv Polytechnic, to whom I owe my introduction to Mykola Matusevych and that whole crowd, was also part of our group. She was a good friend, easy to talk with, and she always responded enthusiastically to Mykola's adventurous schemes.

I should also mention Oksana Franko, who worked as an academic associate at the Central State Historical Archive in Kyiv at that time. I met her during one of our relaxing outings to the Matusevych country house near Kyiv. I valued this acquaintance because Oksana came from the family of Ivan Franko's brother Onufry. We felt that she also valued our friendship, so our group was comfortable hanging out with her. Nevertheless, I feel guilty for destroying her passport. Once, our group was goofing around on the banks of a stream near the Matusevych dacha. At some point, Mephistopheles prodded me—I lost my common sense and felt the urge to "come up with something amusing." I impulsively decided that it would be very funny to grab Oksana, fully clothed, and toss her into the water. I enlisted Mykola's help, and between the two of us Oksana wound up in the water. It was only after I saw her annoyed face that I realized what a blunder I had committed. I felt even guiltier when our victim showed us her waterlogged passport.

Amidst the Ukrainian Fronde

As I already mentioned, perhaps the biggest "sin" attributed to nationally conscious Ukrainians in Kyiv was their efforts to preserve their Ukrainianness.

Today it is difficult to even imagine how defiant this was in the eyes of the general public. The appearance of two young men (not to mention a larger group of people) openly speaking Ukrainian without any inhibitions, and who exhibited interests other than the usual petty ones, was in itself perceived as an expression of rebellion. I can still remember the harsh looks of my fellow Kyivites in public transport, or just on the street, as they tried to distance themselves from us, whether out of pure fear or contempt.

Another of our dangerous rebellions was reading underground literature. At that time, I came across some forbidden literature, such as "Peril from Wisdom" by Viacheslav Chornovil, some excerpts from Valentyn Moroz's articles, Yevhen Sverstiuk's "A Sanctuary in Scaffolding" and "Ivan Kotliarevsky is Laughing," and Mykola Rudenko's "Wind in Your Face," among other works.[35] I was not a particularly avid reader of underground literature, but I did read the things that somehow fell into my hands.

More visible were our open public acts of disobedience. I remember one incident from 1975 or 1976. Some friends and I decided to celebrate the festival of Ivan Kupala.[36] Well aware that we would not be allowed to celebrate this festival in Kyiv, we decided to go to the home village of one of the girls in our group of friends. Amazingly, when we got there, the whole village already knew that some "Banderite" bandits were on their way, and they had been warned that something terrible was about to happen. The KGB's strategy was obvious: to keep us from communicating with the locals. The village was indeed in a panic, as the girl's relatives told us. This was obvious because the village appeared virtually deserted.

There was nothing we could do about this, so we ignored it and went to the river to build a bonfire and proceed with our Ivan Kupala celebration. We were all good singers, and everything looked very lovely, so it must have been enticing. After sunset, some of the younger locals started coming over to us. At first, they stood some distance away, just observing. Then they also built a bonfire. And when it got completely dark, one by one, they started joining us, and ultimately about a dozen young people wound up partying with us to the very end.

---

35 All four authors came to prominence as part of the 1960s Ukrainian dissident movement.

36 Ivan Kupala: pre-Christian summer solstice festival celebrated on July 6–7 across the Eastern Slavic world. Customary components include jumping over bonfires and young women floating crowns of flowers on rivers.

Neither did we neglect the traditional *koliada*, Christmas caroling. As I remember, we celebrated it two years in a row—in 1976 and 1977. Given the conditions in Kyiv in those days, it would have been virtually unthinkable to go caroling on Christmas Day, so groups of us went caroling on December 31. Even on this religiously neutral day, however, it was difficult to go caroling because the KGB did everything in its power to prevent it. Once, on December 31, 1975, the KGB decided that it was time to provoke Mykola Matusevych, so that they would have grounds to arrest him. The previous night I hadn't stayed in Kyiv, so Mykola and I agreed to meet on the morning of the thirty-first. But he didn't show up at the designated place. I ran to his apartment, but he wasn't there; I went looking for him at various other places, but he wasn't there either. I knew that something must have happened.

Realizing that something had to be done immediately, I tried to hail a taxi to go to Olia Heiko, Mykola's wife at that time. But there were no taxis, so I stopped the first car that happened to be going by. The driver agreed to take me, and I got in. Then somehow my intuition told me that I had gotten into a KGB car. I started laughing out loud, and the driver asked me: "Why are you laughing? Soon you might not find things quite so funny!" To which I said, "No need to explain. I understand where I am." This car took me to the Hotel Ukraina.[37] I was brought into one of the rooms for an interview, and I even hoped that I might learn something about what was happening with Mykola. But the conversation was very vague, with no clear purpose. I was beginning to get nervous, but the KGB man tried to calm me down: "No, no, just wait a while." And then he disappeared for a long time. That's when I realized that they were deliberately dragging their feet, so when my interviewer returned, I insisted that the conversation was over and that I was leaving.

I left the hotel with a feeling of disgust that is difficult to describe. It was much later that I read Mykhailyna Kotsiubynska's account, which accurately described my state of mind at the time: "At some point I could not bear it any longer, so I terminated this imposed 'educational' conversation by saying, 'Enough already. Let me go home, I have to wash my hands.'"[38]

---

37 Hotel Ukraina: major hotel in central Kyiv, today the Premier Palace Hotel. Not to be confused with today's Hotel Ukraina on the Maidan, which during Soviet times was Hotel Moskva.

38 Kotsiubyns'ka, *Knyha spomyniv*, 84.

I finally found Olia Heiko and we started calling around to the police. Finally, it became clear why they had detained me for such a long time: it was precisely at that time that they were deciding on Mykola's sentence. He was sentenced to fifteen days for "hooliganism." It was a classic case of staged hooliganism: a man approached him on the street and asked him for a cigarette. As soon as Mykola stopped to get one out for him, the man started shouting (in Russian), "Why are you attacking me?" And lo and behold, the police, and some witnesses, appeared out of nowhere, and Mykola was promptly handcuffed.

Losing Mykola on December 31 was obviously a serious blow to our caroling team, but we decided not to submit to this psychological pressure and to go caroling anyway. We did, however, decide to bring our passports (in case we were picked up), and under no circumstances would we accept any invitations for a drink or anything of the kind. We walked around in a compact group. People reacted warmly to our caroling, and this lifted our mood, to the extent that this was possible in the wake of Mykola's arrest. Still, we were keenly aware that we were being closely watched.

The following year, as we rang in 1977, this time with Mykola back with us, our evening of caroling was rather tense, with a certain premonition of confrontation in the air. Policemen would approach us to say, "Stop it, go home!" But people greeted us cordially; in the stores we were showered with candy, and in public transport we elicited smiles. We also visited many celebrated figures, such as Borys Antonenko-Davydovych, Mykhailyna Kotsiubynska, Vira Hmyria, and Hryhory Kochur.[39] One moment from this evening stands out in my memory: as the evening drew on, we gathered somewhere quiet and sang a carol intended to send wishes of good tidings to our friends in the three concentration camps in the Ural Mountains. I remember that it was nearly 10 p.m., so in the Ural Mountains it was already close to midnight.

Here's another interesting incident from that period: the Mariia Zankovetska Theater in Lviv was staging a visiting production of "Zankovetska," about the famous nineteenth-century actress Mariia Zankovetska herself. This play was rather revolutionary by the standards of the time, and everyone was buzzing about it. I remember one line spoken

39 Vira Hmyria: wife of prominent opera singer Borys Hmyria, who had died in 1969. Hryhory Kochur: leading Ukrainian translator and key figure in the 1960s Ukrainian cultural revival.

by a gendarme: "What counts as a disturbance in Moscow is a revolution in Kyiv." That is, there was greater oppression in Kyiv than in Moscow.[40]

Mykola and I knew that many patriotic people would come to see this play, so we decided to stage a demonstration. One of us came to the play in a yellow shirt and the other in a blue one.[41] Some of our friends saw us even before the show started and said in bewilderment, "You guys are always coming up with something!" As we walked together, our blue and yellow shirts were side by side. Those who knew us understood immediately what it was meant to symbolize.

During the show, when the gendarme uttered the aforementioned line, Mykola and I began applauding loudly. This started a reflex reaction, and the crowd began applauding as well; but after a few moments they came to their senses and quieted down in fear. When the play ended, we brought flowers up to the stage. We stood side by side, our shirts depicting the Ukrainian flag. After we presented our flowers to the cast, we stayed up there on the stage, talking to the actors to give us a reason to keep the flag intact for a few minutes at least. When we returned to the auditorium, one of our friends said: "Hey, you guys, aren't you afraid?"

"What are you talking about?" we replied mischievously. "These are only shirts!"

Around that time, we went on excursions around Ukraine to familiarize ourselves with the country and eventually, during one of them, I met my future wife, Liuba Kheina. In fall of 1976, Mykola and I went on one such outing organized by the publishing house Radians'ka Shkola (Soviet school). This trip was noteworthy because it was the first time that I had ever visited the central Ukrainian city of Poltava. I remember visiting one of the museums, where the guide invited us to play a piano from the museum's collection, which had been played by luminaries like Mykola Lysenko, along with many other members of the Ukrainian cultural elite who used to visit that home.[42] I was emboldened to play a few chords myself, although I did so with great trepidation.

---

40 The line draws an implicit parallel between policy toward Ukraine in the Russian Empire—where the Ukrainian language was banned via the Ems Ukase in 1876—and in the Soviet Union.

41 That is, the colors of the banned Ukrainian flag.

42 Mykola Lysenko (1842–1912): leading Ukrainian composer and arranger of folk music, considered the founder of the national movement in Ukrainian music.

Figure 2.5. Liuba Kheina, my future wife.

During the trip, Mykola and I made it a point to talk with people on the trip that we had not met before and joked with the girls. Some of them we got to know a little better, especially Liuba, who worked as a copyeditor at the publishing house Vyshcha Shkola (Higher education). At that time, we were beginning to put together our caroling team for the coming holiday season, so we invited some of them to join us. Liuba agreed to join, but at the time neither one of us had any idea that the heavens were already beginning to intertwine our fates.

Once, our group went to visit northern Ukraine; we were mostly in the Chernihiv oblast, and our trip focused on Baturyn, the capital of the seventeenth- and eighteenth-century Autonomous Cossack Republic. I remember that our friend Natalia Yakovenko, the historian, spearheaded the trip, the main goal of which was to see the seats of power of the Hetmans, the highest military commanders of Ukraine in the early modern period. I can still remember seeing the half-destroyed, roofless Baturyn fortress. Thankfully, now it has been fully restored. During this trip, an event occurred that exemplified Soviet realities. We were looking for a building associated with Panteleimon Kulish, a renowned nineteenth-century Ukrainian writer, who was responsible for the first Ukrainian translation of the Bible. We asked around among the locals and made a bit of a ruckus, claiming that the building had not been properly maintained. After our visit, we heard that the building had been demolished so that in the future it would not attract undue attention from other enterprising visitors. My conscience still bears the burden of the unintended consequences of our actions.

On March 9 or 10, 1977, Mykola and I went to the Kyiv Philharmonic for a Shevchenko commemoration with some of our friends. This was during the bacchanal of Brezhnev "democracy," so we didn't expect anything good to come out of that evening.[43] Mykola Shamota, the infamous director of the Shevchenko Institute of Literature at the Academy of Sciences of the Ukrainian SSR, who was known for his subservient pro-Moscow attitudes, delivered the opening address. It was therefore no surprise that on an evening meant to be a celebration of Shevchenko, Shamota's speech focused more on Lenin than on the poet. He even mentioned that Lenin loved Shevchenko so much that he went to an evening commemorating him in Kraków, even though the evening itself had a distinct "nationalistic flavor." The whole speech was like this. The concert opened with a song about the Communist Party, followed by some folk songs, but none of the lyrics were written by Shevchenko (unlike many Ukrainian folk songs, which do draw from Shevchenko's poetry). The only traces of Shevchenko were excerpts read from his "Diary"— acceptable because they were in Russian.

43 The year 1977 was one of the high points of Brezhnev's consolidation of power.

It was obvious that the whole evening would proceed along these lines. During the intermission, Mykola and I concocted a plan. As expected, the second half was no better, though towards the end a nice patriotic song was performed. The audience came to life and broke into applause and then started calling for "The Testament" ("Zapovit"), a song based on a Shevchenko poem that was the customary way to conclude commemorative Shevchenko events. The choir responded with another "politically correct" song, sending the message that "The Testament" would not be performed and that the concert was over.

After that song ended, in keeping with our plan, I got up on the stage, lifted my hand in a gesture asking for silence, and asked the people not to leave the concert hall. With a certain degree of sarcasm, I announced into the microphone, "Dear friends, in the opening remarks we heard how much Vladimir Lenin loved Shevchenko's poetry. We should not forget that Lenin liked to listen not only to Beethoven's *Appassionata*, but also to Shevchenko's 'Testament.' So, let's sing it together now." (This was an absolute bluff on my part but totally in keeping with the spirit of the evening.)

I could only see the front few rows, but from the moment I started speaking, I could see people smile and nod their heads approvingly. With the audience's consent, I went to the piano and was poised to strike the first chords. At that moment, a startled young man rushed onto the stage from behind the curtain and shouted in Russian, "The concert is over! No extemporaneous presentations!" Then, a woman ran up to me from behind the curtain, grabbed my hand, and hissed into my ear in Russian, "Stop this at once!" As she gripped my hand, I understood that I could not get into a tug-of-war with her right there on stage, so I went to the edge of the stage, spread my arms, and shrugged, implying that there was nothing I could do about it.

At that moment the second act of our performance began. Mykola jumped up on the stage and addressed the public in his thunderous voice: "Folks, aren't you ashamed?" The audience shouted back: "Yes, we are!" So Mykola and I jumped off the stage, our friends came to the front to join us, and we all started to sing "The Testament." A few seconds later, the entire auditorium joined in.

The young man and woman who had appeared from behind the curtain ran around the stage in despair, shouting at us to stop. The crew started to flash the house lights while the audience was singing. Suddenly they shut the lights off completely, which was a big mistake because in the darkness the sound of hundreds of people singing was simply fantastic. The crew eventually realized this, and as they turned on the lights, I could see that many women were crying. As we finished singing (with no further interruptions), dozens of people reached out to us, saying, "Thank you! Thank you! You guys are great!"

Full of emotion, we waited for everyone to gather their things from the cloakroom before retrieving our own coats, and that's when the third act began. As we exited the Philharmonic, we were stopped in our tracks: the entire audience had gathered in a semicircle, with a clear path down the middle leading to what was obviously a KGB car. No one spoke, but this silence spoke volumes. Finally, we burst out laughing. We understood that no one would take us to this car, and we certainly would not go voluntarily. We turned and headed toward the underground crosswalk as the crowd encircled us in a protective gesture. As we walked, many people came up to thank us once more, and it wasn't until we reached Khreshchatyk Boulevard that the semicircle began to disperse.

With our spirits thus uplifted, we went to the Shevchenko monument, where we sang "The Testament" one more time. No one bothered us there. The reason they left us alone became obvious soon enough: just one month later, Mykola and I were arrested. The KGB could afford to wait a bit.

Chapter Three

The Era of the Helsinki Movement

Responding to the Call of the Day

The year 1976 didn't seem any different than any other year, except for scattered whispers that confirmed that the cup of Ukrainian suffering runneth over. Oles Berdnyk, the science fiction writer who had been expelled from the Writers' Union of Ukraine for his freethinking, had just declared a hunger strike. And on August 13, 1976, his books were removed from all libraries and bookstores and destroyed. Interestingly, the decision to excise this renowned science fiction writer was made by the main administration for the Protection of National Security in Print, at the Council of Ministers of the USSR, even though the relevance of Berdnyk's work to national security was not particularly obvious. Around this time, intellectual and artistic property was destroyed throughout the Mordovian prison camps, resulting in several protests and hunger strikes by those who were affected. For example, news came from the women's camp in the village of Barashevo, Mordovia, that 150 of Stefa Shabatura's paintings had been burned by the KGB.[1] I no longer remember what exactly we did, but Mykola Matusevych and I protested against this vandalism, expressing our solidarity with the artist. Remarkably, she got word of our support, and soon thereafter we got a thank-you note from her.

1 Stefaniia Shabatura (1938–2014): Artist who worked mainly with textiles; active in the 1960s Ukrainian dissident movement. Arrested in 1972 for anti-Soviet activity and sentenced to five years in a labor camp and three years of internal exile.

Lo and behold, our colleague Nadiia Svitlychna finally returned from her four-year prison term, and the Kyiv air was infused with the spirit of the Mordovian "nature preserves," where the seedlings of the Ukrainian opposition were being "safeguarded." We all went to meet Nadiia at the train station, and as one of my friends later wrote, "I still recall the image of a tiny ant bent under a huge backpack, emerging from the train."[2]

Nadiia was a worthy sister to her brother Ivan, who at that time had also been imprisoned, and like him, she carried within her the magic of warm sincerity, which was totally incompatible with treachery. Later her spirit would manifest itself in her inimitable voice, known to those who listened to her Radio Liberty programs after she was fortunate enough to make it to the United States. But on that distant day in 1976, to Mykola and me, Nadiia was a living testament to the courage that the women's camp in Mordovia had become famous for.

That year the sociopolitical winds were gathering, but we still did not know what precise direction they would come from. Today, it is clear that the impulse came from the notion of human rights. At that time, this notion stormed into my life, through three sources at once.

The first of these was the Western media, specifically Radio Liberty, Voice of America, BBC, and Deutsche Welle. The issue of human rights came to the forefront on August 1, 1975, during the Helsinki Summit on Security and Cooperation in Europe, when on behalf of the Soviet Union Leonid Brezhnev signed the Final Act, the third "basket" of which required all signatories to respect human rights.[3] No doubt, at the time Brezhnev had no inkling that some people would take this document (and his signature on it) seriously. It became a litmus paper that revealed everything to the world: "Look, the Soviet Union signed this international agreement, but it continues to blatantly violate human rights." By divulging numerous Soviet violations of the Universal Declaration of Human Rights and the Helsinki Accords to the Western world, we could prove that the Soviet system was antidemocratic and that Brezhnev's signature on any such document was meaningless.

2 Kyrychenko, *Liudy ne zi strakhu*, 194.

3 The first two baskets established ground rules for peaceful international relations between signatories and economic, scientific, and technological cooperation, respectively. The Final Act was signed by thirty-five countries, including the United States, Canada, and all European countries except Albania and Andorra.

Figure 3.1. Nadiia Svitlychna at the Radio Liberty studio in New York, 1992.

Soon after, US President Jimmy Carter—the second of the forces that inspired me to take up the cause of human rights—became an outstanding spokesman for the cause. After he was elected in 1976, he steadfastly sought to fulfill his obligations to defend human rights. He was the first statesman who brought this struggle from the realm of civil society into the realm of international relations. Obviously, he did not manage to achieve all the goals he set for himself; his opposition was formidable. Still, Carter, a deeply devout Baptist, can undeniably be credited with establishing a culture of human rights. This was the tail end of an era that still believed in grand ideas, and worthy civic leaders could still be found to champion them. Jimmy Carter instantly became my hero, and his call to protect human rights resonated with me.[4]

Many years later, in early 1997, I had the opportunity to thank him personally during a brief meeting in the office of the Carter Center in Atlanta. A photograph captured this happy moment, as I shook his hand in gratitude for inspiring me. In the United States his presidency is seen as more of a failure than a success, but this negative assessment does not surprise me because people and things that are oriented toward "the kingdom not of this world" cannot be successful in this world.[5]

The third voice that drew me toward human rights was a Ukrainian one: Oksana Meshko. Mykola and I ran into her one evening in early November 1976 as we were walking down a street in Kyiv.[6] Our conversation did not last very long; Oksana just told us that the eminent dissident Mykola Rudenko was organizing a group that would fight for human rights. She suggested that young people like us were needed and invited us to join in. She told us that once we decided to join, we should go see Mykola Rudenko at his home in Koncha-Zaspa on the outskirts of Kyiv.

As we parted with her and continued on our way, we both felt the first murmurs of our new fate. On the one hand, we had no illusions. We both understood that getting involved with this went far beyond going caroling; we would inevitably end up getting arrested. It was obvious from the start that, sooner or later, this whisper of fate would become the sound of the

4 Today, I am critical of Carter's position regarding Russian aggression in Ukraine. My critique, however, does not apply retroactively. –M. M.

5 Allusion to John 18:36: "Jesus said, 'My kingdom is not of this world."

6 The details regarding our joining the Group differ quite a bit from Mykola's version, but I am focusing on my version, advising you that there also is a different one. –M. M.

Figure 3.2. With US President Jimmy Carter in his office in Atlanta, February 1997.

clanging locks of our prison cells and the weeping of our loved ones. On the other hand, we also understood that if we declined to join this group now, we would never be able to forgive ourselves. After all, it would always gnaw at our consciences that we chickened out and didn't take this step when we had the opportunity. I was twenty-seven at that time, and losing your self-respect at that age was tantamount to drawing a line across your entire life and descending into a state of complete subservience. A person who disrespects him or herself can never be a full-fledged citizen. This is particularly true for men because a lack of self-respect destroys them first and foremost.

In the end, we really had no other choice. As Ivan Hel, another Ukrainian political prisoner, later wrote, "Given the realities of totalitarian occupying regimes, a normal person has no options."[7] We decided to join the group;

7 Ivan Hel', "Opytuvannia," Virtual'nyi muzei Dysydents'kyi rukh v Ukraini, http://archive.khpg.org/index.php?id=1163785533.

from then on, we had to prepare ourselves psychologically for the possibility of being arrested at any time. Once again, and not for the last time, the voice of history won out over the instinct of self-preservation. Today, I am truly thankful to God for having made this decision.

We went to visit Mykola Rudenko in Koncha-Zaspa on November 11, 1976. Once there, we learned from our hosts that on the night of November 10, several rocks had been hurled into their apartment. Mykola Danylovych was not at home at the time because on November 9 he was at Alexander Ginzburg's home in Moscow, announcing the formation of a Ukrainian civic organization supporting the implementation of the Helsinki Accords.[8] This group was henceforth known as the Ukrainian Helsinki Group (UHG). That day, only the women, Oksana Meshko and Mykola Danylovych's wife Raisa, were there. Both of them experienced a stressful night, and Oksana was injured in the shoulder by one of the flying rocks, even though she had taken shelter under some pillows. To capture this incident, upon returning from his trip the next day, Mykola Rudenko decided to create a "political still life." He stacked several volumes of Marx and Engels and then piled all the rocks that had been thrown through the window on top of them. He photographed this composition and captioned it, "Rocks are the weapons of the proletariat." This photo, together with the statement "This is how the KGB saluted the establishment of the Ukrainian Helsinki Group," was sent to the West and subsequently circulated throughout the world. As Mykola and I listened to this story and looked at this photograph, we felt a certain youthful euphoria, and we realized that an important and interesting struggle was about to begin.

Mykola Danylovych asked us a few questions about our backgrounds, and finally it was agreed that we would join the UHG. We accepted the group's mode of operation, most importantly agreeing that it would not function as an underground organization. We signed the group's Declaration, listing our names and addresses, putting us among the ten founding members of the Ukrainian Helsinki Group.

Amazingly enough, Mykola Danylovych remembered something that escaped my memory:

> When I asked Myroslav what brought him to the Helsinki Group, he answered without any hesitation, 'I want to participate in burying the world's last empire.'

8 Alexander Ginzburg (1936–2002): leading Russian human rights activist and dissident, founding member of the Moscow Helsinki Group.

> Later, when we both wound up in the Ural concentration camps, I reminded him of this unusual and perhaps slightly daring statement, but he didn't remember it, while I will remember it all my life. [9]

Well, perhaps I didn't remember it because this phrase was indeed a bit too melodramatic.

It seems that the KGB failed to notice that we had joined the UHG; for a while, at least, nothing happened. We visited the Rudenkos several more times and were always received very cordially and warmly. But this tranquility was just the calm before the storm. As soon as Radio Liberty broadcast the group's declaration, along with the names and contact information of all its signatories, including ours, the situation changed drastically.

I still remember that morning. Mykola and I had spent the night at his sister Tamila's house. I got up in the morning to get ready for work (I still worked at Tekhnika Publishing). It was late autumn, the second half of November, so the mornings were already dark. As I left the building's doorway, I spotted a car that turned on its headlights when it saw me. I had no choice but to walk toward it, into the headlights, as the car started to reverse slowly, still keeping me in its lights. I walked, bathed in this light, until the road curved. This was obviously psychological pressure, and I understood its meaning fully. "So, is this when I'm going to be arrested, or are they just trying to frighten me?" I wondered.

Later, for a month or so, no matter where I went, I inevitably had a "tail." The same thing was happening to Mykola. There was nothing covert about it. On the contrary, this was a direct, open confrontation: they wanted to scare us through this surveillance. Obviously, there is nothing pleasant about being watched, especially when they're so suffocating that they practically step on your heels. But we were young and found ways to make fun of it. For instance, one evening Mykola and I played a prank on our minders: we escaped them and then hid and watched them scurry about. One man ran right past us with a walkie-talkie and we heard him announce (in Russian): "They ran by here somewhere!" I remember that we were amazed that they used so many people with walkie-talkies and vehicles to surveil us. A mighty powerful machine!

A month later, the KGB ended its demonstrative surveillance, and everything became somewhat more relaxed. They left us without any means of subsistence, however: I was fired from the publishing house, and Mykola was

9 Rudenko, *Naibil'she dyvo – zhyttia*, 435.

let go from his job at the House of Sanitary Education, and from then on, neither he nor I could find any employment anywhere.[10] The entire financial burden of supporting us lay on the shoulders of our families, particularly on the Matusevyches.

Founding Members of the Group and Their Documents

Before turning to the UHG's activities, I think it would be appropriate to present some of my views on the issues of documentation. It is important to identify those individuals who can officially be called the founding members: the ten members in the initial group who had signed the declaration, listed in Table 3.1.[11]

Just looking at the group roster, it is clear that the founding members differed quite a bit from each other in terms of their background and experience in political confrontations with the Soviet system. Levko Lukianenko, for example, already had fifteen years of life in the camps under his belt. In a well-known case, he had been convicted much earlier for developing the idea of Ukraine's legal secession from the Soviet Union.[12] In the eyes of the Soviet regime, this was seen as a grave criminal act, punishable to the full extent of the law—namely, execution. Eventually, however, this verdict was commuted to a fifteen-year prison term. In addition to Levko, five other UHG members already knew firsthand what Soviet "justice and compassion" really meant: Oksana Meshko, Oles Berdnyk, Oleksa Tykhy, Ivan Kandyba, and Nina Strokata.

Some people had rather complex biographies, such as Mykola Rudenko, the group's organizer. At one time, he had been a devoted party hack and a fervent Communist who was committed to the system's ideological roots.

10 House of Sanitary Education (*Budynok sanitarnoi osvity*): one of several centers run by the Ukrainian SSR's Ministry of Health to promote public health knowledge among the population.

11 The text of the declaration, and all other documents of the UHG, can be found in *Dokumenty*. English translations are taken from *Documents of the Helsinki Monitoring Groups in the USSR and Lithuania (1976–1986)*, vol. 3: *Ukraine* (Washington: US GPO, 1986–1987) (henceforth *Documents*).

12 In 1961, Lukianenko was expelled from the party and convicted of anti-Soviet activity for arguing that Articles 17 and 25 of the 1936 Soviet Constitution allowed for constituent republics (his work focused specifically on Ukraine) to secede from the Soviet Union.

Figure 3.3. Mykola Rudenko, the head of the UHG.

Figure 3.4. Oles Berdnyk.

Figure 3.5. Petro Hryhorenko.

Figure 3.6. Ivan Kandyba.

Figure 3.7. Levko Lukianenko.

Figure 3.8. Myroslav Marynovych.

Figure 3.9. Mykola Matusevych.

Figure 3.10. Oksana Meshko.

Figure 3.11. Nina Strokata.

Figure 3.12. Oleksa Tykhy.

Once the Soviet government's duplicitousness was out in the open, his inner idealism could no longer tolerate the hypocrisy, and it compelled him to question the legitimacy of the whole regime from a humanitarian standpoint. This same idealism guided Petro Hryhorenko, a former combat general and a committed Communist, who had a wealth of experience opposing the regime.[13] He stood out for his acute sense of ethics. Both Hryhorenko and Rudenko had also had the experience of being declared insane, part of the systemic political abuse of psychiatry in the Soviet Union. Hryhorenko had survived almost eight years in an insane asylum. Rudenko was subjected to compulsory psychiatric evaluations, at which point his first wife left him.

13 Hryhorenko began his military career in 1939 and rose through the ranks during the Second World War; afterward, he taught at the elite Frunze Military Academy. He began to publicly criticize the Soviet regime in the early 1960s, arguing that the disparity between the elite and the rest of the population was not in line with Communist principles. In 1968 he protested the Soviet invasion of Czechoslovakia and was expelled from the party. He was imprisoned and forcibly confined to psychiatric institutions on several occasions.

Table 3.1. Founding members of the UHG.

	Name	Notes	Punishment for UHG membership
1.	Rudenko, Mykola Danylovych	(UHG leader) Writer, poet	Deprivation of freedom (*pozbavlennia voli*) from February 5, 1977, until October 1987
2.	Berdnyk, Oleksandr Pavlovych	Science fiction writer, political prisoner under Beria	Deprivation of freedom from March 6, 1979, until March 14, 1984
3.	Hryhorenko, Petro Hryhorovych	Military general, out of favor by that time, representative of the UHG in Moscow	Stripped of Soviet citizenship on February 13, 1978
4.	Kandyba, Ivan Oleksiiovych	Lawyer, recently released political prisoner	Deprivation of freedom from March 24, 1981, until September 9, 1988
5.	Lukianenko, Levko Hryhorovych	Lawyer, recently released political prisoner	Deprivation of freedom from December 12, 1977, until November 30, 1988
6.	Marynovych, Myroslav Frankovych	Engineer, unemployed at the time	Deprivation of freedom from April 23, 1977, until March 2, 1987
7.	Matusevych, Mykola Ivanovych	Historian, expelled from university and unemployed at the time	Deprivation of freedom from April 23, 1977, until February 1989
8.	Meshko, Oksana Yakivna	Retiree, political prisoner under Beria, mother of political prisoner Oles Serhiienko	Deprivation of freedom from October 13, 1980, until November 5, 1985
9.	Strokata, Nina Antonivna	Microbiologist, then under watch in Tarusa in the Kaluga oblast of the RSFSR, wife of political prisoner Sviatoslav Karavansky	Expelled from the USSR with her husband on November 30, 1979, and stripped of Soviet citizenship
10.	Tykhy, Oleksy Ivanovych	Teacher, unemployed at the time; former political prisoner	Deprivation of freedom from February 5, 1977, until May 6, 1984; died in a prison hospital in Perm

Thanks to the decency of his examining physician, however, he was not sent to a psychiatric institution.

Next to all these prominent individuals with well-known names, Mykola Matusevych and I—two relatively young men—looked rather wan and politically unsophisticated. My own position on human rights at that time was focused more on political disobedience to the Soviet system than on any deeper engagement with the core issues of human rights. The deceitfulness of the Soviet system during my years as a dissident had reached such intolerably grotesque proportions that it was no longer possible to tolerate it and maintain self-respect. Therefore, at the beginning I saw our work not so much as a struggle for some specific political ideals but first and foremost as an attempt to retain our dignity and our right to survive as human beings. In my mind at the time, the pain of Ukrainian national humiliation was inseparable from the anguish of totalitarian oppression.

If I remember correctly, chronologically, Mykola and I were not the last founding members to join the group because Mykola Rudenko was still waiting for Ivan Kandyba to make a final decision. Rudenko personally went to visit him in the town of Pustomyty, near Lviv, to offer him membership in the UHG. At first, however, Kandyba refused, fearing that Rudenko might be a KGB agent. That is why the first UHG communiqué, dated November 11, doesn't include either Mykola's or my name, or that of Ivan Kandyba. They first appeared in the group's declaration. As previously mentioned, Mykola and I joined the group just a few days after it was formally announced, and Ivan Kandyba joined only after confirming with Nadiia Svitlychna that the group was not some sort of provocation. The sincerity of the initiative was also subsequently corroborated by its announcement over the airwaves of the "enemy radio stations."

This was the ten-member roster of the UHG up to Mykola Rudenko's arrest on February 5, 1977. The very day after his arrest, Petro Vins officially joined the group as well.[14] Petro was a brave young man from a respected family, and his joining provided legitimacy for the group in the eyes of Ukrainian society and of the worldwide community. New members

14 Petro Vins was the son of Heorhii Vins, the leader of the Ukrainian Baptists and Secretary of the Church Council. The Vins family had long played a prominent role in the Baptist community, dating back to the Russian Empire. Georgy had clashed with the Soviet regime during Khrushchev's antireligious campaign in the late 1950s and early 1960s. He was first imprisoned in 1966 and rearrested in 1974.

continued to join the group; it is therefore difficult to give a precise list of the group's founding members. Petro was one of the first to join, so I understand that it might seem a bit unfair to him not to consider him one of the founding members of the UHG. Still, if we name him as a founding member, it would be just as unfair not to also list Olia Heiko, Mykola Horbal, Yosyp Zisels, and Vasyl Ovsiienko, who joined the group a bit later. I think that Mykola Rudenko and Oleksa Tykhy's arrests in February 1977 were the pivotal moment that concluded the first phase of the UHG's formation; after that, it underwent some further transformations.

It could be argued that since Mykola Matusevych's and my names were also not mentioned in Mykola Rudenko's announcement of the group's establishment, perhaps we should not be considered founding members either. It is certainly fair to take that argument into consideration; it should be noted, however, that the list in the announcement ends with the phrase "and others." This indicates that Mykola Rudenko didn't consider the list to be finite, and that he was expecting other people to join. Furthermore, I personally consider the UHG Declaration to be the official document that served as a formal record of the group's creation, verified by the signatures beneath it.

In terms of group membership, there is another inequity that should be mentioned. Some of those who chose not to publicize their membership in the group were not listed in the UHG roster. But they worked as diligently as all the others and bore equal responsibility. Raisa Rudenko, the diligent wife of the group's leader, acted as its *de facto* secretary and humbly carried out the bulk of the group's everyday chores. Mykola Rudenko's memoirs have already been published, and they make clear what vital support this small, fragile-looking woman provided to him.[15] It often seemed that she stood her ground much more assertively than the utterly romantic and ideologically preoccupied Mykola did. Her *de facto* membership in the UHG is undeniable, as are the persecutions and the subsequent incarceration that she had to endure. She was mercilessly harassed by the KGB, even when she tried to support her husband by safeguarding the poems he had recently written in prison.

In addition to Raisa, the assistance we received from those who tried to help us publish the group's materials or support us in any other way was priceless. Tamila Matusevych's help was irreplaceable. Olia Heiko, who became Mykola Matusevych's wife during a particularly difficult time for

15 For Rudenko's memoirs, see Rudenko, *Naibil'she dyvo.*

him, stayed very close to us as well. Olia embraced our group wholeheartedly and began to help us fearlessly. Somehow, she managed to rent typewriters, and she would clack away, typing up the Ukrainian Helsinki Group materials. Eventually, after our arrest, I found out that Olia had officially joined the group, and this confirmed how courageous and fearless our devoted friend had been at that time. After all, she had to endure pressure from her parents, particularly from her thoroughly Soviet father.

As I eventually found out, however, it had not been easy even for Olia to join the group. It was equally difficult for Yosyp Zisels, Mykola Horbal, and Volodymyr Malenkovych. For a while, they were considered undeclared members of the UHG. Hanna Mykhailenko, a dissident from Odessa, had a similar status.[16] Today it is rather difficult to reconstruct the logic behind this. As Svitlana Kyrychenko confirms, around November 1976, efforts to recruit new members for the group were in full swing:

> I was not home when, on the eve of the October holidays [to commemorate the Bolshevik revolution], Oksana Meshko came to see my husband, Yury Badzio. She briefly told him about the establishment of the Helsinki Group and suggested that he join the group as one of its founding members. She was distressed because by then she had received two rejections—from Borys Antonenko-Davydovych and Mykhailyna Kotsiubynska. Mykhailyna was very conscious of the "limits of her possibilities": to act with dignity, stand firm in her position, support her friends on both sides of the prison bars, not forsake anything, and not get "into any hot water," because that was not her field of battle. Yury also rejected the idea, because while his unfinished manuscript for *The Right to Live* was still on his desk, it would not be prudent to draw attention to himself with such an act.[17]

It seems that eventually something shifted. As I will relate in more detail a bit later, the psychological atmosphere within the group became weightier, and even the optimists grew aware that membership in the group was tantamount to eventual imprisonment. Furthermore, after the first arrests in early 1977, suspicions arose that the group was riddled with KGB agents. Oksana Meshko, who was considered the group's leader at the time, hoped to protect potential group members (and perhaps also test them) before formally

16 *Odes'ka khvylia: Dokumenty, tvory, spohady v'iazniv sumlinnia* (Odessa: Druk, 2006), 1:15.

17 Kyrychenko, *Liudy ne zi strakhu*, 203.

confirming their membership. Perhaps this was the source of the "undeclared membership" status. This is how Yosyp Zisels remembers that period:

> It was Oksana Meshko's idea. During 1978 I often met with her and passed along information about human rights violations, particularly in the field of psychiatry. Back in the spring of 1978 I offered to join the Ukrainian Helsinki Group, especially since the first cohort had by then pretty much all been arrested. I was not alone; four of us, Mykola Horbal, Olia Heiko, and Volodia Malynkovych, would approach her, and she kept putting us off, saying: "Why do you need this? You will be arrested straight away!" We insisted that there should be continuity— that is, when some people get arrested, the roster of members should be replenished; otherwise, what's the point? If the group existed and its original members had been arrested, then someone had to replace them. It turned out later that she actually had included us in the group, but told us that we were "undeclared members," which was quite absurd, because visibility was paramount, perhaps even more important than any concrete actions. Later, after my first arrest, Zenovy Krasivsky, who also wanted to join the group, managed to finally see to it that everyone got full status. After I was arrested at the beginning of December 1978, it was finally announced that I had been a member since August. I was not the only one; others were mentioned as well.[18]

Various other memoirs will eventually bring other volunteers to light. The lengthy list of female volunteers cited by Vira Lisova is amazing.[19] They formed a new and important echelon around the group, so it would be inappropriate to consider them less worthy or admirable.

Since this book is not a scholarly dissertation about the group but simply a memoir, I will refrain from going into thorough research regarding the various waves of new members as they joined the group. All in all, there were 41 members. I will, however, concentrate on the time frame prior to my own arrest. Here I will only list the overall roster of those who joined the UHG after the first wave of arrests on February 5, 1977. The numbering will continue from the previous list.

I would like to caution readers and researchers about certain anachronisms that might result from applying today's rules to earlier times. Many decided to join the group under circumstances that involved brutal persecutions, even in jail. Frequently they didn't have the opportunity to submit formal applications or to confirm their intent with the group's leader, particularly if

18 Iosif Zisel's, *Iesli ne seichas. . . : Stat'i, interv'iu, vystupleniia* (Kyiv: *Dukh i Litera*, 2006), 50.

19 Lisova, "Zhinky v Rusi oporu."

Table 3.2. Additional members of the UHG.

	Date of joining the UHG	Name	Punishment for participation in the UHG
11.	February 6, 1977	Vins, Petro Heorhiiovych	Series of brief arrests from December 8, 1977, until February 15, 1979
12.	May 14, 1977	Heiko-Matusevych, Olia Dmytrivna	Deprivation of freedom from March 3, 1980; upon her release on March 12, 1983, she was rearrested and held until March 12, 1986
13.	June 1977	Horbal, Mykola Andriiovych	Deprivation of freedom from October 10, 1979; upon his release on October 23, 1984, he was rearrested and held until August 23, 1988
14.	October 3, 1977	Kalynychenko, Vitaly Vasylovych	Deprivation of freedom from November 29, 1979, until April 18, 1988
15.	October 25, 1977	Striltsiv, Vasyl Stepanovych	Deprivation of freedom from October 23, 1979; one day before his release, on October 22, 1984, he was rearrested and held until May 5, 1987
16.	1977	Pliushch, Leonid Ivanovych	Foreign representative of the UHG; expelled from the USSR in January 1976
17.	February 26, 1978	Sichko, Vasyl Petrovych	Deprivation of freedom from July 5, 1979, until July 7, 1985
18.	April 30, 1978	Sichko, Petro Vasylovych	Deprivation of freedom from July 5, 1979, until May 26, 1985
19.	June 1978	Lytvyn, Yury Tymonovych	Deprivation of freedom from August 6, 1979; resentenced on June 24, 1982; died in camp on September 5, 1984
20.	August 1978	Zisels (Zissels), Yosyp Samuilovych	Deprivation of freedom from December 8, 1978 until December 1981; rearrested and imprisoned from October 19, 1984 until October 1987
21.	October 1978	Malynkovych, Volodymyr Dmytrovych	Under threat of arrest, emigrated to Germany on January 1, 1980; for a certain time, foreign representative of the UHG
22.	October 1978	Svitlychna, Nadiia Oleksiivna	Expelled from the USSR on October 12, 1978; foreign representative of the UHG
23.	November 1978	Melnyk, Mykhailo Spyrydonovych	Under threat of arrest, committed suicide on the night of March 9, 1979

—(*continued*)

Table 3.2—*continued*

	Date of joining the UHG	Name	Punishment for participation in the UHG
24.	November 18, 1978	Ovsiienko, Vasyl Vasylovych	Deprivation of freedom from February 8, 1979, until August 21, 1988
25.	February 3, 1979	Popovych, Oksana Zenonivna	Declared a member of the UHG while imprisoned; released on October 2, 1987
26.	February 1979	Karavansky, Sviatoslav Yosypovych	Declared a member of the UHG while imprisoned; expelled from the USSR on November 13, 1979
27.	February 1979	Shabatura, Stefaniia Mykhailivna	Declared a member of the UHG while imprisoned; released on December 2, 1979
28.	February 1979	Rebryk, Bohdan Vasylovych	Declared a member of the UHG while imprisoned; released in 1984
29.	February 1979	Romaniuk, Father Vasyl Omelianovych	Declared a member of the UHG while imprisoned; released in 1981
30.	February 1979	Senyk, Iryna Mykhailivna	Declared a member of the UHG while in internal exile; released on August 17, 1983
31.	February 1979	Shumuk, Danylo Lavrentiiovych	Declared a member of the UHG while imprisoned; released on January 4, 1987
32.	February 1979	Shukhevych (Berezynsky), Yury Romanovych	Declared a member of the UHG while imprisoned; released on October 21, 1989
33.	May 22, 1979	Chornovil, Viacheslav Maksymovych	Declared a member of the UHG while in internal exile; released in 1983 without the right to return to Ukraine (only returned in 1985)
34.	October 1979	Stus, Vasyl Semenovych	Deprivation of freedom from May 14, 1980; died in a labor camp on the night of September 3, 1985
35.	October 1979	Krasivsky, Zenovy Mykhailovych	Deprivation of freedom from March 12, 1980, until November 1985
36.	October 1979	Lesiv, Yaroslav Vasylovych	Deprivation of freedom from November 15, 1979; on the day his sentence expired, he was resentenced and held until 1986
37.	October 1979	Sokulsky, Ivan Hryhorovych	Deprivation of freedom from April 11, 1980, until August 2, 1988

Table 3.2—*concluded*

	Date of joining the UHG	Name	Punishment for participation in the UHG
38.	October 1979	Rozumny, Petro Pavlovych	Deprivation of freedom from October 8, 1979, for three years; released in December 1982
39.	November 1982	Horyn, Mykhailo Mykolaiovych	Declared a member of the UHG while imprisoned; released on July 2, 1987
40.	October 1983	Marchenko, Valery Veniaminovych	Declared a member of the UHG on the day of his arrest, October 21,1983; died in a prison hospital on October 7, 1984
41.	1985	Ruban, Petro Vasylovych	Declared a member of the UHG while imprisoned; released on May 25, 1988 and expelled from the USSR

they were in a camp while Oksana Meshko was in Kyiv. We should calmly accept, for example, Oksana Meshko's edgy comments made in a letter to Petro Hryhorenko: "The listing of the new members that was announced seems to be someone's folly. But this listing is not the final word."[20]

Group members certainly didn't have the Internet, email, or fax. Just having a typewriter was considered a great triumph. Telephone conversations were regularly eavesdropped on by the KGB. Thus, for many members, joining the group was a sacrifice that meant not only great losses for themselves but also great risks for their families. By joining the UHG, every member voluntarily accepted all responsibility for every document the group produced, even if they had not been personally involved in drafting it. The absence of a signature at the bottom of a given document didn't mean that the person who wrote it was not a group member, or that he or she did not agree with its content.

One can only marvel that the Ukrainian Helsinki Group could exist at all, given the horrific conditions of the time. Lyudmila Alexeyeva, a member of the Moscow Helsinki Group and a staunch defender of the rule of law,

20 *Ne vidstupliusia!*, 178.

always emphasizes that she and her colleagues considered the members of the UHG to be kamikazes headed for inevitable sacrifice.[21]

The same threat of anachronism looms when you delve into the group's documents. They should not be read with the eyes of a contemporary scholar or politician. It was as if every word was written in blood because it was such a challenge to work in the group. Every scribble left on the table would be scrutinized by the KGB or confiscated during searches. Any person mentioned in those notes was automatically at risk of interrogation by the KGB. Even visiting someone's home or meeting a person on the street would automatically place that person on the KGB's list of suspects. We were therefore responsible not only for our own lives but also for the lives of others.

One alternative was to memorize everything. Since my youth, however, I have always had a bad memory for names, dates, and faces. I might talk with a person but then in a week forget we ever spoke. So, for me it's a catastrophe if I don't take any notes. The numerous factual mistakes in other dissident memoirs indicates that I was not the only one to have such problems.

Thus, the meaning and historical value of such documents lies not only in their intellectual achievement but most importantly in the effect that they had, namely that they were expressed at that particular historical moment. Statements by the various Helsinki Groups cut through the silence and thus had an explosive effect. The value of their statements lies not necessarily in their documentary excellence (though the latter is often unquestionable) but in the price that was paid for every word.

The first official document of the Ukrainian Helsinki Group was its declaration, written by Mykola Rudenko. Even today, this document seems extraordinary to me. This is what the group set as its aims:

1. Assisting broad segments of Ukrainian society in familiarizing themselves with the precepts of the Human Rights Declaration. Ensuring that this international legal document become the basis for all dealings between an individual and the state.
2. Proceeding from the conviction that peace and stability between nations cannot be achieved without free communication between peoples, or without the free exchange of information and ideas, actively facilitating adherence to

21 Lyudmila Alexeyeva (1927–2018): Founding member of the Moscow Helsinki Group, often referred to as the "grandmother" of the Russian human rights movement. She continued to play a leading role in this movement into the twenty-first century, speaking out for human rights.

the humanitarian articles of the Final Act of the Conference on Security and Cooperation in Europe.

3. Demanding that, during all international conferences where compliance with the Helsinki Accords is to be evaluated, Ukraine, as a sovereign European country and a member of the United Nations, be represented by a separate delegation.
4. Demanding the accreditation of international press representatives in Ukraine and the creation of foreign press agencies, etc., with the aim of ensuring the free flow of ideas and information.

Even today, any civic organization would be proud to achieve such goals.

A diligent reader will no doubt see that the main emphasis of this document is the defense of human rights. Nowhere in the declaration did we talk about the political system of the Soviet Union, nor did we suggest the need to overthrow the Soviet regime. Many nationalists considered this to be the Ukrainian Helsinki Group's major ideological flaw. Once, in the 1990s, Nadiia Svitlychna showed me an audiotape of Yaroslav Stetsko, who was the head of the Organization of Ukrainian Nationalists at the time, in which he scornfully criticized the dissidents for limiting their demands and called on Ukrainians not to trust the UHG.[22] But this was the group's mandate, having declared their goal to be the protection of human rights rather than dealing with political issues; they wanted to function within the law. In the declaration, as in all other subsequent documents, it is stated clearly that we were concerned with specific human rights violations.

All the same, in the declaration there was an implicit critique of the Soviet system and assertion of its unacceptability. For example, we wrote that a Ukrainian writer was jailed in the Soviet Union because his works had been published abroad, in contravention of the precepts of the Universal Declaration of Human Rights or the Helsinki Accords on the right to change country of residence and the free flow of ideas and information. Without explicitly stating it, we made it clear that a totalitarian system prevailed in the country, and it had to be fought.

This notion of the ideological deficiency of the group's documents, from the perspective of typical nationalist doctrine, once played a bad joke on us. To describe this, I need to jump ahead in the chronology and talk about an incident that took place during the investigation of my own criminal case.

The UHG's Memorandum #5 contains a phrase that was conceptually very important to us: "We are not building an underground—and this

22 Yaroslav Stetsko (1912–1986): Leading figure in OUN since the 1930s. After the war, now living in Munich, he headed the Anti-Bolshevik Bloc of Nations.

indicates that we do not intend to overthrow the Soviet order."[23] This phrase was meant to underscore that the group was concerned with the defense of human rights, not politics. At that time, the investigations into Mykola Rudenko and Oleksa Tykhy were already under way, and we thought that a statement like this, which asserts the legal basis of our activities, might have helped our friends indirectly.

This memorandum wound up in the United States, where it was published in the newspaper *Svoboda* ("Freedom").[24] I assume that when the editors came upon this phrase, they thought it was a typographical error. How could it be possible that these dissidents, whom the West considered enemies of the Soviet system, were not trying to bring it down? The investigator assigned to my case, Oleksandr Bereza, thus presented me with "conclusive evidence" of my criminal behavior by showing me a copy of the *Svoboda* article with the words: "We are not building an underground—and this indicates that we intend to overthrow the Soviet order." The word "not" had been omitted from the second half of the sentence, and obviously without it the meaning of the phrase had been completely altered and, I would argue, had lost its meaning altogether. But this alteration gave the investigators a valuable argument: "Here we have direct proof that you stood against the Soviet system!" Only one word was changed, but the contextual and legal consequences of this modification were enormous. I do not mean to overestimate the significance of this incident because in actual fact it did not have a direct impact on our fate: it influenced the rhetoric of the investigation but not the character or the extent of the sentence. It does, however, convey the importance of the printed word.

It was equally important to us that the various Helsinki Groups across the former Soviet Union were the first to attempt to act within the law by clearly stating their principles and goals and declaring their intent. I was impressed with this bold readiness to go head-to-head with the regime. The fact that the system was not ready to deal with open forms of protest only increased the risks we were taking, but it did not change our moral mindset. As it turned out, the situation called for people who would employ legal measures to realize their rights in real life and by doing so reveal the government's inability to protect those rights. In this way, the people who signed the declaration were

---

23 *Documents*, 43.

24 *Svoboda*: Ukrainian-language newspaper established in 1893 in New Jersey; beginning in the 1930s, it was published daily. Read widely by the North and South American Ukrainian diaspora.

a sort of collective litmus test, without which it would have been impossible to establish the "acidity level" of the Soviet system.

Mykola Matusevych confirmed my interpretation: "I didn't seriously consider the Ukrainian Helsinki Group to be an entity that was capable of overturning anything in this world. The greatest justification for creating the Group, in my mind, was simply as a demonstrative public assertion that 'We are not afraid of you. That's all. We are tired of being afraid.'"[25]

It should be mentioned that our group was only one of several early attempts to work within the legal framework of the Soviet system. From an official standpoint, the first effort to organize a human rights defense organization in Ukraine was in December 1971, when Iryna Kalynets and Viacheslav Chornovil formed a human rights organization to advocate for Nina Strokata, who had been arrested for her vigorous defense of her imprisoned husband, Sviatoslav Karavansky. The group was joined by Vasyl Stus, Leonid Tymchuk, and Petro Yakir. But this organization never got off the ground because within several days (in January 1972) most of its members had been arrested. That's why many Helsinki Group members, Oksana Meshko among them, seemingly remembered our group as the first because it actually did something. As Oksana put it, "This was an extraordinary struggle, the first one in our history that was legal."[26]

It had nearly slipped my mind that I had translated the UHG Declaration into English, until I was reminded of it during sentencing at my trial, when it was cited as a "criminal act," and later through Mykola Rudenko's account: "He (Myroslav) was proficient in English and had translated our Declaration into the language of Walt Whitman. Thus, along with the original [Ukrainian version], our American friends also received an English copy of the Declaration. They were so surprised by this that even the radio stations mentioned it."[27] One should not overestimate the significance of my translation, however. I can only imagine how pathetic it must have been, considering my level of English proficiency at that time. Apparently, the only value it held was for the KGB, since in their eyes disseminating this document confirmed my "hostile intentions."

The principal goal of the UHG was to monitor the implementation of and adherence to the Helsinki Accords. That meant issuing memoranda on

---

25 Mykola Matusevych, "Ia vyhrav dvobii z kahebistamy, tomu shcho peremih strakh," interview by Vasyl' Shkliar, *Molod' Ukrainy*, November 6, 1996, 3.

26 *Ne vidstupliusia!*, 288.

27 Rudenko, *Naibil'she dyvo—zhyttia*, 435.

violations of the Helsinki Accords in Ukraine. These might have been overviews (like Memorandum #1) or they might have focused on specific violations of someone's personal rights (as, for example, Memorandum #3 on Yosyp Terelia; #8 on Vira Lisova; or #11 on Nadiia Svitlychna). The group dispatched these documents to the signatory states that stood out in their active efforts to defend human rights, such as the United States, Canada, United Kingdom, and West Germany. Foreign diplomats and journalists in Moscow served as our intermediaries. Thanks to Radio Liberty, Voice of America, the BBC, and Deutsche Welle, information about the creation of the Ukrainian Helsinki Group, as well as the documents we were producing, spread quickly.

At first, people in the West considered our group to be a Ukrainian branch of the Moscow Helsinki Group. On this point, I would like to quote Mykola Rudenko and cite his open letter to "All People of Good Will": "In the reports about the formation of the group, it was said somewhere that we are a 'branch' of the Moscow Group to Promote the Implementation of the Helsinki Accords. This is not true. Our relations are built on friendship and cooperation, not on subordination."[28] Later he also explained this in one of his interviews:

> Since there were no international representatives or journalists in Kyiv, Petro Hryhorenko, one of the Moscow Group members, took it upon himself to serve as liaison between us and them, as well as with the rest of the world. He would "amplify" all our documents immediately. As a matter of fact, at first, word had it that a branch of the Moscow Group had been created in Ukraine. This stemmed from the Western stereotype of Ukraine's subservience to Russia. The Moscow Group, however, immediately corrected this misinformation. From the start we joined as a separate entity, always mindful of our country's future independence.[29]

With time, not only the Ukrainian Group but also all other newly formed national Helsinki Groups, such as the Lithuanian Group (created November 25, 1976), the Georgian Group (January 14, 1977), and the Armenian Group (April 1, 1977), each joined as totally independent entities. And they remained independent, as far as their decision-making processes were

28 *Documents*, 9.

29 Mykola Rudenko, "Proryv do voli (Mykola Rudenko pro Petra Hryhorenka)", Virtual'nyi muzei Dysydents'kyi rukh v Ukrainy, http://archive.khpg.org/index.php?id=1204008234.

concerned, and the Muscovites never meddled in the documents we were producing. This does not mean, of course, that they approved of everything we were doing and writing. Many of the Moscow dissidents felt that the Ukrainian Group focused too much attention on national issues, which they claimed was harming the purely democratic character of the Helsinki movement.

Oksana Meshko wrote to Petro Hryhorenko about some of the conflicts we had with the Moscow group, and I think that it would have been odd if such conflicts had not existed:

> Quite justifiably, our group has some concerns, and it is my duty to mention this. But I bring this up not to vilify anybody, but to forge stronger bonds and foster an alliance. Where our group is concerned, there can be no personal concerns, complaints, or discord—this is my policy and my position. I disregard all trivialities and personal issues.[30]

Later, Yosyp Zisels confirmed the imperialistic attitudes that stood behind the democratic facades of many of the Russian dissidents:

> Even during the dissident era, I realized that Russian dissidents were quite imperialistically oriented. They stood against the Soviet regime but favored the preservation of the Russian Empire. This was a point of discussion for us, because for us dissidents from the outlying regions, such as Georgians, Lithuanians, and Ukrainians, whose ranks I belong to, the demise of the [Russian] empire was a positive thing. We were fighting for the destruction of the [Soviet] empire. For the majority of Russians, however, including the intelligentsia, as well as for various ethnic and religious sub-groups, this idea was considered a tragedy, as Putin himself has declared.[31]

Nevertheless, even though Russian dissidents tried to convince the UHG to move national issues to the back burner, they never escalated to any direct interventions or ultimatums.

Although we were completely independent where the content of our documents was concerned, we were not independent in our ability to transmit them to the West. Here the assistance of the Moscow Helsinki Group turned out to be priceless. By helping us, they demonstrated that their highest devotion was to democracy, and even though they might have considered

---

30 *Ne vidstupliusia!*, 179.

31 Mykhailo Hlukhovs'kyi, "Yosyp Zisels: Donbas—tse nash sektor Gazy," *Glavcom*, January 21, 2015, http://glavcom.ua/articles/25908.html.

the Ukrainian Helsinki Group's preoccupation with national issues somewhat excessive, or feared it might harm the essence of democratic principles, they never attempted to hinder any of our efforts to contact international representatives—or at least I have never heard of anything of the sort.[32] On the contrary, they did everything to make these contacts possible, even offering their own apartments to arrange meetings and press conferences. It must therefore be said unequivocally that without their help, the "national" Helsinki Groups would simply not have been able to function. Moreover, our Muscovite colleagues offered their apartments to those who were passing through Moscow on their way to visit their jailed family members and friends who were serving time in the camps. It was through them that the aid from the Solzhenitsyn Fund was distributed to the family members of those who were incarcerated.[33] For this, the Moscow dissidents deserve our gratitude and praise.

While I was a member of the group, we prepared eleven memoranda. Today, they are all accessible online and in published form.[34] Thus, I would rather not talk about their substance but rather to describe the circumstances under which they were written and as I remember them.

Memorandum #1 was drafted by Mykola Rudenko in November–December 1976. He was always a conscientious and diligent writer. I can still remember him sitting at the table in his apartment in Koncha-Zaspa, the very image of staunchness and dignity. It was at this table that he read Mykola Matusevych and me his poem "The Cross," which was dedicated to the Holodomor, the Soviet-imposed artificial famine in Ukraine in 1932–1933, and discussed Memorandum #1 with us. Sitting at that table he received his many visitors, who by his own words had gravitated to him after the creation of the group was announced: "My apartment in Koncha-Zaspa

---

32 As Oksana Meshko has pointed out, our materials rarely made it to the West, but this may not have been due to Russian ill will. The conditions for dispatching those materials were often inhospitable, and in the West, for a variety of reasons, some materials might not have even been published. –M. M.

33 Solzhenitsyn Aid Fund: Foundation and support network established in the 1970s by Aleksandr Solzhenitsyn and fellow author and dissident Alexander Ginzburg. Solzhenitsyn contributed one quarter of his Nobel Prize cash award and all royalties on *Gulag Archipelago* to the fund, which was distributed to Soviet dissidents by a network of volunteers.

34 For Ukrainian originals of the memoranda, see *Dokumenty*, 22–35, 40–44, 49–63. For English translations of Memoranda #1–11 (excluding #3 and #10), see *Documents,* 15–75.

has become quite populous: many of the relatives of political prisoners have descended on my home, bringing me the latest news about their parents, husbands, and children who had been arrested for political reasons. Recently, we compiled a comprehensive roster of those who were incarcerated."[35]

Another time, while strolling through the Koncha-Zaspa forest, Rudenko discussed the authorship of the group's documents with us. At that time, we agreed that in the event we were arrested and interrogated, we would give evidence because we did not consider the organization an underground entity and didn't see it as antiestablishment. But each person would talk only about themselves and would claim authorship of every document, so that the "blame" would not fall on just one person. I remembered this agreement clearly, and later this was the foundation for how I behaved during my inquest. I mention this conversation because Oksana Meshko remembers that Rudenko apparently believed that none of the group members would be arrested.[36] Perhaps he indeed did not expect us to be arrested, and therefore he was careful not to give any official cause for it to happen. But remembering our conversation, I am convinced that he was nevertheless preparing himself psychologically for his own arrest.

After the declaration and Memorandum #1 appeared, we were obviously all interested in distributing the texts. We thought that the international radio stations and press would be the best conduits for this. Thus, on November 17, 1976, through the initiative of Osyp Zinkevych, who was in charge of an information service called Smoloskyp ("Torch"), an organization called Helsinki Guarantees for Ukraine Committee was established in Washington, DC.[37] Zinkevych served as our main "dispatcher" and bore the bulk of the responsibility for information dissemination. Jumping ahead, in October 1978, an international representative body of the UHG was formed in the United States, composed of Petro Hryhorenko, Nina Strokata, and Nadiia Svitlychna, all of whom had moved to the United States by that time. They were joined by Leonid Pliushch, who had settled in France. They took

35 Rudenko, *Naibil'she dyvo—zhyttia*, 434.

36 Vasyl' Ovsiienko, "Kozats'ka Matir (Oksana Meshko)," Virtual'nyi muzei Dysydents'kyi rukh v Ukraini, http://archive.khpg.org/index.php?id=1121792907.

37 Smoloskyp Publishers: Established in the 1950s in Paris and relocated to the United States in 1960, Smoloskyp focused on publishing Ukrainian samizdat and books that were banned in the Ukrainian SSR. Their publications were then smuggled into the Soviet Union and ended up circulating throughout the North American diasporas.

Figure 3.13. Osyp Zinkevych.

over some of the communications functions and made public appearances in defense of those being persecuted or arrested for defending the rule of law. They also maintained contacts with international organizations. Their organization published a monthly newsletter called "The Bulletin of Repressions in Ukraine," and the publishing company Smoloskyp published all UHG materials in both Ukrainian and English.

Back in Ukraine, however, we also wanted to take part in these efforts, so we re-typed the materials they produced and distributed them among our friends and relatives. Eventually the authorities caught us doing this, which increased the amount of "material evidence" held against us at our sentencing. As we will later see from the trial materials, this method of distributing the group's documents carried great human trauma with it. One example of this was a predicament that Borys Marynovych, one of my relatives, ran into when I gave him our declaration and Memorandum #11 to familiarize himself with. The KGB operatives noted that I had done so, and on the day I was arrested, they arranged for Borys to be taught a showy, even dramatic "lesson." As the *Chronicle of Current Events* reported, during a trip abroad, he was hauled off a train and brought back to Kyiv, where he was subjected to three days of interrogations. Later he had major problems at work, and his sister Lida, trying to keep things from getting any worse, denounced my actions in writing.

Later, when I was already in prison, I learned that Lida was upset over what she had done. By that time, as my acute disappointment regarding this incident had already passed, I wrote in a letter to my relatives on December 13, 1978:

> It's a pity that Lida took her momentary weakness so much to heart. It would be totally ungrateful on my part if those words should negate the love and kindness that she had always shown me in the past. "Do not judge, or you too will be judged." May this Christian wisdom bring peace and reconciliation to us all.

I should also mention an important lesson I learned from Mykhailyna Kotsiubynska. As the youngest member of the Ukrainian Helsinki Group, I wanted to recruit as many people as possible to join the opposition movement, and at a certain point, I disregarded people's right to decide not to throw themselves in the fire. Once, I hoped to secure the signature of one of our acquaintances for one of the group's petitions, and I was not very subtle about it. My behavior might have brought a lot of harm to this person. I had never seen Mykhailyna Khomivna so ferocious. She told me firmly: "Myroslav, instead of loving humanity as a whole, you should love individual people." This was truly a lesson for life!

While Memorandum #1 was being drafted, two open letters were dispatched to the West. The first one, dated November 14, 1976, was from Mykola Rudenko to "All People of Good Will," which outlined the circumstances under which the UHG had been formed.[38] The second one, dated November 17 of the same year, was from Oles Berdnyk to Jimmy Carter, asking the US president-elect to grant him political asylum.[39] Additionally, several samizdat publications passed through our hands, such as Russian scientist Valentin Turchin's pamphlet, *The Inertia of Fear*, the title of which was

38 *Dokumenty*, 19–20; *Documents*, 6–9.

39 *Dokumenty*, 20–21.

a brilliant formulation of Soviet reality, and also *News from Camp 389-37*, which provided valuable information about conditions in the punitive labor camps.[40] At the end of January 1977 Levko Lukianenko sent us his article "Stop the Crooked Legal System," and we reproduced and disseminated it.[41]

At this time, our group leader was preparing a working version of Protocol #1, dated December 15, 1976, which outlined the responsibilities of each of the group members.[42] This document reflected Mykola Rudenko's desire to demonstrate that the group did not hide its activities, choosing instead to conduct them openly. Mykola Matusevych and I supported this protocol because it was obvious to us that since we were the youngest and the most mobile members of the group, it was incumbent upon us to be part of the "information team." Levko Lukianenko had some valid concerns about the protocol, however, drawing our attention to the fact that a document of this sort might provide the KGB with the justification to charge us under Article 64 (taking part in an anti-Soviet organization); this trumped-up charge could then result in longer sentences.[43] Rudenko accepted his argument and Protocol #1 was abandoned. This did not stop the KGB from confiscating a draft of it from Rudenko's apartment during one of their searches, however, and then including it as material evidence during the trial. Lukianenko's intuition was right on target. During Rudenko's meeting with his wife Raisa on July 4, 1977 (after he had been arrested), he informed her that they had initially charged him with "criminal activity" not only under Article 62 ("Anti-Soviet agitation and propaganda") but also under Article 64 ("Organizational activities aimed at committing particularly dangerous state crimes, and also taking part in an anti-Soviet organization"). In the end, however, they withdrew the second charge.

---

40 Valentin Turchin, *Inertsiia strakha. Sotsializm i totalitarizm* (New York: Khronika, 1978).

41 Levko Luk'ianenko, "Zupynit' kryvosuddia!," reprinted in Stepan Sadovs'kyi, ed., *Zupynit' kryvosudiia! Sprava Levka Luk'ianenka* (Munich: Suchasnist', 1980).

42 *Dokumenty*, 35–36.

43 Both Article 62 and Article 64 of the Criminal Code of the Ukrainian SSR fell under the rubric of "especially dangerous crimes against the state," though Article 64 allowed for longer sentences. See "Article 64 of the UkSSR Criminal Code," Virtual'nyi muzei Dysydents'kyi rukh v Ukraini, http://museum.khpg.org/index.php?id=1164245590.

By the end of 1976 everyone was talking about human rights. On December 15, it was announced that Luis Corvalán, who was then the General Secretary of the Communist Party of Chile, had been released and was living in the USSR. Those who listened to international radio stations learned that he had been swapped for the Russian dissident and prisoner Vladimir Bukovsky. In the United States this event marked the pinnacle of Jimmy Carter's human rights campaign. At home, it also became the basis for a mocking rhyme that asked where we could find such an "a-hole and exchange him for Brezhnev."[44]

Soviet propaganda had a difficult time explaining this political exchange because it was obvious that the government had made a major concession. But the KGB was not about to give in, as we soon found out. Between December 23–25, 1976, with the sanction of the Moscow procurator, searches were conducted in the apartments of UHG members Mykola Rudenko, Oles Berdnyk, Levko Lukianenko, Oleksa Tykhy, and Ivan Kandyba. The circumstances and the atmosphere surrounding this spate of searches were documented by Mykola Rudenko in an appeal addressed directly to the Moscow procurator. Furthermore, earlier, on November 10 of that year, the procurator of the Lenin District of the southwest Ukrainian city of Chernivtsi conducted a search of the home of Yosyp Zisels, who would become an official member of the UHG a few months later. Even during these early searches, the KGB was already employing its usual tricks, planting some US dollars inside Mykola Rudenko's desk; "discovering" pornographic postcards on top of Oles Berdnyk's wardrobe; and eventually, during Oleksa Tykhy's criminal trial, presenting an old German shotgun encased in clay, supposedly found in his attic, about which Oleksa knew nothing. Later, criminal cases such as those against Viacheslav Chornovil, Mykola Horbal, Yaroslav Lesiv, and many others, would be completely falsified by means of similar sordid claims. Yosyp Zisels's house was searched under the pretext that he was linked to another suspect who had been accused of possessing pornography. As one of the KGB operatives eventually declared, "We will not be creating any more martyrs."[45]

Group documents mention that Mykola Matusevych and I wholeheartedly supported the hunger strike that Raisa and Mykola Rudenko waged in

---

44 *"Obmeniali khuligana / Na Luisa Korvalana. / Gde b naiti takuiu bl . . . d', / Chtob na Brezhneva smeniat'?"* This rhyme was composed by Vadim Delaunay, a Soviet dissident poet who had recently emigrated to Paris.

45 That is, by targeting people with purely political charges. –M. M.

protest of the horrendous search that had been perpetrated in their apartment in late 1976.

Following the searches, the psychological atmosphere within the group changed dramatically. This is not surprising, given the effect the searches had on everyone. In an appeal to PEN International, dated January 5, 1977, Oles Berdnyk and Mykola Rudenko wrote:

> Almost our entire literary archive has been taken. Dozens of notebooks that contained new ideas for several new works, unfinished short stories and science fiction, tens of thousands of lines of poetry (now impossible to re-create), as well as M. Rudenko's philosophical work "Gnosis and Modernity," were seized. O. Berdnyk's works "Holy Ukraine" and "Alternative Evolution," as well as many others, were all confiscated.[46]

I actually had the opportunity to familiarize myself with "Holy Ukraine," just prior to it being taken away, and for a long time I remembered specific turns of thought.[47] Today, scholars will easily recognize this author of "Holy Ukraine" as the future leader of the humanist organization "Ukrainian Spiritual Republic," whose activities resounded throughout Galicia in the late 1980s and early 1990s.[48]

As mentioned earlier, one of Mykola Rudenko's noteworthy characteristics was the diligence and fastidiousness of his work. That's why all our early memoranda always ended with his characteristic phrase: "The signed original of this document is retained by the Ukrainian Helsinki Group." I think that this addendum was particularly irritating to the KGB because they perceived it as usurping their own exclusive rights to possess documents. These original documents became major targets of the KGB's searches; afterward, the phrase could have been amended: "The signed original is being diligently guarded by the investigative unit of the KGB."

Memoranda #2 and #3 were dated January 20 and 22, 1977, respectively. We worked very diligently on the contents of Memorandum #2, trying to assist Mykola Rudenko in selecting appropriate examples that would best

---

46 *Dokumenty*, 39–40.

47 Oles' Berdnyk, "Sviata Ukraina: Dumy pro Ridnu Matir," in *Sviata Ukraina: Esei i Lysty* (Baltimore: Smoloskyp, 1980), 13–44.

48 Ukrainian Spiritual Republic (*Ukrains'ka Dukhovna Respublika*): A theosophical movement founded by Berdnyk in the late 1980s that sees nations as powerful collective spirits and argues that the pursuit of harmony and unity should be a nation's main goal.

demonstrate that the Ukrainian people were not treated equally before the law. As I read this document today, I think I recognize the ideas that I personally contributed, but I am reluctant to identify them as mine. What if they are just the thoughts of others that became fixed in my memory?

Memorandum #3 was specifically dedicated to the fate of Yosyp Terelia, the head of the Initiative Group Protecting the Rights of Believers and the Church in Ukraine, and to the persecution of the Ukrainian Greek Catholic Church and its faithful more generally.[49] Mykola Matusevych and I met with Yosyp in our apartment. We were left with a heavy feeling, as all three of us were under considerable stress, and we were struggling with conflicting feelings: how to avoid getting into any trouble, evade provocations, and keep from bringing any damage to our cause, while still gathering and transmitting all important pertinent information. Because of this internal conflict, the three of us understandably didn't act as naturally as usual, which was obvious to everyone, and this certainly increased the tension even more. Given the tense conspiratorial circumstances, most of our meetings in those days were conducted under psychological strain.

Terelia came across as a bit strange, relating fairly phantasmagorical tales that were heavily laced with mysticism. In our minds we had to sift out what was credible from the products of his fertile imagination—his mind had been damaged by countless persecutions.[50] It is understandable, therefore, that the text of Memorandum #3 contained only a broad outline of the facts regarding the violations of his rights (which were certainly unquestionable). But we left detailed descriptions of some of the persecutions he had endured up to him and just attached his personal deposition to the memorandum.[51]

Many years later, after Terelia managed to emigrate to the West, I learned that some clerics in the Vatican had similar doubts about his stories. Up until that time, Yosyp Terelia had been the symbol of Soviet persecutions of the Greek Catholics. But the information that he delivered had often become

49 Beginning in the mid-1970s, a movement advocating for religious freedom—and in the Ukrainian case, the legalization of the Ukrainian Greek Catholic Church in particular—began to grow, drawing on the example of the broader human rights movement. Terelia and the Initiative Group were at the forefront of this movement.

50 By 1977, Terelia had spent most of the past fifteen years under arrest, in prison, or in a labor camp, on a variety of charges, ranging from illegal possession of firearms to Ukrainian nationalist propaganda.

51 The text of Memorandum #3 is omitted from *Documents*. For the Ukrainian text, see *Dokumenty* 43. Terelia's deposition is not reprinted there.

so intertwined with his own fantasies that, to a certain extent, one could no longer give full credence to it.

This is an appropriate moment to explain why certain documents, particularly Memorandum #2 and #3, do not include the signatures of Mykola Matusevych and myself. The reason was the psychological atmosphere within our ranks. By the end of January 1977, the general euphoria over the creation of the Group had dissipated. Each member was conscious of being watched, had lost his or her job, or had experienced some other difficulties. Everyone understood that we were all under heavy pressure. Major KGB searches in late 1976, and the confiscation of important documents, put everyone under great stress. We all knew that sooner or later we would all be arrested, but no one knew when. All of this created an overall atmosphere of tension, and we simply could not avoid what was generally known as "spy mania." Since the KGB had focused so much attention on us, it was obvious that they would try to plant some of their agents among us. All it took, therefore, was noticing that someone might be acting a little strangely, and suspicion would immediately start to blossom.

The KGB was very crafty in contributing to this effect. For example, we considered it rather funny when they would play the "Jewish card," by spreading rumors in Kyiv: "So you think this is a *Ukrainian* group? With names like Matuse-e-e-vich, Marino-o-o-vich, etc.?"—pronouncing our names with a distinctively Jewish intonation. In contrast, in the village of Kalynivka, outside of Kyiv, where I lived at that time, my neighbors knew me as "the Canadian spy." All this is to say, responsibility for the extent of "spy-mania" among the dissidents does not fall on us alone but especially on the KGB, which did everything possible to further intensify this feeling. In this instance, Mykola Matusevych and I became the victims of it.

In January 1977, Mykola Rudenko returned from a trip to Moscow, where he had presented our statements, and told us about some of the meetings he had there. At some point I realized that it was all entirely in God's hands, and Mykola Rudenko could be arrested at any moment. What would we do then? We would certainly remain members of the group. But who could we entrust our documents to, and how would we function? I joined Raisa in the kitchen and shared my thoughts with her, asking her for advice: "I don't even know how to broach this with Mykola; he can sometimes be so difficult." "The best thing would be to write him a letter," she replied. "Don't send it by mail, just give it to me, and I will hand it to him. That's what I do when I want to persuade him about something. He might bridle initially, but eventually he simmers down." So, I went home and wrote him a letter, running everything by Mykola Matusevych. The gist of this letter was the following: "Mykola Danylovych, you could be arrested at any time, so perhaps we should know something about our partners in Moscow?" I do remember that I carelessly used the phrase "It would be good to know how this 'dissident kitchen' works." It was in quotation marks, of course, but we passed the letter on to Raisa.

Then all hell broke loose. Rudenko was firmly convinced: "Aha, these boys have been specially dispatched to our group. They hung around, building trust, and now they have been ordered to disclose names and addresses."[52] The next time Mykola and I came to see him, he declared sternly: "I want you to know that you are under suspicion. I will not expel you from the group, but to begin with, I am removing your names from Memoranda #2 and #3. Furthermore, be advised that from now on, every step you take will be monitored, and no matter where you go, we will warn everyone about you."

I ran to Raisa: "I did as you told me!" In a distant voice she replied: "I know nothing." Mykola and I were devastated. It was not enough that we spent every day waiting to be arrested; now our own people were treating us with distrust. On top of that, Oksana Meshko began to suspect us for allegedly not showing up somewhere we were supposed to and deliberately not conveying certain things to certain people. That's how a whole series of seemingly logical allegations got started. From that time on, I have always been amazed by the logic of suspicion: even the most innocent things suddenly take on particular significance. And like the puzzle pieces in a children's game, they seem to fit cohesively into one comprehensive and logical picture. This time, Mykola Matusevych and I were the main pieces in these puzzles.

That is why both our names were absent from Memoranda #2 and #3. Nevertheless, as the verdict in our trial shows, during one of their searches of Mykola Rudenko's house, the KGB found and confiscated an older version of Memoranda #2 and #3, with our signatures still on them, and this version was used to incriminate us in court later. Our signatures on these memoranda were also used as material evidence during Mykola Rudenko's and Oleksa Tykhy's trials.[53]

I no longer remember if I saw Raisa Rudenko or Oksana Meshko prior to Mykola Rudenko's arrest. I do still remember the aloofness in our

52 The most painful aspect of this was that it was precisely the KGB that likely knew the addresses and contacts of our Moscow partners the best. –M. M.

53 *Oleksa Tykhy: dumky pro ridny Donetsky krai*, ed. Vasyl' Ovsiienko et al. (Donetsk: "Donechchyna," 2012), 1:264–65.

communications during that time: even if I said something harmless, I would notice a smirk on their faces, as if to say, "You can say what you want, but we know where you're heading with this!"

I want to emphasize that I forgave my friends for this grievance long ago because I understand the difficult situation they were in at that time. I ultimately reconciled with Mykola Rudenko when we were both in the camps, and with Raisa there was never any need to do so. Years later, when we met again, it seemed that our mutual friendship had never even come under question. I always marveled at this courageous woman, and to illustrate how justified this feeling is, and how futile holding a grudge against her would be, I want to quote what she herself said about her arrest:

> When, during the eleventh search, they finally arrested me, I already knew that this time they actually would, because this search had a different character to it. This time, they took every line that had ever been written in my handwriting, regardless if it had anything to do with the Helsinki Group or not. So I knew that this time they would take me as well.[54]

This, however, came later. First, on February 5, 1977, Mykola Rudenko and Oleksa Tykhy were arrested, and in Moscow the same thing happened to Yury Orlov and Alexander Ginzburg. Not knowing anything about it, Mykola Matusevych and I were walking toward October Revolution Square in central Kyiv (now called "Maidan" or "Independence Square"), when suddenly a group of young men jumped out of a car, twisted our arms, and pushed us into the car. "Quiet, quiet! Don't resist, just get into the car." They took us to the KGB headquarters on Rosa Luxemburg Street (today Lypska Street) and held us in separate rooms. Then they gave us an official warning to sign, the gist of which was, "If you do not stop your criminal activities, you will be arrested." Obviously, we had no intentions of giving up our Helsinki Group membership, nor did we plan to curtail our activities.

Once we got home, we learned that they had conducted searches in Tamila Matusevych's apartment in Kyiv and in my apartment in the suburbs. These searches were subsequently documented in UHG statements. As soon as we found out about Mykola Rudenko's arrest, we immediately went to Raisa Rudenko's house to see how she was coping. Her rather chilly attitude told us that she was still suspicious of us. Yosyp Terelia told us that Oksana Meshko was convinced that we were KGB agents.

---

54 "Spohady Raisy Rudenko", Virtual'nyi muzei Dysydents'kyi rukh v Ukraini, http://archive.khpg.org/index.php?id=1267046381.

Our relationship with Oles Berdnyk, on the other hand, remained unchanged, untouched by any suspicions. We personally saw him as now the de facto head of the UHG (along with Levko Lukianenko), although the general consensus in the group was that after Rudenko's arrest, we would not announce the next group leader's name. I have no idea what Oles's personal opinion on the subject was. In any event, Mykola Matusevych and I remained close to him, and it was thanks to him that our names once again started appearing on UHG documents. We resumed gathering materials for new memoranda. We were grateful to him for all this. (Later, Raisa Rudenko told me that it had been Berdnyk himself who had sown the suspicions against us.)

We also used to visit Levko Lukianenko in Chernihiv, to consult with him about the group's predicament. At that time, Lukianenko was a legend because he had been sentenced to death, but after a long time on death row his sentence was commuted to fifteen years, which he served in full. Since this man had such extensive prison experience, he did not draw suspicion to himself so easily. At that time, he played an important role in my life, not only by calmly opening up to us but also by offering us some truly fatherly counseling: "Boys, are you ready to go to prison? Surely you must realize how all this will end. If you are not prepared to do so, now is the best time to quit." I still remember the tone of his voice and the significance of this decisive moment. I took a moment to contemplate this and then replied decisively: "Yes, I am." I frequently thought back to this moment, particularly during the inquest and during my incarceration, when things got rough. It provided me with inner discipline and strength. This is what it means to pose the right questions at the right time!

As is clear from the style of several of the subsequent memoranda alone, Oles Berdnyk was the main author. The first one in this series was Memorandum #4, on "New Repressions in Ukraine Geared toward Helsinki Group Members," dated February 9, 1977, obviously referring to the February 5 arrests of Mykola Rudenko and Oleksa Tykhy, as well as the new searches connected to their cases. This was supplemented by an "Open Letter to the Governments of all Signatory Countries of the Helsinki Accords," which also discussed these persecutions.[55]

Rather than recounting the contents of these documents—which are worth reading for their detailed factual accounts—I would like to mention a trip Mykola Matusevych and I took to Lviv and Drohobych in late February

55 *Dokumenty*, 44–45.

1977, during which the search cited in Memorandum #4 took place. The goal of the trip was to escape Kyiv for a while because the psychological atmosphere created by our fellow UHG members' suspicions of us was so stressful. We arrived in Lviv and went to visit Atena Pashko, whom we loved dearly, and she asked us: "Boys, what is going on within the group? It sounds pretty bad. Mykhailo Horyn told me that he heard from Mykola Rudenko that Matusevych and Marynovych are supposedly agents. Horyn doesn't know you, but I swore to him that that was not true because I know you very well." Atena got in touch with Horyn, and we all agreed to discuss the situation. We met at a place designated by Horyn—in a field somewhere, where it would have been difficult to listen in on our conversation. We spoke openly and honestly. He confirmed the message from Kyiv, and we explained why we had come under suspicion. Mykhailo Horyn was saddened by this misunderstanding within the group, though at that time it would have been difficult to do anything about it. To Mykola Matusevych and me, the most important thing was that Atena Pashko and Mykhailo Horyn had become our guarantors, confirming that the allegations against us were baseless. It is difficult to overstate the gratitude we felt toward them.

After that, Mykola and I went to Drohobych. At that time my mother was living in temporary quarters while her apartment was being renovated. This is where the search that was mentioned in Memorandum #4 took place, and it was done in a crude, provincial manner. After Mykola, my mother, and I had returned from an evening concert, one of our neighbors popped in and asked us a totally absurd question, which made us all shrug our shoulders in confusion. After a few minutes, however, we realized that he was checking if we were all at home. Suddenly a bunch of functionaries tore into the room and informed us that it was a search. They showed us a document. They all had the typical dull KGB demeanor, even the witnesses. I asked them for their passports, and one of the witnesses got angry: "How dare you ask me for a passport!" I replied: "How dare you? You are required to carry a passport when you come here as a witness!"[56] The group leader was pretending that he had rounded up the witnesses on the street, so he asked them to go get their passports. When one of those witnesses returned with his passport, by some gift of fate I spotted a stamp confirming that he indeed did work for the KGB. He was not an officer, but some lower rank. I hadn't even hoped that I might get so lucky. I turned to the leaders and pointed to that stamp:

56 Legally, searches had to be conducted in the presence of neutral witnesses, whose identities had to be able to be established by their internal passports.

"Whom did you select as a witness? He's a staff member of the KGB! Don't you know the law? A member of the investigating unit is not allowed to serve as a witness!"

I emphatically forbade them to conduct a search, citing a violation of the law. Then Mykola and I were taken to the police precinct, where they searched us, and after several hours they let us go. At my mother's house, meanwhile, they proceeded with the search. It was a basic search, however; they just went through our personal belongings.

Today, it is clear that in spite of all the difficulties and misunderstandings within the group, and the two aforementioned arrests, our work continued in dynamic fashion. Frankly speaking, the chronological listing of all the documents issued by the group in early 1977 is remarkable:

February 10: "An Open Friendly Message" from Berdnyk to the PEN Club International, about Rudenko's arrest.[57]

February 11: Oksana Meshko's complaint to the Procurator General of the USSR, protesting against the unlawful search of her apartment and various other unlawful persecutions.[58]

February 15: Memorandum #5, "Ukraine in 1977—to the Countries Participating in the Summer 1977 Belgrade Conference." This document bears the signatures of all eight group members who were still free. I read somewhere that its author, Oles Berdnyk, had not run the text by all the group members for their approval; I do remember this text, however, so I had certainly approved it.[59]

February 21: Memorandum #6, "On So-Called 'Internal Matters' of the Country," signed by all eight members.[60]

March 1: An open letter from Oles Berdnyk to the presidium of the Parliament of the USSR and to the Congress of the United States, announcing that on March 3, he (Berdnyk) was starting a hunger strike to protest Mykola Rudenko's arrest.[61]

57 *Dokumenty*, 45–47.

58 *Dokumenty*, 47–49.

59 *Dokumenty*, 49–54; *Documents*, 42–53.

60 *Dokumenty*, 54–55; *Documents*, 54–56.

61 *Dokumenty*, 55–56.

March 15: Memorandum #7, "Ukrainian Helsinki Group—the First Four Months," signed by everyone except Ivan Kandyba, who could not be reached. An addendum to Memorandum #7, dated March 10, describes in detail a number of searches conducted at the homes of Mykola Matusevych's parents, sister, wife, and mother-in-law, as well as in my apartment in Kalynivka, "in conjunction with the case against O. Tykhy."[62]

March 15: Memorandum #8, "On the Persecution of Vira Lisova, Wife of a Political Prisoner." Mykola Matusevych's and my signatures are missing (more about that later).[63]

March 18: Memorandum #9, "On Mykola Rudenko's Brutally Unlawful Investigation," document signed by Oles Berdnyk.[64]

March 18: Oles Berdnyk's statement to Volodymyr Shcherbytsky, the First Secretary of the Central Committee of the Communist Party of Ukraine, with copies to the US Congress in Washington, DC, the Helsinki Guarantees for Ukraine Committee based in Washington, DC, and to Dr. Zvarun, the Head of Smoloskyp publishing house and the president of the Washington Committee. In this statement, Berdnyk announced that due to continued persecutions, he would start yet another hunger strike on March 21.[65]

Sometime in March: Memorandum #10. This document is a bit confusing. I personally do not remember its text, and it doesn't seem to exist in any of the official group records. It is possible that one of Oles Berdnyk's personal appeals to leave the Soviet Union might have encountered a roadblock, and the memorandum was intended to serve as a vehicle to that end.

March 20: Memorandum #11, "On the Fate of Nadiia Svitlychna." The memorandum contains seven signatures, with Ivan Kandyba's missing.[66]

Today, it is interesting to compare this list to the words of an interrogator after Mykola Rudenko's arrest, "This time we won't miss the mark the way

62 *Dokumenty*, 56–59; *Documents*, 57–65.
63 *Dokumenty*, 59–60; *Documents*, 66–68.
64 *Dokumenty*, 60; *Documents*, 69–70.
65 *Dokumenty*, 60–61; *Documents*, 230–232.
66 *Dokumenty*, 61–63; *Documents*, 71–75.

we did in 1972—this time your lot won't recover!"[67] As it turned out, their cruel persecutions and intimidations had the reverse effect: the Ukrainian Helsinki Group not only failed to be silenced but burst forth with a slew of new documents and petitions.

The fact that Mykola Matusevych's and my signatures were missing from Memorandum #8 can be explained by happenstance, the inability of the rest of the group to get in touch with us at the appropriate moment. It was actually Mykola and I who had come to Vira Lisova's apartment to document all the illegal pressures the KGB was putting on her. She knew that we were gathering information for future memoranda and was ready for any possible persecutions that might result. Our documentation of these events was confirmed by the KGB itself, when they confiscated the notes that I made in her house during their search of my place. Later this fact was also cited in my conviction: "He, M.F. Marynovych, participated in the preparation of Memorandum #8, when he and another person he refused to name had visited Lisova, and made notes based on their conversation. Those notes were later used for this Memorandum." (I will talk about Vira Lisova's own position during our trial in the next chapter.)

Some of the documents we used for our research in March and April 1977 were a statement from prisoners in the camps, "We, the political prisoners—", and also a statement by the evangelical Christians, "To the Christians of the World," in which the Protestants appealed to their brethren to pray for the incarcerated members of the Helsinki Groups. We also read the manuscript "How Else?" by the persecuted Odesa art historian Vasyl Barladianu and discussed dedicating a separate memorandum to him, particularly after he was arrested on March 2, 1977.

The last group memorandum that I coauthored dealt with Nadiia Svitlychna, who had been persecuted and put into an impossible situation by the KGB. In general, it is these two memoranda about Vira Lisova and Nadiia Svitlychna that I considered our own because Mykola and I were instrumental in their preparation. Back on December 10, 1976, Nadiia had appealed to the UHG (as well as to the Central Committee of the Communist Party of the USSR) with a statement that eventually became famous: "After everything I have endured, I consider it beneath human dignity to be a citizen of the largest, mightiest, and most perfect concentration camp in the world."[68]

67 *Chronicle* 45:232; referring to the mass arrests of Ukrainian dissidents in 1972.

68 *Dokumenty*, 37.

As I remember, this was the first time a "regular" citizen appealed to the UHG declaring that her human rights were being violated. For us, this set an important precedent. Since her first statement was confiscated, on January 5, 1977, she wrote another one, begging the group to help her "find a place in the world where my son and I can live in peace and not be terrified about our future."

Nadiia Svitlychna's extrajudicial persecution only got worse: after her release from prison in May 1976, she was denied permission to live in Kyiv, and she could not get a job, so consequently she was threatened with being put back in prison, this time for "parasitism."[69] She did finally manage to find employment as a cleaning lady in a kindergarten, but after further interrogations she was fired from that job as well.[70] Having to endure such persecutions, Nadiia renounced her Soviet citizenship. For us it was finally time to draft a separate memorandum, which is what the group did, with Mykola's and my active participation.

The intensity of the group's work becomes even more obvious when you consider the amount of traveling we did at that time. In December 1976, Mykola Matusevych went to Moscow to see Yury Orlov. Then in March 1977 on behalf of the UHG I went to the village of Yizhivka in the Donetsk oblast, Oleksa Tykhy's family home, to visit his mother after her son's arrest. (At that time, the village was Ukrainian speaking.) I found her house and asked her how she was coping. Mariia Tykha received me very cordially and trustingly, showing me all her family photos and feeding me.

Along the way to Yizhivka, I stopped in Kramatorsk to visit Serhy Ivanchenko, one of my former army buddies. I didn't hide the fact that I was under KGB surveillance, and he wanted to help me, offering to "hide" me. Eventually, however, in the protocols of my case, I saw a transcript of his KGB interrogation where he recounted our meeting, obviously unnerved. This makes it clear that, as expected, the KGB had diligently been monitoring all my travels.

---

69 The Soviet Union criminalized the refusal to work, seeing labor as an integral part of contributing to a Communist society. Beginning in the 1960s, this statute was frequently applied to dissidents, who were fired from their jobs for their political activism and subsequently charged with parasitism.

70 Decades later, Nadiia Svitlychna gave a wonderful interview that contains, among other things, remarkable information about the dissident movement of the 1960s. –M. M. See Nadiia Svitlychna, interview by Vasyl Ovsiienko and Vakhtang Kipiani, Virtual'nyi muzei Dysydents'kyi rukh v Ukraini, September 23, 1998, http://archive.khpg.org/index.php?id=1121767765.

I don't remember anything about the trips taken by Oles Berdnyk, the unofficial head of the group, or by other group members, but perhaps I didn't even know about them. I did learn from the *Chronicle* that at the end of March, Oles Berdnyk had been summoned to Donetsk to be interrogated in the cases against Rudenko and Tykhy, but he did not go. Oksana Meshko and Petro Vins, who had also been summoned, didn't go either. In April, however, Berdnyk was picked up in Kyiv and forcibly delivered to Donetsk, where he was interrogated and then released.

Around March 20, 1977, the Helsinki Group asked me to go to Moscow and Tarusa, a town around 140 kilometers south of Moscow that was home to many dissidents, to meet with Petro Hryhorenko and Nina Strokata. At that time, I had already been fired from my job, so I had plenty of time and energy on my hands.

I was anxious on my way to these meetings. General Hryhorenko's name alone was enough to intrigue me. First of all, that name legitimized the dissident movement: if even generals, who were in a position to enjoy all the privileges and benefits of their position, were beginning to criticize the Soviet system, that demonstrated that something must be wrong with the system as a whole. A system like that cannot have a future if the highest military ranks and the creators of the hydrogen bomb (like the leading dissident Andrei Sakharov) rise up against it. Secondly, it was significant that Hryhorenko was not some bureaucratic hack latching on to whoever was in power at a given moment, but a combat general. This reassured me that he, a Soldier with a capital "S," who had courageously looked death in the eye, would not waver from the perilous truth. Thirdly, the general's name bore echoes of that Ukrainianness that was so dear to me.[71] To me, he was yet another fellow countryman who refused to tolerate deceit and injustice, in spite of the fact that he now lived in Moscow and Ukraine was but a distant memory of his youth. For this reason, even prior to our acquaintance, his name evoked a spirit of kinship in me.

Hryhorenko's decision to join not only the Moscow Helsinki Group, but also the UHG was a tribute to his national sentiments, which were consolidating quickly at the time. This was different, of course, from the feeling of national superiority or other exaggerations that usually accompany bursts of nationalistic feelings from the average neophyte. His embrace of Ukrainianness was somewhat similar to the attention he dedicated to the

71 Hryhorenko is an obviously Ukrainian surname.

issue of the Crimean Tatars.[72] The principal motivating factor in both cases was his keen empathy for those who endured state-sponsored oppression. I suspect that had he lived in Central Africa, he would likewise have sided with mistreated indigenous tribes. For him, the predominant feeling was ethical rather than ethnic.

Moscow received me with a chill, and I'm not just talking about the weather. I could never be a mere tourist in this odious capital of the "Evil Empire." I suffocated in that all-encompassing imperial chill, as if it were freezing out the sense I had that somewhere close by, the key to Ukraine's future was being safeguarded in one of the Kremlin's vaults. In this megalopolis, particularly when looking at the spiky towers of the Kremlin, an even greater chill enveloped my being at the thought that an insignificant powerless ant like me was trying to stand up to this mighty machine. No, I had no intention of retreating; on the contrary, I felt great pride that I had been granted the honor of being part of a small cohort of intrepid beings. What was daunting was the contrast of scales. What's more, this timorous provincial chap was about to enter Petro Hryhorenko's home, with full awareness of the chaotic worldview that reigned in his own head and thus the sense that his UHG membership was more like an honorary advance payment.

Our first encounter immediately confirmed my lack of maturity. After receiving me hospitably, courteously, and trustingly, Petro Hryhorenko gave me one of his texts to read. I remember that it dealt with the internal passport system as a marker of a police state. I was shocked and didn't even attempt to hide my astonishment: "Can a country actually exist without an internal passport system?" Petro Hryhorenko only smiled and eagerly delivered a short lecture about the basics of democracy. I no longer remember the gist of what he said, but what amazed me was that at no point did he ever convey to me the naïveté of my question, neither through words nor with his facial expression. He never made me feel like an ignoramus straining to enter the ranks of human rights defenders. This served as a dual lesson for me: one lesson in democratic theory and one on human dignity, the importance of which seemingly went unnoticed by Hryhorenko.

72 The Crimean Tatars had been expelled en masse from the Crimean Peninsula in 1944; a 1967 decree removed restrictions on their returning to the peninsula, but the Soviet government refused to reestablish Crimean Tatar autonomy there and provided minimal assistance to those who wanted to relocate to the peninsula. Many Crimean Tatars returned to the peninsula but were denied residence permits, which made them the target of arrests in the 1970s.

The main aim of my visit was to familiarize him with the gist of UHG Memorandum #11, about Nadiia Svitlychna's case. I don't remember any of his comments or that he was unwilling to sign it; I would have remembered these things. Courageously overcoming my bashfulness, I briefly apprised him of the situation within the UHG, knowing full well that he served as a spokesperson for the group and that his voice would be heard not only in Moscow but—because of the presence of international diplomats and journalists there—around the world as well.

The Hryhorenko apartment was humble, certainly not one befitting a general. The host's robust figure seemed to fill the entire space, although he was not alone in the house. That day, I met his wife, Zinaida; their ailing son, Oleh; and Aishe Seitmuratova, a Crimean Tatar. Zinaida Hryhorenko was an exceptional hostess, and her courtesy was simply bewitching. Her honesty and candor were remarkable, and after just a few minutes with her, you felt you had known her for a long time. Even two decades later, when we spoke on the phone during one of my visits to the United States, it was apparent that even that short visit had been sufficient for Zinaida to maintain this unique trust in me for a lifetime. This woman deserves to be remembered affectionately, as Mykola Horbal has captured so well:

> Even the years could not hide her former beauty. She was always attentive and inquisitive. Eventually I found out that she was Russian, and that Petro Hryhorenko was her second spouse; her first husband had been shot as an "enemy of the people." "I thought that I might be able to hide behind the broad shoulders of a General," said Zinaida, "but this husband also turned out to be a lover of truth." This detail helped me understand the phenomenon of the disgraced Soviet general. This woman must have certainly sown the seeds of doubt in his heart about Stalin's infallibility and showed him how to look more closely at "the most democratic society of the world." Perhaps it was thanks to the experiences of this woman, who had survived all sorts of atrocities and repressions, that Hryhorenko began to contemplate the true meaning of life, his roots, and the fate of his native Ukrainian culture. Their Moscow apartment was a safe haven for all those who were persecuted and hounded by the totalitarian regime, and not only Ukrainians.[73]

At that time, Petro Hryhorenko was closely associated with the fate of the Crimean Tatars, who had fallen victim to Stalin's ravings over the collective guilt of that entire nation. The general's decision to openly support

73 Horbal, *Prezentatsiia zhyttia*, 211–12.

the Crimean Tatars in their right for rehabilitation and their return to their ancestral lands symbolized the better traditions of the Moscow dissidents and transformed them (that is, the dissidents) into a beacon for many human rights supporters scattered throughout the Soviet Union. In my mind, this decision also subconsciously awakened his Ukrainian consciousness because, as is often the case in our society, the concept of justice won out over the idea of the interests of the state. It cannot be denied that the government had triumphed in its aims: with the deportation of Crimean Tatars from their homeland, the potentially dangerous Muslim factor had been removed, the glory of Russian military might had been definitively established in Sevastopol, and the territory of Crimea had been cleared for Kremlin dachas, All-Union health sanatoriums, and single-family homes for "worthy pensioners."[74] How could a dutiful citizen complain about that? But Petro Hryhorenko's moral outrage spoke out loud and clear: "This is not fair!" The voice of his civic consciousness served as the foundation for his noteworthy public actions.

At that time, however, I still had a poor understanding of these issues; in my conversations with Aishe, therefore, I tried to steer clear of any discussions of the Crimean Tatars, although I did feel an almost instantaneous friendship toward her. All the same, Petro Hryhorenko was the central focus of Aishe's attention. Her unequivocal love and respect for her host was obvious, and for me it took on symbolic meaning. Eventually, while in prison, whenever I heard how the Tatars revered Petro Hryhorenko, and how he was a national hero for them, Aishe would always come to mind. I didn't remember her face, but I remembered clearly the conscious or subconscious signs of love that she bestowed upon the general.

After Moscow I was supposed to go to Tarusa, where Nina Strokata, one of the UHG members, was living under administrative surveillance after her release from the camps. My task was to acquaint her with the memorandum. So General Hryhorenko and I discussed how I should get there. All in all, my stay at the general's hospitable home didn't last very long. We had a short working discussion, which continued around the dinner table, and then I was on my way. As often happens, I had no way of knowing that my first meeting with him would also be my last. The broom of the Kremlin machine, diligently clearing living space for the "happy and carefree

---

74 After the deportation of the Crimean Tatars, Crimea became perhaps the principal holiday destination in the Soviet Union; the ability to vacation or retire to the peninsula was seen as a reward granted to loyal Soviet citizens.

Soviet citizens," swept away all the "undesirable and unworthy," sending us in opposite directions: I was sent to a camp in the Ural Mountains, and Petro Hryhorenko was banished to America, where he languished in his final days, deprived of his Soviet citizenship. It was from Nadiia Svitlychna that I learned about his last years in that country. She loved Petro Hryhorenko and his family and always tried to maintain close contact with them. He died the same year that I returned to Ukraine from my internal exile in Kazakhstan. I was able to pray at his gravesite in Bound Brook, New Jersey in the early 1990s, when I visited the United States for the first time.

After arriving in Tarusa, I located Nina Strokata's apartment. She was in internal exile in the same town as the Russian dissident journalist Kronid Liubarsky. They met and hosted me, and during our conversation, one of them finally asked me: "What is going on with you all in Ukraine?" They went on to tell me that as they were watching me, they noticed that I was acting normally. "But we received word from Mykola Rudenko, telling us that Myroslav Marynovych is on his way to visit you, but be careful because we suspect that he might be a KGB agent." I just raised my hands: "Believe it or not, but that's how things are there."

We had a very honest and open discussion, and they were extremely candid with me. They gave me some letters, but it would have been better if they had not: the following day, when I traveled from Tarusa to Serpukhov (a larger town outside Moscow), I was searched. And obviously all those letters were confiscated. This is what happened. At the Serpukhov train station, the police approached me and told me that they had witnesses who had testified that they saw me selling gold items; therefore, they had to search me. I realized that they were obviously just looking for a reason to search me. In Memorandum #1, Mykola Rudenko wrote about similar incidents:

> After an illegal search, former political prisoner Oleksa Tykhy was arrested on suspicion of robbing a store. A guard then began to beat him. When Tykhy protested to KGB Lt. Col. Melnyk, V.O., the latter responded with brutal obscenities and shouted, "And who do you think you are?" Actually, this detention was necessary for the KGB to confiscate Tykhy's manuscripts. In two days, he was released, but his manuscripts were not returned.[75]

After I was brought to the police station, they sarcastically asked me why I had come there, where I had been, and what my goal was. I also resorted to sarcasm because I knew how this would end. During our conversation, the

75 *Documents*, 33; *Dokumenty*, 34.

issue of the Holodomor was brought up, and the militiamen became angry, claiming that calling it a deliberate famine was unfair to the Soviet government because even though the farmers' food was taken away, they had been compensated with some clothing. I told them that even if that were true, how nourishing could this clothing have been if all their food had been confiscated and they were dying of hunger? This was the sort of discussions we had, mostly on the ideological level.

Searching my briefcase, they found some materials and told me, "Well, here we have something anti-Soviet, so we are required to call in the KGB." It took an hour for the KGB to arrive, and after looking things over, the agent told me, "This is quite serious, we have to search you. Take off your clothes." I told them that I would not do that, and they would have to undress me themselves if they wanted to. We argued for a long time, and eventually I realized that I was losing time and that nothing good would come of this, so I said sharply: "There's so many of you here, big guys, and you aren't even capable of searching one single person? I need to return to Moscow." This got them angry and they yanked off my clothing, of course finding the hidden papers. Among them were copies of Memorandum #11 and the letters that Nina and Kronid had given me. The loss of the letters bothered me greatly because I would be required to prove to my UHG colleagues that they had indeed been confiscated, as opposed to my turning them over to the KGB myself. Already under suspicion in Kyiv, this caused a lot of anguish for me.

All my agonizing, however, was futile. First of all, the *Chronicle of Current Events* described the search and the confiscated letters.[76] Secondly, as the *Chronicle* also confirmed, searches of Nina and Kronid's guests had been an everyday thing at that time, and this did not surprise them:

> On 29 May, in Moscow, Pinkhas Abramovich Podrabinek and his son Kirill . . . were detained at the Kursk station on their return from Tarusa. At the police station in the railway station they were told that they were suspected of carrying narcotics and body searches were carried out. An outline for a scientific samizdat journal was confiscated.[77]

I should also mention one other prearrest episode: my attempt to apply for a job as a poster hanger. As I remember, it happened shortly before my arrest, when I saw an advertisement in the Kyiv City Information Bulletin seeking someone to hang posters on bulletin boards. I brought my passport

76 *Chronicle*, 45:233.

77 *Chronicle*, 46:34.

and diploma and presented them to a nice-looking Russian-speaking manager and told her, "I would like to work for you as a poster installer." After checking my documents, she cried in amazement, "With a diploma of higher education?" I told her, "Yes, with a higher diploma. Let me step out into the hall for a minute, and you call the KGB, and ask them if I could be allowed to work as a poster installer. I am tired of being fired all the time. So please call." She stared at me in amazement, and said in Russian, "No, I like you, and I am not going to call anyone, I'm just going to hire you." So, I got the job. For the next two days I was assigned to work with another person to get the hang of pasting those flyers. Then on the third day, I was to be given my own district.

But that Saturday morning, April 23, 1977, fate had a different plan for me: I was arrested. I subsequently took great satisfaction in insisting that all my KGB records should list me as a poster installer. They were not too happy about that because it put them into a rather ludicrous predicament. I could never understand why the KGB considered even this job so dangerous. Eventually I found out from my interrogator: "Who knows what you might have posted?"

Chapter Four

Arrest, Investigation, and Trial

"So This Is What One of These Looks Like"

On the morning of April 23, 1977, Mykola Matusevych and I were at his sister's apartment in Kyiv, where we had spent the night. At 6:30 a.m. we heard the doorbell. Tamila got up, went to the door, and asked, "Who's there?" On the other side of the door, a woman's voice answered: "Telegram." When Tamila opened the door, the room was instantly filled with KGB officials, all dressed in black. Again, we heard the standard: "Quiet, quiet!" Mykola's voice was not easy to quiet down, however.

This had been one of the KGB's typical tricks. On December 28, 1976, Mykola Rudenko had written of a similar incident in his appeal to the Moscow procurator: "Those who were conducting the search tore into the apartment under false pretenses: the civilian witness Prykhodko knocked on the door, claiming she was delivering a telegram. This was a lie that attests to the collusion between the witnesses and those who were conducting the search."[1]

Interestingly enough, many years later when I was in the Netherlands, I heard that one of the markers of a democracy is that when someone knocks on your door, you think it's the post. I liked this because in my case that's about how it was, except with opposite results.

We were informed that the apartment would be searched, as would we, but at a different location. We got ready, though Mykola made them wait until we had our breakfast. After we finished our coffee, they escorted us

1 *Dokumenty*, 38.

Figure 4.1. The KGB (now SBU, Security Service of Ukraine) building on the corner of Volodymyrska and Irynynska Streets in Kyiv.

out to their car. As the lady of the house, Tamila remained in the apartment while they conducted their search. We were taken to the Kyiv city branch of the KGB and each placed in a separate room so we could cool off.

Then Oleksandr Fedorovych Bereza walked in. From that moment on, he would be the investigating officer in charge of my case, #51, in which Mykola Matusevych was my codefendant. Bereza presented me with a warrant for my arrest, issued by the procurator, dated April 22. Two thoughts raced through my head: "So this is what one of these looks like" and "How will my mother and my sister Nadiika deal with this?"

The conversation that followed was fairly short, although it was actually the first inquest; I no longer remember its gist. I was taken to the SIZO[2], the pretrial detention center, in the inner courtyard of the KGB headquarters, where I was received by Colonel Sapozhnikov, the head of the SIZO. Another

2 SIZO (slidchyi izoliator): "investigative detention center" where political arrestees were held and interrogated prior to their trials. Not to be confused with ShIZO (shtrafovoi izoliator), isolation cells used for punishment in labor camps.

thorough search was conducted, even examining what Vasyl Ovsiienko likes to call the "unmentionable places." With this I began to get used to what Patriarch Josyf Slipyj describes in his memoirs: "I remember how miserable it was to feel their villainous hands all over your body."[3] (Eventually, I became fascinated by comparing the patriarch's and my impressions of various situations in camp; given his prominence, however, I always imagined his stress was much greater.) Eventually they took me to a cell that already housed a Russian-speaking prisoner, Valery. I later learned that Valery was a currency trader.[4]

The iron doors slammed shut behind me, and I found myself in another world—in a totally different lifetime. Out of muscle memory, my body kept twitching for a week; I kept ruminating on what still needed to be done and what needed to be passed on to whom. The persistent psychic overload I had been under, felt by every UHG member, was constantly present. After a week, I finally calmed down and made my peace with the situation: "Hey, man, you're going to be here for a long time, and there's nothing you can do to change that, so stay cool." After that I actually experienced a psychological release of sorts because from now on everything would be comprehensible and predictable. Gone were the days of uncertainty—no longer did I have to get up in the morning wondering if today was the day they would arrest me. It was over and done with.

The distinctive noise of the cell door slamming behind you has one other effect: you realize that you are now facing the all-powerful authorities on your own, without the friends and colleagues among whom you played certain social or political roles. You are now facing your interrogating officer and the entire KGB machine in all its strength. You have no one to lean on, just your own will and conscience. So, you are suddenly faced with one important question: what principles in the political positions you espouse are really yours, and what are you prepared to suffer for? What has been imposed upon you by others, so you're actually indifferent to it? That's when I remembered Levko Lukianenko's portentous words when Mykola and I wanted to join the UHG: "Boys, are you ready to go to jail for this? Do you understand how

---

3 Iosyf Slipyi, *Spomyny*, ed. Ivan Dats'ko and Mariia Horiacha (Lviv/Rome: Vyd-vo UKU, 2014), 157.

4 Currency trading involved buying foreign currency from visitors to the Soviet Union and then reselling it at profit. This was outlawed by Article 88 of the criminal code, "Violation of the regulations governing currency operations," and was punishable by up to eight years deprivation of freedom.

all this will end?" The time had come to prove that my affirmative answer at that time was not just empty boasting.

Luckily, however, even though your trustworthy mentors are not physically beside you, they are there for you in spirit. You are with them in your thoughts. When asked why some prisoners didn't break, Eduard Kuznetsov, a prominent Soviet Jewish dissident, summed it up aptly: "It all depends on the reference group you associate yourself with, and whose respect you hope to retain. If you have a group like this, like it or not, you will strive to live up to them."[5]

I grew accustomed to my new, much simpler lifestyle. My SIZO cell was fairly bright and rather large: two beds, two cabinets, and a frosted glass window. According to the rules, a duty guard had to look through the hatch in the door every few minutes to see how the prisoners were behaving. In the morning and in the evening, everyone was led to the toilet and washroom; once a week we were allowed to take a shower. We were taken there together with our cellmates, and the guard warned us with a cynical smirk "not to enjoy yourselves too much!" Three times a day the hatch would open for a food delivery. I don't remember what they fed us, but I do remember that I had a hankering for honey, and I would get angry with myself for having been so picky and not eating enough of it when I had the opportunity.

The lights were not turned off all night—I had to get used to that somehow. Somewhat later in camp I heard a story, related sarcastically by Semen Gluzman: from one of Comrade Corvalán's publications we learned that Generalissimo Pinochet's Chilean prisoners had been subjected to the cruel torture of not having the lights in their cells turned off all night. Whereas we Soviet prisoners, who were used to other, more conspicuous cruelties, considered bright lights in the cell at night to be the norm.[6]

During my stay in the SIZO, which was a bit less than a year, I shared my cell with three different cellmates: Valery, Vitaly, and a third man whose name I don't remember. They had nothing to do with politics—they had been nabbed for illegal currency trading and other such infractions. They were most likely thrown in together with me as a result of deals they had made with the KGB. This is not to say that they actively tried to solicit any

5 Eduard Kuznetsov, "Geroistvui do kontsa ili prevrashchaisia v stukacha," interview, *Jewish.ru*, September 4, 2015, https://jewish.ru/ru/interviews/articles/175548/.

6 Semen Gluzman, *Risunki po pamiati, ili Vospominaniia otsidenta* (Kyiv: Izdatel'skii dom Dmitriia Burago, 2012), 178.

information from me, or to make my life unbearable. By and large, our conversations were neutral and nonhostile. Prior to his arrest, Valery had been a friend of the son of Ukrainian party boss Volodymyr Shcherbytsky, and he told me many interesting things about the lifestyle of the progeny of the powerful elite and about their increasingly criminal ventures and drug-fueled gatherings. My third cellmate, on the other hand, alienated me completely with his total ignorance—I couldn't even imagine that a person could finish school and still not know that the moon rotates around the earth.

Generally speaking, in this prison they treated me and my cellmates superficially "within the bounds of Soviet rules" (at least in my presence): we were addressed with the polite form of "you" or as "citizen." I suspect that in my case such politeness was less the result of the high standards maintained at the Ukrainian SSR's main SIZO than of the KGB's desire to demonstrate that the UHG's claims of prisoner mistreatment were libelous. Eventually my interrogating officer underscored this: "You are a witness to the fact that no illegal methods are being used towards you. Therefore, everything that you have been writing is nothing but libel."

Mykola Matusevych, on the other hand, was beaten at least once. A few months after our arrest, he shouted to me in the hallway: "Myroslav, they are beating me!" In protest, I pounded on the door and declared a three-day hunger strike. By chance, I found out that at that time Mykola had also declared a hunger strike. It was the procurator himself who gave it away. When he came to my cell to find out what was going on, he asked me: "So how long do you intend to keep this hunger strike up?" I told him that I was staging a protest but not intending to commit suicide. "So, I will not strike forever, just three days." He grunted and immediately said: "Looks like a conspiracy." That's how I knew that Mykola was also on a hunger strike. This was actually the only time during my investigation that I resorted to this type of protest.

There's not much that I can say about the prisoners I didn't share a cell with. Later I found out that Hely Sniehyrov, a renowned writer and filmmaker, was treated brutally in that very SIZO around the same time I was there. He was suffering from prostate cancer, from which he died soon after. He was subjected to great agony not only because of his illness but also because of the torture inflicted upon him: the KGB promised to provide him with all the medical care and painkillers he needed in return for his "sincere repentance." Sniehyrov's letter of remorse, which was forced out of him in this fashion, was published on April 1, 1978, in the newspaper *Radians'ka Ukraina* (Soviet Ukraine) under the title "I Am Ashamed, and I

Condemn."[7] This exemplifies the KGB's fundamental precept of taking an "individual approach" in dealing with prisoners. In memory of the horrific suffering Sniehyrov experienced just before his death, may his name remain forever unblemished.

I suspect that, in my case, the KGB had some hope that I would crack, and perhaps I somewhat fostered this illusion through the way I behaved. On the whole, I am neither aggressive nor a hothead. If spoken to in a courteous manner, I will not be the first one to lose my temper. Perhaps my mild demeanor created the illusion that I would eventually give in if they just worked on me a little bit more. They had not yet realized that courteous behavior is not incompatible with holding firm to one's principles.

I was summoned for interrogation about once a week. After I managed to pull myself together and got used to the prison environment, I considered this to be annoyingly infrequent. After all, due to the lack of information, life in my cell was often boring, since nothing ever happened. I had access to the two official newspapers, *Pravda* and *Izvestiia*, but they were obviously not enough to quell my hunger for information, whereas the interrogations were actually very entertaining. I was guiltless and had nothing to hide, my conscience was clear; it was interesting, therefore, to leave my cell, walk down the hall to the case officer's chamber, and find out something new for myself from his line of questioning. In exchange for this novelty, I could even put up with the shouts of "hands behind your back!" and the numerous pat-downs on the way to his chamber.

That I found these interrogations interesting, rather than anything more sinister, relates back to what I previously called the "personal approach." For other inmates in this prison, the KGB's method of interrogation was far from entertaining. In the case of Oles Shevchenko, for example, "Throughout the investigation he was denied medical assistance, although he had heart problems and stomach pain. On April 5, 1980, Easter Sunday, during a KGB interrogation in the SIZO, he suffered a heart attack and lost consciousness. An ambulance was called. Shevchenko filed a complaint with the procurator over these extremely cruel methods, but he never received a response."[8]

7 Helii Sniehir'ov, "Soromlius' ta zasudzhuiu," *Radians'ka Ukraina*, April 1, 1978.

8 Oles' Shevchenko, interview by Volodymyr Kaplun, July 15, 2007, Virtual'nyi muzei Dysydents'kyi rukh v Ukraini, museum.khpg.org/index.php?id=1184522126.

In my case, while I was being escorted to the case officer's chamber and back, there were no surprises: no inadvertent meetings, no scripted dramas. There was, however, one incident in which the officer who was escorting me there took the opportunity while we could not be overheard to express empathy toward me: what a pity that I, such a young man, was ruining my life in vain. To be sure, it would be easy to chalk his behavior up to a KGB-staged attempt to soften their prisoner psychologically. I am still convinced, however, that he spoke sincerely and was not following any specific orders. His was the rationale of a typical Soviet individual for whom the primary rule for survival was not to stand out and not to get involved in any confrontations with the all-powerful regime: you would most certainly lose.

The aforementioned Oleksandr Fedorovych Bereza was in charge of the interrogation. He was Ukrainian, which was clear from his fluency in the language, and he spoke calmly and carefully, as did I. There were times when we even joked with each other, and once he even told me a joke that was almost anti-Soviet. I quickly caught on to the simple sequence of his questioning, and once in a while I would gently rebuke him by suggesting a question that he might have forgotten to ask me. As all his questions were extremely serious, laden with bureaucratic pompousness, this doubled the farcical nature of the situation: it appeared that the accused was attempting to sink himself by suggesting these questions.

Occasionally Mykola Matusevych's interrogator, Leonid Berestovsky, would show up during my interrogations. I suspect that he wanted to hear my answers to some of the main questions I was being asked. Later I learned that Mykola had decided not to answer any of their questions at all, and decades later he explained his position:

> I did not give them any testimony and hardly even got into any discussions with them, except I would occasionally allow myself a psychological duel with them. I would tell them, "If you need these games, then go ahead and play them, but without me. You guys are all shooting at my goal, and then you expect me to pass the ball to you as well. No way!" My silence was much harder on them than on me. They would press on my sore and sensitive spots, mentioning my mother and my sister. . . . They begged me to at least discuss football with them. There were many interrogations with a rotation of investigators, like corralled horses, and I was disappointed. I had prepared myself for a challenging and difficult confrontation, but when I saw this bunch, I became totally bored.[9]

9 Matusevych, "Ia vyhrav dvobii," 3.

During my interrogations I maintained the position that had been previously agreed upon with Mykola Rudenko. Officially, I argued that we were not an underground organization and that we declared this publicly in all our documents; I said we did not oppose the Soviet government per se but rather the human rights violations that had been perpetrated by representatives of that government. I therefore didn't think it necessary to play the "underground" game and keep quiet about everything. On the contrary, I asserted that the UHG was a legal civic organization that promoted the implementation of the Helsinki Accords, signed by Brezhnev himself, and that the group had publicly presented its Declaration of Intent. Surely a civic initiative could not possibly be bad; surely it was not forbidden in the Soviet Union? (I'm itching to put a sarcastic smiley face here.)

At the same time, I was not completely naïve, so from the start I warned the interrogator that I would talk only about myself and that I would not sign any protocols that mentioned other people's behavior. That's why my sentence repeats the same formulas over and over, "In early December 1976, Marynovych, M. received from a person he refuses to name—" and "He disseminated it among people he did not name—" After all, I was aware that other people had the right to behave differently, and I had no right to stand in their way. By and large I stuck to my policy; I only violated it once or twice by accident, and of course later my slip-ups kept me awake at night.

As I mentioned in the previous chapter, I insisted that I was the author of all eleven UHG memoranda. It was easier to articulate this than to stick by it. Oleksandr Bereza mocked me good-naturedly when he heard my assertions. What bothered me most was the nagging feeling that I was trying to claim other people's accomplishments as my own. But I stubbornly asserted, however, that I had indeed been the author of whatever document they asked me about. Obviously, my interrogator understood all of this very well, and thus in the verdict against Mykola Matusevych and me one encounters more realistic formulations such as:

> In the second half of January 1977 the accused, Matusevych M. I., and Marynovych M. F., discussed Memorandum #2 with Rudenko M. D.—an anti-Soviet document, which had been drafted by the latter, intended for mass distribution. By approving and signing it, they became collaborators and co-authors in the drafting of this hostile document.

If you look at the protocols of my interrogations, however, you can see my testimony in which I claimed that I was the one who had drafted those documents.

Other UHG members, particularly Mykola Rudenko and Oles Berdnyk, maintained a similar position. My sentence contains a note that my authorship of the Helsinki Group's documents was confirmed "by evidence given by Berdnyk O.P. during a previous interrogation, and was also confirmed by him in court, declaring that the authorship of Memoranda #4, 5, 6, 7, 8, and 11 is collective in nature and that the co-authors of the Memoranda are the persons on whose behalf these documents had been drafted." Likewise, Levko Lukianenko, appearing at Mykola Rudenko's trial, also confirmed that "all members of the Group that signed the documents were its co-authors."

During a later interview, however, Oksana Meshko once made a statement that I should now respond to. She said:

> Members of the Helsinki Group had agreed not to provide any statements to the KGB. Some of the earlier prisoners did testify, signing their statements at the end of the inquest. We, however, remained silent. Matusevych did not sign any of the protocols, and I understand that they raked him through the coals for it. Lukianenko did the same. During his trial in Horodnia, he told them: "I beg you, take me back to my cell and conduct this trial without me."[10]

I suspect that we are dealing with a certain memory lapse here. It's entirely possible that after our arrests, seeing how the KGB was manipulating our testimony, the other group members decided not to give any testimony at all. On the other hand, perhaps this was Oksana Meshko's personal decision based on her previous arrest experience. Nevertheless, the courageous and noble position taken by Oksana Meshko and Mykola Matusevych, in refusing to provide any statements, cannot be considered as having been agreed upon by the entire UHG.

My insistence that I had drafted and personally typed all the UHG materials created new and rather amusing difficulties for me. After all, now the investigation had to prove that I was indeed the one who had actually typed it on the exact typewriter that had been previously confiscated from us. To do so, they had to conduct an official verification test. One day they sat me down in front of a typewriter and asked me to type some text, and I was faced with a new dilemma: I was fully aware that it was really Olia Heiko and not I who had typed that text. If I typed the way I usually do, the experts would certainly be able to determine that I had nothing to do with typing that text, and then my testimony would be invalid. The only thing I could do to save myself was to try a different way of hitting the keys, one that

10 *Ne vidstupliusia!*, 308.

might have some similarities with Olia's typing method, and then her style might be seen as similar to mine.

That day, I sweated so much I was as soaked as if I had taken a bath. At that time, I was not a very skilled typist, and on top of that I had to wrack my brain to try to invent novel typing techniques. You can only imagine the joy I felt when I read the case notes, which stated that the expert witness determined that "it was impossible to conclude that Marynovych had typed the documents." In other words, it was not confirmed that I did it, but it was not denied either. This is why the sentence frequently repeats the following: "For the purpose of mass distribution of this libelous document, Marynovych reproduced at least nineteen copies in Ukrainian and Russian on a typewriter rented by Matusevych's wife, Olia Heiko." Certainly, during her trial Olia got her due, and the crime of typing those documents was eventually assigned to her. To me, however, it was psychologically important that I did everything possible to take the "blame."

Eventually I learned from the interrogator that I had been given the status of an "exceptionally dangerous state criminal" (unless, of course, I were to repent). I found this ironic and extremely funny, and once I even commented on it: "It seems that murderers are not considered as dangerous to the Soviet authorities as we dissidents are." To this Bereza shook his head and replied in all seriousness: "Yes, murderers are not as dangerous as you are because they don't infect others, like you do."

During my interrogations, I often pointed out certain irrational aspects of the investigation. For example, Bereza would often repeat the following: "We are putting you on trial not because of your beliefs; you are free to think what you want. We're putting you on trial for what you are saying—that is, for your concrete actions." I joked in return: "Well, then the Soviet Union has clearly made a scientific discovery and managed to perform a unique lobotomy, separating thought from speech."

It was interesting to read later that the same formula of Soviet "lawfulness" was used during the investigation of Mykola Rudenko (as well as of many other detainees). This is how Rudenko explained it in his final statement:

> I have been interrogated for over three months, and every day the KGB officers tried to impress upon me the following truth: "we do not convict you for your thoughts; we convict you for your actions." As a human being, you not only have to think, but you also have to express those thoughts. Otherwise there would be no difference between a human being and a turtle.[11]

11 Rudenko, *Naibil'she dyvo–zhyttia*, 542.

In my conversations with the case officer, he suggested that in reality we should be tried according to Article 64 of the Criminal Code of the Ukrainian SSR, "Creation of an Anti-Soviet Organization." This article carried a stronger punishment than Article 62, "Anti-Soviet Propaganda," with which we had been charged at the beginning. At that time, the KGB insisted that the Ukrainian Helsinki Group should be treated as an anti-Soviet organization, even though Brezhnev himself had signed the Final Act of the Helsinki Accords in 1975. The KGB had apparently decided not to go that route. Still, this did not stop the KGB from utilizing this subject as a weapon to deepen Mykola Rudenko's mistrust of Matusevych and me. Thus, in the transcript of Rudenko's trial, the *Chronicle of Current Events* cites an interesting episode:

> Rudenko asked the court to read out the evidence which Matusevych and Marynovych had given after their arrest, so that the witnesses who were members of the Ukrainian 'Helsinki' Group might know about this evidence, as it was slanderous, provocative and terrifying; it said that the Ukrainian 'Helsinki' Group was not a public group but an underground anti-Soviet group.[12]

One can only imagine what they must have told Rudenko about us! Furthermore, the annotations to this excerpt from the *Chronicle* include an important note: during a visit with his wife on July 4, 1977, Rudenko "stated that he did not believe that Matusevych and Marynovych had given the slanderous testimony ascribed to them and considered that it was a provocative invention of the KGB."[13]

Indeed, the KGB was doing everything in its power to discredit the incarcerated UHG members. The typical rumors were that we had "given in" or that we had "started to testify" against other group members. When Olia Heiko tried to send a package to her husband for his birthday, the KGB told her, "He is behaving himself very nicely." This was an intentional lie because that very day, Mykola Matusevych was beaten in his isolation cell for being "uncooperative." Obviously, we had no way of straightening out such rumors while incarcerated, which made signs of our friends' trust all the more valuable to us. I will relate one such example, even though I learned about it much later. In 1977, when one of my army buddies, Gennady Plotkin, visited Drohobych, where I had previously lived, he tried to look me up; then, through Radio Svoboda, he found out that I had been arrested. He didn't stop looking for me even after he emigrated to the United States. He finally

12 *Chronicle*, 46:15.

13 *Chronicle*, 46:20.

contacted Petro Hryhorenko, who answered his letter, and this letter perfectly captures the spirit of this nearly forgotten period:

August 20, 1982

Dear Gennady,

Of course I know Myroslav Marynovych. I am a member of the Ukrainian Helsinki Group, and since my exile from the USSR, I represent the Group in the West. At the time when you were looking for Myroslav (summer 1977) he had already been arrested, and I was still in Moscow, fighting for the release of the incarcerated Group members, including Myroslav. He has been sentenced to a seven-year prison term and five years of internal exile. According to the most recent information, he is in the Chistopol Prison. [This was incorrect; I was never there—M. M.]

You ask if there is any possible way to get in touch with him by mail. There certainly is. You and I, thank God, live in a free country, where communications are not restricted. This country has a legal agreement with the USSR regarding mail exchanges, and [the USSR] is supposed to receive and deliver mail to their citizens sent by the US Postal Service. However, given the fact that the USSR is likely to violate all agreements, the US Postal Service recommends that their citizens send letters and postcards by registered mail, requiring confirmation of receipt, and packages and large envelopes should additionally be insured. In case of non-delivery, they can be reimbursed.

I don't know what your financial capabilities are, but if you have them, send a package to Myroslav's wife. When you write, please remember that things will be censored (how you were looking for him, contacting his wife, etc.). Do not mention Radio Svoboda when you talk about how you found him. Better claim coincidence: you met a fellow countryman, and he turned out to know Marynovych. If by chance they should require his last name, give them my name and patronymic (not my last name) in Ukrainian transliteration—"Petro Hryhorovych."

Good luck! If you do get in touch with him, you will be doing a noble deed by uplifting the spirits of a good man, although he is holding up quite well. He conducted himself quite valiantly during his trial, and now in camp as well. He participated in the formation and in the work of the Ukrainian Helsinki Group.

May God bless you and your family. Greetings also from my wife, Zinaida.

Yours truly, P. H.

Needless to say, this letter is very dear to me. I read it only after Petro Hryhorenko had passed into eternity, and it was like getting a greeting from him from a place where there is no longer any pain or suffering—and, most importantly, where there are no searches, snitches, spies, psychiatric wards, Communist foolhardiness, or the polished devilishness of the KGB.

Further interrogations in Mykola's and my case showed that we were both being additionally charged with "crimes" perpetrated on the territory of the Russian Soviet Federative Socialist Republic: Mykola for visiting Yury Orlov, the head of the Moscow Helsinki Group, and me for visiting Petro Hryhorenko in Moscow and Nina Strokata in Tarusa, as well as for the "libelous documents" that were confiscated from me in Serpukhov. Thus, our charges also included Article 70 of the Criminal Code of the Russian Soviet Federative Socialist Republic.[14]

They took a more aggressive stance toward Mykola because they were also charging him with a "hooligan crime" that he allegedly committed in the Carpathian Mountains in 1972.[15] I found out about this during my inquest, and this gave me an opportunity to further chide Oleksandr Bereza for letting a "criminal" guilty of a "hooligan crime of particularly grave proportions" (which was supposedly well documented) roam around freely for the past five years, potentially subjecting unsuspecting Soviet citizens to a new attack by this "unchecked hooligan." It was obvious that the KGB had been holding on to this "hooligan" story to use it at an opportune moment.

Once in a while Bereza lost his temper, especially when I staunchly defended one of my positions. One time he exclaimed: "Stop making a hero of yourself! Who do you think you are? Stronger people than you have broken down! Look at Ivan Dziuba: even he acknowledged his mistake, and you certainly are no Dziuba!" To which I responded assertively: "It's true, I am not Dziuba, and therefore I will not break down!" It wasn't until I was released that I found out that Mykola Matusevych had been subjected to similar tactics:

> I suspected that all they really wanted was a small breakthrough, for me to crack at least a little bit, so that they could then show my friends and my community

14 Each Soviet republic had its own criminal code. Article 70 of the RSFSR Criminal Code, "Anti-Soviet agitation and propaganda," was the equivalent of the Ukrainian SSR's Article 62.

15 "Hooliganism" functioned as a catchall category for behavior that the Soviet regime found objectionable. It was regulated by Article 206 of the Criminal Code, which defined it as "willful acts grossly violating public order and manifesting an evident lack of respect for society."

> that even though they thought I was as solid as a rock, here you have it. . . . Eventually we will crush all of you. I realized that the strategy the KGB had created was not only aimed at me alone, but also at my family and friends, and particularly at those already incarcerated. "They are not your equal, Mykola. Look at yourself, prison is certainly not for you!" All they really needed was for me to break down, to retreat, even though the moral blow was aimed at others.[16]

Surprisingly enough, it wasn't until a recent conversation with Vasyl Ovsiienko that I realized I had barely escaped a psychiatric evaluation. I still don't know why Bereza never brought this up. Knowing this, I can honestly say that God was merciful to me, and I avoided the infamous Serbsky Institute of Forensic Psychiatry, known for the horrific tortures inflicted on other political prisoners.[17] I do, however, remember discussing General Petro Hryhorenko's case with my interrogator. With an expression of grave seriousness on his face, Bereza claimed that the general was indeed mentally ill, and this gave me further opportunity to make fun of Soviet psychiatry as well as the KGB's methods.

While my interrogator declined to use the psychiatric angle, he did try to pin homosexuality on me, which in the Soviet Union was regarded as a criminal offense. He officially cited testimony given by one of our acquaintances Liudmyla (I don't remember her last name). Along with one of her friends, she used to stop by the apartment where Mykola and I lived. I have no idea if these women had been sent to us specifically, or if they just had us in their sights; whatever the reason, her testimony claimed that Mykola and I were homosexuals. Eventually, after I became familiar with my case, I found out that the interrogator brought this issue up with anyone he happened to be questioning regarding our case. Most people denied such allegations. These denials, however, would not have stopped the KGB had a command to act on the accusation been given. Luckily, this did not happen.

During my interrogations, I sat at a small table near the door. Such were the rules. One time, wanting to stretch my legs, I asked if I could walk around the room. Bereza allowed it, even though this was generally forbidden. While walking around the room, I succumbed to the temptation to glance out the window, which looked out on Irynynska Street, in central Kyiv. After several months of isolation, seeing a living street was mind-blowing. Today I can

16 Matusevych, "Ia vyhrav dvobii," 3.

17 Serbsky Institute: The Soviet Union's main center for forensic psychiatry, located in Moscow; it was the main institution responsible for psychiatric evaluations of dissidents, resulting in the involuntary confinement of thousands of individuals.

Figure 4.2. A typical strolling courtyard. Photo credit: Nikolay Postnikov.

walk past the SBU building on Volodymyrska Street (currently the Security Service of Ukraine) without any emotion, but it is only with great trepidation that I look at Irynynska Street.

My impression from seeing the living city was all the more intense because for a long time I had refused to go out for the "prescribed" walks. As I remember, I was indignant at that cement abyss, all wrapped in barbed wire, where I was supposed to "enjoy" my promenade. After a few months, when I sensed that depriving myself of fresh air was beginning to damage my health, I changed my mind and started going out for those walks. And there, the first time out, I was rewarded: in a far corner of this cement void I spied a feeble little tuft of grass that had installed itself in a tiny mound of dirt blown in by the wind. I was completely awestruck because I never expected a feeble little weed to be so beautiful.

In the Meantime, Out in the Free World

It would be appropriate here to say a few words about what was going on beyond the walls of the KGB prison. On April 23, 1977, the same day I was arrested, my sister Nadiika's apartment in Rivne was subjected to a sudden raid by the KGB, like a lightning bolt from the sky. The search was long and thorough. Then Nadiika was hit with horrific news: her brother, "an exceptionally dangerous state criminal," had been arrested. My mother found out the following day, and a dark cloud descended on both their worlds. Nadiika's career as a teacher was immediately called into question. After all, the authorities considered schools to be an ideological bulwark. I suspect that she was able to retain her position only because they knew that the stronger the sanctions against my family, the stronger my own resistance would be. The KGB had hoped to break me down, so in their mind, the carrot would produce better results than the stick.

Going through some archival materials after my mother's death, I found a notebook where my mother described her interrogation by Bereza on June 8, 1977. Obviously, I was moved by these notes. There was nothing new in the interrogation itself: my mother tirelessly defended me, enumerating my exemplary behavior and showing Bereza all my letters and certificates of commendations, sincerely trying to help me. What I find most significant was her description of events on the day of my arrest and the following days:

> On that day my Nadiika was subjected to a raid that lasted from 7am until 7pm. They took all of Myros's [pet name for Myroslav] letters. As I always did on Sundays, I booked a telephone conversation with Nadiika for 12 noon, and that's how I found out about Myros's arrest.[18] I took a train to a nearby city, where Nadiika met me, all in tears. We sat on a bench talking for about an hour, and then took the train to Rivne. We talked for a long time, crying all night and not sleeping. Monday morning I returned back home. From then the difficult days began, with every thought about our beloved little boy.

Some friends and acquaintances distanced themselves from my mother and sister, but others, thank God, became closer and even more supportive. Luckily Nadiika's husband, Leonid, was not frightened by all this and did not abandon her. Later, my mother told me that some people crossed the street when they saw her coming. Several family members became critical. But in many other cases people tried to encourage her. For example, Mrs. Domanska, the mother of one of my classmates, saw my mother on the street and admonished her: "Why are you walking around with your eyes downcast? Lift your head up high! You have nothing to be ashamed of! Your son is a hero!"

18 Long-distance telephone calls needed to be arranged in advance with an operator.

In conjunction with our case, that same day, April 23, 1977, several other individuals, including Mykola Matusevych's parents, were subjected to searches, as was my own apartment in Kalynivka. Other searches included the homes of Borys Antonenko-Davydovych, Mykhailyna Kotsiubynska, Liuba Kheina, Yevhen Obertas, Hanna Kovalenko, as well as my relative, Borys Marynovych. In addition to those whose homes were searched, others were also questioned about our case, including Levko Lukianenko, Oksana Meshko, Nadiia Svitlychna, Lidiia Ruban (Petro Ruban's wife), Vasyl Ovsiienko, and Liudmyla Riabukha, Ovsiienko's niece. Some of them were questioned several times: Svitlychna twice, Antonenko-Davydovych three times, and Obertas a full six times. During those interrogations, the KGB revealed that "hostile materials" had been confiscated from those arrested. Some of the witnesses were warned not to disclose any information about the case, and they were asked to sign an affidavit to that effect.

Each person was exposed to great stress, and everyone had to endure some unpleasantries at work as well as new persecutions in the public sphere. A few days after our arrest, on April 29, 1977, a slanderous article appeared in *Literaturna Ukraina*, penned by a certain Hornovy, entitled "You Don't Get Money for Nothing."[19] In it he accused Mykhailyna Kotsiubynska and Borys Antonenko-Davydovych of receiving bribes from abroad. They wrote a rebuttal, but when no replies were forthcoming from the editors, they visited the publishing house. The letters from "outraged readers" that the author based his article on could not be produced.

This wave of persecutions was best described by Mykhailyna Kotsiubynska:

> The repressive noose began to tighten around me starting in 1977, when they arrested some of the Helsinki Group members. Officially, I had not been a member of the Group, but I had ongoing contacts with some of their members, particularly with Myroslav Marynovych and Mykola Matusevych, who were renting a room in an old building just across the street from me; I felt at home in their youthful, loose company. On April 23, [the KGB] searched my house and found a copy of the UHG declaration. Suddenly, during the lunch hour a few days later, the staff of the publishing house was gathered to discuss firing me from my job for my anti-Soviet activities. My daughter, who came to support me, told me that no one in the back rows had voted, but those who were in the management's line of sight, wanting to create a good impression, reluctantly raised their hands in favor of my termination. Two individuals voted against: Liudmyla Korobova, the secretary and my colleague from the editorial

19 Hornovyi, "Za 'tak' hroshi ne daiut'," *Literaturna Ukraina*, April 29, 1977.

> board, and Liuba Kheina (later Marynovych). She stood up and demonstratively raised her hand against, a truly heroic act. One can only imagine what they did to her later.[20]

In a sign of protest against her husband Mykola's arrest, Olia Heiko-Matusevych quit the Komsomol, declared a hunger strike, and on May 14, 1977, presented an appeal to Amnesty International, in which she announced that she was joining the Ukrainian Helsinki Group. At that time, many new members were flocking to join the group, ready to use nonviolent resistance to cast light upon the inhuman reality of the Soviet regime.

The UHG issued numerous announcements about our arrests and released documents that included protests against these new persecutions. Among them was an appeal to the Presidium of the Council of Ministers of the USSR, as well as a petition (Letter #2) to the governments of all the Helsinki Accords member states.[21] On June 3, 1977, a separate warning appeal was sent by Oksana Meshko to the upcoming Belgrade Conference.[22] On June 29, a number of the Moscow Helsinki Group members reviewed the situation in some of the other Helsinki Groups. Describing what was happening in Ukraine, Oksana Meshko, the informal head of the UHG at the time, wrote to Petro Hryhorenko: "God alone can see how difficult it is for all of us and for me personally. . . . But I will not betray my own nature. I shall not yield, because there, behind the barbed wire, are our best people—those whom I love and who love me."[23]

All this was invaluably significant: not only did the cruel repressions against us fail to break the group members but amazingly gave them a second wind. (Thirty-six years later, the same effect seemed to repeat itself on the Maidan, when, in 2013–2014, millions of Ukrainians staged a nationwide protest, ousting President Yanukovych and his pro-Kremlin administration. The harsher the government repressions, the bolder and more widespread the public reaction.)

Our mothers—Mykola's and mine—as well as other family members met to discuss ways to liberate us. Relations among them were not always easy: if

---

20 Kotsiubyns'ka, *Knyha spomyniv*, 83.

21 *Dokumenty*, 67–72.

22 *Dokumenty*, 75. Belgrade Conference: From October 1977–March 1978, the Conference on Security and Cooperation in Europe held its first follow-up meeting to review the Helsinki Accord.

23 *Ne vidstupliusia!*, 178.

one person did not sign a protest appeal, it could result in psychological pressure or even reproaches. Our relatives and friends tried to do everything they could to help us, but everyone did it in his or her own way and in accordance with their own political views and mindset. It was therefore inevitable that there would be differences in their actions. It would be unconscionable to reproach them for anything they did.

Eventually, an organized system of community support for the families of those incarcerated was established. The names of our families were included in a listing of those who were receiving assistance from the Solzhenitsyn Fund. It would have been impossible to survive on that assistance alone, but its psychological significance was enormous. Gratitude should be given to those Muscovites and their emissaries in Ukraine who facilitated the distribution of this aid. At various times, Vira Lisova in Kyiv, Olena Antoniv in Lviv, and Yevhen Zakharov in Kharkiv were among the people who helped distribute this assistance.

There were also cases of spontaneous support. One time in Drohobych, my mother was approached by an elderly man who whispered that the local underground Greek Catholic community had collected a financial contribution for her. He handed her an envelope with some money and then quickly ran off. My mother was touched to the bottom of her heart.

There was also a diaspora support network that had been set up. Dr. Anna-Halja Horbatsch (an unofficial Ukrainian cultural attaché in Germany), Zinoviy and Lydia Marciuk of Munich, Zenovia Bihun from the United States, Osyp Krasiy from Great Britain, and many other humble and ordinary people: all were messengers of our gracious God, who was watching over our families. They gathered and dispatched many packages containing everyday essentials for those in Ukraine who were under constant KGB pressure. They bared their hearts and souls in many postcards and letters. In the dissident circles it was enough to mention their names—like "Ms. Halja" for instance—and everyone understood immediately whom they meant. People's faces would brighten up, and their souls would be filled with a warm wave of gratitude.

Turning Points

Let us return, however, to my SIZO cell, where I still could not have even imagined what turns of fate awaited me. August 1977 was approaching and with it came some radical changes in my mindset and spiritual world.

Figure 4.3. With Anna-Halja Horbatsch after my liberation.

During one interrogation, Oleksandr Bereza was trying to clarify my stance on the Pentecostals' appeal "to Christians of the World" to pray for the incarcerated members of the various Helsinki groups.[24] This is, almost word for word, how I responded to his question: "I am very grateful to the Protestant Christians for their support, and am quite touched by it. I am rather indifferent toward religion, however." I am sure that many readers will think that such words sound a bit strange coming from the grandson of a priest. Nevertheless, that's what the true state of my soul was at that time: on the one hand, I never liked it when people ridiculed the church; on the other, I could live quite comfortably without God, or rather without mentioning His name.

But God was preparing a major shakeup in my life, one that thoroughly changed my mindset and my life in general. It was truly a rebirth, after

24 In the 1970s, the Protestant community in the Soviet Union was actively in contact with Protestant organizations in the West, seeking assistance in obtaining permission to leave the Soviet Union because of widespread persecution. In this instance, the Protestant community used its connections to raise awareness of the fate of the arrested UHG members.

which I could no longer idly glance at the words of the Bible: "The wind blows where it chooses, and you hear the sound of it, but you do not know where it comes from or where it goes. So it is with everyone who is born of the Spirit."(John 3:8) It is difficult, however, to describe these experiences. Even in camp, when I tried to share my feelings with Mykola Rudenko, words were somehow inadequate. Standing before me, after all, was a person who had experienced a similar transformation and who understood me from the get-go. At that time, I already realized that I had to put something that cannot be dissected into words. I would not have mentioned this event had Rudenko not insisted. He later included my description in his own memoir.[25]

It happened on August 24, 1977. I had just returned from an interrogation and, riled up by the conversation with my investigator, was pacing up and down the short little Champs-Elyseés of my cell, entirely lost in thought. My contemplations carried me to Mykola Rudenko's *Economic Monologues*, an exemplary samizdat publication. The *Monologues* dealt with a theoretical duel between Karl Marx and François Quesnay, the French physiocrat, concerning the remarkable ending of the fourth volume of *Das Kapital*, where at the end of his life Marx acknowledges his blunder. The French philosopher categorized the social classes differently than Marx did: not according to the means of production but by the very type of production. Pacing about my cell, I was not just trying to map the "cells" of various classes to Quesnay's scheme but also beginning to see the dynamic relationship between different classes more clearly—or, more accurately, how the "overflow" of people from one cell to another worked. At first, the majority of people were concentrated in the cell of agriculture; then the workers (proletariat) started to play the main role, to be substituted, finally, by the professionals, who use their brains. Their cell was permanently growing. My own brain was working intensely and precisely, and I could envision those cells clearly without even charting them on paper. Since this scheme incorporated the most important tendencies of our era, my sense of approaching the truth evoked a heightened feeling of spiritual euphoria. At the very moment when all those cells merged into one, something inside me cried out: "And that's total fusion!" And my vision suddenly changed.

I saw the whole earth clearly, as if in a hologram, with the entire surface covered, like grass on the steppe, by a swaying mass of humanity split apart by their divergent passions and oriented every which way. But this chaos did

25 Rudenko, *Naibil'she dyvo–zhyttia*, 529–40.

not last long. Suddenly in one spot on the globe—Ukraine—a large figure appeared. Even though I was far removed from having any religious experiences at that time, I could recognize that this figure was Christ.

At the same time, the entirety of this "swaying" mass of humanity, like little metal slivers in a magnetic field, converged on that figure. Within the globe as well as inside me, I felt a terrific tension, and then suddenly a flash of light covered the entire globe. A strong jolt made me recoil, and as I closed my eyes, I lost consciousness.

From that moment on, and for the next three days, I found myself in a trancelike state. In my thoughts (or rather in my feelings, and my being) I was hovering above the earth. But at the same time, back in my cell, I was performing all the usual everyday functions. I retrieved my meals from the hatch, walked around, ate, slept, washed; but as I learned later, I did not react to my cellmate or respond to any of his worried questions. I had the feeling that some unexplained information was being transmitted into me, not presented as individual thoughts but offered as a total compendium. It is actually impossible to describe this condition in words because they would only distort the picture.

I came to on the fourth day, when I realized that I was hearing a monotonous ringing of bells, and I asked my cellmate, Valery, "Why are the bells of St. Volodymyr ringing so long?" In response I heard his relieved reply: "Finally, you woke up! What's with you, are you going mad?" That's when I found out that I had spent the previous three days in a somnambulistic state. Later, in camp, Mykola Rudenko told me that at some point he had also experienced a similar state and that I had been very lucky: at such a young age (I was just twenty-nine then) a jolt of light like that could have resulted in insanity.

The following days in my SIZO cell blended together. I would wake up with a thought that I could never previously have had. The smallest detail from my daily routine could evoke an inundation of philosophical or, rather, metaphysical contemplations. It seemed that the information that had entered my mind as a bundle during that extraordinary state was now unspooling one piece at a time. Today I am no longer afraid of using the word "revelation" to describe what was happening, but at that time it was daunting. It took a long time to get used to the ease with which I was able to absorb things that had previously been unattainable to me. I was able to find explanations for my fate and my actions: they no longer seemed coincidental but took on a huge providential dimension. It felt almost like absolute determinism, which confirms each of your steps or actions as inevitable.

Here is one example that stands out in my mind. One autumn day, my thoughts led me to the periodic table. I already thought of it as just a partial representation of a more universal law that governed all facets of life. The obvious similarities between certain phenomena evoked a deluge of hypotheses in me: the group of elements headed by lanthanum contains fourteen additional elements that are united under the common name "lanthanides." Analogously, the series headed by Russia also included fourteen elements (the other national republics of the USSR), which are known around the world by the collective name "Russia."

I played with this table for a long time, but I was frustrated by the fact that I couldn't recall certain spots on the chart, and I felt that I absolutely had to fill them in. I pleaded with my interrogator Bereza to send a message to my family, asking them to bring me a copy of the periodic table. The request was rather unusual for a "politically engaged" person, so Bereza asked me with some confusion: "Why do you need it? Can you guarantee that you will not use it against the interests of this interrogation?" I found this question so funny that I refused to give him this assurance. But this meant that I wouldn't be given the table.

A week passed, and then a guard came by with the prison library trolley. As usual, it contained some Stalin-era novels, depicting the heroic deeds of Communists during collectivization and industrialization. Suddenly I saw a book entitled *Dmitri Mendeleev* from the popular biography series *Lives of Outstanding People*. I grabbed it like a hawk, not believing my luck. I quickly read it to the end, but the entire table wasn't depicted in it, only some individual parts. So my suffering continued. Then, during one interrogation, Bereza told me, "Here, your family sent you some popular scientific journals. I looked them over, and now you can have them." You can only imagine my excitement when, back in my cell, I opened one of the journals and saw the exact portion of the table that I was looking for. I was completely blown away. And this is only one illustration of the significance of some of the events that I experienced from then on.

The entire subsequent process of making new discoveries resembled the unwinding of a ball of yarn. Day by day, thought after thought, the information that had been installed in me in practically one instant was now unraveling slowly within me. Interestingly enough, my train of thought would always lead me to the wisdom revealed to us through the Bible. To be sure, at that time I still didn't have a comprehensive understanding of that book. Everything I knew of it came from literature, from general cultural knowledge. My secularized brain was all the more flabbergasted when it encountered elements that I had dismissed in the past, such as the story of Adam and Eve and the conniving serpent.

I didn't even notice that I was becoming a devout person. My faith came to me not as the result of the feeling of powerlessness a prisoner experiences when facing the KGB's lawless machine, left with no other hope except for God, but as the result of His obvious presence.

Nothing stays the same forever, however, and in a month or two doubt started creeping back into my soul. I thought to myself, Hey, why are you calling it a revelation when it was most likely the hallucinations of an overwhelmed mind? You had been incarcerated in this cell nonstop for over four months, without any fresh air; you were agitated when you returned from your interrogation; so this was nothing but an overheated physiological reaction. Thank God you didn't crack up. I had to wait until the next revelation, which happened later in camp, to realize that those were not hallucinations at all. But more about that later.

I remember another episode from this intellectually volatile period. Since I had a lot of free time, by chance I started calculating the "biblical beast"—the number 666. It was Pierre Bezukhov from *War and Peace*, which I was rereading at that time, who drove me to it.[26] The book uses a generally recognizable way of tallying that number by apportioning numerical values to the letters of the alphabet. This method, however, was never convincing to me because the scope for random interpretation was too large. Furthermore, it is difficult to say with any certainty which language the ancient Hebrews used to code the Beast's name in Revelation. I therefore started contemplating what in our current life linked us with the life of the ancient Hebrews. Then I realized that it was the sun and the moon because God gave us those two to count time, and it is their observable movement on the horizon that has remained unchanged for two thousand years. So, I decided to look for some calendar associations. I remembered that the Hebrew calendar was lunar—in other words, the month was calculated on the basis of 29 days for one month, and 30 days for the next, with 29.5 as the median.

I then began to consider the Antichrist as an entity but from the opposite point of view. It became clear to me that from an ideological point of view Vladimir Lenin fit the bill as the Antichrist. Not in the medieval sense, with horns and a tail, but as a real historic figure who rejected Christianity and then imposed a radically anti-Christian ideology on people.

---

26 In *War and Peace*, Bezuhkov, having become a Freemason, notices that adding up the numerical values of the letters in "l'empereur Napoléon" equals 666.

Since I had chosen to think about it from the perspective of the calendar, I now had to try to solve the riddle by calculating how long he had lived. He was born on April 21, 1870, and he died on January 22, 1924. According to our calendar that made fifty-three years and nine months. How many months would that be in the Hebrew calendar? I calculated the number of days he lived (factoring in the leap years, of course) and got 19,634 days. I divided that by 29.5 and got 665.56. In other words, Lenin died in the 666th lunar month of his life!

As I was calculating the numbers and got the first two sixes, my whole body shuddered.

These stories, as incredible as they might be, are but pale illustrations of what was going on in my soul. This was just the beginning of a phenomenon that is our Lord's gift to those who are unfairly incarcerated. Later it manifested itself vividly in my camp life. Being shut in a prison cell doesn't deprive a person of liberty; on the contrary, it liberates you from the unnecessary ballast of unimportant concerns, thus making you free.

From the time of these blessed insights, I became aware of a crucial imperative: to observe everything happening around me with greater vigilance because some important lessons might be hidden there. Just as God's laws are written in the natural living phenomena that surround us, so too are God's hints inscribed in the people that we are destined to meet, in the problems we encounter, and in the unforeseen breakthroughs with which God turns the pages of our life. Our task is to recognize these clues and then to properly interpret them.

Tyrants Are Also Afraid

Toward the end of August the interrogations suddenly stopped. When my case officer, Bereza, announced this development, he even dropped a hint: "Perhaps they will not put you on trial after all." Since I had been keeping up with the newspapers, I understood what he was getting at. The CSCE Belgrade Conference was about to begin, and the American delegation brought a list of all incarcerated Helsinki Group monitors whom the West was demanding be released and documents from the various Helsinki groups. Moscow was prepared to release us because they suspected that they would have to make some concessions during negotiations.

As it turned out, up until Christmas there were no interrogations—I just sat in my cell. Then on January 5, 1978, the questioning started again, and

I realized why: the Belgrade Conference had ended, and everyone had gone home to celebrate Christmas. It became obvious that although the voice of the Soviet prisoners had been heard at the conference, the prisoners themselves had not actually been protected. It appears that the American delegation was the only one that had appealed for our release, while Europe preferred to stick to its beloved *Realpolitik*.

This incident taught me once and for all that one can never trust the self-assured bragging of tyrants who profess that they will not react to any international pressures. Tyrants can also be frightened, perhaps even more deeply than the rest of us. If the Western delegations had acted more cohesively, the fate of all the incarcerated Helsinki Group members might have turned out much differently.

In actuality, my interrogations resumed, and the process promptly came to its conclusion: my "crime" had been established. The time had come for me to familiarize myself with my case documents. To that end, each day I was taken to a different facility, where I was put in a special room to go through the various volumes of Criminal Case 51. I remember experiencing a psychological shock the first time I peered at the world through the cracks in the metal frame of the police van. Kyiv residents looked like nothing had happened. Young people were embracing each other, and women carrying shopping bags were scurrying about their chores. Kyiv, and the whole world, didn't even notice that I, an innocent person, had been languishing in a prison for almost a year now. I was dumbfounded; the shock was enormous. I realized, however, that there was no point holding a grudge against the Kyivites. Logically, I understood that my feelings stemmed from self-absorption in my own pain, but emotionally it was hard to accept this.

Familiarizing myself with the case was a tedious task: I read each of the eight volumes, while the investigator sat nearby also busy reading something. The protocols of other people's testimonies were most captivating: their fates shone through the bureaucratic language of the investigation. Some people attempted to maintain their dignity and cautiously tried to circumvent the minefields set up by the investigator. This is how I remember the testimonies of Natalia Yakovenko and Mariia Labovka. In other friends' protocols I could sense their desire to help Mykola and me: how their hearts must have pounded in an effort to help us, and how they must have feared causing us any harm. Once in a while you can sense the fear the interrogated person feels for himself, and then you see a readiness to uphold the interrogator's version of events, followed by insincere remorse for having been imprudent enough to be acquainted with us. At that point, you turn the page not only of the protocol itself but also on the whole period of your life that had connected you to that person.

One day, while leafing through those pages, I came upon a handwritten note. When I opened it, I saw what looked like a plan of action in Bereza's handwriting: "Show films about the struggle against nationalism to M. M. and M. M." Then he suggested installing one of their own people into our cells; they would pretend to also be prisoners and would try to find out something from us. In other words, they would plant moles. I was overjoyed at this discovery, but now what should I do with it? I knew that I would not be able to smuggle this note out with me because on my way to the cell I would be searched more than once. I therefore decided to simply enjoy the pleasure of the moral high ground. I took this note, went up to my interrogator, and told him: "Mr. Bereza, I found a fascinating piece of paper here; I think you might also be interested in reading it. I have already gotten a kick out of it." With that, I put the paper in front of him. His reaction was remarkable. He turned red as a beet and couldn't look me in the face. He put away that blasted note without a word and then quietly pretended to get back to his reading.

Although I was not able to use that note to write a scathing appeal to the procurator, I never regretted acting as I did. This was an emotional victory, which is more valuable to me than any momentary legal triumph in a battle with the KGB.

Before I finished familiarizing myself with my case, I was able to resolve another dilemma. At one point, the interrogating officer introduced me to a lawyer who the prosecution suggested would defend me in court. Our conversation was rather brief. I saw before me a man who outwardly seemed composed but was really frightened to the core. I was queasy at the thought that in court he would try to ingratiate himself with the judge, pleading that the judge take my youth and inexperience and the good recommendations from my employers into account. I rejected the lawyer unequivocally, proclaiming that I would defend myself in court. This is what was ultimately decided, and I am sure that the lawyer left the room relieved as well.

Finally, the day came when my "work" with Bereza officially came to an end. Our leave taking was cordial. In a pleasant tone (and earnestly, since he believed he was in the right), he asked me again to reconsider my position and repent, to which I just waved my hand. I also remember that Bereza asked me about my plans for the future, to which I replied rather nonchalantly: "Well, in about ten years I will come to your office and invite you out for coffee." He laughed, knowing all too well that prisoners who do not repent receive the maximum sentence—twelve years, in my case. The funny thing is, however, that my prediction turned out to be accurate, and eventually I did fulfill my promise—but more about that later.

The procurator, Yury Antonenko, the First Deputy of the Kyiv Region Court, who later handled my case in court, was present during this conversation. He also asked me a question: "If you do not repent, you will be punished. So what is your goal in that case?" My reply came spontaneously and amazes me to this day: "Not to become embittered."

The Trial

Mykola and I were not tried in Kyiv but in the regional court in Vasylkiv, about forty kilometers southwest of the capital city. The official justification for this was that Mykola was registered as living in Vasylkiv, and I myself lived in Kalynivka, just outside Vasylkiv.

Ukrainian folk tradition holds that you should receive a blessing before embarking on a journey, and indeed I did. My impressions of it were so strong that eventually I wrote about it in my first camp essay, "The Gospel According to a Holy Fool":

> At the very moment that the creaking police wagon was taking me from the Kyiv SIZO to court, I glimpsed the gold cross of St. Sophia's Cathedral through a small chink in the metal armor. It sailed by in a few seconds, against a background of indifferent playful clouds, but I understood that I was seeing it for the first time: imprisoned, to make me grovel forever, I finally learned to look upward.
>
> Thank you, my Ukrainian Infinite Wisdom! You understood better than all of vain and foolish Kyiv how much I needed Christ's blessing during this festival of injustice.[27]

I was placed in a local prison, which was nothing more than a hole in the wall. The room was rather small, with cots for an undetermined number of prisoners and the infamous *parasha* (the toilet bucket)—the ever-present heroine of prison folklore. For a few nights I shared the cell with another supposed defendant, who was never able to shake his prison guard demeanor—he practically reeked of it. I never let on that I remembered the note I had discovered in my files, where Bereza outlined his strategy for us.

27 See full text in the appendix.

Figure 4.4. The St. Sophia Cross.

I even gave my cellmate an innocuous message "for the outside." During the rest of my trial, I had the cell to myself, as there were no other volunteers to endure the smell of the *parasha*.

I am not going to list everyone involved in the trial, but I should say a few words about the judge. He had an odious surname, Dyshel (which was very close to the Russian word *dyshlo*, meaning drawbar, a wagon coupling), and all of us future political prisoners couldn't get enough of the direct allusion to a Russian proverb: "A court is like a *dyshlo*—whichever way you turn it, that's the direction it will go." He was also the judge at the trials of Nadiia Svitlychna, Yevhen Sverstiuk, Semen Gluzman, Liuba Seredniak, Mykola Plakhotniuk, Vasyl Stus, Leonid Pliushch, Heorhii Vins, and perhaps also Viacheslav Chornovil. He was truly the "godfather" to most Ukrainian political prisoners, and his name was an endless source of jokes for all his "clients."

The trial began on March 22, 1978, and it had the character of a typical Soviet farce. The court proceedings were considered open, and the rather large courtroom was jammed to the hilt with KGB associates; I suspect some "reliable" lawyers and law school students were there as well. There was not one familiar face. This upset me, and even the first day I protested that none of my family was here. I was a novice when it came to court proceedings, however, and I did not know how to handle myself in the courtroom.

Before the court session began, Mykola Matusevych, my codefendant, was also brought in. He was brought in by force because he refused to walk. To be honest, my heart skipped a beat when I saw him with his hands twisted and heard his angry outbursts. I was also taken aback by his appearance: his hair had not been trimmed (perhaps deliberately), and it hung down his back; the overall effect was almost phantasmagoric.

When the trial started, Mykola immediately announced that he would not be party to such a farce. This is when I understood that as defendants, we took different positions and approaches in justifying and explaining our behavior. The court disregarded Mykola's statements. He kept protesting and finally asked the judge, "What will it take for me to be taken away from here?" Judge Dyshel replied: "You would be taken away from here if you insulted the court." Mykola just laughed. "Wow, as simple as that?" He proceeded to lash out with such profanities that the judge quickly lost his patience and ordered Mykola's removal. He was absent from the courtroom until the verdict was read.

Mykola didn't know what strategy I was planning to employ, and perhaps he became frightened that my mildness would betray me. While he was being led away, he just shouted: "Myroslav, do not belittle yourself!" But my course had already been set, and I didn't want to deviate from it.

That first day I appeared as both defendant and self-appointed counsel. Matusevych's defense attorney also took part in the proceedings. But as I listened to his weak defense, I gave thanks to God that I had been able to dodge my own "defense lawyer."

Today I no longer remember all the details of that trial—and the isolated moments that I do recall certainly do not paint the whole picture. Obviously, I maintained the same position I did during the inquest; in other words, I insisted upon the legal human rights defense aspects of the Ukrainian Helsinki Group. One incident does remain clear in my mind, perhaps because it was so funny. While attempting to justify my position yet again, I wanted to refer to a quote from Lenin that was relevant and would have directly vindicated my actions. I started, "Even Lenin himself said—" Suddenly Judge Dyshel, realizing what was about to follow, cut me off and shouted in his pathetic falsetto, "Do not utter the name Lenin! Coming from you it sounds like blasphemy!" To me, this is a brilliant confirmation of the French historian Alain Besançon's thesis on the quasi-religious basis of Communist ideology. [28]

I best remember specific moments from the testimony of several witnesses on the second day. The most noteworthy of these, in terms of its relevance to my further involvement in the trial, was that of Nadiia Svitlychna. She was summoned as a witness to confirm Matusevych's and my criminal activity in connection to the preparation of UHG Memorandum #11. Nadiia, however, lodged a protest in court, complaining that some of our friends, who were standing outside and freezing, were blocked from entering the courtroom. The judge attempted to explain that the "room was already overcrowded." But Nadiia's protest had already accomplished the most important thing: this vital information had reached my ears. I stood up and announced that I refused to participate in a closed trial. After that, I appeared in court every day. But after every statement the judge uttered, I stood up and repeated the same phrase: "In connection with the fact that this is a closed trial, I refuse to take part in any court proceedings."

My protests did have an effect. Eventually my mother and sister told me that in the evening on the same day I started protesting, the KGB finally notified them that the trial had begun. Up to that point they didn't even

28 Alain Besançon, *Le Malheur du siècle: sur le communisme, le nazisme et l'unicité de la Shoah* (Paris: Fayard, 1998), 65–71.

know. They were brought from their respective cities to Kyiv, and the following day I saw them in court. Before my eyes actually focus on them, in my soul I saw two shiny colorful spots. They were trying to smile so that their grief would not show and to convey their support. I think that Nadiika was dressed in pink, or at least she was radiating pink, and that's how I remembered her.

There are certain differences between how I remember the court proceedings and the description of the trial compiled by one of my anonymous friends. My mother and sister appeared in court as witnesses, but this has been totally erased from my memory. Perhaps I was not actually listening to what they were saying, instead savoring their appearance while simultaneously commiserating with their grief.

It didn't matter that the KGB had so efficiently delivered my family to the courtroom; I still refused to participate in the process. The judge would get angry: "Why are you still refusing? Look, your family is here now!" I would reply: "Yes, my family is here, but all my friends are still standing at the door and are not allowed in." This was the main reason I did not participate in the court proceedings.

I recently learned that the trial of the "Odessa triad"—Nina Strokata, Oleksa Riznykiv, and Oleksy Prytyka—was almost identical:

> A rather large crowd of people would gather outside the court, and they even dared to cheer the defendants on. Even though the court was declared open, those wishing to enter were refused, because all the seats had already been taken by the "men in civilian suits" [i.e., KGB officials]. Riznykiv frequently proclaimed that he would not participate in the hearings until his father, his sister, and his wife would be allowed in. As a result, they were ultimately permitted to enter.[29]

Much later I learned that during my trial the dissident Liuba Murzhenko tried to get permission to be present in court, but instead she was taken to the police station and held there for the rest of the day. And only recently I read in dissident journalist Alexander Podrabinek's memoirs about his efforts to come see me in court:

> 1978 was full of trials. On March 22, Ukrainian Helsinki Group Members Myroslav Marynovych and Mykola Matusevych's trial was held in Vasylkiv, near Kyiv. I went to the trial together with Tania Osipova. We didn't have any

29 *Odes'ka khvylia*, 27.

> hope of getting into the courtroom, but we thought that we might at least stand there together with some of our Ukrainian friends; that didn't happen, however. As soon as we approached the court, we were detained by the police, and without any explanation we were taken back to Kyiv. At the train station we were held at the police station, and the "powers that be" told us to purchase tickets for Moscow. Tania and I objected: "We are not planning to return to Moscow just now, so why would we buy any tickets?" After a lengthy and difficult argument, the Kyiv police finally purchased our tickets, and we were escorted to the train.
>
> At the train station it was as crowded as usual. Several police officers trailed us through the throng, but at some point, they stopped paying attention and ended up in front of us. At the next staircase I pushed Tania to the side, and we did not follow them up the stairs, but instead ran down to the exit. We soon lost ourselves in the crowd, and a few minutes later we wound up outside in some alley, where we grabbed a taxi and disappeared into the city center.[30]

But let us return to the witness testimonies. Nadiia Svitlychna was both intrepid and confident; she confirmed that she was the one who submitted her statement to the UHG but did not reveal the name of the person to whom she gave it to. Nadiia expertly deflected all of Judge Dyshel's attacks. For example, he read out a remarkable excerpt from her UHG appeal ("After everything that I have endured, I consider it below human dignity to be a citizen of the largest, mightiest, and most virtually unassailable concentration camp in the world.") and took issue with this appraisal, but Nadiia retorted, "This trial of Marynovych and Matusevych is a prime example of that!" The judge was amazed that her four years of incarceration had "not taught her anything." As expected, the so-called impartial audience voiced its dissatisfaction, and it was obvious that Nadiia's attitude and Soviet reality were totally incompatible.

Vira Lisova, another Helsinki Group defendant, was also called in as a witness. Her persecutions were the subject of the UHG's Memorandum #8. After greeting me very cordially, she spoke boldly, though it was clear that she was afraid of causing me any harm. She did not know that I had confirmed the authenticity of my signatures on all the documents or that I had testified that I had gathered the information for her memorandum. She was

30 Aleksandr Podrabinek, *Dissidenty*, ed. Elena Shubina (Moscow: ACT 2014), 237–38.

therefore reluctant to answer the judge's questions. To help her out, I called out to her: "Vira, say everything as it was." Seeing that I said this in a genuine manner, she talked more freely, and she spoke very well. She confirmed all the information that was presented in the memorandum dealing with the persecutions she had endured from the KGB.

Oles Berdnyk's walk up to the witness stand was majestic, if not dramatic. Before listening to the judge, he turned and acknowledged me in the eastern fashion, bringing his two palms together at his chest. Then he turned to the judge and asked him in a thunderous voice: "What are you trying him for?" The judge was flabbergasted. Berdnyk behaved as if he were the main procurator in the courtroom, and this was really beautiful to see. However, it was obvious that given his attitude, he would not be a free man for much longer. This was further confirmed by the reaction of the alleged "outraged Soviet citizens" who sat in the courtroom.

Mykhailyna Kotsiubynska was another witness who caused the procurators a fair bit of grief. The procurator was eager to back her into a corner. With great relish he detailed the protocol of the search that had been conducted in her apartment, when they found the text of the Ukrainian Helsinki Group Declaration inside an old boot hidden in a dusty attic closet. Mykhailyna was uncomfortable listening to all this, and she became flustered and agitated. With a sneer, the procurator then slammed her with his "killer" question: "If you say that there was nothing criminal about the Group's Declaration, then why did you hide it so far away?" He expected Mykhailyna to become jittery and cautious, trying to find an explanation, but she straightened out her shoulders and replied defiantly: "Yes, I am very sorry that I hid that document so far away. I should have framed it and placed it in the most prominent spot in my room." It was a thrill to watch the procurator, who practically turned green. You can only imagine the gratitude that I, the defendant, felt while listening to these words.

Borys Antonenko-Davydovych had also been summoned by the court to appear as a witness, but he did not show up, claiming illness. His testimony was, however, read in court, and in it he refused to name the person who had given him the Ukrainian Helsinki Group documents that were later confiscated from him. Yevhen Obertas also refused to divulge any names. He was questioned in court regarding our involvement with the group, as well as about Mykola's "crime of hooliganism" (more on this later). Yevhen spoke courageously, acknowledging that Mykola and I were his friends, and that he fully supported our activities. He refused to testify in our case, and for that he was rewarded with a prescription of "corrective work."[31]

My ex-wife was also called as a witness, and I was amazed at the dignity she exhibited during her examination. She had not been involved in the dissident movement, but she had a strong moral character and was able to recognize the difference between good and evil. She spoke cautiously and did not allow herself to be manipulated by the court into saying anything against me.

I hardly remember the testimonies given by Mykola's family—his parents Nastia and Ivan, his sister Tamila, his uncle and cousin, and his wife, Olia Heiko. Perhaps some incomprehensible memory block took hold, as it did with my own family's testimony. I do remember that Nastia and Tamila Matusevych acted with dignity and courage, and Olia was daring and bold, so much so that the judge pointed toward the defendants' bench and said: "If you are a member of the Group, then you certainly belong over there."

By the way, the *Chronicle* recorded another exchange that escapes my memory:

> Olha Heiko refused to answer the Procurator's question, "Do you still consider yourself a member of the group?" Judge: "Defendant Marynovych, what can you say about this?" Marynovych: "I refuse to take part in a closed court session." Judge: "Marynovych, I cease to understand you. On your word hangs the fate of your comrade. It is one thing if she is simply a witness, but it is completely different if she is a member of the group; then her place is side by side with you and you keep repeating your 'I refuse.' When it was a question of your own interests you could well say 'this is ethical, but that is not ethical.' But not to take account of your comrades — is that ethical in your opinion?" "It is not the place of a Soviet court to talk of ethics," Marynovych added to his usual formula.[32]

It was difficult to watch the testimony given by the husband of one of Mykola's cousins, L. Studzinsky. He was unwilling to acknowledge publicly that he was the one who had secretly handed over a copy of the UHG Declaration to the KGB. Mykola had given him that copy to forward to his

31 At the KGB's urging, the staff at Obertas's workplace, the Kyiv Institute of Electrodynamics, collectively condemned Obertas's testimony at the trial as "hostile to Soviet order" and told him he had to "disclaim his remarks at the trial, write an appropriate statement, and in this way 'correct' his 'behavior.'" See *Documents*, 166.

32 *Chronicle*, 49:7–8.

uncle and cousin. Smirking and patronizing him, the judge kept pressuring him to acknowledge this, but Studzinsky held off, incriminating himself even further until he finally broke down and reluctantly confessed.

The court hearing for Matusevych's "crime of hooliganism" was long and tedious. The "plaintiff," V. Danyliv, a man from Ivano-Frankivsk, appeared, along with some eleven other witnesses. This five-year-old case involved several Russian tourists who had been visiting Kryvorivnia, a colorful ethnic village in the ethnic Hutsul region of the Carpathian Mountains. When they spotted a local woman smoking a pipe, in Hutsul fashion, they began to ridicule her. Mykola stepped in and cut them short. The ensuing mêlée resulted in some punches being thrown. Some prudent individual split them apart, and that was the end of the story. In the falsified case that was now presented by the KGB, however, everything sounded much more sinister and politicized. Judge Dyshel was dying to turn the incident into a felony case.

When this case was presented, the accuser was the first to appear in the courtroom. The judge asked him a standard question: whether he saw anyone familiar on the defendants' bench. Danyliv looked at me (I was obviously the only one seated on the defendant's bench) and said: "Yes, that's Matusevych sitting right there." This created a rather comical and confusing situation, especially after several other witnesses replied the same way. During the break, the KGB had to brief them. When Danyliv realized that he had confused me with Mykola, he kept glancing at me with a guilty expression, not really understanding what was going on.

On the whole, his testimony was thoroughly incompetent. He was clearly uncomfortable describing the scuffle in the words that the judge was feeding to him. Nor was he willing to consider himself a victim. During a recess, the KGB worked on him, and then things moved more smoothly. Then there was a series of additional witnesses, and I saw the whole gamut of manifestations of *homo Sovieticus* unfold, like a deck of cards being shuffled before my eyes.

On the other hand, the witnesses that appeared on Mykola's behalf were valiant and honest. They included Nina and Yevhen Obertas and Valentyna Hirenko. They all denied that the scuffle had been "exceptionally dangerous" or that it had had a "politically motivated" subtext. Quite significant in that regard was the testimony from Valentyna Hirenko, in which she denied her friend Mykola's alleged anti-Russian motivation. She herself was Russian speaking and spoke Russian in court.

Be that as it may, Judge Dyshel finally pushed the case to his desired end, and on March 29, 1978, the court reconvened to announce its verdicts. Mykola Matusevych was returned to court, and I remember the loving gaze with which his mother Nastia virtually embraced her son.

I had no illusions regarding the verdict. Since I had not repented, I knew that I would receive the maximum sentence. I was, however, afraid that they might give me a lesser term than Mykola. This would have been distressing to me because our posture during the whole process had been so different. Had they given me less, I would never be able to explain that I had not betrayed him and received a lesser term for "good behavior." Mykola's sentence was read first, and in accordance with the appropriate Article 62, part 1 of the Criminal Code of the Ukrainian Soviet Socialist Republic, and Article 70, part 1 of the Criminal Code of the Russian Soviet Federative Socialist Republic, and also Article 206, part 2 of the Criminal Code of the Ukrainian Soviet Socialist Republic (Matusevych's hooliganism felony charge), he was sentenced to the maximum seven-year prison term in a strict regime camp, plus five years of internal exile.

I froze in anticipation of my own verdict. When I heard seven and five, I was actually ecstatic. Thank God, we got the same! However, when I looked at my mother and Nadiika, my joy suddenly evaporated because they obviously had not expected the maximum. My mother's face wilted, and Nadiika later remembered that at that moment only one thought had been racing through her mind: "My God, why so much?"

At the last moment, Mykola Matusevych managed to ask, "What about a closing statement?" But at that point he was simply shackled and led out of the courtroom. He didn't know that any final words would have had to be presented at the previous court session prior to the reading of the verdict. Eventually this is how he would describe that moment: "I was brought in just for the sentencing, and unfortunately I was not allowed to voice my concluding remarks, since this is when I had hoped to say something 'heroic.' I was extremely disappointed because to be perfectly honest, I really wanted to give them a piece of my mind."[33]

I had declined to make any final remarks, repeating my refrain of not participating in their closed court proceedings.

And with that I returned to my cell as an unrepentant "exceptionally dangerous state criminal."

---

33 Matusevych, "Ia vyhrav dvobii," 3.

Eventually I learned from the *Chronicle* how our case had been ideologically justified to the "toiling masses" in the press:

> A week before the trial the district newspaper *Shliakh Ilicha* (Path of Illich, i.e. Lenin) published an abusive article by P. Barzinsky, entitled "Black Ingratitude" about M. Matusevych and his family. On 19 March the article was reprinted in the regional newspaper *Kyivs'ka Pravda*.
>
> On 15 April the newspaper *Shliakh Ilicha* published another article by Barzinsky, "Spiteful Critics," in which not only Matusevych and Marynovych were stigmatized, but also "their confederates, especially the anti-Soviet [Oles] Berdnyk and [Yevhen] Obertas. The article said that letters had reached the editor from people demanding that Berdnyk and Obertas "answer for their actions before a court."[34]

I didn't bother filing an appeal—there was no point. I think that Mykola's lawyer filed an appeal, but this was certainly not at Mykola's request. Thus, after the trial, I remained in prison until June 8, 1978, while the Court of Appeals, in the typical Soviet style, "left the verdict intact."[35]

In this interim period, another event gave me the chance to see my mother: my father died suddenly of a heart attack. Obviously, they did not allow me to go to the funeral; they didn't even notify me of his death. Soon after the funeral, however, my mother managed to arrange a meeting with me, which was granted to us at the prison warden's office. She watched me with trepidation, worrying how I would receive this news. I remember telling her, "May he rest in peace; now I no longer have to remember all the bad things he did to us!" This meeting ended with a rather volatile conflict with the prison chief, Colonel Sapozhnikov. As my mother was leaving, she embraced me and whispered something into my ear. I did not understand her words, but the warden heard her whisper and began to shout at my mother. I reacted immediately, telling him that he dared not insult my mother. I was immediately taken away, and my intrepid mother was left behind to smooth things over with the angry KGB man.

Before long, the day for my sentence to begin rolled around, and like all other convicts before me, my head was shaved. They started addressing me as "citizen convict" (Rus. *grazhdanin osuzhdennyi*), and I awaited my imminent deployment. A new chapter in my life was about to begin.

---

34 *Chronicle*, 49:9.

35 Because they were codefendants in the case, Matusevych's appeal automatically implicated M. M. as well.

Intermezzo I

On the Road to Camp

On June 9, 1978, I was taken from my SIZO cell and sent off to camp. My first impressions of this transfer were extremely intense. That day, before the prisoners were dispatched, we were all taken to a remote spot on the periphery of the Kyiv train station. Since this was an open area, we were all told to crouch down, and the whole group was surrounded by soldiers with guard dogs. I was just on the edge of the crowd, where I could see the dogs growling angrily right next to my face—an indelible memory.

Finally, they took us to the Stolypin wagon, and since I was considered an "especially dangerous state criminal," I was locked in an isolation cage.[1] Ordinary criminals were put in large holding pens with cots. There were so many of them that they could hardly fit. Next to me there was a small cage for women, with two of them in there. One of the women was probably a first-time convict, as she was crying the whole time. But the other one looked more at home. When the criminal inmates spotted the women, they immediately began hitting on them, telling dirty jokes, and asking them to sing "Daisy White" (Rus. *Romashka belaia*), a prison song with lascivious lyrics that was popular at the time. When the women did not comply, the criminals started singing it themselves, relishing the effect it had on the women. After each bout of dirty jokes, the frightened woman in the neighboring cage cried even more.

The guards paced up and down the corridors, peering through the wire mesh. They wearily exchanged the usual expletives with the prisoners. As the train started moving, one of the guards cracked open a window to let in

1 Stolypin wagon: a train car designed to transport prisoners, named after Petr Stolypin, prime minister of the Russian Empire in the early twentieth century. Stolypin oversaw large-scale reforms that included encouraging peasantry to resettle in Siberia in exchange for free land; these settlers were transported in special train cars. Perhaps because the train cars were carrying prisoners also bound for Siberia, they became known as "Stolypin wagons."

Figure I1.1. The "Stolypin," a special wagon for transporting prisoners.

some fresh air—right next to me, luckily enough. I climbed up to the top bunk and soaked in Kyiv's hills and the bell towers of the city's churches as they glided past me. Once the train crossed the rail bridge, with a deep sense of longing I bade an extended farewell to the Dnipro River and to my beloved Kyiv.

During the night I was astonished that the guards ignored prisoners' pleas to take them to the toilet. Such things were only allowed in the morning, and if anyone wanted to go earlier, that was his own problem. The relentless pleas of those who were suffering eventually ceased, and I can only imagine how they must have resolved their problem.

Later I read Patriarch Josyf Slipyj's own account of those transfers: "Each relocation was truly a horrifying cross to bear, and just writing about this is painful; to be cold and hungry and surrounded by bandits, without the possibility of dealing with even the most essential needs; the guards' bullying, etc."[2] It is truly difficult to imagine a person of the patriarch's stature having to endure this.

By morning, our train had reached Kharkiv, and the prisoners were finally led to the much-needed facilities. I retrieved my soap, towel, toothpaste, and toothbrush and stood there waiting my turn. The soldier who opened my cage glared at the things in my hands and came out with a whole string of vulgarities. I couldn't understand what I had done wrong, so I just looked at him, which only made him even more furious. I finally understood that it was the toiletries. I put them aside and followed him, and everything became clear: there are no doors to the toilets—you do your business with a guard right there, pointing a Kalashnikov at you. As for washing, it was simply not permitted. That's when I understood what a provocation my toiletries had been for him: to see a towel folded over my arm, soap, and the audacity of a toothbrush and toothpaste! What? "You intend to remain a human being? Abandon all hope, ye who enter here!"

Every political prisoner endured this moment. There comes a time when you are forced to choose: you will either be destroyed by the denigration of your human dignity, or you will tell yourself once and for all what your fellow prisoners before you had said: "No! They will not succeed in humiliating me!" You learn how to create a psychological barrier to help you endure endlessly being forced to undress, constant searches, and never-ceasing abuse. Your mindset becomes: "You can do anything you want to me, but you will not take my dignity away from me."

At the same time, I am convinced that this work was unbearably humiliating for the guard assigned to toilet duty. He did, after all, have to stand there for hours and carefully watch all the prisoners relieve themselves. Perhaps that—or any other of the many indignities—was what made the guards so cruel. I remember once, during one of the transfers, for no apparent reason, a guard dragged me out to the vestibule of the train car, pointed his rifle straight at me, and yelled: "You anti-Soviet bastard! I will kill you here and now!" And you have no idea what's going through his mind, whether he means it or not because it's clear that he is either wasted on narcotics or stone-cold drunk. It was well known that this was common practice in prison: as Slipyj wrote, "The prison authorities perpetrated such heinous atrocities that they would massacre prisoners like flies; they were psychopaths and debauched criminals."[3]

2 Slipyi, *Spomyny*, 188.

3 Slipyi, *Spomyny*, 198.

In Kharkiv I was housed in a well-known transit prison with the euphemistic name of "Cold Mountain" (*kholodna hora*).[4] A young and inexperienced prisoner, I was put in a cell with another detainee. Our conversation automatically veered toward the usual topic for such meetings, with each of us describing his criminal case. Normally, a feeling of comradeship is established under such circumstances—after all, we were both in the same boat. So, I good-naturedly listened and nodded along as he described his story: in his hometown of Chișinău, there was a certain scoundrel who annoyed everyone, and nobody could straighten him out. At some point, my cellmate found himself at a party with this rascal, who true to form began to annoy everybody. "Finally, I couldn't take it any longer, so I just took a bottle and hit him over the head and killed him."

I just froze: *there was a killer sitting right in front of me.* He just kept on talking, staring me in the eyes: "Evil has to be destroyed, right?" Caught by surprise, my bewilderment was greater than you can possibly imagine. Since then I have no patience for those righteous and all-knowing do-gooders who profess that "you should not tolerate any evil. Evil must be destroyed." I cannot simply nod my head in agreement with this anymore.

I did not stay with the murderer long; as an "especially dangerous" criminal I was placed in a separate cell, and for the first time in a long time I heard music being played over the loudspeakers. Apparently, I had not been housed on death row, as most political prisoners who passed through this prison were. Once, I heard one of my favorite songs and got emotionally carried away—I started dancing in my cell. Even now, whenever I hear that song, I imagine myself dancing.

After Kharkiv, my route ran through other transit prisons, such as Syzran, Kazan, and Perm.[5] We stayed in each prison for just a few days, depending on how quickly they could collect a large enough group of prisoners for the next transfer.

I have forgotten everything about the Syzran camp except for one incident: once again I was "inadvertently" placed in a general cell with the criminal inmates. I say this ironically because normally a mistake like this would

---

4 Kholodna Hora is the historic name for a neighborhood on the west side of the city of Kharkiv; the prison there was initially constructed in the late eighteenth century and housed many Soviet Ukrainian prisoners en route to camps farther east.

5 Syzran, Kazan, Perm: Cities in the RSFSR, all well-known transit points for Soviet prisoners.

not have been possible. According to the rules, criminal and "especially dangerous" prisoners were supposed to be separated. Often, however, trying to teach the political prisoners a lesson, the guards would suddenly "forget" this rule, expecting the criminals to "have some fun" with the political prisoners. This is precisely what happened with me this time. As they brought me into the cell, the guards loudly announced the criminal code and article of my sentence for everyone to hear, so the criminals knew I was a political prisoner. I remember the harsh, unfriendly looks they gave me as I entered the cell. One of them demanded that I surrender my belongings to him. I tried to protest, but they slowly and silently created a tight circle around me. I realized that there was no point in resisting and quietly handed over my bundle. They didn't take everything; only the most valuable things, such as a warm sweater my mother had given me.

I cannot refrain from comparing this with another incident that happened much later, during another transfer. In one of the transfer prisons, I was again "mistakenly" placed in a large cell where the criminal elite—the "thieves within the law"[6]—sat in the center. They had also heard what I was sentenced for, but in contrast to the previous group, they invited me to join them as they passed around *chifir*.[7] Taking my two sips at every round, I answered all their questions: where I'm from, why I was locked up, and so on. They listened to me carefully without interrupting until I started describing the Ukrainian Helsinki Group's activities, when one of the criminals burst out: "The fact that you are against the Soviet system, that's good, but fighting them with words, that's absurd! It's dynamite you need against them!"

In contrast to my faint memories of my stop in Syzran, I remember the prison in Kazan very well. Perhaps that's because another funny incident took place there. I was being held in a separate cell, which contained nothing more than a mattress on the floor. As usual, the food was delivered through a hatch in the door. One day, the guard opened it at an unusual time and just left it open. I got curious and got up from my mattress. I looked through the hatch and was dumbfounded. Just opposite me was another cell with the hatch open, through which a female prisoner was looking at me amiably. I

6 Thieves within the law (Rus. *vory v zakone*): "high-ranking" criminals who control life within the prisoners' community. Normally, a prison administration unlawfully cooperates with this criminal elite by offering drugs or other temptations in exchange for "keeping order" among the prisoners.

7 *Chifir:* a strong hallucinogenic tea.

waved to her and asked her how she was, but after a while, clueless as to what to do, I waved goodbye and settled back down on my mattress.

A while later, the guard muttered something angrily and slammed the hatch shut. After a few minutes he opened my door and ordered me to get out, leading me to the cell across from me, but now it was empty. "So, what do you smell?" he asked, as I stared at him, still not understanding. "Do you smell the broad? You worthless prick!" He led me back to my cell, having lost all interest in me. This is when I realized that I was no longer at the Kyiv KGB prison; now I was in the world of simple human reflexes, and the guard was hoping to make some money off it.

At some point during this extended transit, I had a particular experience of what it means to be on the threshold of life and death: I was pushed into a metal compartment intended for the "especially dangerous" prisoners inside a *voronok*.[8] Even though the compartment was meant for one person, there were three of us in there. It was impossible to stand side by side; we had to stand on top of each other, and each of us was trying to climb up from beneath the other. Since we were traveling on old bumpy roads, trying to free your body from under two others was a challenge. The heat inside this compartment was unbearable because there were only a few small holes drilled in the metal door that might have provided just enough air for one person. But there were three of us that had to breathe in there, and the trip lasted some two or three hours. Each of us was suffocating, attempting to position his mouth or nose close to those life-saving holes. It was extremely frightening: could this be my end? Despite my fear, however, I felt no regret for taking this treacherous path.

I have no special memories from my first stay at the Perm transit camp. The next thing that I do remember is being in the ShIZO[9] of camp VS 389/36 in the village of Kuchino in the Chusovoi district of the Perm region,[10] where I was brought on July 6, 1978, and placed into quarantine.

8 *Voronok* (raven): common slang term for trucks that carried prisoners.

9 ShIZO (*shtrafnoi izoliator*): punitive isolation cell, not to be confused with "SIZO," pretrial detention.

10 In the early 1970s, special prisons were set up in the Perm region in Russia, intended for "especially dangerous state criminals." On June 13, 1972, under top secrecy, an echelon of several hundred "strict regime" prisoners were placed in three camps near the town of Chusovoi, under the jurisdiction of the Skalny camp administration. Those camps were Camp VS-389/35 (in Vsekhsviatskaia village), Camp VS-389/36 (in Kuchino village), and Camp VS-389/37 (Polovinka village), commonly referred to as Camps 35, 36, and 37. These

Figure I1.2. "Stakan" enclosure for "especially dangerous" prisoners in the avtozak prisoner car. This is a modern avtozak with bigger holes for fresh air.

Figure I1.3. ShIZO (penal isolation building) in the Kuchino concentration camp where I stayed for the quarantine (contemporary view). Photo credit: Ilia Buianovsky.

It lasted for a week, and it was psychologically unbearable: on the other side of the fence were those for whom my soul had been reaching toward for over a month now, while I made my way from Kyiv. There were political prisoners in this camp whose stories and cases I had heard about on the free radio and

prisoners were all activists from various human rights defense and national liberation movements, *samizdat* authors, writers, poets, journalists, lawyers, philosophers, psychologists, physicians, and teachers, all convicted for "anti-Soviet agitation and propaganda." Also with them were the resistance fighters—UPA members and Nazi police who had been incarcerated after the war for "treason against the fatherland." They were all finishing up their lengthy (fifteen- to twenty-five-year) sentences. These were not just camps but actual prisons with extremely severe conditions. Camp VS-389/36 was divided into two parts: "strict" and "special" regimes. See *Rukh oporu v. Ukraini, 1960–1990: Entsyklopedychnyi dovidnyk*, ed. Osyp Zinkevych (Kyiv: Smoloskyp, 2012), 561–62. –M. M.

Figure I1.4. Semen Gluzman. Photo credit: Alexander Chekmenev.

about whom the UHG had written in our statements and memoranda. And here, where they were almost in reach, I just had to wait.

Once a day I would be taken to an outdoor courtyard for a walk. One day, during my walk, a small window to one of the cells opened, and I saw not a face but just someone's lips: "I'm Semen Gluzman, and who are you?" After I identified myself, he told me: "Have you heard that all the members of the Helsinki Group have been nominated for the Nobel Peace Prize?"[11] "No!" This was a level-seven earthquake on the Richter scale. After I returned to my cell, I started thinking frantically: "God, to be a Nobel Prize winner! If they really do award it to us, then will they have to release us so we can go receive the prize?" Bewilderment, hope, and yes, the temptation of glory. The next few days turned out to be extremely important for the rest of my life, serving as an inoculation of sorts. If we inject a few bacteria into our bodies, our organism manages to find the strength to fight the infection and develop

11 The Helsinki Groups were repeatedly nominated for the Nobel Peace Prize, including by members of the US Congress in 1978; this may have been the root of Gluzman's information.

immunity to it. I am certain that this was the Lord's intention in injecting me with a small dose of this temptation of glory through the rumor that we might win this prize.

"Who do you think you are?" This was the phrase that my case officer Bereza had used on me, and I also heard it many times throughout my trial in a variety of humiliating formulations. On top of that, I was also hyper-aware of my civic immaturity. I therefore succumbed to the thought that soon I might be forgotten altogether. And here, all of a sudden, to be nominated for the Nobel Peace Prize! People are weak by nature, and completely racked with emotion, I began to assess whether there was enough space on my chest to pin this most important of prizes.

It's a good thing that I survived that period of ostensible inoculation. After a few days, when I was finally transferred from quarantine to the actual camp, I came face-to-face with normal camp conditions. Then everything returned to normal, and I felt embarrassed by my weakness. Eventually the Nobel Peace Prize was awarded to Menachem Begin and Anwar Sadat for the Camp David Accords. I actually thanked the Lord for that period of temptation. By that time, I had already developed enough "antibodies" to take the news calmly—and, later, to endure many other infectious bouts of glory.

Part Two

The Universe behind Barbed Wire

Chapter Five

The Labor Camp Up Close

Finally, on July 11, 1978, they transferred me to the residential zone of notorious Camp 36, a strict regime camp.[1] It is impossible to convey my feelings as I crossed the entry gate from the ShIZO barrack where I had been quarantined into the camp.

I remember it vividly: this was not the beginning of a new chapter of my life but rather the beginning of a new life altogether. No doubt that's how Neil Armstrong must have felt when he first stepped on the surface of the moon. Even though I was well aware that this place was a valley of new suffering, my soul was filled with joy and hope, anticipating the people I would soon meet; today, I would say this was hope in God's grace. A dark ironic metaphor for this feeling is captured in an excerpt from the letter that I sent to my family on February 12, 1979:

> It was once believed that there was a spot in the Ural Mountains where the most fortunate people in the world lived in comfort and love, but it is nearly impossible for outsiders to get there, beyond the forests and the snows. Only a mythical bird can bring you there on its wings.

When I was brought in, most prisoners were at work in the labor zone. This gave me an opportunity to arrange my meager belongings and prepare myself to meet them. I was assigned to a barrack where a cot and a small cupboard had been allocated to me. Soon enough, all the prisoners returned from the work zone. A group of "disobedient" prisoners (i.e., the dissidents) greeted me warmly and enthusiastically, and I later found out that there was a unique ritual for new arrivals:

---

1 The *Chronicle* (51:74) lists the date of my arrival as July 6, but this was the date when I was put in quarantine isolation. I was let in to the residential zone on July 11. –M. M.

Figure 5.1. The way I entered the camp; my barrack is on the right.

> Welcoming a newly arrived prisoner was always a special sort of camp festivity. Some traditional tea, kept for just such an occasion, would be brewed; the Ukrainians in the camp would gather in a circle, with the newcomer in the center—and all attention was focused on him. He would be carefully scrutinized, his every word carefully evaluated. And all this, with their silent gazes, was meant to say: "No matter what, we shall survive. We are your friends, and you can count on us."[2]

In my case, the reception was exceptional, as I was the first member of a Helsinki Group to arrive in the zone. Since I was seen as a human rights defender, the Ukrainians were not the only ones who greeted me. I was invited to an unusual feast of fried mushrooms prepared by my new friends. What kind of mushrooms could grow in a concentration camp? At first the guys just smiled mysteriously, but later they showed me the meager "gifts of nature" that grew in the yard. They did indeed belong to the fungus kingdom, but they looked far from edible. Seeing my trepidation, the boys explained that the mushrooms are first boiled twice and then fried thoroughly on top

2 Horbal, *Prezentatsiia zhyttia*, 122–23.

of that. I didn't dare reject their hospitality, but in my head, I had a nagging feeling that my first day in camp might also turn out to be my last.

This is how I became acquainted with the place where I was destined to spend the next six years of my life. At that time, I had no idea that the zone I had been brought to was infamous for its extreme brutality. This is how Yevhen Sverstiuk described it:

> Zone 36 was the most like a concentration camp, the most evil. It was a penal zone in every way: the regime was punitive; the supervision was punitive; the work and censorship were punitive; as were the living conditions, and any contact with the outside world and with one's family: all were punitive. We were not just serving out our terms—each day was filled with punitive measures. The Soviet penal system was an environment steeped in hatred towards human beings.[3]

Camp Organization

Some good soul had the foresight to sketch out a plan of Kuchino Camp 36, so I can rely on it now. It should be taken into account, however, that at different periods this facility underwent certain changes. It seems to me that some elements of this plan were arranged differently during my time there, but I cannot rely on memory alone. I therefore look at the current setup of what remains of that camp with a certain amount of nostalgia.

The population of this camp varied widely, but during my time it averaged about sixty persons. They were all split between two wooden barracks (detachments 1 and 2), each of which was further divided into two units of fourteen to sixteen individuals each. We slept on cots that were arranged in pairs along the length of the barrack, with two cupboards separating each pair. There was only one period in which all the prisoners were set up in bunk beds in just one barrack.

During my first month, I was lucky: the bed I was assigned to was next to the Ukrainian poet Ihor Kalynets.[4] This arrangement didn't last long, however, because he was already reaching the end of his term, and by early August he was transferred. My neighbor amazed me with his inner composure and his serene self-assurance. His authority within the zone was indisputable. We

3 Yevhen Sverstiuk, interview by Vasyl Ovsiienko, December 23, 2012.

4 Ihor Kalynets (b. 1939): poet from western Ukraine arrested as part of the 1972 wave of repressions against Ukrainian cultural activists.

had many discussions, and I am still a bit embarrassed of the eccentricities of my worldview that I often shocked my tolerant friend with.

Each residential barrack had a reading room, which the inmates jokingly dubbed "the Lenin room." I associate this room above all with Yevhen Sverstiuk who, to the total despair of the guards, was occupied there every day, religiously writing his subversive epistles. His handwriting was completely undecipherable, and it would reduce the guards to sheer despondency. It was, after all, crucial for them to determine whether these scribbles had any anti-Soviet qualities to them. You should have seen the smile on Yevhen's face as he observed the decoders' torments.

Each barrack also had a room with washbasins. Urinals first appeared in the barracks toward the end of my term, and before that you had to go "against the wind." Regardless of the time of year, you had to make your way to a separate toilet at the far reaches of the camp. In both units of each barrack, behind glass partitions there were what we called "sarcophagi"—special cabinets with small compartments where the inmates could store their food provisions.

Additionally, in the residential zone there were barracks that housed the cafeteria, a storage area, the baths, a library, the medical unit, and of course facilities for the guards. All these buildings flanked the main axis, a road that ran from the gate and sentry post to the work zone.

In the dining hall there was more or less free seating, although newcomers were relegated to the vacant seats. I remember only one person at my table in my first months at the camp: Wolf Zalmanson, from one of the "First Leningrad Trials."[5] Our food sometimes included a fair share of tripe, which I abhorred. But this revulsion didn't last long, as a letter to my family, dated September 30, 1979, reveals:

> I will surely make you happy by telling you that nowadays I eat all the meat that happens to fall onto my plate. I resisted it for a long time, giving the meat away to others, and I would line up the onions from the soup neatly on the edge of my plate. But since June, I have given this up, and now my plate is clean, if you disregard the bay leaf, which I doubt that I would eat anyway. In other words, as they say here in such cases: at last they "set me straight."

5 First Leningrad Trial: 1970 court proceedings against a group of sixteen Soviet citizens (most of whom were Jewish) who, after having been denied permission to emigrate from the Soviet Union, attempted to hijack a small passenger airplane in order to escape to Israel.

Figure 5.2. Yevhen Sverstiuk.

Amazingly enough, the camp library had some interesting and valuable books and journals. As a rule, the inmates could subscribe to some newspapers and journals through Soiuzpechat and books via the all-Soviet organization Kniga-Pochtoi (Books by mail).[6] (Obviously this only included Soviet publications.) We were in a political zone, and the dissident inmates were highly educated professionals from the most diverse scholarly fields. Therefore, they subscribed to the most valuable materials ever published in the country—both books and periodicals. When transferred to another camp, you could take only whatever you could carry in your own two hands, so most of the literature prisoners had acquired was left behind in the camp library. That is how I, for example, managed to read such rare publications as a multivolume collection of Nikolai Leskov's works,[7] Lev Gumilev's *Ethnogenesis and the Biosphere of Earth*,[8] and *The Armenian Genocide in the Ottoman Empire*.[9] (I actually read this work in the camp prison, and I almost fainted when I read about all the atrocities it described.) There were even English-language volumes of Agatha Christie stories that had been published in the USSR, and we used them to practice our English.

There was a volleyball court in camp, which was popular with the inmates in the summer. You could take a walk there and chat with your friends or take the ironically named "Ho Chi Minh Trail," which had been well trampled by years of prisoners treading upon it. At certain times, the camp's loudspeakers would broadcast the all-Union radio programs. I associate this with a memory that I conveyed to my family in one of my letters, dated September 30, 1982: "I'm walking along the street and suddenly I hear the renowned 'Zaporozhian March.' What optimistic and heavenly music! You hear the first few chords and positively sprout wings!"

---

6 Soiuzpechat: Soviet agency responsible for distributing periodicals across the Soviet Union; it operated kiosks as well as postal subscription services.

7 Nikolai Leskov: nineteenth-century Russian writer best known for his short fiction.

8 Gumilev, son of poets Nikolai Gumilev and Anna Akhmatova, pioneered the controversial notion of ethnogenesis, an account of human history focused on the formation of ethnoses through behaviorist factors. His views are laid out inthe work mentioned by M. M.: Lev Gumilev, *Etnogenez i biosfera Zemli* (Moscow: Mishel, 1979).

9 Primary source collection on the 1915 Armenian genocide. Mkrtich Gegamovich Nersisian, *Genotsid armian v Osmanskoi imperii: Sbornik dokumentov i materialov* (Yerevan: Izd-vo AN Armianskoi SSR, 1966).

Nature and Climate

From my first days in the zone, I was fascinated by the Ural sky. During the day, the clouds hung so low over the earth that it seemed like you could catch one just by reaching upward. At night, the sky would transform itself into a brilliant planetarium, and under its cupola the whole Milky Way sparkled directly upon you. The air was clean, unpolluted by industrial smog; I had never seen such a clear atmosphere before. Once, as I walked out of the barrack at night, I was astonished by the sense that I was the first Adam on earth with no one else around, just the sky and its starry dome. Another time, as I was lying face up on a bench, I felt a strange trepidation, as if the sky would fall on top of me together with all the stars.

All these impressions later filled the pages of my letters to my family:

> The clouds in the sky here are phenomenal; you could gaze at their astonishing beauty for hours, if a primeval instinctual fear of the mysticism of the heavens didn't take hold of your subconscious. Tonight is unforgettable. I woke up, as if jolted, at the exact moment of the full lunar eclipse. It is a pity that your vision cannot remember this diffused red blur forever. The tranquility of the night heightened these impressions. I walked out into the yard, and despite my recent experiences, I felt as if I were the only person around, touched by the grandeur of the world. Thoughts like these do not come to mind very often; otherwise, you would shrivel up with loneliness. (September 17, 1978)

> Spring in the sky bodes the return of its majestic beauty. Now the clouds are playful, as if Rococo designs suddenly appeared in the heavenly spheres. (May 20, 1979)

> On the morning of July 31, I saw the solar eclipse, which in these parts was only a partial eclipse, and it gave me a remarkable feeling. It is, after all, the last eclipse of this millennium, and certainly the last one in my life. To me it is a novel and somewhat shocking feeling—to see something for the last time. As far as I know, the eclipse was not visible in Western Ukraine; at best the sun probably appeared just a bit clipped. Here the sun appeared as a crescent, and then it became quite dark. The noise from the machinery [in the camp] created a stark contrast with the general stillness of nature, as if immobilized in anticipation. (August 14, 1981)

> The morning greeted me with a symbol clearly carved in the sky: the crescent moon and Venus. It was the same symbol as the day when Yevhen Sverstiuk left. (November 21, 1981)

Mixed feelings were evoked by the Ural Mountains silhouetted against the horizon. The mountains reminded me of the Carpathian Mountains near my native Drohobych, so the sight comforted my eyes but not my soul: rationally, I was acutely aware that this was just an imitation. Hence the rather sad tone of my letters:

> Even though the weather is quite nice—the last sunny days of autumn—I nevertheless didn't even want to go for a walk today. I finally had to force myself. Inadvertently I recalled Ihor Kalynets, who would also get depressed by the forest blazing with yellow leaves. (September 26, 1979)

The climate in the Ural foothills is strictly continental: the summers are hot and the winters very cold. The inmates had a difficult time enduring this, and the old timers would share their survival skills with the newcomers. Obviously, in our letters to our families we had to embellish these descriptions with humor, romanticizing them because reading these letters caused a storm of emotion:

> Right now, Kuchino is inhaling the haze, holding its breath, and noticing how the crescent moon shakes down the frost with evil foreboding. The day before yesterday it was -21, yesterday -31, and today -38 Celsius. I pulled on my quilted pants and heavy felt boots, although I could have still held off on that, and immediately entered a different dimension. It took me a quarter of an hour to move several meters, leaving me quite breathless, but still quite warm. (December 13, 1978)

> I finally got used to the local winter, and I now consider a temperature of -31C to be positively Tashkent-like [giving an example of a sub-tropical zone]. A temperature of -50 to -51 was the lowest so far, and at this temperature it is difficult to breathe, so I try to avoid doing so outdoors. Holding my breath, I jump outside, dash to my destination, and only then resume breathing. (January 1979)

> We had a terrible blizzard here. You step into the deep snow, and a moment later there is not even a track left. I thought about you and imagined an explosion of emotions if you ever saw me in this snowy kingdom. The feeling when

you tumble in it is somewhat like the luxury of rolling onto a Persian kilim. (February 12, 1979)

There is a lot of snow, and at twilight the wires [of the camp fences] look like festive New Year's garlands. (December 17, 1979)

Unlike our relatives who came to visit, we obviously never saw the village of Kuchino itself, but from their descriptions we knew that people lived in dire poverty there. There was even a joke about it among the inmates: we were not the only ones who carried the burden of incarceration—our camp administration did as well. Here is a description of the road leading to the camp, written by a former inmate, my friend Aleksei Smirnov:

> Chusovaia Creek is half the width of the Moskva River. Every few kilometers there is a hamlet. Many of the houses are in disrepair—the rooftops are caved in, the walls stand crooked, and the rain soaks the black beams. We all had to exit the bus because the driver refused to drive us any further; it was still five kilometers to Kuchino. We did manage to talk him into taking us further, and these last kilometers are the most difficult. The whole time, after each turn, you expect to finally see the buildings, the fences, and guard posts of the camp to emerge. Then, quite suddenly, we arrived at the gates of Perm Political Camp of Strict Regime VS-389/36. [10]

The *Chronicle* noted that in spring 1979, Chusovaia Creek flooded, and the administration had to save the camp from inundation:

> Camp 36 is situated by a river in very marshy surroundings. During this year's spring floods the camp was inundated—the water came to about knee height. The whole camp was evacuated to a nearby hilltop for a week. All the prisoners were kept together in one Army tent. They were guarded by soldiers with dogs, and a few days later a barbed-wire fence was erected.[11]

Curiously enough, being taken outside the camp didn't make an earth-shattering impression on me, and I have no special memories of that incident. So I was not surprised by what I later wrote to my sister, Nadiika: "Recently I

10 Aleksei Smirnov, "'La dumal, oni khuzhe,' (Poezdka v byvshii polit-lager')," *Fond Sozidanie*, September 5, 2001, https://web.archive.org/web/20071112184304/http://www.fondsozidanie.ru/old/21/5.htm.

11 *Chronicle*, 53:89.

had the opportunity to see a slice of a different world, which was not part of the camp, and believe me, I looked at it with complete indifference."

By contrast, the feelings I had toward some of the creatures that assisted the camp administration in torturing us were much stronger. They also got a certain amount of space dedicated to them in my letters:

> One thing that drives me crazy is mosquitoes. The sun is shining, and you could just lie there and enjoy the fresh air, but this "Egyptian scourge" considers you a bottomless, free supply of blood. Not long ago, I saw an enlarged photo of a mosquito head in a newspaper, and I thanked the Creator that this ugly creature only comes in microscopic form. (June 21, 1981)

> Likewise, it is not very easy for my fellow travelers, the mosquitoes. They have to replenish what they missed during the rains by sucking enough blood from us to qualify us for a medal as "Meritorious Blood Donors of the USSR." (June 12, 1983)

This was similar to the torments endured by previous generations of prisoners, like Metropolitan Slipyj: "During the summer, the mosquitoes and other tiny flies were a great nuisance. They would crawl into all our orifices and sting us mercilessly."[12]

Prisoner Profiles

It is difficult to divide the prisoners up even into rough categories because each category had its exceptions. To simplify, the zone was essentially divided into two major groups: those who behaved themselves and didn't cause the administration any problems, and those who rebelled and waged various protests. Consequently, each group was treated differently by the administration, and the rules were applied selectively. Obviously, each group had a broad range of different personality types within it, since each person is unique.

The first group included those who had been convicted for so-called war crimes. This included alleged Nazi collaborators, those who had worked in the auxiliary police, etc.[13] They had been convicted under Article 64 of the

12 Slipyi, *Spomyny*, 213.

13 Auxiliary police (Ger. *Ukrainische Hilfspolizei*): local police force established by the Nazis in 1941 in the Reichskommissariat Ukraine.

Criminal Code of the Russian SFSR, "treason against the Motherland," or analogous articles. These were mostly older people who did not oppose the administration, quietly behaved themselves, and were literally living out their last days. They were collectively called the "old timers" (*staryky*).

Among them were those who admired the dissidents and supported them whenever they could. I still have a certain sympathy for Ivan Braga, a Belarusian who was imprisoned because he had agreed to guard a German warehouse as a ten-year-old boy; and Ivan Dadonov, a Russian, who quietly looked after me in an almost paternal fashion. Aleksei Smirnov has offered a fair description of these supposed Nazi sympathizers: "Their incarceration is one of the most heinous and as yet unexamined crimes of the Soviet regime. There are real grounds to assume that, by and large, these people were innocent."[14]

It was from among those old timers, however, that the KGB often tried to recruit its spies. During the period when we were all sleeping on bunk beds, the bunk directly below me was occupied by a certain Baranov, who was undoubtedly reporting to the authorities on all my movements. He ingratiated himself to the KGB openly and with great relish; he belonged to the category of men who were referred to in the Gulag as "bitches." Around that time, Igor Guberman, the camp poet, even dedicated one of his poems to them:

There is no life without bitches,
And bitches are all around us,
If they should suddenly disappear,
We ourselves would have to turn into bitches.[15]

Still, there was a group of old timers who categorically refused to spy for the KGB and the camp administration. They even refused to write appeals asking for reprieves, and once in a while they participated in protest actions organized by the dissidents. This, however, didn't happen very often, and I think they considered some of those initiatives rather childish. These men had mainly been arrested for their participation in various national military

14 Aleksei Smirnov, "Vybor," *Nevolia* no. 31-2012, http://index.org.ru/nevol/2012-31/18-smirnov.html.

15 *Zhizn' ne obkhoditsia bez suk, / v nei suki s nami popolam, / i esli b ikh ne stalo vdrug, / prishlos' by ssuchivat'sia nam.* Igor' Guberman, "Zhizn' ne obkhoditsia bez suk," *Gariki na kazhdyi den'*, http://guberman.lib.ru/gariki/1KD/01_06.htm.

formations like the UPA or the Lithuanian "forest brothers" —people whom the war had touched in some way. [16] They were, naturally, older, finishing up twenty-five-year sentences. In this category I would include the Lithuanian Stasys Morkūnas, the Latvian Yury Būmeisters, and the Armenian Grigory Avakian.

Among the Ukrainians in this group, there were two men who served as examples to me as I tried to resolve my dilemma of whether I should become embittered or not—something I had once mentioned to my procurator in Kyiv. One of them was Pavlo Strotsen, a UPA fighter from the Ternopil area. His unwavering principles fused harmoniously with his natural goodness and optimism. This man amazed us all with his dignity and steadfastness.

The behavior of Onufry Kulak, another UPA fighter from the Ivano-Frankivsk region, was much different. He was also unwavering in his convictions, and he deserves respect and admiration for this. But his psyche was distorted by his hatred for the Soviet regime and its representatives. All you had to do was mention the guards, and Onufry's hands would start shaking, and he would curse them with the strongest words he could find. I could not but thank the Almighty for providing these two models for me, Strotsen and Kulak; I naturally gravitated toward the former. It was only a bit later that I opted definitively for his model, however.

The second major category, which was much more interesting and generally referred to as "the dissidents," was also diverse. It was mostly made up of younger people, those who had been incarcerated and charged as I was under the "political" article of the Soviet republics' criminal codes: "anti-Soviet agitation and propaganda, aimed at undermining the Soviet regime." In addition, there were also a few individuals who were not technically dissidents: they had been charged with treason, rather than anti-Soviet agitation. But the political motives behind their cases were obvious. Together, these men made up the majority of the militant segment of the camp's population and were the object of vigilant attention on the part of the KGB and the camp administration.

I will not distinguish between the two types of charges when discussing the members of this group because sometimes the prisoners charged with "anti-Soviet propaganda" were actually politically passive, while the "traitors to the Fatherland" were sometimes actively involved in political struggle. It all depended on the individual.

16 "Forest brothers": Baltic partisans engaged in guerrilla warfare against the Soviet Union, particularly between 1944 and 1953.

During the first year of my incarceration, my closest friends were mostly prisoners from Ukraine:

Yevhen Sverstiuk—a Ukrainian writer, one of the *shistdesiatnyky,* sentenced in Kyiv for preparing and distributing samizdat.

Ihor Kalynets—a Ukrainian poet, one of the *shistdesiatnyky,* sentenced in Lviv for writing and distributing "anti-Soviet" poetry.

Valery Marchenko—a Ukrainian journalist sentenced in Kyiv for preparing and distributing "anti-Soviet" materials.

Semen Gluzman—a Ukrainian-Jewish psychiatrist sentenced in Kyiv for conducting an independent psychiatric evaluation of General Petro Hryhorenko *in absentia*, which diagnosed the general as mentally healthy.

Yevhen Proniuk—a Ukrainian philosopher sentenced in Kyiv for "conducting anti-Soviet agitation and propaganda, intended to weaken and undermine the Soviet government."

Hryhory Prykhodko—a radio engineer from Dnipropetrovsk oblast sentenced in Kaluga for "conducting anti-Soviet agitation and propaganda, intended to weaken and undermine Soviet government."

Anatoly Zdorovy—a Ukrainian physicist sentenced in Kharkiv for his fight against Russification.

Oles Serhiienko—a Ukrainian mechanical engineer sentenced in Kyiv for editing Ivan Dziuba's essay "Internationalism or Russification?" He was Oksana Meshko's son.

Mykhailo Slobodian—a former police officer from Ivano-Frankivsk oblast sentenced for forming an underground organization whose members displayed the forbidden Ukrainian blue and yellow flag.

Aleksei Safronov—an ethnic Russian from Crimea.

Members of other Soviet republics were also included in this group:

Wolf (Zef) Zalmanson and Yosef Mendelevich—two Jews from Riga sentenced in the above-mentioned First Leningrad Trial.

Mikhail Kazachkov—a Jew from Leningrad sentenced for providing information to foreigners in order to facilitate his efforts to emigrate abroad.

Vladimir Balakhonov—an ethnic Russian and a Soviet UN diplomat in Geneva incarcerated for his unsuccessful attempt to request political asylum.

Šarūnas Žukauskas—a Lithuanian sentenced for his participation in the "ethnic studies" cultural movement in Kaunas.[17]

Kalju Mätik—an Estonian sentenced for his involvement in the Estonian democratic movement.

Artem Yuskevych—a Ukrainian living in Estonia sentenced for his involvement in the Estonian democratic movement.

I often spoke with Norair Grigorian, a former Armenian KGB agent who at some point grew tired of serving that hateful system and started spying for the Americans. I trusted him, seeing that he earnestly participated in some of our protest initiatives. But his KGB past obviously prevented him from making many friends in the zone.

Over time, the cohort of prisoners in the zone changed, as some of them, such as Ihor Kalynets, Yevhen Sverstiuk, Yevhen Proniuk, and several others, were sent to their internal exile, while others filled their places in the zone during 1979 and 1980:

Zenovy Krasivsky—a Ukrainian from Galicia sentenced for the fourth time—this time for his membership in the UHG.

Bohdan Klymchak—a Ukrainian convicted in Lviv for crossing the Soviet border in Central Asia.

Mykhailo Monakov—a Ukrainian from the Odesa region sentenced for showing caricatures of Brezhnev to his tourists while working as a guide.

---

17 Interest in national or ethnic studies of a particular minority group within the USSR was considered a manifestation of nationalism.

Oleksandr Zahirniak—a Ukrainian sentenced for attempting to hijack an airplane on its way from Petrozavodsk to Leningrad.

Sergei Kovalev—a Russian from Moscow convicted in Vilnius for his activities in defense of human rights.

Aleksandr Ogorodnikov—a Russian from Moscow sentenced for creating a samizdat magazine promoting the rebirth of Orthodoxy.

Yury Fedorov—a Russian from Leningrad, yet another member of the First Leningrad Trial.

Vadim Arenberg—a Jew from Leningrad convicted for his attempt to hijack an airplane to take him to Israel and then demand the liberation of Nathan Sharansky, Ida Nudel, and Vladimir Slepak, who had been arrested for their efforts to emigrate.

Leonid Lubman—a Jewish engineer from Leningrad sentenced for allegedly "revealing national secrets" during contact with foreigners.

Antanas Terlackas—a Lithuanian sentenced for his illicit participation in the National League for Lithuanian Liberation.[18]

Viktor Niitsoo—an Estonian incarcerated for his bold public statements of opposition.

For a while, Kovalev was the informal leader of our group. He had a keen sense of human rights issues and was familiar with all the legal mechanisms of defending human rights. No wonder that during his tenure the zone received a lot of coverage in the world media. Later, when he was transferred to the Chistopol prison, a new contingent of prisoners was delivered to the zone. Among them were:

18 Terlackas was one of around forty-five Soviet citizens from the Baltics who signed an appeal on the fortieth anniversary of the Molotov-Ribbentrop Pact (in 1979) asking the international community to "nullify the results" of the pact and "give the Baltic nations the right to self-determination." He was arrested soon after. *Chronicle,* 54:98.

Viktor Nekipelov—a Russian from Moscow sentenced for his human rights defense activities.

Oles Shevchenko—a Ukrainian convicted for his human rights defense activities.

Genrikh Altunian—an Armenian Ukrainian arrested in Kharkiv for the second time for his legal rights defense activities.

Mykola Rudenko—a Ukrainian from Kyiv sentenced in the Donetsk oblast for establishing the Ukrainian Helsinki Group.

They added new strength to the contingent of prisoners who initiated acts of resistance against the administration. For this, Viktor Nekipelov and Genrikh Altunian paid the price of being shipped to the Chistopol prison. Then more new faces appeared in camp, and those closest to me were:

Zorian Popadiuk—a Ukrainian from Galicia arrested for the second time on trumped-up charges of "anti-Soviet agitation and propaganda."

Aleksei Smirnov—a Russian from Moscow arrested for his legal rights defense activities.

Fr. Alfonsas Svarinskas—a Lithuanian priest arrested for the third time for his decisively nonconformist position and his membership in a Catholic organization that defended the rights of religious believers in Lithuania.

Ishkhan Mkrtchian—an Armenian arrested for organizing a youth opposition group.

Vardan Arutiunian—an Armenian arrested for participating in the Armenian national movement.

Tiit Madisson—an Estonian arrested for "anti-Soviet agitation and propaganda."

Vazha Zhgenti—a Georgian arrested for his participation in the Georgian liberation movement.

Boris Chernykh—a Russian writer from Siberia arrested for organizing an independent literary seminar in Irkutsk.

Every so often, Jonas Simokaitis from Lithuania; Appolony Bernychuk and Yury Zalepa from Ukraine; Dmitry Donskoi, Valentin Zasimov, Rostislav Yevdokimov, Aleksandr Nilov, Vitold Abankin, and Vladimir Yelchin from Russia; and Nuraddin Aliyev from Azerbaijan would all join us in some of our initiatives.

Considering that Ukrainians usually constituted the majority of the prisoners in the political camps, it is easy to understand why I didn't feel particularly homesick for Ukraine. Everything dear to my heart was close at hand, even "our" Ukrainian KGB! It was also important for me that eventually Mykola Rudenko ended up in our camp, though not right away. By then he understood that the suspicions he had harbored against me had been unfounded, and my behavior in camp confirmed this. Thus, our relationship was uncomplicated from the start, and eventually it became truly cordial. His former suspicions were never brought up.

The zone was a virtual Soviet Babel, and so it was difficult to categorize some of the people there. My barrack mate, for example, Petro Chorny, a mathematics teacher from Kirovohrad oblast in central Ukraine, kept a distance from all our dissident activities. And yet, in spite of his aloofness, no one ever suspected him of collaborating with the KGB. His incarceration for the "preparation of anti-Soviet materials" serves as yet another example of the crimes of the system: Chorny was just a lone thinker trying to conceptualize the world in an unusual way. His arrest probably got some KGB opportunist an extra star on his uniform.

On the whole, I had close ties with the Ukrainians in the zone. I had a trusting relationship with Hryhory Prykhodko, whom my mother always mentioned with much gratitude. As it turns out, after his liberation he contacted my mother and told her all about me in great detail. I also had a friendly, trusting relationship with Mykhailo Monakov. He did not take part in any active confrontations with the authorities, but at the same time, he waged the most important battle in camp: the struggle to remain an honest person. The young Russian Dmitry Donskoi and the Estonian Tiit Madisson, about whom I have nothing but pleasant memories, also behaved in a similar fashion.

Two of the Russians, Igor Ogurtsov, a committed monarchist from Leningrad, and Grigory Isaev from Kuibyshev (now Samara), a zealous fighter for pure Leninist ideals, presented the greatest challenges for us run-of-the-mill dissidents. They ended up in camp at different times, both for their criticism of the current government. So, in this respect they were both on our side. But their goals were something we could never share.

Ogurtsov dreamed of the restoration of the Romanov dynasty, while Isaev hoped to restore the Soviet government to its former "ideal" version of early Bolshevism. They participated in most of our initiatives, as long as there were no ideological implications that they found unacceptable. Generally speaking, they served out their terms with dignity, though at one point, against all our warnings, Isaev tried to get into a game of complicity with the KGB; in the process, he almost compromised his credibility in the camp. Toward the end of my term an even more exotic prisoner arrived in the zone: Vladimir Yelchin. He was an opera singer from the depths of Russia. I was captivated by his baritone, but he, like any professional, was not very keen to demonstrate his talents.

Given the harsh camp conditions, it would have been strange if none of the prisoners developed certain *idées fixes*. For example, Vladimir Balakhonov was convinced that the administration was endangering the prisoners by making the cooks add special pharmaceutical substances into our food that would later lead to hemorrhoids or dysentery, exposing us to additional torture. Likewise, Leonid Lubman was convinced that the KGB was penetrating his thoughts with the aid of radio waves. In his memoirs, Yosef Mendelevich quotes phrases that we often heard from Mr. Lubman: "And then those monsters started torturing me again. A radio receiver was mounted into my upper jaw, transmitting radio signals that cause a toothache. Then they provoked diarrhea. They are doing this because I am revealing all this to you. But I cannot remain silent; it is my civic duty!"[19] Another prisoner, Jonas Simokaitis, kept finding evidence of KGB provocations against him. Once he claimed that during the night someone had poured water into his shoes. I can still hear his shouts of complaint the next morning.

I would like to emphasize that there was nothing unusual about these complaints. The punitive system in the camp was so all-encompassing that the human psyche could not always cope with it. In such cases, a person needs simple answers that bring psychological comfort and comprehensibility, providing answers to virtually all stressful situations. In mentioning these cases, therefore, I certainly do not want to denigrate my camp colleagues. For example, Aleksei Smirnov had some laudatory words for Leonid Lubman:

> In camp he was an exemplary prisoner—really compassionate. He never squealed on anyone. During his transfers he "walked" [from one camp to the

19 Iosef Mendelevich, "Operatsiia 'Svad'ba'," *Istoriia Evreiskogo Naroda*, http://jhist.org/zion/zion008_08.htm.

next] empty-handed, with just a small satchel, never accumulating any extra junk. He would send all the guards to hell (or even further). He never got out of the ShIZO—he had accumulated well over a year in the *kartser*. He never crossed the line in prison, and he always dreamed about America—and now he is dying there of a grave illness.[20]

The Camp Administration and Guards

The sixty of us "especially dangerous state criminals" were guarded by seven layers of barbed wire and apparently some 120 guards and administrative personnel. Given these measures, who could ever doubt that these "criminals" were "especially dangerous"? No wonder Oleksa Tykhy wrote ironically in one of his letters, "They are guarding us very efficiently—no chance that anyone could steal us."[21]

The camp commander was a certain Major Zhuravkov, and his deputy was Major Fedorov, both Russians. Often they played good cop/bad cop, with Fedorov in the latter role. They could not have switched parts because Zhuravkov was not malicious enough by nature. Of course, he performed all his expected duties diligently, often doing despicable things. But you got the feeling that it didn't bring him any pleasure.

At that time, the head of the special regime division was Major Dolmatov.[22] After Zhuravkov died, Dolmatov became the director of the entire Camp 36, but he did not live very long either. Zhuravkov's and Dolmatov's names will forever be associated with the Ukrainian poet Vasyl Stus because it was during their tenure that the poet died there. It is obvious that the Communist powers-that-be committed crimes against the Ukrainian poet: during the night of September 4, 1985, Stus died in an isolation cell in the VS-389/36 special regime concentration camp.

In contrast to Zhuravkov, Fedorov was the devil incarnate. Never before or since have I ever met a person who exuded such deep-rooted satanic evil as he did. This man was a classic sadist: he derived obvious satisfaction from

20 *Kartser* means "punishment cell"; Aleksei Smirnov, "Lageria 80-kh," (Personal website of Aleksei Smirnov), http://gendirector1.blogspot.com/p/80-1982-6.html.

21 *Oleksa Tykhyi*, 121.

22 Camp VS 389/36 contained prisoners who were assigned to both "strict" and "special" regimes. The latter section was designated VS 389/36-1.

Figure 5.3. The Chusovoi camp cemetery.

the suffering of others. He would periodically burst into the zone looking for prey like a vampire searching for an exposed vein on his victim's neck. There were rumors that he had once been the director of a women's colony but had to be dismissed for overstepping his professional duties. One shudders at the thought of what those excesses might have been. Oksana Meshko shared this dread because she witnessed what occurred at the hospital of the women's camp in Ukhta, northern Russia: "I saw such merciless depravity, virtually an open cesspool, and I was astonished at the depth of human debauchery, when a human being loses its semblance to God, and stands naked, facing the fear of dying, desperately trying to survive at any cost."[23]

My opinion of Fedorov was shared by many other prisoners. This is how a group of political prisoners from Camp VS-389/35 (where Fedorov also worked for a time) characterized him, based on the research done by Yury Orlov, Mykola Matusevych, Petras Pluiras-Plumpa, Valery Marchenko, and Zynovy Antoniuk (they managed to get their work out to the free world, and it was published in samizdat; henceforth I will refer to it as the Orlov group research): "Major Fedorov is perhaps the cruelest of all the

23 *Ne vidstupliusia!*, 35.

tyrants in the Soviet political camp system; he personally meted out most of the punishments."[24]

In his memoirs, Norair Grigorian cites an interesting item about Fedorov: "By some miracle, the Armenian Grigory Avakian managed to procure some seeds to grow nutritious plants, and he planted them in a work area near the boiler room where he worked. At one point, Major Fedorov discovered these plants and trampled them with his boots. And with that yet another example of 'transgression against the regime' was discovered and destroyed."[25]

It was Yevhen Sverstiuk, however, who finally pinned the tyrant to a pillar of disgrace. In order to convey the appropriate effect, his entire letter should be quoted, especially since it has never been published:

> October 14, 2002
>
> To the Attention of Major Fedorov:
>
> Citizen Fedorov! Sorry, but I don't know your first name and patronymic. It was never used at work.
>
> Do you remember this prisoner, who was in your Kuchino Camp 36 in the 1970s? Surely you remember Yevhen Sverstiuk. He was held under double and exceptional surveillance—both by the KGB and by the camp administration.
>
> And I certainly do remember you, not because we were many and you were only one. The "children of many nations," who departed for Ukraine, Armenia, Lithuania, Estonia, Israel, France, and America, all remember you. They left, and they took your tyrannical image with them.
>
> Apparently you made a smooth transition into our "democratic state," avoiding Nuremberg, a confession, the gallows' noose, or any other symbols of contrition conjured up "over there in the West." Apparently you have convinced yourself that penal systems have always existed and always will.
>
> But we remember you as a diligent and inventive tormentor, for whom the rules of the regime were just a pretext and license to destroy life and separate it from everything that is humane. To undermine, abandon, compel, force, deprive, and confiscate: these were the notions that constantly flitted through your head and glinted from your eyes.

---

24 "O polozhenii zakliuchennykh v lageriakh SSSR," *Dokumenty Moskovskoi Khel'sinskoi Gruppy (1976–1982)*, ed. D. I. Zubarev and G. V. Kuzovkin (Moscow: Moskovskaia Khel'sinskaia Gruppa, 2006), 362.

25 Norair Grigorian, "Vospominaniia," 2015, https://www.facebook.com/groups/312182498867001/permalink/804836596268253/, 20.

Remember how I once tried to bring you down to a normal human level by asking you: "Major, what day is it today?" The day was Wednesday, and we both knew it, but all the same, you decided to lie, and said Thursday, just so that you could spoil the game of an "enemy of the people."

You even regarded our mothers, sisters, and wives as enemies, and looked at them with one harsh thought: search them.

In the springtime, when a prisoner could hardly drag his feet, that's when you would come to life. Do you remember how one evening you were told that the prisoners had taken to drinking birch sap? There were plenty of birches to go around. You and your lieutenants swept down on us like a typhoon, shouting: "I will give you something to drink! I will." They did not chop the birches down, of course, but they did put them under security, and our cups were confiscated.

Major, do you remember our triumphant farewell? You had been preparing for it. About half a month before the end of my term, you slated me for a transfer, and I was brought to your office. The guards and the officers were all there in full force, including the physician and the camp barber. And then you, Major, triumphantly told me that you had decided to give me fifteen days in solitary confinement for my "systematic disruption of the regime." The physician had been asked to monitor the show you then staged. Everyone was waiting. Then you gave the order: "Shave him!" The lieutenants stood with handcuffs, waiting for me to resist. And you were clearly expecting a violent reaction from me. Coming from you, Major, that command sounded like a combat officer's battle cry: "Fire!" This was your attempt to provoke me, demonstrating disregard for the rules. The rules were not to shave a prisoner two or three months prior to his release.

And that's when I spoiled the show for you, Major. I sat down just like one normally sits in a barber's chair and then silently went off to my solitary confinement.

You had hoped to deprive the prisoner of the one privilege that was still left to him, but it turns out that it no longer had any value for me.

At that moment I saw a spark of something almost human in your eyes: confusion.

I saw similar bewilderment when you burst into our barrack to squelch our opposition, but we then declared a hunger strike.

"Aren't you even going to protect your health?"

"What for?" I replied.

"What do you mean, what for? You have to live!" you proclaimed in a weird voice.

"Why?"

And then I saw in your eyes a tyrannical feebleness.

You know, later I once went back to visit "our" zone and was amazed that there was nothing left of the seven layers of barbed wire. No doubt it took a lot of work to remove and destroy the tons of metal. It looks like there must have been a moment when you actually expected to be brought before a court of justice, and once again you felt a sense of confusion. But it passed.

The birch trees and everything else stand there, but without any guards, and such deterioration and weeds reign in your fiefdom that your favorite penal domain is scarcely recognizable.

The same devastation exists in your soul, Major. Everything turned out to be worthless weeds! But the evil, Citizen Major, that has permeated your soul, and which you inflicted upon those who were wounded by fate, this destructive evil has been forever tied to your name.

I don't think there is any need for a hangman's noose. You carry it in your memory. It will always be with you, even if they grant you the rank of Colonel.

It's a pity, of course, that hardships have not brought you to repentance. Certainly the soul God gave you is just like the one I have, and everyone else. May God forgive you for not acknowledging that precious gift . . .

And we—I am convinced that my thoughts and feelings are shared by all former prisoners—we forgive you.

But for justice's sake you should be left there, in Camp 36, all by yourself with your memories, as a relic. You should reflect and make an accounting—remembering everything that you did and to whom.

October 14, 2002
Yevhen Sverstiuk
Kyiv, Ukraine[26]

Another camp commander—an unofficial one, though nevertheless very real and often the most important—was the relatively young KGB Captain Surovtsev. He was responsible for all ideological aspects of the camp, and in those days, ideology permeated everything. Not only did Surovtsev come from the Ternopil oblast, but he also spoke flawless Ukrainian with his fellow countrymen. I suspect that the KGB thought that this would foster trust among the Ukrainian political prisoners. All feelings of kinship vanished, however, when you made sense of what this "compatriot" was saying. For example, once, Surovtsev told me that the number of letters I would receive "depended on my behavior"—in other words, my readiness to collaborate with the KGB. Several decades earlier, Patriarch Josyf Slipyj aptly described

26 This letter was taken from the personal archive of Vasyl Ovsiienko. It is being published for the first time in English.

this sort of "compatriot": "Generally speaking, guards from Galicia could not be surpassed in their treachery and brutality. They were real turncoats."[27] Surovtsev was a faithful servant of the Soviet regime who, as I learned after my release, went to live in Moscow after fulfilling his duty in the camps, not having the guts to return to independent Ukraine. That's not very surprising, since he had been in the zone during Vasyl Stus's murder.

Captains, known as "scheduled assistants to the camp commander" (Rus. *dezhurnye pomoshchniki nachal'nika kolonii*), comprised the rest of the camp administration team. During my time, this included Dolmatov (later promoted to major), Chepkasov, Chugainov, Rak, Galedin, task force leader Rozhkov, and deputy political leader Nikomarov. There were also some *praporshchiki*, among whom I remember Novytsky, Chertanov, Kukushkin, Samokar, and Makhmudov.[28] (Vasyl Ovsiienko's memoirs list more names.) Several of them will appear later as the "heroes" of my stories, so here I will just mention that the spectrum of compassion (or rather the lack thereof) they showed was extremely broad.

One time, I was "lucky" enough to witness how quickly human dignity can be destroyed. The door of the cell where I was sitting together with some other prisoners was opened by a young new warrant officer from Ukraine. He demanded something of us, claiming that he was ordered to do so. Sergei Kovalev asked him, "What if they tell you to kill us, will you do that too?" The lad lowered his head and said "No." We got scared for him: what if some of his colleagues had overheard this? Then, a few months later, while processing me for solitary confinement, the same officer along with two others stripped me naked and pitilessly made me take off my warm underwear and put on a skimpy robe, even though it was winter. Our young lad, together with the others, was mocking me, thoroughly enjoying his unlimited power. The transformation of his humanity was really striking.

I remember that one of the officers got on Yevhen Sverstiuk's nerves to such an extent that he shouted at him: "I had no idea that something in human guise could stoop this low!" The camp is a testament to the fact that there is no such thing as the lowest rung.

It goes without saying that I mostly think of the officers, or *menty* (cops) as we called them, in a negative light. But in all fairness, it must be said that

---

27 Slipyi, *Spomyny*, 221.

28 *Praporshchik*: military rank falling between officer and noncommissioned officer, akin to a warrant officer.

not all of them had lost their humanity. First among these was the Russian Sergei Sviridov, whom Genrikh Altunian described best:

> I remember one unusual incident regarding communications with the prisoners. Once, on the evening of January 4, 1982, Viktor Nekipelov, Sasha Ogorodnikov, Mykola Rudenko and I were sitting in the internal colony prison, when the door opened, and a young guard, Sergei Sviridov, walked in and asked us to follow him to the duty room. [. . .]
>
> The four of us walked into the duty room and were amazed: The windows were shuttered, the room was flooded with light, and the table was laden with a large skillet full of fried potatoes, a chunk of butter, some cucumbers, and a bottle of vodka. As it turned out, Sviridov had invited us for his birthday. We had a wonderful time, not worrying that someone might catch us. The ShIZO is completely isolated from the rest of the zone, and it locks from within, so no one can enter it from the outside. [. . .]
>
> [Sviridov] would always help us whenever he could. His kindness came back to haunt him, however. At some point, [the prisoner] Aleksandr Ogorodnikov asked him for a Russian-English dictionary, a thick volume by Muller. This dictionary was discovered during one of the daily prison searches and they suspected that it had bypassed a censorship inspection. One of the guards remembered seeing the book in Sviridov's quarters. It would certainly have been very difficult for him to procure this book in Chusovoi [a town near the camp] or even in Perm, but this only spared him from a tribunal. Sviridov was no longer permitted to hang out with us, and shortly thereafter he was transferred to serve in another location.[29]

I also remember the one and only deal that I made with a *praporshchik*, when I was in the PKT (*Rus. pomeshchenie kamernogo tipa*, camp prison) for the second time in mid-1979. We were going hungry at the time, and with the aid of this guard, I sent a letter to Halia Levkova, a Russian-speaking friend in Lviv with whom I had studied at the Polytechnic Institute. I asked her to convey a message to my family asking them to send me a food parcel, giving her the appropriate address. As I had hoped, Halia turned out to be a trustworthy friend and passed my letter on to my family, so about a month later I received a portion of my parcel from the guard.

Obviously, the entire administration—from the camp commander down to the lowest guard—officially considered us criminals and slanderers. This was the rhetoric they used when testing themselves and checking their own

29 Genrikh Altunian, *Tsena svobody: Vospominaniia dissidenta* (Kharkiv: Folio, 2000), 160–62.

ideological views. But fate granted me a unique opportunity to hear what task force leader Rozhkov really thought. As I strolled around the camp, I witnessed a peculiar scene: Sergei Kovalev, in the presence of many other prisoners, was arguing with the task force leader about the UPA. Seeing me approaching, Rozhkov gestured for me to come closer so I could serve as an arbiter in their argument. He said, "Here comes Marynovych, and he will not allow any lies." This was how he described a "criminal slanderer"! Even today, I consider this moment a quintessential victory over my overseers. He gave me a glimpse of something that had never been revealed and confirmed that at least some of our oppressors were fully aware that they were dealing with innocent people—in other words, they knew perfectly well what they were doing.

Camp Life and the Daily Schedule

We were woken up at 6 a.m. every day, and the duty officers and guards took churlish pleasure in catching anyone who lingered in bed for even a moment. It goes without saying that they only targeted those who had not "embarked on the path of correction" (i.e., repented and become cooperative)—this gave them an additional pretext to punish them. A carelessly made bed served the same function. During these inspections, Captain Rak, a Ukrainian, took particular pleasure in this sort of harassment.

Not much time was allotted for morning ablutions because the general inspection started at 6:35 on the dot. Obviously, being late for inspection also merited additional punishment. I learned that in some camps they held "curative" calisthenics set to typical bombastic Soviet march tunes. I don't remember if we had calisthenics in Zone 36—I suspect not.

In the strict regime, camp convicts' uniforms were not striped, as one might expect. Such garb is worn in the "special regime" zones. For us it was solid dirty gray, and the only "embellishment" was our nametags. For hats we were given the so-called cardinal's hat (*kardynal's'ka shapka*).[30] In the winter everyone wore quilted coats and hats with earflaps.

We all walked to breakfast in formation. After breakfast, we again formed lines and walked back to the barracks in step. At 7:25 all convicts had to gather by the gate leading to the work zone. Here there was a roll call, and every prisoner had to pass through a shack where the guards dutifully frisked

30 Cardinal's hat: named for its resemblance to a Vatican official's skullcap

everyone. Overall, there were at least four inspections every day: entering the work zone every morning, leaving for lunch, returning again after lunch, and then finally at the end of the workday.

Eventually you get used to this ritual, as one gets used to their morning toilette. If something happens, and you don't get patted down, you feel as if something is missing. One time while in the work zone, I decided to write yet another "malicious slander that vilified the Soviet administrative and civic order." I put the piece of paper into my pocket and forgot about it. During the search, the guard felt the paper, took it out, and asked me unenthusiastically, "So what do we have here?" I looked, and a chill went through me, but I caught myself. "Oh, that's nothing!" I said, as I grabbed the paper out of his hands, stuffed it into my mouth, and carefully chewed it up. I must have looked totally absurd because the guard burst out laughing and just waved me on. Now I understand how lucky I was that time. Perhaps there was a certain languidness in the air because other camp accounts report a different outcome: "D. Hrynkiv was thrown into the isolation cell for chewing up his notes in front of a guard—that is, 'resisting a representative of the administration.'"[31]

I no longer remember when lunch started and how long it lasted. Nor do I remember when they took us from work back to the residential zone. I do remember that the workday was eight hours long, six days a week. I will talk about the working conditions a little later.

For a certain period in 1979, the administration tested out a new work schedule. The new system differed by the addition of ten minutes' "preparation time" before breakfast, before being led to work, and before work itself. Officially they justified it by saying that the older prisoners needed more time to get ready. In reality, the goal was to shorten the free time in the evening, which the administration thought the prisoners used in an "unauthorized manner." According to the new schedule, the workday ended two hours later. Mykola Horbal best described the end of the workday: "At the close of work, the atmosphere was quite a bit more animated than at the start. The promise of rest and sleep, hope of a letter from the outside, and the anticipation of some good news added a certain euphoria to one's attitude. In this deep isolation from the outside world, the zone was like a large sensitive membrane."[32]

31 "O polozhenii zakliuchennykh," 365.

32 Horbal', *Prezentatsiia zhyttia*, 219.

For a certain period, between dinner and the evening inspection, at around 6:30 p.m. they organized political lectures for the prisoners; skipping them would result in severe punishment. This was an old Gulag tradition, which had also annoyed Patriarch Josyf Slipyj: "They organized lessons in Communism, and you had to attend them and listen to some nonsense from ignorant idiots."[33] The political prisoners waged a lengthy war to have these political lectures stopped, and eventually they succeeded. Their success was not due to the wishes of the prisoners who could not stand this primitive harangue: more importantly, the administration did not like them either. It was nerve wracking for them to conduct these political lectures in front of prisoners who ripped apart every word coming out of the lecturer's mouth. The prisoners delighted in mocking the unconvincing Soviet ideological slogans, showering the lecturer with sarcastic comments, or backing him into a corner with pointed questions. After such verbal flagellations, the lecturer often left drenched in sweat and without any burning desire to return.

Our after-work free time was divided between discussions, penning secret missives to the free world (or the "big zone," as we usually called it), reading books and periodicals, and later watching TV news. Even then, as Valery Marchenko remembers, the camp administration did everything in its power to keep us from being bored:

> Credit is due to the genius of the Soviet concentration camp: personal searches several times a day, confiscation of petitions to higher authorities as well as all writings found on the prisoners, and even gynecological inspections of our wives and mothers who would come to visit us, all thoroughly filled up the prisoners' days. Prisoners who collaborated with the KGB and the political task force chief were recruited to gather and prepare information on those who were under suspicion.[34]

We would talk either in our barracks or out in the open. Prisoners could walk around the residential zone freely, and by the time I arrived at the zone, there was a walking path that the prisoners had worn down (ironically referred to as the "Ho Chi Minh Trail"). We were forbidden to visit other people in their barracks, however. We obviously all violated this rule and duly paid the price.

Evening hours were like "post-graduate studies" for us, full of intense work on our own personal growth and our intellectual development. Liberated

---

33 Slipyi, *Spomyny*, 225.

34 "O polozhenii zakliuchennykh," 361.

from daily chores, the prisoners dove into textbooks and manuals. After the suffocating Brezhnev era, free and unrestricted conversations were a great treat. After all, everyone had already been punished for his freethinking, so there wasn't much more to fear. You can only imagine the discussions that blazed among us, how high our thoughts would soar, and how many lofty ideas and remarkable stories were given voice on the Ho Chi Minh Trail. All freethinking prisoners really savored this unique part of the camp. To confirm this, I will cite just one comment made by Yevhen Sverstiuk:

> The concept of intellectual fortitude and independence was only considered sinful and impossible by those who had latched on to Marx's and Lenin's words, like a blind man clinging onto a pole. This notion was cultivated both in the zone and in prison. It is here that you can see the rift between the prisoners of conscience, i.e. people who answer to their conscience, and the lackeys, who constantly make compromises with their conscience.[35]

Those dissident discussions were remarkable because we were all united in refusing to accept the Soviet realities of the day. We were united in our total rejection of Communist, totalitarian, imperialist, and atheist rule—except for a few, such as the monarchist Igor Ogurtsov. But whenever the conversation turned to how our eventually liberated countries should be constructed, our ideas and ideological positions would diverge. In camp this was accepted as normal because you had already paid for the right to your personal opinion by your incarceration; it was therefore considered an inalienable right. It was only in the 1990s, in the early days of Ukraine's independence, that it came to be considered a negative that a difference in viewpoint meant that the dissidents could not emerge as a single consolidated opposition force.

In a political camp, there was no greater offense than harboring a piece of paper that had been meticulously scribbled on. Every such piece of paper was seen as harboring the "crime of anti-Sovietness" and was therefore confiscated immediately for further scrutiny. The prisoners, in turn, tried to produce as many such little notes as possible. Early on, I was enlisted into the "holy of holies" of camp life, preparing information for the *Chronicle of Current Events*. This was an expression of complete trust in me because only the most trustworthy individuals were recruited for this task. When I arrived at the zone, the team included Yevhen Sverstiuk, Semen Gluzman, Yevhen Proniuk, Aleksei Safronov, Hryhory Prykhodko, and several others.

35 Ievhen Sverstiuk, *Na khvyliakh "Svobody": Korotki esei* (Lutsk: BMA 'Teren', 2004), 198.

They not only chronicled events in camp but also drafted a variety of other texts, such as appeals, petitions, etc. This was a skillfully constructed conveyor belt, which the KGB never managed to deal with effectively. Semen Gluzman described it well: "We, the hungry, the persecuted, the gray, lived for the Word: the Word of pain and truth that we were able to dispatch into the world."[36] He remembers that Ivan Svitlychny jokingly dubbed this writing factory a "PEN Club."

Our sacred mission was to transmit information on the prevailing conditions in Soviet concentration camps to the West. We took this mission seriously, and objectivity was paramount in describing events; we expressed our emotions only in our own personal accounts. We were convinced that the truth about the crimes of the Soviet system would inevitably serve as a nail in its own coffin. At the same time, however, we didn't have much hope for salvation from the West. There was a popular saying in camp: "The British Queen will not declare war on the USSR over this."

The greatest credit for the *Chronicle* in Zone 36 goes to Mary, the cat. She turned out to be the ideal sentry. She would show up for "work" in the morning; she favored the same "Lenin Room" that the *Chronicle* writers occupied in their free time. Her ability to sniff out a guard was amazing. I have no idea how she knew, but as soon as a guard would leave his hut (some thirty to forty meters away), our kitty would immediately start stressing out, even if she had been totally quiet prior to that, sitting or curled up in a ball asleep. Her anxiety signaled that a guard had left his post, so it was necessary to immediately hide what we were writing. At some point, however, Mary unfortunately disappeared without a trace.

It goes without saying that we monitored all political news carefully and diligently, and our discussions about it were lively and emotional. We would often spot legal issues that we had previously overlooked, and we shared our observations with each other. I remember how disappointed I was when I heard about the Iranian revolution in 1978–1979. It was not so much the revolution itself as the ineffectiveness of the US State Department that bothered me. Exactly a week prior to the insurrection, they had issued a report stating that everything was under control in Iran and that the Shah's rule was not in jeopardy. And then a few days later came the revolution that changed the face of the whole Muslim world.

This incident taught me to be skeptical of any conspiracy theory: that somewhere in Shangri-La, or Washington, or Israel, or anywhere else in the

36 Gluzman, *Risunki po pamiati*, 15.

world, there is a group of people allegedly controlling world events. The Iranian incident proved that it's impossible to have a group of people anywhere on the planet that could plot world events with 100 percent accuracy. I do understand that attempts of this kind have occurred, but in the end, people always find themselves helpless before the will of God. For me, therefore, the Almighty is the sole creator of history.

During good weather in the summer, the younger prisoners would come together on the volleyball court. My memories of this have completely evaporated, so I was surprised to read about it when I recently browsed through my letters:

> On sunny days, we all tromped around on the volleyball court. I, of course had to go and sprain my big toe, and now I've been limping around for a week. (June 21, 1981)

> I am fine; still hitting the volleyball. Today we even formed two teams: those over 40, and "those whose whiskers are yet to sprout." (July 21, 1982)

> I am healthy and doing well, and I'm still playing volleyball almost every day. But I'm dealing with radiculitis—that damned thorn is rearing its ugly head again. Shameless! So why am I even bothering to play volleyball? (August 8, 1982)

> While playing volleyball, I sprained my right thumb. (July 10, 1983)

In my case, free time also meant that I could sing a bit. For a while, there was an accordion in the zone, and I would play it to experience a typical Ukrainian catharsis. By singing nostalgic Ukrainian folk songs, including some based on Shevchenko's poetry, I could cleanse my soul and gaze at God's world as if the sun had emerged again after the rain. Sometimes appreciative listeners would gather around. I remember that Yury Būmeisters, the old Latvian, loved to listen to my singing. He was moved by those sentimental Ukrainian songs. In July 1982 when Vladimir Yelchin, the conservatory-trained opera singer with a strong and resonant baritone, arrived in the zone from the depths of Russia, Būmeisters remained jealously loyal to my unsophisticated singing over the vocally refined opera singer.

About halfway through my term, a TV arrived in the zone. It was mostly the guards who got to enjoy it, but once in a while we also got our turn. We would listen to the *Vremia* evening news, and from that we often learned

Figure 5.4. With Yury Būmeisters in Riga, 1988.

fascinating things—such as the deadly hunger strike by a group of Irish political prisoners, ten of whom died in HM Prison Maze in Northern Ireland in 1981. We listened to such news with an understandable amount of empathy.

I also remember funny moments during the 1982 World Cup in Spain. The second matches of the day were aired after our curfew, so we tried to make a deal with the duty guards to get permission to watch them as an exceptional favor. We didn't always succeed, but since Captain Rak was an avid soccer fan, he was the one most likely to let us watch, provided we had not staged any protest actions that day. The funny thing was that we were not able to show any emotion. Obviously we were pulling for anyone except the Soviet team, but we certainly could not show any joy when they were losing to a "capitalist team" or express any distress when they scored a goal because we would instantly be ousted from the room. All we could do was to silently glance at each other in triumph or in disappointment, or shake hands, as long as the guards didn't see us. It turned out that we had to shake hands often, and in my letter to my family dated March 13, 1982, my words were rather pessimistically foreboding: "I even watched soccer, the World Cup, and once again, I became aware of a simple reality: that the team I'm rooting for invariably loses."

To my amazement, I discovered that the zone was not necessarily just a place of tragedy and suffering. We laughed and joked, and poked fun at each other, and mercilessly made fun of the guards. The young and healthy prisoners were particularly full of *joie de vivre*; the ailing ones, understandably, were not up to it. These feelings were even mentioned in my letters home: "Since a person cannot live without emotions, I also experience some joy here and I feel it just as strongly as you do there" (September 1, 1983).

For some reason, I remember one particularly shrewd and friendly prank that brought much joy to the young jokesters, particularly Sashko Zahirniak. A sleeping prisoner would be abruptly woken up and told, "So-and-so told me to wake you up because you have to go pee. I told him that it's not necessary. Am I right?" The crux of the prank lay in the fact that in order to comprehend this convoluted phrase, you had to be fully awake. The victim was seized with rage, and then the pranksters would burst out laughing.

Curfew sounded at 10 p.m., and that's when the guards started hunting for those who might have "violated the regime" by not being in their beds or who had gotten up for a nighttime conversation. The *Chronicle* recorded one of my violations after my release from the ShIZO, and now I don't know how I can redeem myself before humanity for such a transgression: on November 10, 1978, I "was reprimanded for eating after lights out, and for being rude to Captain Chugainov."[37] Oftentimes, when the guards needed to fulfill their quota of rule breakers, they would turn the light off a few minutes early and then write up everyone who was caught out of bed.

Sunday was a free day, and for that we had the Communist Party to thank. They certainly could have taken it away, as they did in the gulags in the 1940s. On Sunday, the "sheared folk" (i.e., the prisoners) were somewhat reinvigorated, and everything looked as Oksana Meshko described it: "It was always quiet in the zone, except for the seventh day, when the Almighty and the prisoners rested, and then the zone would become a bit more animated."[38]

37 *Chronicle*, 51:80.

38 *Ne vidstupliusia!*, 54.

Chapter Six

In the Vise of the Strict Regime

Camp Food

Food was prepared by a special team of prisoner-cooks assigned to this work duty. I am certain that our cooks, like the Lithuanian Antanas Terlackas, did everything possible to prepare meals that were more or less edible, given the ingredients they had access to. Obviously, that was not an easy task. Luckily, the *Chronicle of Current Events* recorded some notes that provide a good overall picture. Here are just three illustrations:

> [Based on M. Kiirend's report to the Executive Committee of the Soviet Societies of the Red Cross and the Red Crescent, dated December 31, 1977.] Kiirend gives a table, which he composed, based on the official food menus. It indicates the average quantity of food which a prisoner receives daily. The author takes into account the fact that the prisoner actually receives even less than this, as part of the food is inedible. Kiirend concludes from his calculations: "The energy deficiency is 436 calories, or 15%; the protein deficiency is 27.2%, the figure for animal protein being 68%; the fats deficiency is 64%, and that of mineral salt is 53%; the following vitamins are deficient: Vitamin A (100%), Keratin (78%), Vitamin B1 (8%), B2 (47%), PP (48%), C (63%)."[1]

> 11 June [1979]: Inedible food in the refectory. Mass food poisoning. Six people were sent to hospital.[2]

1 *Chronicle*, 51:95.

2 *Chronicle*, 52:33.

> In October and November [1978] the quality of the food deteriorated; the choice of groats was limited, and out of the kinds of fish prescribed for supper the prisoners were almost always given so-called herring, which disintegrates as soon as it is cleaned. As reported above, large worms were found in the food on several occasions. Fat disappeared from the shop; for two months only about 200 grams of margarine per prisoner were sold.[3]

There is a humorous story associated with the aforementioned worms: having discovered them in our bowls, we summoned Captain Rak, who was on duty that day. He lifted the spoon containing the worms that we had collected as "material evidence," popped them into his mouth and chewed them up, and announced: "Those are not worms, that's porridge!" He destroyed our "libelous evidence." The whole zone had a lot of fun with that.

Interestingly enough, I later learned from Semen Gluzman's memoirs that this sort of "self-sacrifice" on the part of our guards had not been unusual; it also occurred in Zone 35:

> During such rotten dinners, we would normally just eat the gruel and then leave. One time Valery [Marchenko], without telling anyone at the table, placed some rotten green fish on a piece of newspaper and took it to the camp headquarters, where a KGB officer was holding a briefing. He offered it to him as a snack. A few minutes later the camp duty officer, Patskov, together with a witless physician and a KGB officer, entered our dining hall. Assessing the situation, officer Patskov and the physician said that they should also like to try this fish, and then quietly devoured it. Valery, who was present at this spectacle, loudly remarked: "This is what it means to be infinitely loyal to the Communist Party! Here's a beautiful example of real Communists' fortitude and lack of disgust!"[4]

My youth and good health had their benefits. I digested this food quietly, considering the impoverished portions as a sort of ascetic diet. I even joked about it in one of my letters to my family:

> I would like to tell you about a quote from the magazine *Za Rubezhom* (From Abroad) about some American scholars' research. I found it so funny that I thought you should get to be amused as well: "The long-term restriction of food portions remains the only way one can delay aging." There is no evil that does not turn out for the best! (September 30, 1982)

---

3 *Chronicle*, 51:81.

4 Gluzman, *Risunki po pamiati*, 180–81.

Those prisoners who had a weak stomach fared the worst. For example, Zenovy Krasivsky could not eat food that contained any onions, while for others this was a treat. Thus, he solved this problem by giving away all his food that contained onions, trading it for food without any—mostly food parcels people got from home.

Younger and stronger prisoners were fortunate because bread slices were provided in one large pile, and everyone could take as much as he wanted from this pile. Since most older men usually took fewer slices, this left more for the younger ones. Even though the bread was prison issue, utilizing the most inferior grain, which made it heavy and underbaked—as Patriarch Josyf Slipyj put it, "containing anything but flour"[5]—it is hard to convey just how helpful this mutual aid was.

A prisoner could supplement his rations by purchasing food in the camp kiosk, but this could be done only once a month, limited to five rubles per person, perhaps to prevent anyone from thinking that life was all milk and honey. Realistically, this amounted to one kilo of margarine and one kilo of apple jam. If you were a smoker, you could purchase *makhorka*, cheap tobacco that would later be rolled up in strips of old newspaper. If you chose to purchase any Astra cigarettes, you would certainly have to sacrifice buying any other products.[6] I was one of those people who made that sacrifice, since I smoked at that time. The camp administration considered such purchases a luxury, and therefore depriving you of this privilege was one of their favorite methods of punishment. It is not surprising that being allowed to make purchases at the camp kiosk was a rare event, almost like a festive occasion.

Snacking was possible only in the storage area, and this is where our tea parties would take place. At the zone, tea was served in a special ritual. Zorian Popadiuk even reproached us, saying that for us, tea had become akin to alcohol. And it must be acknowledged that well-brewed tea did indeed raise a prisoner's stamina. *Chefir*, the extremely strong, invigorating brew favored in the criminal camps, was not prepared in the political camps. We limited ourselves to a matchbox ration of tea per aluminum cup of water. Since there was a shortage of sugar in camp, tea was mostly drunk without it. But if anyone had been fortunate enough to procure some sugar cubes, they would be placed in the center, and we jokingly called it "sugar to look at." We mostly used sugar lollipops that could be purchased in the kiosk. According to the

5 Slipyi, *Spomyny*, 160.

6 Astra: one of the most widespread Soviet cigarette brands, producing fairly inexpensive unfiltered cigarettes.

purchase quotas, only a fifty-gram packet of tea could be purchased at one time, which made it a great scarcity indeed. This is why tea became known as the "thirty pieces of silver," because that's how the KGB would reward their snitches for the information they provided.

Tea was also associated with a special distinction: a prisoner's "seniority" was measured by the accumulation of tea stains in his metal teacup. Only a veteran could pride himself with a teacup thoroughly blackened by tea stains. At first, as a rookie prisoner, I did not know about this tradition (which was apparently adopted from the criminal camps) and committed an unforgivable *faux pas* against Sergei Kovalev. I was sick and had stayed home from work. Wanting to do something nice, I decided to wash all the dishes. Kovalev's cup was completely black inside, so I had to use a lot of elbow grease and sand to scrub off the many layers of tea stains. Sergei was devastated when he returned from work and hardly recognized his cup, finding it snow white: he was transformed from a veteran to a virtual novice.

Obviously, there was no alcohol in camp; true to his character, Captain Surovtsev, however, managed to pull another trick. Word got out among the prisoners that one could get a bottle of liquor by going to a particular location. I no longer remember who spread the news, or where you had to go to get it. I personally could get along without alcohol, so I was not tempted, but some dozen prisoners did fall for it. The following day I thanked God for my abstention, when the smiling Surovtsev approached everyone on his list who had succumbed and proceeded to humiliate them with great relish.

We planned well ahead as the New Year or any religious holidays approached. I was known in the zone for the "cakes" that I would create. For a while before the holidays, we collected bread leftovers, dried them on the radiators, and then crushed them into "flour," which I would later mix with water to create cake patties. Those would later be layered with a "cream" made of margarine mixed with apple butter. It was considered a special holiday delicacy, though today I wouldn't even dream of eating a single morsel of this culinary concoction. Sometime after our liberation I received a letter from Boris Chernykh, a writer from the Urals, who had been one of my prison mates, and he fondly remembered my cakes. In 1979 I made *kutia*, a traditional Ukrainian Christmas Eve porridge, in a similar fashion. This is how I described it in a letter to my family: "Even the *kutia* was an imitation: some breadcrumbs, cocoa, honey, raisins, and sugar. Everyone loved it and I became known as the Master Chef."

Lest the reader be shocked at this list of delicacies, I should explain. They became available every now and then thanks to yet another "humanitarian act" toward the prisoners devised by the Soviet penitentiary system: if a prisoner had fulfilled at least half of his term, he was allowed to receive a five-kilo food parcel once a year, as well as a one-kilo packet twice a year. The permitted items were strictly controlled, so relatives used all their creativity to devise a way to circumvent these rules and send the most nutritious items to their loved ones. For example, here is a list of the prized items I had received, as I reported to my family in a letter dated October 26, 1981:

> Two jars of oil, some butter wrapped in paper, bacon, cheese, a small bag of garlic and onions, caviar and sardines, two types of cookies, apples, a pomegranate, raisins, St. John's Wort, two pairs of socks, insoles, and two pens.

The mysterious term "two types of cookies" has to be explained because it is a vivid example of my relatives' inventiveness. Having received, among other things, some wonderful home-baked cookies, I decided to savor them after my dinner. To my surprise, they just disintegrated in my mouth, spilling the salty taste of a beef bouillon cube into my mouth, an item that was on the forbidden list. Apparently, there was an advisory guide circulating among our families with ways to mask some of the valuable items on the forbidden list, which our loved ones nevertheless wanted to send to us. Our clever women devised a system that allowed them to camouflage bouillon cubes in home-baked cookies, thus (for a while at least) pulling the wool over the eyes of even the most experienced prison guards. As Svitlana Kyrychenko confirms, this sisterhood of mutual assistance was truly phenomenal:

> Our wives, fiancées, sisters, or just friends, such as Mykhailyna [Kotsiubynska] and Liudmyla Lytovchenko, stood shoulder to shoulder, forming a tight circle of kindred spirits on this side of the barbed wire, linked to the other circle of men and women on the other side. We were like one large family. All this was invaluable to us because it bolstered our optimism and helped our children in their own self-actualization.[7]

Eventually we learned that these diligently selected and restricted products were banned out of sheer envy on the part of the camp administration. The Chusovoi district of Perm Region was at that time a quintessential "armpit," whence none of the delicacies enjoyed by the Moscow elite ever made their

---

7 Kyrychenko, *Liudy ne zi strakhu*, 347–48.

way. These pitiful folks had never seen some of the products that they had to divvy out to none other than the "enemies of the State," the "criminals." It's not difficult to imagine their despair. Their reaction to this justifiable feeling of envy and resentment was described in an article that appeared in a Ministry of Foreign Affairs journal for prisoners entitled "Toward a New Life" (Rus. *K novoi zhizni*). The article was analyzed in the *Chronicle*:

> The article claims that "dissidents" in the camp receive parcels and printed matter worth 250–400 rubles from abroad every month. The "dissidents" overeat, pass food on to "their own people," even in the punishment cells, and sell the rest to other prisoners. In order not to attract undue attention, the "dissidents" deceive the warders, who think that they go to the bathhouse to wash, whereas in fact they go there to eat their supplies.[8]

The only truth in this pack of lies was the fact that prisoners did indeed share their products with their colleagues. One person's treat was considered a celebration for all because the dissidents considered themselves one family, and sharing delicacies with others was a universally accepted tradition. Yevhen Proniuk, the Kyiv philosopher, could not rest until all his food was distributed. I used to get angry with him for categorically refusing to take anything from me or the others in return whenever we would receive our parcels. Neither I nor anyone else was able to break this stubbornness of his.

Needless to say, depriving a prisoner of his parcel was as important in the hierarchy of punishments levied by the camp administration as being deprived of access to the camp kiosk. Borys Monastyrsky had no family to send him a parcel, nor did he have any cash to purchase things at the prison canteen because all the money that he earned had been confiscated to pay for his trial. Thus, in May 1978 he appealed to the Soviet Red Cross, asking them to send him a parcel. After confiscating his letter, Nelipovych, the deputy political task force commander, told Monastyrsky that he was not permitted to receive parcels from the Red Cross.

Luckily, those who for some reason could not receive parcels from their own families could, however, receive them from other prisoners' families. Thus, for example, my mother was able to send a hot water bottle to Mykola Rudenko, and during the last months of my incarceration she sent food parcels to Oleksandr Zahirniak, who lived in my barrack. Oleksandr and I were good friends, and once in a while we would challenge each other's strength; after our liberation, he even asked me to be godfather to his son Myroslav. As

8 *Chronicle*, 54:58.

I was putting together these memoirs, I wrote to him, asking him for some photographs, but alas he had already passed on to another world.

Since I had survived my first day after eating those fried mushrooms, I often cooked them myself whenever the Almighty offered them on the little patches of parched earth. In my letters to my family I frequently mentioned other gifts that grew during the parsimonious Ural summer:

> The cooks have mastered the secret of preparing borshch from nettles and other weeds, which pleases us to no end. As far as berries go—as Nadiika was asking—perhaps they do grow around the village, but here in the zone there is not a single plant. Why would they sprout here, when in our overjoyed fervor, we would have only trampled them down? (July 23, 1981)

> I dried some medicinal chamomile, without the flowers; it grew plentiful this year. It's a pity, though, that the linden trees froze this past winter, as their flowers used to sweeten the chamomile and made a rather fine brew. (July 21, 1982)

The little greenhouse that was built in 1981 went a long way towards providing us with some additional food, and I talked about it in my letters to my family:

> We recently got a little greenhouse, and now every so often we have a pinch of greenery in our dining hall, shared by all of us. (July 23, 1981)

> This year we have a good crop of greenhouse cucumbers. For a while now, we have been getting cucumbers, either fresh or lightly salted. Tomatoes I have only had once, and we are still waiting for fresh cabbage and potatoes. (August 23, 1983)

Correspondence

In the strict regime camp, prisoners were permitted to send just two letters a month. The architects of this regulation felt that sending more than two letters per month might create a sanatorium-like atmosphere. All letters were read by a censor; at Camp 36, this role was long filled by the daughter of Camp Commander Zhuravkov. Her work was monitored by Captain Surovtsev, the KGB overseer. All too often, our letters were confiscated due to "suspicious content." Early on, if a letter was confiscated, you could send a second one in its place. My very first letter from camp was confiscated for "suspicious content," thanks to my rapt impressions of the Ural sky. I described Jupiter and Venus floating brilliantly across the sky and the unusual curvature of the new moon. A few days later, Captain Surovtsev chided me sarcastically: "Well, Marynovych, how naïve do you think we are that we would not catch your code names of 'Jupiter' and 'Venus'?" How could I not be embarrassed, as a political prisoner, for permitting myself these poetic references?

Soon enough, Surovtsev must have realized that he was dealing with a true weirdo because soon thereafter, he allowed my next letter to go through, where I wrote to my family:

> Please send me some information about music history and music notations. I am interested to know: 1) When and by whom was five-line music notation developed, and who devised the seven original notes? 2) What is the basic meaning of the treble and bass clefs? 3) Why is C positioned on the first line below the treble clef? 4. Why is A used for tuning? 6) Why is there no black key between E and F, and B and C? 6) What are the rules of harmony governing the transition between major and minor keys?

None of this had anything to do with any sort of a code. At that time, I was exploring my own private realm, designing my own worldview. God alone knows what could have taken hold in my head if I had had the internet at that time.

After a while you were no longer allowed to substitute a new letter for one that was confiscated. The Perm Region Procurator's office issued a special explanation that all letters presented to be mailed, including those that are confiscated, as well as any subsequent ones, should be tallied in the total quota. No one can accuse Soviet lawmakers of not earning their keep. I even mentioned this new ruling in my letter to my family, dated May 16, 1982: "We were informed that if my letter is confiscated, I will no longer be allowed to write a new version of it, and my quota would be forfeited."

If the censor confiscated two letters in a row, the author of these missives would disappear to his family for a long, worrying month and in many cases longer. If, however, he was punished with a long stint in the PKT, his quota was reduced to one letter every two months. In such cases, his handwriting would become minuscule, and the page would be filled with thoughts that ran no risk of being deemed "suspicious."

Often, in order to avoid confiscation, the censor simply blacked out the "suspicious" words. The new censor who replaced Camp Commander Zhuravkov's daughter was particularly notorious for overstepping her bounds in this respect. I only learned about these redactions when I recently began to reread my letters. At this point it is no longer possible to reconstruct the gist of those lost thoughts, but it is obvious that this censor scratched out all foreign words that I might have used, harmless or not. Just to be on the safe side, in my July 4, 1982 letter she scratched out the word *bud'mo*—"cheers." Just try to make sense of that.

As soon as my postal address became known in the free world, the letters started coming, and each one brought an informational and emotional tsunami with it. The letters from my mother and Nadiika enveloped me with their love, and my friends Mykhailyna Kotsiubynska, Natalia Yakovenko, Liuba Kheina, and Olia Heiko sent me warm words of support. Unexpectedly, Oksana Meshko sent me a postcard. At first glance, its words seemed fairly neutral, but reading into it, and looking at certain small nuances and the way she addressed me, it was clear that she was apologizing to Mykola Matusevych and me for not having trusted us and was hoping that we did not hold a grudge against her.

According to the law, the number of letters a prisoner could receive was unlimited, and perhaps that's how it might have gone, if not for the censors. The *Chronicle of Current Events* described a few transgressions against me, which were typical camp realities for many other prisoners as well:

> A letter from Matusevych's sister in Kyiv was confiscated from Marynovych.[9]

> The following letters were confiscated: . . . and to Marynovych from T. Matusevych and E. Obertas in Kyiv.[10]

> It was announced that letters to Marynovych from his mother and from O. Matusevych (Kyiv) . . . had been confiscated.[11]

It goes without saying that letters from abroad, with some rare exceptions, were never delivered. The *Chronicle* mentions Valery Marchenko's appeal to the Secretary General of the UN, Kurt Waldheim, dated December 10,

9 *Chronicle*, 51:78.

10 *Chronicle*, 51:81.

11 *Chronicle*, 52:42.

1978, in which he asked the secretary to protect letters to the camp from abroad that were confiscated by the censor:

> Knowing that many people living outside the USSR are constantly writing me letters and not having received even one letter from them over a period of five and a half years, I ask for your intervention, to enable me to make use of the relevant articles of the Declaration of Human Rights and of the Helsinki Agreement.[12]

Interestingly enough, the Perm Region Deputy Procurator General, Mr. Savelov, who was responsible for all prison oversight, justified his confiscation of Valery's appeal by saying that "it was addressed to an organization that was not competent in dealing with such issues."

The Orlov group research highlighted this issue as well:

> Prisoners hardly ever receive letters from abroad, with the exception of letters from Israel, which are confiscated slightly less frequently. The whole of the time they were in camp, the following received not one letter from abroad: Kiirend, Marchenko, Antoniuk, Grabans. Ogurtsov occasionally received a letter from Poland. Plumpa received only one letter from abroad in all those years, dated 6 February 1976, from Switzerland.[13]

It is worth saying a few words about the exception of letters from Israel. As with religious literature (which I will return to), I expect that international pressure on the Soviet Union played a part here. But this was not the only factor; the clever actions of some correspondents also played a role. I remember when a letter from Israel arrived at the zone from Yakov Suslensky, a former prisoner. This letter was not only allowed through but with a special recommendation from the administration to "heed the words of an experienced man." Why? Because Suslensky, knowing all the idiosyncrasies of camp life, dedicated his first paragraph to standard lines about the importance of contrition and only wrote about his life in Israel later in the letter. We caught the irony and the phoniness of his preamble right away, so we chuckled over his inventiveness. The camp administration, however, took it in earnest because this was their standard language.

---

12 *Chronicle*, 52:60.

13 "On prisoners in Soviet camps," 85.

For a while, we were allowed to insert small items into our registered letters, such as a small scrap of burlap I enclosed in a letter to my mother, upon which I had embroidered the "philosopher's spiral" in blue thread:

> I have plenty of thread here, so last week I started embroidering, using burlap, which I have plenty of because I use it to wipe my tools. I am convinced that I'm producing masterpieces, because that seems to be the general consensus here. Perhaps my keen desire to embroider stems from the lack of beauty here, but it is probably just temporary. (December 13, 1978)

It goes without saying that this little embroidery was no doubt soaked with my mother's tears more than once. At one point, my mother even took it to Kyiv to show it to some friends and relatives there. Eventually the administration's liberal policy of allowing us to enclose such items in our letters was stopped, and we were also prevented from receiving the stereocards that were popular at the time.

Children's drawings brought us much joy, though even here the administrators worked hard to prevent any excessive emotions from the prisoners:

> I wait for the drawings with bated breath; at the same time, however, I'm prepared to be disappointed. We were recently informed of a new ruling that states that if there is no text included on the same page, children's drawings are deemed "superfluous irrelevancies." I am concerned that our children might not even be aware of this. (December 7, 1981)

The letters sent out, and those received in camp, were considered great blessings for both sides. I could no doubt fill a whole chapter with fragments that reflect my impressions, revealing the emotions I feel when I hold those letters from Ukraine in my hands. Here, however, I will present just two of my favorites:

> I am holding before me the next batch of your letters, which I received today, December 5, and the emotions that they evoke resemble those of little children who refuse to settle down into their beds. They want to hear a story with a happy ending and a fairy godmother. In my hands I hold the photo of my dear mother, which I have embraced and kissed numerous times. I am searching for new wrinkles on her face, bestowed upon her by my turbulent fate, and in them I find a muted maternal reproach. I'm glad I have it, and my sadness represents the joy that every Ukrainian experiences when he hums one of those melancholic Ukrainian songs. (December 13, 1978)

> Shevchenko used to carry newly received letters with him for days while strolling the Kyrgyz steppe, not opening them, just savoring the promise that they might hold within.[14] A similar thing is happening in the Perm region. Today, while scrubbing the floor in my cell after they white-washed the walls, I suddenly heard the screeching of iron as the doors were opened, and a batch of letters landed in my wet hands. I deposited them onto the table and continued scrubbing, cursing every damned speck of paint that was embedded into every crevice on the floor. In the meantime, I greedily studied every envelope, extending this sweet torture beyond dinner, which was brought just as soon as I had dried my hands, and only then, while having my first cigarette, did I open my first letter. (October 9, 1979)

Letters coming out of the camp were equally important to our families because they conveyed all available information about us. The camp authorities would scrutinize every word and nuance because while we knew what was going on with us, they could only hypothesize. This is why I told my family during our first visit that it was much more difficult for them: my life was like a clean white sheet that would be filled with the black ink of their dark assumptions and emotions.

My mother and I had agreed upon a secret code for some short and extraordinary messages, but otherwise my family had to extrapolate information from my innuendos and cautious descriptions. For example, I used the phrase "my strong desire to retain my figure" to camouflage the fact that I was in the *kartser*. Saying that I "break down my endless dreams about food into small portions" indicated that I was on a hunger strike at that time. I never knew if it worked or not, but my letters were full of such convoluted conspiratorial phrases:

> I was not deprived of the parcel, but I will not receive it until December 18. A similar comment may be made regarding our future visit: they did not cancel it. It was just delayed in conjunction with a change in the regime of my upkeep. I cannot go into any more detail. (September 1, 1979)

> Since February 11, the regime of my upkeep was changed once again, just as the last time. This means that I will be able to write two times per month no sooner than six months from now. This time, the term will definitely be delayed. As sad as it is, I have no choice but to give up the hope of seeing you in 1980 as well. (February 28, 1980)

---

14 Taras Shevchenko spent nearly a decade in internal exile in Central Asia following his arrest for participating in the fledgling Ukrainian national movement in the 1840s.

Obviously, prisoners themselves could not send any packets from camp. Given how strictly our letters were censored, this created a desperate situation, as the camp became a "black hole" from which no information could ever escape without the censor's eye passing over it. No wonder the prisoners would beat their heads against the wall in an attempt to circumvent this blockade. Every so often, some prisoner would succeed in making a deal with one of the guards to dispatch a letter or parcel to his family or friends. This was always risky, however, because according to KGB mandates it meant the guard was violating the regime.

Once, in 1978, we recruited one of the guards to help us send a book. We devised a full operation whereby we removed a portion of the book's cover and replaced it with densely scribbled accounts of the camp. All this was very skillfully done by Mykhailo Slobodian from Galicia. The whole packet was addressed to Maia Vovchyk-Blakytna, a friend of Yevhen Sverstiuk in Kyiv. Later, however, we found out that the packet had wound up in the hands of the KGB, and it had elicited as much joy as ridicule from the KGB officers. Their joy was partially due to having intercepted "enemy information" but also because Mykhailo had apparently been so proud of his masterwork that he had secretly signed it, claiming authorship. Mykhailo and the other authors of this document paid a high price for this venture.

Family Visits

The KGB and the camp administration paid even more attention to prisoners' visits with their families. Obviously, visits were permitted only to immediate family members and never to distant relatives or simply friends.[15] According to the rules, a strict regime prisoner could receive one extended personal visit per year that could last for up to three days, although in practice we were happy if we were granted at least one day. Additionally, two short-term visits of up to two hours, conducted via telephone through a glass partition, would be granted every six months.

But the difference between "the right to have a visit" and actually getting it was huge. The reason was simple: the KGB wanted to hinder any exchange of "dangerous" information in and out of the camps at any cost. The prisoners, on the other hand, were trying to receive or impart vital information at any cost. This was like a "calf butting his horns against an oak tree," to

15 Visits from lawyers were officially permitted, but rarely granted. –M. M.

paraphrase the title of Aleksandr Solzhenitsyn's memoir. So, it would have been rather naïve of a prisoner to remind the authorities that they were obligated to grant him a visit. Oftentimes the authorities would openly explain their actions, as happened to Zorian Popadiuk. In May 1978, his mother had come to see him at the Vladimir prison.[16] The camp administration suddenly found some trivial reason to deny him the right to see her: they claimed that on her way to the prison, she had stopped in Moscow and visited numerous anti-Soviet dissidents, gathering all kinds of information from them. In the future, she would consistently be denied the ability to see her son.[17] Norair Grigorian mentions a similar situation with his relatives:

> My elderly parents came to see me in 1980. In a letter they told me that the administration had given them permission. They had to fly from Yerevan to Moscow, then connect to another flight for Perm, followed by a train to Chusovoi, and then from Chusovoi to Kuchino by truck. Then, wouldn't you know it, the administration dumps me into an isolation cell for 10 days, and my elderly parents were sent back. . . . On the way home my father had a heart attack![18]

To prevent any visits, the administration occasionally even resorted to more exotic methods, such as declaring a quarantine. As can be seen from one of my letters, the prisoners would then resort to sarcasm:

> We were informed that in conjunction with the untoward epidemiological conditions in the Chusovoi Region, no visits would be granted until further notice. It seems that the Chusovoi region has certainly been jinxed. These pesky bacteria seem to re-visit our region with a certain mysterious frequency. Why wouldn't they infect, for example, someplace like sunny Switzerland, where prisoners have bi-monthly visiting rights, not counting Christmas and Easter vacations? In other words, how vile can these bacteria be? (December 30,1980)

But whether the administration liked it or not, some visits actually had to be granted, and then the areas near the visitation rooms were supercharged with high-stress energy. Before any contact, both the prisoners as well as the visitors were thoroughly searched. Everyone, including women and children, had to fully disrobe, and wives, mothers, and sisters were even subjected to

16 Vladimir prison: large prison in the city of Vladimir, two hundred kilometers east of Moscow, dedicated to housing "especially dangerous state criminals."

17 "On prisoners in Soviet camps," 83.

18 Grigorian, "Vospominaniia," 15.

gynecological inspections. The room was replete with listening devices and was under constant surveillance. There would be instances when the guards would storm into the room when the conversation paused abruptly, or if the administration thought that some illicit information was being conveyed at a given moment. And, of course, everyone was searched again at the end of the visit.

I find it incredible that I do not recall every visit with my family. It would certainly seem that I should remember every moment of such visits. But memory can be fickle. It is, however, true that during my entire stay in the camp, I had just three personal meetings with my mother and my sister Nadiika, although I do not remember how many days each one lasted. I also had two short meetings through the glass partition, once with my mother and once with both my mother and Nadiika. The three additional personal visits that, legally, should have been granted to me, and numerous short-term visits, were disallowed in a variety of ways, sometimes through claims that I had "violated some rules"; or when I happened to be in isolation or in the camp prison, my visits would just be suspended.

Luckily, since I first arrived in the camp in summer 1978 and had not yet managed to accumulate any penalty points, I was able to have a visit with my mother and sister, Nadiika, on August 16 of that year. It only lasted one of the three allowable days, however, because even then, I was already regarded as a potential rule violator. The lady guard who checked my family in before the visit told them that "he is such a nice lad but such a criminal!" This striking description of me remains one of my favorites to this day.

During the searches, families were subjected to all the typical humiliating procedures, such as a total strip search, meticulous inspection of every seam in their clothing, and a thorough check of all the foodstuffs that were brought. The procedure was particularly mortifying to Nadiika because her spine was crooked due to her scoliosis, and to display it, even to a female guard, was extremely stressful for her. But they endured it all just so they could see me. Thankfully, a procedure mentioned by Norair Grigorian in his memoirs was no longer practiced at that time:

> The KGB is a conscientious organization. In their attempt to prevent any leaks of information from the camp, they decided to inspect all female visitors in a gynecological chair. The wife of one of the dissidents asked the male guard who was inspecting her: "So, do you see any Communism down there?" This practice did not last very long, because protests in the West resulted in Soviet diplomats being assaulted, so this odious practice was eventually abandoned.[19]

19 Grigorian, "Vospominaniia," 15.

My family and I spent this welcome day in a room especially designated for such visits, and I never heard any criticism or reproach from them. Their love, tenderness, and care toward me seemed to have increased a hundredfold. They both watched me with great joy as I savored all the goodies that only a mother's hands could have prepared. I no longer remember what we talked about because everything has just melded into one shining image of love.

During this meeting, I had two important goals that, given the listening devices, were difficult to accomplish. First, I had to develop a secret code with them that would simplify the exchange of important information in future correspondence. I had devised this code prior to our meeting, having consulted other prisoners about it. I managed to convey it to them, and this code simplified our communications throughout my prison term.

Second, I had to provide my mother with a capsule containing secret information about camp life, as well as some directives to be passed on. I had swallowed this capsule just prior to our visit. I managed this task as well, and my poor mother was a bit taken aback, not totally understanding why she had to swallow this less-than-appetizing capsule. She did it, however, trusting her son. Before our visit was up, I explained everything to her in truncated phrases, thus fulfilling my mission toward my prison mates. At that time, however, I still did not appreciate the emotional turmoil I had subjected her to.

Eventually I learned that on her way back to Moscow, while attempting to wash the capsule in the train toilet after retrieving it, it slipped through her fingers, and our information floated out onto the tracks and into oblivion in the Russian wilderness, waiting for the Second Coming. My mother was devastated, her blood pressure spiked, and she could never forgive herself for neglecting to fulfill an obligation that had been entrusted to her after so much difficulty.

Interestingly enough, in my subsequent letters I hardly ever mentioned this visit. I recently found a psychological explanation for this in one of my letters to Nadiika:

> I hope you are not too surprised that I am so restrained when remembering our meeting; I cannot be otherwise. Believe me, sometimes I chase those memories away, reflexively—like jerking your hand away from a flame. (September 1, 1978)

My next personal visit was granted around April 15, 1981. By that time, I had lived through 1980, which had been a difficult year for me, which I will talk about later. I don't remember too much about this visit, but I did come across a rather interesting comment about it in one of my letters:

> I found Mama's words, "I did not ask how you are sleeping," very funny. It strikes me that the best proof was the fact that all three of us did actually fall asleep, even though I drank all those cups of coffee! (May 17, 1981)

Then, just seven months later, on November 15, 1981, I received a short visit from my mother; it is connected with a compromise that was painful for me. I knew that my mother was eagerly awaiting this meeting, even if it was only two hours long, having taken her three full days to get there. But when they warned me that this meeting would be granted only if we agreed to speak in Russian, I rejected it and refused to go. Some of the guards in Camp 36 were from Ukraine and certainly would have understood Ukrainian. Furthermore, Captain Surovtsev himself, as I previously mentioned, also came from Galicia. I therefore considered the administration's fickle demand an attempt to "re-educate a nationalist."

About half an hour later, I received a note from my mother in which she asked me to come after all. I gave in, doing it strictly for her. We spoke in a room that was divided by a glass partition. Obviously, we could not embrace and kiss each other, and we had to speak through a phone. This was a bittersweet joy, riddled with great torture for me: I could never have imagined that being forced to speak in an alien language with my mother could be so painful—a language that symbolized national oppression and subjugation at that. My mother butchered the Russian language, but seeing her so happy was my only consolation and absolved my conscience of this compromise. I was fully aware that this demand that we speak Russian was not a unique event. Vazha Zhgenti, for example, was also forced to communicate with his mother in Russian. She was a peasant woman from the hills of Georgia and hardly knew Russian at all. I also knew that Yevhen Sverstiuk had refused to do so when he was in the same predicament. Eventually, the New York Ukrainian newspaper *Svoboda* ("Freedom") wrote about this in 1977:

> On April 14, 1977, when Lilia Sverstiuk traveled three thousand kilometers from Kyiv to visit her husband, Yevhen, her visit was denied under the pretext that her husband had been deprived of visiting privileges. A while later, Lilia was informed that she could see her husband, but only under the condition that they would speak Russian. She agreed but was later informed that the meeting would not take place after all because her husband had refused to speak Russian. Lilia had to leave, and Sverstiuk, protesting the unlawful deprivation of his legal

> visitation rights, declared a hunger strike, which was supported by some twenty other prisoners. Then on April 30, the camp director, Poliakov, sent Lilia a telegram informing her that another meeting had been scheduled for late April or May. It took extreme measures—a hunger strike by some twenty individuals—to make the camp commander put an end to the lawlessness.[20]

In the Orlov group report, P. Plurias-Plumpa wrote about one of the short visits granted to the Armenian Markosian:

> In May 1978, R. Markosian had a two-hour meeting with his brother but was not allowed to shake his hand. They were also forbidden to speak in their native Armenian. The supervisor present at the meeting continually warned them that if they uttered even one word of Armenian, the meeting would immediately be cut short.
>
> As a rule, during short meetings, only Russian is allowed to be spoken. If the children or relatives of a non-Russian prisoner cannot speak Russian, there is no way for them to take part in a conversation.[21]

I do not want to say that refusing to speak Russian during a visit was a litmus test of patriotism. Yury Badzio and his wife Svitlana took a different stand, which I do not condemn in any way:

> They warned us to speak only Russian. We had no problem with that, Yury and I both agreed, particularly since there is a certain benefit to be had: if you speak very fast, you can use Ukrainian words that the guards don't understand but pronounce them in such a way that they sound like Russian, and then you can convey many personal things. All you have to do is stay calm and collected.[22]

I have a cherished memory from our short Russian-speaking visit: my mother brought a piece of embroidery with her, part of a yellow embroidered shirt with colors that I had dreamed about while in prison and had asked her to bring. In the zone, the color gray dominated everything—even in summer, when everything was green, the colors of flowers were nowhere to be seen. The warm colors of the embroidery on a yellow background burst before my eyes into a joyous array of emotions. I was mesmerized looking at it and objected vehemently when my mother tried to hide it away. I alternated

20 "Ukrains'ka hromads'ka hrupa znovu tavruie rezhym bezprav'ia, podaie fakty," *Svoboda*, June 25, 1977, 1.

21 "On Prisoners in Soviet Camps," 366.

22 Kyrychenko, *Liudy ne zi strakhu*, 377.

between glancing at the embroidery and at my mother for the rest of the visit. The very same day, I wrote about it in a letter:

> Only after leaving our meeting, dear Mama, did I realize how stressful these two hours had been. But I will not talk about it in this letter, because it will make it too heavy. I will tell you all about it at our next meeting, if I should be granted one in the next two and a half years. For two hours, my chest was filled with warmth, as your wonderful soul radiated from your eyes. For two hours, our hearts belonged only to us and to our merciful God. Close by, our dear Nadiika seemed to be there as well, clasping her hands, as if her look pierced time and space. This was the most important thing, because in our triune world the look was first, and only then came the word. (November 15, 1981)

I can still see that exquisite embroidery before my eyes. I could fully appreciate it only after the meeting when I had calmed down a bit. But even the most magnificent masterwork would pale in contrast to the loving and tender maternal hands that were holding it.

The third meeting I had with my mother and Nadiika was on April 4, 1982. Recalling it in my subsequent letter, I used the same simile as before: "The new phase of our correspondence, my dear ones, begins with the same painful feeling I mentioned previously; once again our last meeting is like a burning hot iron."

Apparently, both my mother as well as Nadiika were there for my second brief visit, which happened on October 13, 1983. Once again, the prevailing emotions totally paralyzed my long-term memory, but fortunately, there is a short mention of it in one of my letters:

> It's wonderful that we managed to string together a few words at all. But it's not a matter of words when the eyes consciously or subconsciously focus on the fine nuances of each facial feature, and the soul alone vibrates in our magical trilateral glances. (October 30, 1983)

Among all the letters my mother diligently saved, there is one small note that my mother had inserted into one of Nadiika's letters: "I join Nadiika in expressing my appreciation for those two hours of our conversation. In about six months, we should be able to talk as much as we want." There is another mention of this meeting in one of my other letters:

> It seems I have so gotten used to this seven-year incarceration that I no longer remember when I last allowed myself to fantasize about nice clothes or using a silver tea spoon. Quite recently, at our last meeting, when you, Nadiika, were

talking about the things that had been purchased for me, I understood it in my brain but not in my heart, because it still had an embargo on simple human aspirations. (February 4, 1984)

Camp Medical Services

It was assumed that initial medical services would be provided by a physician in the infirmary. During the early years of my incarceration, the camp physician was Dr. Petrov, a short, chubby man, who stood out for his distinctive sense of humor. For example, when I developed gum disease after a hunger strike, he told me during a consultation with a smirk, "All you need is some vitamins—strawberries, for example."

Eventually Dr. Petrov inadvertently revealed his true self. This happened on the day when we learned from the Soviet newspaper *Izvestiia* that our colleague Yosef Mendelevich, who was transferred out of our camp in February 1980, had not only been expelled from the Soviet Union but was subsequently received by President Ronald Reagan. The Soviet press was raging that the US president had received "a convicted criminal." Vadim Arenberg, a young Jew from Leningrad who was uplifted by the news about his friend and mentor, came to see Dr. Petrov for a consultation and shared this news with him. Dr. Petrov was dumbfounded by this and then mumbled: "Well, I don't think I did him any harm." This phrase was worth its weight in gold. Mendelevich himself cites another quote from Dr. Petrov in his memoirs: "I'm a member of the Cheka first and foremost, and only then a physician."[23] I suspect that he must have uttered this with great pride.

Eventually a certain Pchelnikov became the head of the medical unit, although it's hard to call him a doctor; rather, he could better be described as a KGB medical stooge. Had there been a second Nuremberg trial, he would have merited a place among the defendants. Pchelnikov was probably not even aware to what extent the fires of hell openly radiated from him, as demonstrated by an incident with Viktor Nekipelov. In fall 1981 Nekipelov was already gravely ill and had been admitted to the camp hospital. One time when I visited him, I gave him my crucifix as a gift. With trembling emotion Viktor put it around his neck, as if renewing his baptism. Then, the following day, he told me that when Pchelnikov made his rounds and saw the

---

23 Mendelevich, "Operatsiia 'Svad'ba.'"

Figure 6.1. Ronald Reagan and George Bush receive Josef Mendelevich and Ida Nudel in the White House. Photo credit: The American Jewish Historical Society.

crucifix, the doctor drew back, pointed to the crucifix, and cried: "I refuse to treat you! Let Him treat you." It is hard to say what astonished me more: that this so-called physician refused to uphold his Hippocratic oath, or this atheist's seeming acknowledgment that God actually does exist.

In terms of the conditions of medical services in Zone 36, it is worth quoting several eyewitness accounts:

> 31 August [1978]. KGB officers from Latvia and Ukraine (Ivano-Frankivsk region) arrived in the camp. Those from Ukraine had a talk with Slobodian, during which a certain Kovtun told him: "We will give you medical treatment if you help us." [Slobodian needed surgery for a cyst on his large intestine, as well as his tonsils.][24]

> 21 June [1982]. In connection with the Day of the Medical Worker [a Soviet holiday], [some dozen inmates, including the author —*M. M.*] sent complaints to different Procuracies about the medical service in Camp 36: the regular absence of the head of the medical unit Pchelnikov at the appointed reception

24 *Chronicle*, 51:76.

> hours and the impossibility of sick prisoners being received by him in the morning before work, the lack of the most essential medications in the medical unit and at the chemist's at work, the lack of a dentist, the poor laundry service and unsatisfactory sanitary conditions, the general policy of the administration to refuse to hospitalize or send dissidents for examination.[25]

Clearly, selective medical services, as well as selective punishment, were the norm. This notion had certainly penetrated the structural mindset of the powers that be on all levels. The administration was totally convinced that our ideological incongruence with the Soviet status quo gave them a justifiable legal basis for constantly devising new ways of punishing us. (What is astonishing is the way this justification for selective jurisprudence in Ukraine was later adopted by President Viktor Yanukovych in 2010–2014, echoing the status quo of those earlier years. The names of the countries and the colors of their flags had changed, but the government's ideological reasoning had remained the same: punitive medicine and punitive lawlessness remained in place.)

We were also amazed by most of our guards' perverted understanding of the rule of law. Even if you took into account the fact that we might have violated the law, the courts had already punished us by depriving us of our liberty. Everything beyond that, like selective medical services, refusal to provide first aid, subjecting us to freezing cold and hunger, and depriving us of family visits, were extralegal persecutions and certainly not part of our sentences; therefore, they were not congruent with any civilized international law. Our tormentors, however, considered these additional persecutions to be the norm; you put yourselves beyond the law, so why are you now appealing to it? Yevhen Sverstiuk described this very aptly:

> In the West, depriving you of your freedom is the punishment. In the Soviet Union, however, where the whole country has been deprived of all its freedoms, the concentration camp serves as a means of degrading the individual and instilling fear. Our highly skilled tormentor, Major Fedorov, pondered new ways to punish [any prisoner] who "had not embarked on the path of correction," and stood in the way of others becoming snivelers and spies.[26]

Valery Marchenko's situation was also outrageous in this regard. He had a grave kidney ailment that went untreated, and it resulted in constant agony,

25 *Chronicle*, 64:93.

26 Yevhen Sverstiuk, interview by Vasyl Ovsiienko, December 23, 2012.

which ended only with his death. Likewise, Oleksa Tykhy was brought to his death by endlessly postponed surgery. Attention was finally brought to this issue by the press and relatives' complaints. As if anticipating his own fate, Valery Marchenko commented in the Orlov group's report on a similar situation with Stepan Mamchur:

> The atmosphere of abuses and violations of legality which prevails in the [camp] bears its own evil fruit. The death of Mamchur is instructive. After being called several times, the guard eventually came to the sick prisoner, then came the duty officer, then the deputy political officer, and after quite a time had passed they found the duty nurse, Kuznetsova. She did not know what to do, and asked [another prisoner] Cherkavsky, " Should we give him a jab of magnesia?" Then, finally, T. A. Solomina appeared (a non-specialist doctor who was in fact a graduate from the faculty of sanitary hygiene) who, seeing the critical condition of Mamchur, managed merely to order " hospitalization." But the patient, who had been suffering from a violent headache, followed by hallucinations and nausea, lost consciousness. . . . He began to have convulsions and his face became distorted. These were clear symptoms of a stroke (for several years, Mamchur had been an invalid due to high blood pressure) but they had remained undetected by the nurse and the doctor for nearly three hours, until the consultant Utyro arrived. As a result no first aid was given. The post mortem showed a brain haemorrhage.
>
> This is an appropriate point to give a brief account of the contacts which the deceased had had with the representatives of the camp's medical service. Mamchur usually received his monthly diet rations no more than twice or three times a year. In January 1977 he was in hospital and for three months before his death on 10 May 1977 he asked in vain for his diet rations. Authorization came through the day after he died.[27]

The deaths of a host of older prisoners serving twenty-five-year terms, those who perished partly due to the lack of proper medical help, went mostly unnoticed. The *Chronicle* was the only source in which short notices of their deaths were listed.

Here are some poignant illustrations of camp life during my tenure there that underscore the cynicism of the KGB and the camp administration.

Mykola Rudenko had an inoperable double hernia in his groin that would become strangulated every so often, turning him into a virtual invalid. This was the result of an injury during the Second World War; he had been diagnosed as a permanent invalid, making him unemployable. This ruling

27 "On Prisoners in Soviet Camps," 360–61.

should also have been applied to his place of confinement because a war injury was not dependent on a person's legal status. But there were certain conditions that complicated this, and in Rudenko's case, what mattered first and foremost was his refusal to embark on the "path of correction." This alone absolved his tormentors of any moral obligations, and his war injury provided them with endless opportunities to continue to torment him intentionally. Rudenko had difficulties sitting for a long time, and when he walked too much, he had to lie down. He also did this in the ShIZO, where there were cement blocks instead of chairs, and no one could sit on them for long. This is how Oles Shevchenko remembered it: "It was extremely painful to sit on those cylindrical stone stools because we no longer had any muscle or fat left, so you were sitting on bare bones. Those hard seats had no backing, so you had to sit directly on your bones, and that's very painful."[28] Since our cots were lifted during the day, like it or not, Rudenko had to lie down on the cold floor. Sooner or later, the guards took notice of this, and since it was forbidden to lie down during the day, new punishments were levied on him for violating the regime.

Those of us who shared a cell with Rudenko defended him as best we could. What was most outrageous about this was that this cruelty resulted from an injury that the writer had sustained while "defending the Soviet homeland." In my appeals, I always pointed out the ironic fact that in Rudenko's case, Brezhnev's refrain, "No one and nothing is forgotten" (Rus. *Nikto ne zabyt, nichto ne zabyto*), had gotten so twisted that it took on a totally different, mocking meaning.[29]

The fact that Rudenko had not repented, and that his newly written camp poetry had wound up in the West, made the KGB livid. The poet's wife, Raisa, had been arrested for merely doing something the Universal Declaration of Human Rights guaranteed: distributing her husband's poetry and ideas regardless of political borders.[30] The logic of punishment took precedence over all common sense, and thus on March 1, 1982, they revoked

28 Oles' Shevchenko, interview by Vasyl Ovsiienko, October 21, 1998, Virtual'nyi muzei Dysydents'kyi rukh v Ukraini, http://archive.khpg.org/index.php?id=1362779377.

29 Brezhnev's refrain: popular slogan that became an integral part of the Soviet politics of memory of the Second World War during the Brezhnev era.

30 Specifically, Article 19 maintains that "everyone has the right to freedom of opinion and expression; this right includes freedom to hold opinions without interference and to seek, receive and impart information and ideas through any media and regardless of frontiers." "Universal Declaration of

Rudenko's designation as an invalid (as if his chronic war injury had suddenly miraculously healed all by itself) and deemed him fit for work. Now he was required to put in an eight-hour workday. This was pure and simple retaliation that had no moral justification even within the Soviet system of values. It was reminiscent of what Patriarch Josyf Slipyj had asserted two decades earlier: "Whenever articles about me appeared in the Soviet press, the repressions against me became unbearable, and everyone feared me like fire itself."[31]

From that day on, Rudenko was punished relentlessly, either for not fulfilling his work quota, or for attempting to take a break and lying down for a while at an "unauthorized" time, when the pain in his spine had become unbearable. Thus, in the hands of the authorities, medicine became a blatant way to punish and torture one of the defenders of the motherland.

Rudenko's was not the only such case, as Valery Marchenko demonstrates in the Orlov group accounts:

> [Some prisoners] were all at one time declared invalids, but then they were deprived of Group 2 disablement status; invalids in this group are only required to work if they feel up to it. The illegality of such decisions is obvious, since Svitlychny has not grown eight new fingers, Pidhorodetsky's hump has not disappeared, Gimpu has not suddenly acquired a stomach which has been operated on and the progressive deterioration of Filonenko's bone marrow has not been halted. Incidentally, when Filonenko was deprived of Group 2 status, the results of blood test were entered on his medical card, tests which, for all the years of treatment in clinics, had never been carried out.
>
> Falsifying the results of tests—entering them up as better than they really are—is a widespread phenomenon in the central hospital and in the medical departments of Camps 35, 36, and 37. For example, in the case of Marchenko's illness, facts were entered which did not correspond to the truth. The results of tests carried out in the Kyiv Institute for his kidney disease prior to his arrest contrast strikingly with similar ones carried out in the KGB isolation prison in Kyiv while he was there for treatment consultations.[32]

Human Rights," Documents, United Nations, https://www.un.org/en/universal-declaration-human-rights/.

31 Slipyi, *Spomyny*, 187.

32 "On Prisoners in Soviet Camps," 360.

The history of Viktor Nekipelov's illness in 1981 is yet another example of punitive medicine. Here are some of the brief accounts of its chronology given in the *Chronicle*:

> 17 September. . . . Nekipelov was put into the medical unit suffering from sharp pains in the region of the kidneys and urethra. There was no medical assistance available in the medical unit, and no diagnosis was made. Nekipelov was blamed for having called out the doctor at night. In order that Nekipelov should be given a pain-killing injection, the prisoners in the zone were obliged to warn the administration several times of the possibility of a strike. Nekipelov's condition was deteriorating all the time, while the doctors had not even made a rapid analysis of his urine.
>
> 25 September. A strike was declared [by 16 inmates] to demand that a qualified urologist should come to see him. [. . .] That same day, Altunian, Rudenko, and Fedorov [active members of the strike] were sent to the [ShIZO] for 15 days.
>
> 26 September. Three more strikers [including the author —*M. M.*] were also thrown into the ShIZO for 7 or 10 days.
>
> 27 September. Because of the absence of a local doctor at the time when Nekipelov's illness became critically more acute, a hunger-strike was declared (the participants were the same as before, excepting those who were in the [ShIZO]). Safronov was thrown into the ShIZO for 5 days.
>
> 29 September. Ogorodnikov and Shevchenko were put in the [ShIZO] for ten days. Later that day the hunger-strike was called off (Ogorodnikov continued it until 1 October).
>
> 30 September. A urologist arrived. A diagnosis was made and Nekipelov was given assistance.
>
> 1 October. In response to this the strike was called off.
>
> 9 October. [Having been branded as the strike organizers,] Altunian was given four months in the [PKT] and Rudenko was given six months.[33]

---

33 *Chronicle*, 63:153.

This is how much blood, sweat, and tears was required to ensure that basic medical care was provided to a critically ill person. Incidentally, this was the first phase of an illness that resulted in the death of this brilliant Russian poet a few years later. Generally speaking, the prisoners' struggle to try to ensure even the most basic medical services throughout the penal facilities was next to impossible. As you can see from this saga, winning this sort of duel with the administration was only possible through extraordinary efforts and the complete solidarity and active involvement of all prisoners. During my incarceration, there was only one precedent when the administration officially acknowledged our justifiable demands, at least partially:

> 19 July [1982]. Because of prisoners' complaints to the procurator regarding poor medical services, a committee from the Perm medical authorities monitoring the forced labor correctional facilities came to visit the camp. It included the department inspector, Mr. Grigorev, and Ms. Golubova, the procurement inspector. To respond to the allegations of misconduct, Inspector Grigorev summoned prisoners Altunian, Balakhonov, Marynovych, and Ogorodnikov. He acknowledged Dr. Pchelnikov's frequent absences during clinic hours, a lack of proper medical kits at the workplace, unacceptable laundry services, and assured us that ailing prisoners would no longer be sent to work in the morning, and those who required special nutrition would receive it. Golubova, however, insisted that the medications supplied to the medical centers had been properly organized.[34]

The prisoners also demanded the services of a dentist. Given the quality of the food and the lack of vitamins, our teeth became particularly vulnerable, and a dentist's care was crucial. Once, however, this medical service turned out to bring additional problems for Viktor Nekipelov:

> There is no dental surgeon in the camp. The specialist who came opened up Victor Nekipelov's painful tooth, took the broken denture for repair, promised to insert a filling the next day and bring the denture back a month later, then disappeared altogether.[35]

I wrote about the same practice in one of my letters to my family:

---

34 "Permskie lageria," *Khronika tekushchikh sobytii* 65, http://old.memo.ru/history/diss/chr/index.htm. (Volume 65 of the *Chronicle* was not published in English.)

35 *Chronicle*, 64:84.

> My teeth are a real problem for me. One tooth has a small cavity which doesn't hurt much, but when a dentist came to the zone recently, I refused to go to see her, because she will leave a temporary filling and then disappear, leaving me to tend to it by myself, to remove it and plug the hole with some cotton, and wait a few months for someone else to arrive and to take care of it. It's the same as having the tooth removed right away, because that's what's going to happen in the end anyway. When they pull a tooth, by the way, they do give you a pain killer—do not fret. (June 21, 1982)

Nevertheless, later letters make clear that our protest did have some positive results, and unlike in Nekipelov's case, when they wanted to punish him for instigating a protest, my case ended well:

> Conditions change all the time, and my mood grows more somber every day. There is, however, one bright moment: We have a dentist here and two of my teeth have been treated, and plastic fillings were installed. This is the first time that we have such a competent specialist here. He not only treats you well, but also makes you feel safe, forgetting for a while where you are and what a horrible chair you are sitting in. For the time being, my teeth are fine, so please do not worry. (July 21, 1982)

As I never stayed in the central hospital that services all three camps of Zone 389 (35, 36, and 37), I will refer the reader to the Orlov group's report to learn more about conditions there.

Since our letters were censored, we were extra careful when writing about the medical services. First of all, we did not want those letters to be confiscated, and then we did not want our families to worry about us. Even if I did mention difficulties, I personally wanted to couch them in a bit of levity. My letters to my mother and Nadiika, relating my encounters with the dentist, were full of humor:

> I recently started dental treatment, but it was only the beginning—I will get further chances to dazzle my dentist with many charming smiles. Our initial conversation was quite interesting: "Pardon me, I just ate some garlic." She answered from five meters away: "Yes, I noticed." (December 12, 1978)

> Since every respectable old age should be spent toothless, I decided that it was my duty to get rid of one more tooth. Finally, the dentist arrived, and tickled my ears with the most enjoyable sound of all, that of his drill, and thus I was enriched with yet another filling. Luckily, I was amazed that during his probing of the root canal, I did not feel much pain, so I asked him to check if my original

> pain might have been coming from another tooth. Suddenly, your son, with his sniveling soul, was soaring somewhere above the clouds, from where God's earth doesn't seem very Godly at all. This is how I lost my last wisdom tooth, and so I am humbly hopeful that from now on, wisdom will bring nothing but pure joy for me. (August 7, 1983)

Obviously, my teeth were not the only problems I had because every so often the normal seasonal ailments would also latch on to me. I talked about them in a humorous tone as well:

> Spring has sprung, and in addition to the jolly chirping of birds, the most widespread sound is that of the hacking coughs and sneezing of the *homo sapiens.* This year, too, we were not deprived of such concerts. My nose was one of the first to greet spring with ever-flowing streams. The fact that it started right on Easter brought me to despair. Nowadays, I walk around with a swollen nose, and when I shave, I turn the mirror in such a way that I can avoid looking at this abomination. (May 22, 1983)

Every so often, however, things were not so funny, and then my tone became more somber. That's what happened in summer 1981 when I suffered from depression. I no longer remember the cause of it, but it may well have been a crisis of worldview. Or perhaps, like the disciple Peter, I just stopped being convinced that I could walk on water. I came to this conclusion after reading my letters from the time:

> The reason my letters were held up was the bad feeling I had. At first, I was just in a bad mood and irritable, which was followed by intermittently deepening depression and uncontrollable outbursts of emotion. Finally, I had nothing left in me, so I went to the doctor, and now I am taking some tranquilizer injections. It is difficult to diagnose my state—perhaps it's an accumulated nervous condition. For months now, all the negatives have piled up, and one thread or another was always breaking, and those threads are not unlimited. It seems like a murky shroud has blocked me from you, and you from me, because there have been few letters from you as well. It goes without saying that I am in a state of some foreboding, and it's quite obvious because with every fiber of my being, I feel that something bad is about to happen, and I have no clue where it might be coming from and how it is going to hit me. (August 14, 1981)

> I am feeling a little better—hopefully the crisis has passed. Once in a while, I still explode, but at the same time, I feel the flicker of a smile deep within me, because I certainly must look quite funny when out of the blue and

without any control, I impulsively start flinging my arms and begin to mumble something ridiculous. (I would give half my kingdom for steady nerves.) (August 27, 1981)

People say I have lost some weight—or at least I don't have that swollen look anymore. My mood seems to be a bit steadier, and the last few days it has actually been quite good. Please don't worry about me—I am getting back to myself again. During my depression I must have looked like Sisyphus when the stone slipped through his hands and rambled down the mountain. (September 20, 1981)

"Reeducation" through Forced Labor

Work in the camp was both forced and obligatory. The work week consisted of six days, eight hours per day. According to official policy, it was intended to "rectify the behavior" of "malingerers" and "evil libelers," although our master tormentors were skilled in converting work into yet another instrument of torture.

According to the law, half of all our earnings were to go to the coffers of the Ministry of Internal Affairs and, theoretically, the other half, after taxes, was to be deposited into the prisoner's personal account. If the courts determined that the prisoner was liable for all court costs, however, those expenses would be automatically withdrawn from the prisoner's personal account, and he would get nothing. Remarkably enough, my court fees were deducted twice—once from me in prison and then again directly from my family. As my letters indicate, it took years to get that money reimbursed. With any money a prisoner had in his account, he could purchase food from the camp kiosk, not to exceed five rubles per month (four if you were under special regime and two if in detention). That money could also be used to purchase books through Kniga–Pochtoi, or to subscribe to periodicals through Soiuzpechat.

Production quotas were another major drama in the labor rules. "Malicious and willful under-production of the quota" was a typical citation that merited additional punishment for those who refused to "embark on the path of correction." The *Chronicle* was replete with reports of this "violation," and the administration did everything it could to make those quotas as difficult to achieve as possible. Production norms might be raised without any improvement in the work environment, and evaluations might be lowered capriciously as well. Here are some illustrations from the *Chronicle* that show how production norms were increased randomly and how the prisoners persistently objected to such outrageous behavior by the administration:

> The productivity norms in the camp are rising sharply. Thus since 1 December 1977 the norm for lathe operators has risen 45% and for stokers—100% . . . I. Ogurtsov refused to fulfil the impossible 200% norms, and for that, on 16 December, he was thrown into the [ShIZO] for seven days.[36]

> [From a report written by Mykhailo Slobodian:] On March 10 this year [1978], I, a sick man, was put in the [ShIZO] for 48 hours for not being able to fulfil the production norm, due to poor health, and for demanding medical assistance because of ulcers and glands . . . I am deprived of access to the camp shop because I, a sick man, was unable to fulfil the production norm. In winter it is 8°-9° in the barracks, instead of 18°. In winter the temperature in the workshop dropped to zero (the water froze). In this temperature one must work eight hours at the panel assembly. Moreover we are not issued warm clothing (felt boots and quilted jackets) and those who manage to obtain some are put in the [ShIZO] by the administration.[37]

Trying to fulfill the quotas was another way in which prisoners demonstrated solidarity. There were always some prisoners, especially the younger and more proficient ones, who managed to fulfill their quotas, and when needed, they would then help others. Usually this help went to those who were being punished, particularly when they had a scheduled family visit coming up. At the same time, this put these hardier workers into another moral dilemma: hard labor combined with a lack of nourishing food was a direct path to exhausting themselves, while a few moments of rest were invaluable. Thus, by helping others, they deprived themselves of their own opportunity for some precious rest.

Reaching his quota did not mean that the prisoner could avail himself of the rest he deserved. The *Chronicle* cited numerous instances illustrating this paradox:

> 23 February [1979]. Kovalev and Marynovych were reported for being absent from their work places for 21 minutes (on a day when both had overfulfilled the norm).[38]

---

36 *Chronicle*, 51:96.

37 *Chronicle*, 51:88.

38 *Chronicle*, 52:45.

> 18 July [1981]. Lieutenant-Colonel Fedorov arrived in the workshop a few minutes before work broke off and reprimanded Marynovych for having stopped working, even though he had fulfilled the daily norm earlier than the regulations stipulated.[39]

The work zone in Camp 36 consisted of three barracks housing the workstations and a sawmill at the far end of the camp. Over the course of my incarceration, I wound up working in all these locations. At first, I worked as a lathe operator. From a long piece of metal, I had to cut pieces of specific configuration and size. It would not have been too bad, had the two pieces of metal not been of different thicknesses, and not been melded together in the middle, making the seam so thick that the cutter often broke. That cursed seam caused me much grief, and it wasn't until 1983 that a better cutter was brought in.

Oddly enough, I no longer remember who taught me lathe operating skills. It might have been Ihor Kalynets, or possibly Wolf Zalmanson. I don't remember because it was the cursed seam that absorbed most of my attention. As a rule, I usually managed to fulfill my quota, although with some difficulty. Interestingly, whenever I remember my post at the lathe, it always evokes some weird memories.

First of all, at that time, 1978, I was plagued with intermittent, unpredictable fainting spells. They were not very frequent, only once every month or two, but when they did occur, it was important to recognize the initial symptoms, stop the apparatus, and sit down because the machine spun with great speed, and there were many sharp edges and metal pieces all around. Should you fall, you might not be able to get up again. But God was kind to me, and I would always groggily regain consciousness in the presence of one of the other prisoners.

Second, I remember a funny collision between Genrikh Altunian and some of the other prisoners. Genrikh was a God-given engineer with golden hands, and he literally suffered when one of the machines broke down. He considered this a personal challenge and would be agitated until he got it working again. This brought us into conflict with him because we considered these equipment breakdowns legitimate opportunities to take a rest. We would try to make him understand this but to no avail. He did not have any evil intentions, nor was he trying to ingratiate himself; for him it was just unacceptable to have any machine be out of service in his presence.

---

39 *Chronicle*, 63:151.

Figure 6.2. The work zone.

Third, I remember standing by the lathe and mentally composing a secret greeting to Solidarity in Poland, which had grabbed the world's attention at the time. We were captivated by their struggle and wanted to congratulate our distant ideological comrades and offer them our support and solidarity. I still do not know if our telegram ever reached the Polish strikers, but I am certain that our efforts must have been duly registered up there in the heavenly spheres.

I returned to my job as a lathe operator a few more times and, as my correspondence shows, by the end of April 1983 I had actually passed a test and earned a level-two lathe operator certificate, but I never actually received the certificate itself. The lathe operator's job was considered difficult, so it earned you the right to purchase an additional four rubles' worth of food and to get some milk. In March 1982, however, these perks were canceled. Perhaps the Soviet lawmakers had decided that working as a lathe operator had suddenly become easier.

My next job was in the sawmill. All we had to do was to cut logs into boards, but the work was exhausting. I worked there a relatively short time—I myself had asked for this placement during my last winter in camp, and I had a special motivation:

> I am healthy and doing well, and I intend to become even healthier, because I have a new work assignment. I asked to be transferred to the sawmill—to be in the fresh air and to smell the fragrance of cut wood. So that's what I have been doing since January 5th. Who knows, perhaps one day these skills might come in handy in my internal exile. (January 8, 1984)

I spent much more time assembling various parts for electric irons. There were two stages in that process, and I will quote the *Chronicle* to describe the stage that was universally hated by all:

> In the autumn a group of prisoners was transferred to a new job (the camp produces components for electric irons). To assemble one component a prisoner has to put in three or four 3-millimetre screws, using a semi-automatic screwdriver, and attach a cable to two of them. He must then twist the cable. The norm for the job is 700 components. None of the prisoners is able to fulfil this norm—the largest output does not exceed 400 components. Group 2 invalids (whose working day is half as long) have to fulfil half the norm, but in order to do this they continue working after dinner.
>
> In an attempt to make the prisoners fulfil the norm, the administration makes use of the fact that 'even' the invalids fulfil their norm. Some female workers, who performed the same job at a 'free factory' [i.e. one not part of the penal system] and fulfilled the norm in a day, visited the camp at the invitation of the administration.
>
> The prisoners regard their transfer to this new job as a punishment, for it requires practice and a particular skill, whereas they had got used to their previous job and were able to fulfil the norm. Similarly, the prisoners who were in their turn transferred to the old job are still unaccustomed to it and unable to fulfil that norm.[40]

Another way of assembling those irons was to gather some parts on a special bench and then to activate a press with your foot that would meld them together into one unit. Here the quotas were also quite high, but with experience your hands could work automatically, leaving your head—the source of all your anti-Soviet thoughts—unencumbered. Indeed, it was while

40 *Chronicle*, 54:58.

Figure 6.3. One of the assembly platforms.

assembling these units that I was able to conceptualize the initial ideas for my first camp essay (more about this later).

In addition to these jobs, there were a few intermittent ones, one of which is cited in the *Chronicle*: "12 September [1978]. . . . Grigorian and Marynovych received a warning for refusing to dig a hole when the subsoil waters were high and it was pouring with rain."[41] This was a totally absurd

41 *Chronicle*, 51:77.

Figure 6.4. The "forbidden zone."

situation: due to the excess water in the hole, the task was completely futile. In the eyes of the administration, however, it made a lot of sense because this sort of "rehabilitation through hard labor" gave us the opportunity to become "normal Soviet citizens."

Among the jobs that were offered to the inmates were some that, according to internal prison etiquette, were considered unworthy of a political prisoner. For example, it was deemed inappropriate for a political prisoner to work as an artist illustrating various Soviet symbols and slogans. There were unwritten taboos against any work associated with barbed wire, since it symbolized our deprivation of freedom, as well as any work in an area that was between the two rows of barbed wire. By law, if a prisoner should find himself in that area, the guards had the right to shoot him without any prior warning. Anyone working in that area had to be considered trustworthy by the administration, and thus the assumption was that he was collaborating with the authorities.

It is this taboo that is at the heart of the story of a moment of weaknesses, which was perhaps my one and only serious moral defeat in camp. This was in the fall of 1982. Oles Shevchenko had injured his arm, and in order to ease the pain he took to wearing a winter coat before we were allowed to do so. Oles had been forewarned a few times, and finally, when he was alone, they forcibly tore the coat off him. He came to us visibly upset, told us that his arm had been reinjured in the process, and asked us for help. Obviously, to show our solidarity with him, we all went on a work strike, demanding that the perpetrator be punished for using excess force and hurting him. I was not totally convinced that Oles did the right thing, however. I thought that he had consciously embarked on this confrontation and that he was too agitated to behave appropriately. I was not pleased with this. But not supporting the strike was unthinkable, so I also stopped working. Eventually most of the strikers wound up in the ShIZO, but we were used to this.

We sat there for our first fifteen-day term, and then we repeated this four more times, each time refusing to go to back to work. I was in a foul mood, and I realized for the first time how quickly a person loses his stamina when he is not totally convinced of the moral justification for his actions. But I was certain that I would be able to survive those sixty days of punishment, which at the time was the maximum allowable for solitary confinement. Then, alas, on the fifty-ninth day of our confinement, it was announced by the procurator that, according to the new law, ShIZO terms were no longer limited to sixty days.

This is when I broke down. It was the first time while in camp that I was not able to continue with a protest action—and this was because I was not completely convinced that my position had been correct. I thought about it all night, and in the morning, I conferred with my colleagues and told them that I intended to break my strike but that it did not mean that I was backing away altogether. Everyone understood except for Vadim Arenberg, a young prisoner, who mumbled, "This isn't worthy of you!"

I suspect that our conversation was overheard by one of the guards because the next time punishments were meted out, Major Fedorov, the deputy chief of the camp, came up with a clever plan. When urged to go back to work, everyone refused except me. I was immediately sent to work in the forbidden zone between the two layers of barbed wire, where a prisoner was not supposed to go willingly. Had I refused to, I would have been thrown back into the ShIZO, the very place I had been trying to flee. I was powerless to refuse, so I was taken to the prison courtyard right in front of the prison windows. They ordered me to move coils of barbed wire from one place to another. The job made no sense, except that it forced me to violate all our camp standards of behavior—not only breaking the strike before everyone else but also agreeing to work in the forbidden zone and handling the barbed wire, which a prisoner was not supposed to do willingly. This was undoubtedly Fedorov's diabolical plan to latch on to a prisoner's weak moment and finally bring him down.

I was fully aware of their plan and suffered greatly from it. As I handled the coils of barbed wire, I visualized Christ's crown of thorns, and my heart was drenched in tears. At the same time, I vowed that I would not break down. "In the end, you will see that you have not broken me." At that moment, I had not yet realized that Fedorov's demonic plan had a sequel. It turned out that while I was lugging that barbed wire, they brought every prisoner to the window so that they all could see what I was doing, and they kept urging them, "Look, Marynovych is working in the forbidden zone, and you could be doing the same thing." To my friends' credit, they all objected to this attempt to humiliate me before their eyes and insisted that this spectacle be stopped.

Within a week, I managed to renew my psychological energy, and then Major Fedorov called me in. Glaring at me, he tried to test the ground to see if anything had actually changed. But nothing had changed. I was still on the opposing side of the camp struggle, and I was not the only one that had to make such choices. This is how Eduard Kuznetsov remembers it:

> I knew that as soon as the KGB notices your weakness, they will immediately start to cajole you and attempt to break you down so that they can mold you into a rag, one of their slaves. In other words, you have no way out. If in your folly you join the ranks of heroes, stay in the upper echelons of the struggle, you have nowhere to go. You cannot withdraw, there is no middle of the road, there is no way back. This is how the regime spawns its own enemies, and then pushes them into a corner, without any chance for them to withdraw. Whether you like it or not, you have to be heroic to the end. Or else become a collaborator.[42]

Today I am totally convinced that this moment of weakness was essential for my spiritual well-being and was also a great lesson for me. Our moments of defeat are crucial because they promote our further development. No wonder Kierkegaard considered the acknowledgment of one's sin to be the highest form of Christianity. No one is able to maintain the same level of strength at all times. On the contrary, success is followed by failure, or sometimes even total collapse, and it is important not to tell yourself after a collapse that you might never be able to rise again. The invisible but redeeming hand is always close by.

42 Kuznetsov, "Geroistvui do kontsa."

The six years of hard labor in camp had cost me a lot of blood and sweat, but they never managed to instill the Communist ideology in me. (The first year of my seven-year sentence included my interrogation, so I did not work then.) Soviet social Darwinism (or any other form of it) was a dead ideology and therefore could not fulfill its intended goal. If there was anything positive that actually managed to emerge in the noxious environment created by this system (such as any literary works of art), it was possible only in opposition to this environment and only because the human spirit is able to instill life in even the most atrocious and devastated social wasteland.

But the final chapter of my work saga will end on another note. When a prisoner's term came to an end, the administration was supposed to provide the sum total of all his income earned from hard labor performed in camp. Since our earnings were extremely low (a prisoner was not allowed to receive more than three quarters of the salary paid in the open market), the total that a prisoner received was ludicrous. Personally, after six years of tortuous hard labor, all I sent my sister was three hundred rubles, which was equal to about three months of regular earnings. None of the five-ruble kiosk expenses per month, or any subscription or purchase of books, could justify this pitiful sum.

Chapter Seven

The Pinnacle of the Struggle

When I began writing this section, I thought about dividing it into two parts: one describing our various forms of resistance to the authorities and the other covering the punishment we received in return. But it proved impossible to separate the two because one flowed from the other. In other words, the struggle itself, and then the ensuing punishments, were inseparable elements that penetrated all aspects of camp life for every prisoner.

As I have previously mentioned, everyone in camp already knew about the Helsinki Group activities and that some of their members had been arrested. My status, as a person who had spoken up in defense of the prisoners and their rights, was very high. At the same time, this made me accountable to them: I couldn't make any mistakes or show any fear. This was why I immediately got involved in the camp struggle. Beyond the punishment that would inevitably result from it, my elevated status also brought me some unexpected difficulties. Early on, Yevhen Proniuk stunned me with a solemn pronouncement: I should immediately start readying myself for future political activity. It was as if a sort of *noblesse oblige* required me to do so. I remember my surprisingly categorical answer: "No way!" Somehow, I never envisioned myself in politics.

Political engagement is one thing, but working to protect human dignity and my rights, which in our Soviet reality had a clear political dimension, was another matter. In this respect, I had no other choice: I simply had to defend my status as a political prisoner and dissident. Today, I am aware that a number of former Ukrainian political prisoners refrain from calling themselves "dissidents," calling themselves "fighters for the Resistance Movement" (Ukr. *Bortsi Rukhu oporu*) instead. I accept this designation and agree that the term "dissident" might be semantically deceptive (as Ihor Kalynets and Ivan Hel claim) when applied to committed national freedom fighters. I do not agree, however, with retrograde and anachronistic attempts to denigrate the label as immature or unworthy. In my memory, in Zone 36, this term was considered both mature and honorable. To illustrate this, I would like to quote Ihor Kalynets's declaration of February 28, 1978, protesting against Levko Lukianenko's arrest: "It seems to me that it is high time to see sense and cease the harassment of dissident Ukrainian patriots."[1]

I also consider it anachronistic to instrumentalize the notion of human rights and reduce it to something that is politically expedient, as some Ukrainian activists have done. For example, Levko Lukianenko was firm on this point, and in an interview Ivan Hel also asserted that "The defense of human rights was just a tactical move; it served as a cover-up and way to protect yourself from execution because it certainly did not protect you from the concentration camps."[2]

As far as I am concerned, when you have to pay the price of your freedom and the suffering of your loved ones, any idea you might believe in ceases to be strictly theoretical or tactical. The *Chronicle of Current Events* clearly shows that in the late 1970s, the concept of human rights was at the core of most political struggles, and it consumed the minds of all Soviet political prisoners. Once again, I will cite from a declaration written in summer 1978 by Oleksa Tykhy and Vasyl Romaniuk, who at that time were imprisoned in Mordovia.[3] This declaration was their attempt at a generalization, and it was recorded for posterity by the *Chronicle*. The authors claimed that under the present situation "Ukrainian patriots were obliged to assume moral responsibility for the fate of the nation." The authors declared:

> We are democrats. For us, the UN's Universal Declaration of Human Rights and its covenants and other documents on the independence and sovereignty of nations and peoples represent the highest principles of community and international social life. We dissociate ourselves from the policies and practices of the Soviet communist party in the nationality question, and from its interpretation of the idea of democracy.[4]

---

1 *Chronicle*, 48:79.

2 Ivan Hel, "Opytuvannia," Virtual'nyi muzei Dysydents'kyi rukh v Ukraini, http://archive.khpg.org/index.php?id=1163785533.

3 Vasyl Romaniuk (1925–1995): Ukrainian dissident, involved first with the Ukrainian national movement and later with the UHG. In 1992, he became one of the founders of the Ukrainian Orthodox Church-Kyiv Patriarchate and subsequently served as patriarch of that church (under the monastic name Volodymyr) until his death.

4 *Chronicle*, 51:91.

Here it is clear that the concept of human rights is indivisible from the idea of nationhood. Today, when the notion of human rights might in some circles be considered hostile to the interests of Ukrainian nationhood, the above phrase might almost sound heretical, even though this declaration was written by two great Ukrainian patriots who stood firm in their nationalist positions. Personally, I am convinced that most of the prisoners of the day did indeed subscribe to this idea of the fusion of nationhood and human rights. Two declarations, both dated 1978 and signed by me and several other prisoners of Camp 36, use the same language:

> Without spiritual liberation, both national and religious, there can be no national or individual freedom, there can be no question of respecting human rights.
>
> It took us some time to come to the conclusion that the communist dictatorship—a committedly atheist regime devoid of spiritual values—undermines the foundations of a nation to no less an extent than forced Russification.[5]

All theoretical arguments vanished because the epicenter of and yardstick for our struggle had always been human dignity, which is the cornerstone of national and democratic principles. At the same time, both national and democratic principles could, should they be interpreted dogmatically, compromise human dignity, and thus cause harm to basic human rights.

The Struggle for Dignity and Human Rights

Filled with a sense of moral obligation toward my conscience and my colleagues, I actively joined them in opposing the camp administration. At the time I arrived in camp, the prisoners' massive campaign to be recognized as political prisoners, initiated by Viacheslav Chornovil, had basically been squelched by the administration.[6] This campaign brought much deserved recognition to Chornovil, whom the Russian Jewish writer (and fellow prisoner) Mikhail Heifets even called "the Prisoners' General,"[7] as well as some

5 *Chronicle*, 52:54.

6 That is, political prisoners rather than simply criminals.

7 In fact, it was Captain Pikulin, the commander of Camp 19 in Mordovia, who first gave Chornovil this epithet; Heifetz publicized it. Pikulin asked him, "Why did you, Heifetz, claim the status of a political prisoner? You are

other prisoners who had endured horrific suffering, such as Ivan Svitlychny, Zynovy Antoniuk, and Semen Gluzman. Even without this struggle for status, I had the opportunity to embark on "the education of a young warrior," including protests, appeals to procurators, and labor and hunger strikes.

I didn't meet Viacheslav Chornovil in the camp, but I heard a lot of legends about him. Some of the prisoners recalled that as they would just be getting started on discussions about particular issues, he would already have come up with solutions, which after all subsequent discussions and considerations would turn out to be the best ones. The same later happened in the Verkhovna Rada, where he served as a deputy for much of the 1990s. He was a brilliant political pundit, a self-made man from central Ukraine who, having suffered the torments of a struggle for his own rights, was polished into a political diamond.

Appeals to the procurator and to the higher Soviet authorities were a popular undertaking among the prisoners. None of us had any illusions as to their effectiveness, but by expressing our grievances and telling the authorities what we thought about them, we could at least vent some of our psychological stress and unburden our hearts. We rejoiced at how clever we were in finding creative expletives to apply to the KGB administration. At the same time, we never deviated from the truth because the truth itself could be more condemning than any words. Likewise, reality could be more cynical than any description thereof.

We never deceived ourselves: we were fully aware that the procurators considered our appeals to be the pathetic pleas of wretched chronic complainers who were hell-bent on vilifying the Soviet system. Often, they would not even bother to skim our appeals and would simply send back one of their standard replies: "Justly sentenced." This standard reply often took on ironic overtones, as the following letter from Valery Marchenko to Oleksandr Yakymenko, the Head of the Supreme Court of the Ukrainian Soviet Socialist Republic, dated March 20, 1978, seems to indicate: "Perhaps you would like to differ from your silent colleagues and send me some kind of reply. However, I must warn you that if you intend to write 'you were justly sentenced', you will not be displaying any originality."[8]

completely devoid of independence in action, self-esteem. You do everything according to the orders of your Prisoner General, Chornovil!" Mikhail Heifets, *Izbrannoye*, vol. 3: *Ukrainskie siluety. Voennoplennyi sekretar'* (Kharkiv: Folio, 2000), 78. –M. M.

8 *Chronicle,* 49:33.

By and large, there was no limit to how many letters we could send to the procurators. The outcome, however, is another story. Yury Orlov wrote aptly about this in his report:

> Prisoners' appeals to the procurator, an entity charged with ensuring that lawfulness is maintained in the various prison facilities, usually result in a statement from the procurator that reads "Convicted appropriately." All other entities in the USSR to which a prisoner has the right to direct his appeals usually send these appeals back to the regional procurator, or to the prison authorities. Then, to teach the prisoner a lesson, he is punished for making libelous accusations. Such a reaction from the government authorities who should in fact be protecting human rights during the inquest, the trial, and in prison, is actually the main reason for growing criminal recidivism. The fact that the procurator dispatches responses that support the malfeasance of the Ministry of Internal Affairs results in prisoners' protests, and indeed their rejection of the system standards as a whole. Then, when provoked in such a manner, it is very easy for the authorities to "legally" punish such a prisoner.[9]

To confirm Orlov's assertion, I will cite two entries from the *Chronicle*:

> On 29 May [1978] [Semen] Gluzman was shown documents from the camp informing him that his statements to the Ministry of Health and the Presidium of the Supreme Soviet had been confiscated as "distorting Soviet reality," while the rest had been confiscated as being "ideologically harmful."[10]

> On 16 March [1979] Marynovych was deprived of a scheduled visit for "cynical and insulting expressions" allegedly contained in his statement to the Presidium of the USSR Supreme Soviet regarding the imprisonment in prisons and camps of women and old men.[11]

But confiscating our appeals or simply ignoring them was not enough for the powers that be. They pressed on, and pretty soon a new restriction was introduced: you were not allowed to appeal on behalf of other prisoners. Semen Gluzman could not but relish the irony of this, in a letter to the director of the USSR's camp system:

9 "O polozhenii zakliuchennykh," 360.

10 *Chronicle*, 51:68.

11 *Chronicle*, 53:92.

> In connection with a point contained in the new Rules on Internal Order ("Order No. 37"), which forbids the giving in of statements about circumstances concerning other people, Gluzman expresses the supposition that camp informers will now be called upon to give information only about themselves.
>
> In this way, formerly immoral activities which rotted the soul will henceforth be replaced by useful and moral work with prisoners, which has as its aim goodness and lawfulness.
>
> Am I correct in my interpretation of the intentions of the Minister of Internal Affairs in the new rules?[12]

Still, even these preventive measures were not sufficient for the administration. Indeed, the *Chronicle* diligently recorded all confiscated letters, and prisoners' dispatches noted scores of letters that had never been delivered to them. In order to curtail this leakage of information, the authorities invented yet another law: going forward, a prisoner was not allowed to mention to anyone that one of his letters had been confiscated, even to inform his family about it. The reasoning on this was explained to Semen Gluzman on January 22, 1979, by the Perm procurator Yazev in terse and brutal fashion:

> The censorship service is too soft. If I was in the censor's position, I would confiscate more. And you have no right to tell people in your letters about the confiscation of other letters. This amounts to divulging information about camp life.[13]

The camp calendar had fixed dates for our one-day hunger strikes: January 12 was Ukrainian Political Prisoners Day. Originally established by Viacheslav Chornovil, it was honored mostly by Ukrainian prisoners. August 23 was the anniversary of the Molotov-Ribbentrop Pact, a day when our Baltic friends would strike, with our unequivocal support. September 5 was known as Red Terror Decree Day, in memory of the decree signed by Lenin's supporters on that day in 1918.[14] October 30 was recognized as Political Prisoners Day across the Soviet camp system, and December 10 was known as Human Rights Day. As Yevhen Sverstiuk later described it, "Commemoration of these dates was a form of self-identification among

12 *Chronicle*, 51:98.

13 *Chronicle*, 52:67.

14 Red Terror Decree Day: commemoration of the Decree of the Council of People's Commissars "On Red Terror," which called for the systematic imprisonment and/or execution of "class enemies."

all political prisoners, as hunger strikes were considered a demonstration of implacability."[15]

Obviously, we never forgot to commemorate such generally recognizable Soviet holidays as May 1 (Labor Day) and November 7 (October Revolution Day), which we would also "hail" with general strikes and mass protests. Often we would announce ad hoc events, such as prior to the CSCE conference in Madrid.[16] The first initiative of this sort that I ever participated in lasted from July 23 to August 1, 1978, a week of international solidarity against Soviet Russian imperialism and colonialism.

Honestly speaking, it was in the zone that I fully learned to understand the meaning of the Bolshevik decree "On Red Terror." To be sure, other terrorist acts had occurred throughout history, going back to the start of human preoccupation with politics. But it was in the horrific twentieth century that this "decree from nice uncle Lenin" transformed terrorism into state policy, thereby opening a Pandora's box that humanity has not been able to close to this day.

The *Chronicle* reproduced excerpts from a letter Yevhen Sverstiuk sent to the Legislative Proposals Committee of the Soviet Parliament, dated September 5, 1978:

> This is the brightest, reddest, the most far-reaching of the great Lenin's decrees. It was because of this decree that a new age of all-permissiveness and unlimited power over people was unleashed in the twentieth century. It remains for future researchers to discover how people degenerated and acted meanly and obsequiously from fear and horror before this "revolutionary justice," which has administered wave upon wave of terror over 60 continuous years.

He went on to propose that the decree, "which has fully completed its murderous circle," be repealed. Fourteen other prisoners from Camp 36 sent similar letters to the parliament of the USSR likewise requesting the abolition of this decree.[17]

As soon as Sergei Kovalev showed up in camp, he joined Yevhen Sverstiuk and me in drafting a letter to the president of the United States, Jimmy Carter, dated December 5, 1978, for Human Rights Day on December 10:

---

15 Sverstiuk, *Na khvyliakh "Svobody,"* 197.

16 Madrid conference: 1980 follow-up meeting to discuss the implementation of the Helsinki Accords; successor to the 1978 Belgrade meeting.

17 *Chronicle*, 52:59.

> On Human Rights Day, please accept our tribute of great admiration for you, Mr President, and for your administration: in a world becoming wrapped in lies, you have allowed yourselves to make human rights and moral considerations the basis of your international policy. Responding to the great problems of the century on the level of an amoral game of denunciation, our system of self-legitimizing lawlessness does not wish to understand that the seeds of violence are more dangerous than pollutions of the atmosphere, and that the question of human rights needs more open discussion than ecological questions, since only a free man, who knows his rights, has the strength to accept and to carry out his duty. It is in the resurrection of human faith, honour and duty that the hope of our world lies.[18]

Today, in the era of the Revolution of Dignity, when millions of young Ukrainians gathered in Kyiv's central square in 2013–2014 to demand justice and Ukraine's European integration, I am not ashamed of my words. On the contrary, I am delighted that the million-strong Maidan has incorporated these words as its own legacy.

The *Chronicle* also mentions that the prisoners of Camp 36, together with those of Camp 37, commemorated a "Day in Defense of the Helsinki Groups" on September 20, 1979: "Grigorian, Ismagilov, Kovalev, Marynovych, and Yuskevych staged a one-day hunger strike and sent statements about it to the administration."[19] All such initiatives were regarded as violations of the regime and proof that the prisoners involved had not yet "embarked on the path of correction." It was to this category of prisoners that a variety of selective punishment methods was most often applied. In the eyes of the administration, I was one of those who belonged to this group. Once, the Political Task Force commander called me in and disclosed that I had officially been deemed to be someone who "exerts negative influence on the negative prisoner element of the camp." I just burst out laughing and told him: "You certainly don't know any algebra—two negatives create a positive! Ergo, my influence should be considered positive!"

In a typical Soviet prison camp, convicts were not only surrounded by visible layers of barbed wire but also by invisible, yet equally barbed restrictions: "That is not allowed!" "That is against the rules!" A prisoner encountered these everywhere. It is virtually impossible to enumerate all the possible "violations" that would most certainly result in punishment. For example, "violated the dress code" (e.g., an undone button on one's collar), "bed not made

18 *Chronicle*, 52:59.

19 *Chronicle*, 54:58.

correctly," "did not stand up when greeting someone of authority," "lay down during forbidden time," "stayed in bed after reveille," "got up after lights out," "was late to roll-call," "visited another barrack," "organized a gathering," "disrespected an officer," "ignored a duty officer's command," "did not fulfill his quota," "abandoned his work station"—just to name some of those supposed violations.

There was an extensive menu of punishments: verbal warning, censure, withdrawal of kiosk privileges, confiscation of parcels, cancellation of short or long-term family visits, being put in the ShIZO (with or without a work requirement), incarceration in a PKT for up to six months, and ultimately, incarceration in a centralized prison such as the Chistopol Prison, typically for three years. It was the administration's prerogative as to the type of punishment one received, and they did not necessarily follow any ranking scheme.

Nevertheless, no matter how long the list of punishments was, this was never enough for the administration. The "especially dangerous" prisoners turned out to be such a nuisance for the guards that they would dip into yet another arsenal to find additional punishments. Receiving or being denied medical services, cold and hunger tortures, worsened work conditions, increased work quotas, wanton confiscation of letters, blocking of any communications with one's family, or deliberate dissemination of false information, as well as the placement of psychologically incompatible prisoners together in one cell, forcing non-Russian prisoners to communicate with their relatives during their meetings only in Russian: all of these and more became supplementary methods of punishment. The list is virtually endless. Once again, I will cite some of the Orlov group's observations:

> The atmosphere of impunity in which the administration operates turns all the guards, not to mention the officers, into torturers, their professionalism depending on the degree of their malevolence. "Let me have him for my detachment and he'll become as good as gold," said Lieutenant Kuznetsov to the chief officer of another detachment, referring to V. Pavlenkov, and this was no idle boast. Detachment officer Kuznetsov, perpetually drunk, would amuse himself by seeking grounds for punishments. On Christmas Eve Soroka put a candle and the branch of a Christmas tree on his bedside table—solitary confinement. A carelessly made bed—solitary confinement. Collar unbuttoned—solitary confinement. What little cause one needs to punish "state criminals."[20]

20 "On Prisoners in Soviet Camps," 359.

I would like to explain the phrase "disseminating deliberate disinformation," as it pertained to one's family. They employed an impeccably polished mechanism that would intensify the psychological suffering of an "unrepentant" prisoner. One typical scenario was to deliberately provoke spouses at home to give the semblance of infidelity, which the KGB would later "candidly" bring to the prisoner's attention. Viacheslav Chornovil, Mykola Rudenko, and Yevhen Proniuk and their wives were among those who were subjected to this. Later, Chornovil himself was cast in the role of the unfaithful spouse when an attempted rape was staged during his internal exile.

I witnessed a particularly slick plot that Oles Shevchenko was subjected to. In 1981 Oles knew that his wife was ailing, and then suddenly her letters stopped coming. After a while, Oles was called in by the camp KGB, who informed him that his wife was gravely ill, near death, unable to write to him, and that he should be ready for the worst. "Now you have to think about your two small daughters," they told him, who would inevitably have to be sent to a state orphanage forever. Should he want to help them, all he had to do was repent and stop resisting the KGB, in which case he would be released. Oles left the meeting pale as death. Having told us about this meeting, he paced around the camp in deep deliberation. Finally, he rejected their offer.

One can only imagine what was in his soul at the prospect of sacrificing his loved ones. In the end, however, truth prevailed in Oles's heart. After some time, the letters from Oles's wife resumed. It turned out that all this had been a diabolical trick. The KGB simply used his wife's minor illness to manipulate and try to break a recalcitrant dissident. It is hard to imagine the trap that Oles would have been caught in, had he acquiesced. Norair Grigorian mentions similar psychological pressure:

> Once, as I found myself yet again in an isolation cell, a KGB man with a beaming face handed me a letter from my wife in which she announced that she was breaking up with me. I was heart-broken and beat my head against the wall; it took a long time for me to come to. I was not even allowed to get any letters from my daughter; they simply changed her name. This was a very sad story.[21]

It was extremely difficult for prisoners to endure such moral trauma. It is one thing to sacrifice yourself because you are only responsible before the Almighty and your conscience. But it's another thing altogether to sacrifice your loved ones. Your actions destroyed them and their professional

21 Grigorian, "Vospominaniia," 14.

Figure 7.1. Oles Shevchenko with his family during his internal exile in Kazakhstan.

careers and could sometimes bring them to the brink of death. Who gave you the moral right to do this? This torment was reflected in one of Valery Marchenko's letters to his mother:

> Suddenly, for the first time I saw you in tears. Believe me, it was like an open wound, and I can't ever remember such anguish. I returned to my cell and asked God: "What is the purpose of this world, when a person like you has to suffer? Why do I exist when I have to inflict such pain on those I love the most?"[22]

Some families expressed this agony through a perpetual rebuke: "Because of you, I . . ."; "If it weren't for you, I . . ."; "You didn't even think about us." It is obvious that people's lives were indeed being destroyed. My friends' families, such as the Sverstiuks, Svitlychnys, Marchenkos, Shevchenkos,

22 Valerii Marchenko, *Lysty do materi z nevoli* (Kyiv: Fundatsiia im. O. Olzhyvcha, 1994), 253–54.

Gluzmans, Popadiuks, and many others, just like my own family, were truly blessed because their spiritual life underwent its own metamorphosis: the sacrifice of one of their own became a voluntary sacrifice for the whole family, and feelings of pity and grievance were transformed into gratitude to the Almighty for the ability to offer Him this sacrifice.

This is not an overstatement on my part, although in our time people seldom (and usually spontaneously) reach that level of spirituality, which in the past happened very consciously. It suffices to recall just one line from a prayer of the young Roman Sheptytsky, who took the monastic name Andrei and went on to become the head of the Greek Catholic Church, just before taking his vows: "Almighty, please choose from our family your priests, apostles, and holy martyrs."[23] Who among our contemporaries would actually beg God to have any of their relatives die a martyr's death? Sheptytsky's is certainly a voice from another era, from another spiritual plane. Yet even today there are some such instances, as in the case of some of my friends and indeed my own family. Take the sacrifices of my mother and my sister Nadiika, who, thanks to the purity of their souls, rose to a spiritual level:

> In tribute to our womenfolk, not heroic in the least in their daily chores, when everything seems to go smoothly and effortlessly, without any drama or posturing—but none of them ever faltered. I felt as if I were in the cell next to my husband, and the others felt the same—inseparable and indivisible.[24]
>
> By and large, our "politics" was rooted in the ethics of morally conscious individuals who cannot remain silent when evil reigns in their society. Thus, when the men found themselves behind bars and could no longer express themselves freely, the only thing the women in their lives—wives, friends and colleagues—could do was stay loyal to their incarcerated menfolk and to the values they had fervently espoused. We upheld them, confirming their legacy and passing it on to their children.[25]

In March 1979, we got word in camp that Yevhen Proniuk's father had died. Yevhen was in isolation at the time. I asked the administration to allow

23 Roman (later Andrei) Sheptytsky (1865–1944): head of the Greek Catholic Church from 1901 to 1944. Vasyl' Lentsyk, *Vyznachni postati Ukrains'koi Tserkvy: Mytropolyt Andrei Sheptyts'kyi i Patriarkh Iosyf Slipyi* (Lviv: Svichado, 2001), 24.

24 Kyrychenko, *Liudy ne zi strakhu*, 392.

25 Kyrychenko , 461.

me to see him at least briefly so that I could psychologically prepare him for this news, but my request was denied.

The ShIZO in Zone 36, where prisoners served out their punishments, had a long history; it's a pity that the walls cannot speak. Luckily, however, those cells' residents did not stay silent, and the *Chronicle* has safeguarded a detailed description of this penal facility and the various regimes that reigned within:

> The camp prison building [which houses the ShIZO and PKT] was constructed without a damp-proof course between the walls and the foundations. Consequently in the cells, especially Nos. 2 and 13 (the end ones), the lower part of the walls and part of the floor never dry out. Water often streams down the walls. Higher up the walls it is always damp in the corners. There is ice on the walls in the winter. Sometimes even the water in the jug freezes.
>
> There is always a foul smell in the cells, since the toilet has no flushing mechanism. The smell becomes particularly strong when the cesspit is being cleared out. Water to flush the toilet is turned on in the corridor by the guard on duty, at the request of the prisoners. This often requires a lot of insistence. There is a small hinged window for ventilation. It is impossible to open it fully because of the bars on the outside, besides which the cell gets cold very quickly. In the summer there are swarms of flies and mosquitoes.
>
> Dead mosquitoes are sometimes the cause of an additional period in the [ShIZO]—for "unsanitary conditions in the cell." The cells are cramped. The only available space to walk in is three paces long. The total area of a cell is 11 square metres (2.5 sq. m. per person and another 1 sq. m. for the toilet—a bucket and a washstand). The floors are made of wooden boards, with many gaps between them.
>
> A [ShIZO] cell's entire "furnishing" consists of a stone table, supported on one thick leg, which looks like a large mushroom, and four stone posts to sit on. It is impossible to eat at this table, since the stone posts are situated too far away. Consequently, many prisoners squat in front of a stone stool and place their bowl of gruel on top of it. When the bunks are let down at night, the lower bunks rest on these stone posts (during the day they are up against the wall and locked in position). The [PKT is] a little more "comfortable": there is a cupboard on the wall for crockery, coat hooks and a small table. Moreover, the prisoners succeeded in getting wooden planks fixed across the stone posts, which makes them into benches.
>
> The daily regime in the [ShIZO] differs markedly from that in the [PKT]. Prisoners in the [ShIZO] are issued with thin cotton clothing which is already worn out and invariably the wrong size. There are usually no buttons, everything is held together with string. If the temperature in the cell falls below

Figure 7.2. The ShIZO (penal isolation cell).

the regulation level of 18°C the prisoner can campaign for his pea-jacket. But in order to do this he must first get someone to measure the temperature. At night, when it is coldest, this is impossible. The administration's thermometer, moreover, gives unrealistically high readings and the guards constantly "forget" about this fault.

In the [ShIZO] bed linen and mattresses are not allowed, the beds are knocked together from planks of varying width and are difficult to sleep on. The prisoners are not taken out for exercise (in the [PKT] the exercise period is one hour). The crockery is taken away after meals and kept in a cupboard in the corridor. The prisoners' toilet requisites are also kept in this cupboard. Books and notebooks are forbidden in the [ShIZO] (prisoners in the [PKT] are allowed books and notebooks and may use the library). Writing letters is forbidden (one letter every two months may be sent from the [PKT]), prisoners in the [ShIZO] are only allowed to receive incoming correspondence and publications that they have subscribed to. The guards, however, often "do not know" this rule. It is forbidden to use the camp shop (prisoners in [the PKT]

> may spend two rubles a month). Visits, parcels and packets of printed matter are forbidden, both in the [ShIZO] and in the [PKT].
>
> A stay in the [ShIZO] may also include going to work. In such cases the food ration is the same as in the [PKT]. Prisoners who refuse to work are punished with an additional period in the [ShIZO]. In the [PKT] work is compulsory. No privileges are granted for overfulfilled norms, but underfulfilment results in a decreased food ration (no sugar and significantly less of everything else).
>
> Hot food is given on alternate days. A sample menu: 150 grams of bread and a bowl of greasy soup in the morning; 200 grams of bread, soup, and about five spoonfuls of buckwheat as a second course at midday; in the evening 100 grams of bread and a small piece of fish weighing 30-40 grams, usually rotten. The following day the prisoner is given 450 grams of bread, 20 grams of salt and some hot water. The "hot" food and "hot" water are usually brought to the [ShIZO] barely warm.
>
> The camp administration and the Regional Procuracy consider that the conditions in the [ShIZO] "fully conform to the established norms." The camp Head, A. G. Zhuravkov, even said once: "The conditions are simply ideal."[26]

In his memoirs, Genrikh Altunian also described the tyranny of the thermometer in the isolation cells during the winter. Once he complained about "torture by extreme cold," so the guards showed him the thermometer as per regulations. Looking at it, he could see with his expert eye that there was no mercury in the thermometer. The gauge was permanently set to eighteen degrees Celsius—conveniently enough, the temperature below which cold-weather gear had to be provided.[27]

On the basis of numerous testimonies that we managed to disseminate to the outside world prior to my arrival at the camp, in 1976 the Moscow Helsinki Group issued a document entitled "On the Conditions of Upkeep for Prisoners of Conscience," summing up the overall conditions and issuing its verdict:

> The International Covenant on Civil and Political Rights, which, per Article 1(a) VII, of the Final Act of the Conference on Security and Cooperation in Europe, the Soviet government is obliged to adhere to, states that: "No one shall be subjected to torture or to cruel, inhuman or degrading treatment or

26 *Chronicle*, 52:38–39.

27 Altunian, *Tsena svobody*, 159–60.

> punishment . . ." (Article III.7 of the International Covenant on Civil and Political Rights)
>
> Furthermore, the Final Act of the Conference on Security and Cooperation in Europe envisions the "effective exercise of civil, political, economic, social, cultural and other rights and freedoms all of which derive from the inherent dignity of the human person" (Article 1(a) VII).
>
> The cited information, which is based on many documents and materials, indicates that according to the Public Group to Promote Fulfillment of the Helsinki Accords in the USSR, there have been gross violations by the Soviet government of Article 1(a) VII of the Final Act of the Conference on Security and Cooperation in Europe.[28]

Now I would like to offer a few of my own remarks about my stay in the ShIZO. At one point, the layer of frost on the cement was thick, and the thin robe that was issued to us failed to protect us against the cold. We lodged a protest claiming that the guards had set the temperature in the radiators as low as they could without them freezing, essentially creating an environment aimed at "re-educating" us through torture by extreme cold. We finally managed to get Dr. Petrov to come check the temperature and render his verdict. I remember that when we showed him the frost on the walls, he just shrugged and said dispassionately, "So what, that's nothing! You can live with that!" This confirms that the physicians were often more ruthless than the guards.

While in the ShIZO, I was amazed to learn that the newspaper could be an excellent protector against the cold. From then on, I always subscribed to *Literaturnaia Gazeta* (Literary gazette) because its pages were the widest. If you pulled up your knees and covered yourself with the pages, it did help a bit: unless, of course, the guards on a particular night decided that covering yourself up with a newspaper was "against the rules."[29] The newspaper was not able to solve this problem on a long-term basis, however, and when the cold became unbearable, you had to get up in the middle of the night and do calisthenics to warm up.

The uneven boards on our cots were another hardship. They dug into your body, making it impossible to sleep. There was also the problem of what to

28 "Ob usloviiakh soderzhaniia uznikov sovesti, 17 iiunia 1976," *Dokumenty Moskovskoi Khel'sinskoi Gruppy (1976–1982)*, ed. D. I. Zubarev and G. V. Kuzovkin (Moscow: Moskovskaia Khel'sinskaia Gruppa, 2006), 34–35.

29 Later on, they figured it out, and reading newspapers in the *kartser* was forbidden. –M. M.

put under your head because pillows were not allowed. Even all this was still not enough for the rule-makers, and they always managed to come up with new rules:

> Inmates in the ShIZO are not allowed to have any visits, send any letters, purchase additional food or any other essential personal items, receive any parcels, have any table games, or smoke. They are not given any bedding and are not allowed to go outside for a walk.[30]

The two feeding regimes were known as "restaurant" and "hunger." One time, when sharing a cell with Sergei Kovalev, I witnessed the guards tormenting him by mixing up which food he was meant to get on which day. By nature, Sergei was methodical and languid. He took more time to evaluate a given situation than most people. But once he did, no one was his equal. That particular day had been a "hunger" day, but for some reason he received some warm gruel. He carried the bowl to the table, not fully aware of what was happening, as the guard said sarcastically, "Well, Kovalev, are you taking the soup, even though you are not supposed to get it today?" This humiliated Kovalev, and I never saw him get so angry.

It was in the lock-up that I first noticed how a person swells up as a result of a long period on a prison starvation diet; as Patriarch Josyf Slipyj aptly remarked, "There was not enough food to sustain life, but too much to perish."[31] We experimented by eating each item separately to draw out the feeling of fullness.

The smoking ban in the penal isolation cell was also difficult for the smokers. As one of them, I know firsthand how tough it was. This deprivation certainly did not help our mental state. On three different occasions, I vowed to stop smoking, especially when I returned to the zone after long-term confinement in the isolation cells, but my resolve quickly crumbled with the joy of seeing my friends—telling myself that I'd have "just this one," or "how can I not have a smoke on New Year's?" Just typical.

There is a long story behind my first time being sent to the isolation cells. At the end of August 1978, the residents of the Team 1 barrack were told that they would have to temporarily move to another barrack while our old one was being refurbished. We were told that we would have to sleep in bunk beds. Some ten inmates, including me, refused to go, claiming that this was an attempt by the administration to make our living conditions worse. A

---

30 "Ob usloviiakh soderzhaniia uznikov sovesti," 45.

31 Slipyi, *Spomyny*, 185.

prolonged struggle resulted: the water and heating were disconnected, the windows were removed (it gets rather cold in the Urals even in August), and all our personal belongings were thrown outdoors while we were in the work zone. Obviously, all our kiosk privileges, family visits, and parcel entitlements were canceled. Then, on October 25, the main protestors, Yevhen Sverstiuk, Oleksy Safronov, and I, were given fifteen days in the ShIZO, for which we were taken to the neighboring Zone 35.

We were transferred in a covered truck, and this reminded me of the tortures that we had endured in the notorious Stolypin wagon, which I discussed earlier. After about an hour I had to go to the toilet, so all three of us began pounding on the truck wall, asking for the truck to stop. Our guards paid no heed, claiming that it was against the rules. Riding along the bumpy roads became rather unbearable for me. I desperately cast about for a solution and finally found a few cracks in the floorboards, and while my friends turned their heads, I tried to target those cracks while relieving myself. This task turned out to be rather difficult, given the condition of the Ural roads; they were certainly not American interstates.

That year, an early winter had descended on the Urals, and the ground was covered with fresh snow. I was alone in my assigned ShIZO cell, my soul craving peace and tranquility, and I was rewarded with a magnificent sight when I gazed out of my cell window. It was a moonlit night, and the virgin snow sparkled like billions of diamonds, as if in response to the bright stars glittering in the sky. All of this was infused with a bright blue haze, as if I were seeing everything through a filter. This sublime beauty and the feelings it evoked in me simply cannot be put into words. To top off this incredible beauty, one of the stars burst across the sky, leaving a meteoric flash in its wake. I suddenly remembered my sister Nadiika, and I silently sent my thoughts to her.

Perceiving the world through the bars of a cell window creates a unique impression. Even the most callous person can suddenly be transformed into a lyric poet. The soul courageously reaches out for what it lacks by creating a different reality—one in which it can feel safe and protected. As I wrote in my letters:

> I often gaze at the sky, and the magnificent midnight twilight contradicts the notion that blue is a cold color. Once, I was stopped cold by the landscape of bright blue evening snow, the twirling of snowflakes against the lights, and the unyielding barbed wire. I could never have imagined that barbed wire could look so poetic. Every fiber of my being sang "Ave Maria"—and

now the organ chords of that song always accompany my finest moments. (February 12, 1979)

> Yesterday evening I received a star as a gift. Our evenings are already quite dark, and as the clouds parted temporarily, before going to sleep, I suddenly saw one solitary star in the sky, something that we had not seen since June. All this reminded me of Shevchenko's poem, "My evening star" (*Zore moia vechirniaia*), as if the star was itself singing that poem, and I fell asleep enveloped in such emotions that would be impossible for someone who had never experienced life behind bars. (September 9, 1979)

Eventually, when back in the "big zone" (as we referred to the Soviet Union in general), I really missed the intense feelings I had experienced there.

It is indeed a curious paradox that it was in the ShIZO or the PKT that I experienced such gentleness and heightened feelings. I am convinced that this elevation and gentleness are the essence of that evangelical blessedness that is invariably granted to those who are unjustly punished.[32] I was not alone in experiencing such bliss. Viktor Nekipelov once read one of his poems that also reflects this gentleness and evangelical note in the melody of the soul:

> They said that prison is full of agony of wrath!
> They claimed it's the citadel of hopelessness!
> But prison is the symbol of love and patience.
> It is the highest school for hope and gentleness.[33]

The intensity of feelings in camp is amazing: the exalted and beautiful lives alongside the ugly and inhuman, and God alone knows how all this can combine in one's soul. A perfect example of this synthesis was Nekipelov's birthday on September 29, 1982, which we protesters celebrated in isolation. Those of us in a different cell from Viktor wondered how we might celebrate the poet's birthday. We didn't have many options; after all, we were locked up! I had suggested that an appropriate gift for a poet might be a poem. Perhaps we could write a verse each and then read it to him the following day.

---

32 A reference to Matthew 5:10, "Blessed are those who are persecuted for righteousness' sake, for theirs is the kingdom of heaven."

33 *Govorili: Tiur'ma – eto ston ozlobleniia! / Utverzhdali: ona – tsitadel' beznadezhnosti! / No tiur'ma – eto simvol liubvi i smireniia, / Eto – vysshaia shkola nadezhdy i nezhnosti.* Viktor Nekipelov, "Tiurma," http://old.prison.org/lib/nakip1.shtml.

Everyone liked this idea, and we each set out to compose our own verse. It wasn't easy because Rudenko and Nekipelov were the only professional poets in the zone. It was not possible to write our poems down, so we just had to memorize them. By the following morning, everything was ready. There was only one way we could recite the poems: through the toilet. Through this hatch the sound resonated in such a way that you could hear it in every cell. We got Viktor's attention through our regular method of tapping on the pipe. Each of us leaned over the latrine and recited his poem in an emotion-filled voice. Viktor, bent over the toilet, listened to the poems with tears in his eyes.

Nowadays, when I am speaking at public events, it is next to impossible to relate this story: audiences find it difficult to envision such a revolting scene. At that time, however, we did not see the ugliness, or smell the stench; all of this vanished before the magic of our friendship and love.

Amazingly, I still remember my poem:

Someone purged himself of a slave's blood
A small drop that was poisoned.
A spider balked: it's too weak.
It puts the spider to sleep.
  But here's some innocent blood – and it's tasty.
  But it smells of Styx and Charon
  It will make a weak thread
  And this the people with stars on their lapels cannot condone.
There should be some thick and rich blood
Nurturing blood, infused with love.
Full of honey, left by a lover's lips
And a son's gentleness which I took with me.
  Intoxicated he will start to weave
  On his loomed shawl
  Incredibly painful crosses
  From your untainted blood.

On three occasions I was dispatched to the PKT, each time for six months. The PKT cells and the ShIZO cells were pretty much the same, except for the regime. At night, we were issued a mattress and a cover, and the food ration was bigger than in the ShIZO, although it was still smaller than in the zone's regular regime. We were allowed a daily thirty-minute stroll. The PKT had a radio, and we could listen to programs broadcast from Moscow.

Figure 7.3. Parasha (toilet) in the kartser (cell).

My first stint in the PKT began on June 18, 1979, about a year after I arrived at the zone. The official grounds for my confinement was that some of my writings found by the guards were deemed to have been anti-Soviet in nature. On June 22, I started a solidarity hunger strike in support of Sergei Kovalev, who had begun his own hunger strike a week earlier. (Kovalev was desperate because all his letters and visitation rights with his family had been blocked.) A bit earlier, a meeting with his lawyer, who came to see him in the zone, had also been blocked. The tension in camp at that time was extremely high, and my solidarity with Kovalev helped alleviate my own anxiety—I did not want to be a witness to his psychological torment while remaining passive.

I remember that I had previously waged a twenty-day hunger strike to protest the fact that I was not permitted a Bible. During my hunger strikes, I discovered an amazing thing: no matter how much a person might love cookies and other sweets, by about the third day of a hunger strike, you dream of nothing but bread. The smell of bread is with you all the time. Actually, waging a hunger strike in a cell (rather than in the general camp area) brings an additional challenge: your food is brought into your cell and left on the table. You can smell it all the time, and even the most disgusting gruel smells divine.

Five days after the start of a hunger strike, and every three to five days thereafter, inmates were force-fed.[34] I refused to eat willingly, but to prevent losing my teeth (as had happened before to others), I did not protest when

34 In his review of my memoir, Vasyl Ovsiienko stated: "Personally, I did not conduct long-term hunger strikes. Vasyl Stus, however, ended his hunger strike at the beginning of 1983, on its eighteenth day. He had not been force-fed. 'How pathetic is it to terminate one's hunger strike without having achieved anything. I will never bother doing this again,' he told me in 1984. Then he died in his isolation cell on September 3, 1985, just seven days into a hunger strike. In the autumn of 1983, Yurko Lytvyn was force-fed on the sixteenth and twenty-fifth day. Then, on the twenty-sixth day he ended his hunger strike. Ivan Hel was force-fed for the first time on his thirty-second day! His hunger strike ultimately lasted for 100 days. Normally, they would force-feed you every three or four days. Mykhailo Horyn had a heart attack on the tenth day of a hunger strike during his investigation in 1981, and after that he never embarked on any long-term hunger strikes. During his investigation in 1988, Ivan Makar conducted a thirty-five-day hunger strike! In camp, we reckoned that force-feeding would normally start after eighteen to twenty-two days." –M. M.

they stuck a tube into my mouth and down my throat, then they poured liquid gruel in. To be honest, while my conscious will opposed this, my physical body actually enjoyed the feeling of the warm porridge. Somehow it did not want to accept the logic of political resistance.

Kovalev endured his hunger strike for twenty-seven days, finally ending it on July 11, when he was granted a meeting with Reznikova, his Moscow lawyer, after all. That's when I also ended my hunger strike. That night, when I finally did eat something, I became ill. My stomach and my heart ached; my stomach started hemorrhaging, and I lost consciousness some three times.

The rest of my stay in the internal prison was rather uneventful. I was alone in the cell, and at that time I was avidly reading the *Anthology of World Philosophy*. That is when I developed a unique perception of the world, in which you seem to be removed from the world itself and observe events from a distant vantage point. The tiny planet Earth, you yourself, and God formed a triangle. How could you be lonely? This feeling is well illustrated in a fragment of my letter to my family:

> Regarding my leisure time, Mama dear, it is quite simple—it consists of books and pacing around my cell. But the "free spirit of my unfettered mind" [a reference to Lesia Ukrainka's poetry] creates unlimited space for my mind to soar, so I am totally unconscious of the mileage I'm logging. These days I seem to live in a utopian world—perhaps because I am reading Shevchenko's stories. The stories that in the past I had been uninterested in, now find resonance in my soul, thanks to my current emotional state. Shevchenko's epistolary work is still awaiting my attention. (July 9, 1979)

A few months later, my "romance with myself" was almost interrupted. One day, the guards informed me that Ivan Popadychenko, a Ukrainian sportsman who for some strange reason wound up in a political labor camp, would be placed in my cell. Ivan usually joined us wholeheartedly in our struggle with the administration, and every so often he also managed to get himself caught up in the disciplinary system. But it was already clear that I and several others, such as Oles Serhiienko, were not on the same psychological wavelength with him. So the idea of finding myself in the same cell as him for a few months seemed unbearable. I realized that it would be much easier for me to declare a hunger strike than to have Popadychenko as a cellmate. I duly informed the administration of this. In this instance it worked, and I finished my term alone.

My decision was forced by the circumstances and was psychologically motivated, but it was certainly nothing to be proud of. Even then I was beginning to develop an attitude that later, under different conditions, I explained in a letter to my family:

> Fate sends us such difficult people so that we might be able to measure the depth of our patience as well as our love for humanity. Oftentimes, during such difficult moments, I feel that I am part of some cosmic test, that the story of Job repeats itself in our lives again and again. Most importantly, it is vital to remain calm during these challenges, because only then can wisdom reign. (June 12, 1983)

The Popadychenko case was a single instance of my internal contradictions, even though there were numerous such cases in camp. In 1980 I was faced with another challenge: I had to share my PKT cell with Bohdan Klymchak and Mykhailo Slobodian. The two of them were psychologically incompatible; more precisely, Bohdan could not stand Mykhailo. He was annoyed by everything Mykhailo did. He even covered his ears when Mykhailo was washing or eating. He closed his eyes so he wouldn't have to see him. Finally, Klymchak cordoned off a third of the cell and said, "Please do not trespass on my space." He would turn to face the wall. Even though all three of us were Galician Ukrainians, it did not make things any easier.

I am relating this story not to cast any aspersions on Bohdan Klymchak but to show that this was a deep-seated chronic psychological trauma, not just a capricious quirk. Life in camp was far from easy. You had to constantly be ready for unpredictable, sudden provocations from the administration and to regularly cope with the psychological stress of various punishments. Even after many years, after my liberation, my friends would always marvel, "You always look as if you're expecting to be punched." So, it is understandable that relationships within the zone did not always come easily under so much psychological stress. Locked up in a cramped space for years on end, always seeing the same faces, people had to adapt their methods of communication, and not everyone was psychologically compatible. Conflicts were numerous. When astronauts are sent into space for an extended period of time, the organizers are careful to select psychologically compatible personalities. In camp, however, the administration chose incompatible individuals in order to inflict maximum stress and torment on the inmates. This is what happened with Slobodian and Klymchak.

At the same time, far more examples of personal nobility and magnanimity are preserved in my memory. Take, for instance, certain episodes from Valery Marchenko's experience of fate. In spring of 1979, we set a date for a hunger strike and began preparing for it. A week prior, Valery, who was already suffering from a serious kidney illness, was dispatched to a hospital in Perm and was therefore out of reach. I no longer remember what the administration did, but we abandoned our plans for a hunger strike. Most likely, we resorted to some other means of protest. After a while, Valery returned from the hospital and asked us how our hunger strike had gone. Chastened, we explained that the circumstances had changed, and so had our plans. Valery replied with surprise: "But I kept the hunger strike in the hospital—after all, we had agreed!" This created a rather awkward situation. We had totally forgotten that, knowing about the hunger strike, a person of such nobility and commitment as Valery Marchenko would certainly fulfill his obligation, even though he was gravely ill, and no one would know he was doing it. Such high moral virtue is mind-boggling.

At that time, Valery and I talked a lot about the broken lives of our mutual Kyiv friends. We used to joke that we would celebrate at each other's weddings, knowing full well that such a luxury as getting married might never be possible for us. After Valery was sent to his internal exile, these jokes echoed in some of my letters to my family:

> Valery recently sent me a letter, but it hasn't reached me. I have already grown accustomed to this and will somehow manage, but it will be a blow to me if he should get married before I am able to come to his wedding. Still, a guy like Valery should always be desired and a bit inaccessible; how can he belong to just one woman? (November 22, 1981)

Like many other political prisoners, Valery began his prison term with certain doubts and compromises. Subsequently, however, his spiritual journey progressed rapidly. His behavior between his two stints in the penal system, from 1981 to 1983, showed particular commitment. Most dissidents knew they would be arrested, but on top of that Valery knew he would likely die in prison because of his grave illness. My mother was a witness to this because he told her with great irony that he was fully aware where he was "emigrating to." To my mind, this distinction was enormous. Most political prisoners joined forces for a common cause while they were relatively healthy, but Valery embarked on this struggle while gravely ill. Everyone knows how stamina and attitude change even when we just have the flu, for example. One can only imagine what torment a person with a life-threatening illness must bear. Valery endured it all; his was not just a struggle (and certainly not a kamikaze feat) but martyrdom.

Jumping ahead, I should note that Valery paid his filial obligation to his mother in full. His mother was the one who had taught him how to walk, take his first steps into independent life, and stand firm with self-assurance. Eventually, the roles were reversed, and he was the one who taught his mother how not to be afraid and not to succumb to the typical paralyzing fear that deprived Soviet citizens of their intellect, conscience, and self-respect. He taught her how to take the first steps of civil disobedience and to stand firm and with dignity:

> You are my only one, but I don't want to listen to anyone or anything that says that you can compromise spiritually for the sake of being near your mother. Surely no mother needs a depraved bloke who just holds on to her skirt, and when asked if the previous thirty years had been a sham, would just roll his eyes and mumble something about an illness and various other difficulties. Surely this is not the life you would wish for your son![35]

This is how Valery described his alternatives. In the Soviet system, people endured many spiritual challenges when they succumbed to KGB pressures, convincing themselves that they "were forced to be a support to their dear ones." They turned away from their rebellious ways and tried to live docile lives, repentantly begging for their freedom. Yet later, in desperation, they fell victim to alcohol, bringing their families the "gift" of having to witness their slow disintegration as their backs bent under their burden of futility. Or there was the option of following in Valery's footsteps: not betraying his ideals, consciously facing death, and later serving as a beacon from heaven, guiding his mother into her old age and helping her stay strong knowing that both Valery's and her own sacrifices had been acknowledged by the Almighty and are an ornament for His Kingdom. This is how mother and son have remained in my memory: strong and enlightened.

My own experience in the camps can be divided into two periods. In the first, I lived life according to the camp's unwritten rules, in opposition to the camp administration. Yevhen Sverstiuk's description is apt:

> My participation in camp was quite active—I took part in hunger strikes, in mass actions, and in constant opposition to the camp administration. At the same time, I never initiated any conflicts with the administration. My aim was never to get into any confrontations with the guards or the officers. I avoided all contact with them. I would pass by the camp director, Kotov, after which he

35 Marchenko, *Lysty do materi z nevoli*, 254.

Figure 7.4. Valery Marchenko and his mother Nina during his exile in Saralzhin, 1979.

would catch up with me and admonish me, "Sverstiuk, what is your reason for not greeting me? Do you think that this will benefit the cause of an independent Ukraine?" "No, I just don't think Great Russia needs it."[36]

36 Nataliia Pavlenko, "'Khochu sydity v tiurmi za Ukrainu'—Ievhen Sverstiuk, 85 rokiv, pys'mennyk, dysydent," *Kraina*, March 3, 2015, https://gazeta.ua/

Such God-given composure as Sverstiuk had was not universal, however. More commonly seen were demonstrations of the prisoners' unbreakable resistance, such as open hostility toward the guards, defiant behavior, and an arrogant attitude toward the camp KGB representative, Captain Surovtsev. In the beginning, I also demonstrated this boldness, although deep inside I felt that I was really playacting. But I was convinced that I had no other choice: I felt that the alternative would have been seen as betrayal.

Then around the beginning of 1980, Zenovy Krasivsky, a veteran prisoner, showed up in camp. At that time, he was serving his fourth term, having served at the Arkhangelsk Lumber Camp, Vladimir Central Prison, and the Smolensk Psychiatric Center. He was considered a totally trustworthy person. He sought me out after arriving at the zone. It only took a few seconds of looking into each other's eyes and embracing for us to become fast friends. I immediately noticed that his behavior was a bit different. There was nothing artificial, nothing done just for the sake of creating an impression. He even engaged in friendly conversation with Surovtsev, said hello to him, and even joked a bit. It would certainly have been inappropriate to accuse Krasivsky of betraying our cause, so after rallying some courage, I just asked him: "Pan Zenko, aren't you afraid that you might be misunderstood in the zone?"[37] He just looked at me with a puzzled expression and answered with another question: "What, don't you trust yourself?" I was amazed—so that was the answer, just being yourself! The key was to be honest and not just try to look like you were. Whom, after all, was I trying to convince of my unbreakable "rebelliousness"? The behavior that came naturally to me did not require demonstration of this haughtiness and ideologically motivated arrogance. That is, there was an internal contradiction, but it was in my behavior, not Zenovy's!

Eventually, I realized that the position he took resembled that of Christ. After all, it was Christ who had dared to enter the tax collector's house, contravening all unspoken taboos.[38] He was able to do this because he believed in himself and didn't bother to cater to people's image of him. Furthermore, I realized that now, in normal conversations with my captors, I was able to

---

articles/opinions-journal/_hochu-siditi-v-tyurmi-za-ukrayinu-evgen-sverstyuk-85-rokiv-pismennik-disident/598007.

37 "Pan": Honorific roughly equivalent to "Mister"; particularly in Western Ukraine, "Pan" followed by the first name is a customary form of address

38 Referring to the story of Zacchaeus told in Luke 19:1–10.

Figure 7.5. Zenovy Krasivsky with his wife, Olena Antoniv.

convey things that were more jarring to their consciences than before, when I had just sneered at them. I was also able to better maintain my own dignity.

Thus, thanks to the simple formula I learned from Pan Zenko, I embarked upon the second phase of my incarceration, seeking my own style of resistance. I continued to participate in all camp hunger strikes and protests. For me, that year, 1980, was the most difficult of my entire camp ordeal. My resistance had reached its peak, and punishments were meted out one after the other. With my new outlook, however, I perceived all this in a totally different psychological light.

Some of the fruits of that journey shape my character to this day. At the same time, I also had some painful breakdowns that took a long time to recover from. This was a remarkable experience, one that I would have never been able to have in the free world. The words that I had previously written to my family took on even greater significance:

> I have ceased to be amazed at the vortex of my fate; on the contrary, I have started to be curious as to which of the numerous pitfalls that a person might fall into is the one that is made for me. I have even begun toying with the possibly sinful notion of scrutinizing the lawfulness of Providence, to see the world from its perspective. (July 2, 1979)

By that time, both Viktor Nekipelov and Genrikh Altunian had been transferred from camp to prison. None of my other friends were in the camp anymore. Being as depressed as I was, I thought that perhaps this was a good time for me to get sent to Chistopol prison, too. Then suddenly I came into conflict with the administration. One morning I felt that I had a temperature and decided not to go to work, even though the medics stated that I was well enough to do so. I rebelled and did not go to work after all, and for this I was deprived of a meeting with my family. I had warned them ahead of time to think twice before punishing me because in that case I would opt to go to jail. My plan did not succeed, and a new cycle of my protracted resistance began. The spiritual toll it was taking on me can be felt in a letter to my family from that time:

> This is the third time that I have been deprived of our meeting. I did receive your letter, Mama dear, where you asked me to see to it that a meeting would be held, but honestly, I could do nothing about it. Therefore, my conscience is clear. I am at peace, and even though our cup runneth over, I ask God to help the two of you to bear this news with equal stoicism. I can say nothing about my future letters. If you should not get any for a long time, please muster the last scraps of your patience and wait. I am fine, although a few days ago I came down with a touch of flu, but I got over it. For two days I did not go to work and had to stay in bed. Today, Monday, I'm back at work. I treated myself with my own methods. (January 14, 1980)

The punishments were coming at me left and right:

> The sun has once again turned toward autumn, and my gaze is focused on the second half of the calendar, wondering what other troubles are still hiding for me in mighty Pandora's box. (July 4, 1980)

I had not left the *kartser* for months; I was given another six months in the PKT, and on one occasion, Surovtsev told me: "No, we will not send you to Chistopol!" By that time, my physical condition had deteriorated to the point that I was all swollen, and some of my physiological functions had been disrupted. Eventually, however, I realized that my attempts to get into prison were misguided. I gave up on the idea of going to prison and returned to the zone, and I'm not sorry for that.

The next wave of unending punishment came in 1982, after my previously mentioned efforts on behalf of Oles Shevchenko. This is what I wrote to my family at that time:

Do not worry, I am fine. I am writing this right away, because I know how concerned you must be, not having received any letters from me for such a long time. Obviously, I could not write because I didn't have the right to do so [as I was being held in isolation for thirty-four days —M. M.] and those long epistles that I composed in my head while reclining on my cot obviously did not make it to you. I was actually pleased that they did not get to you, because when I received your letters, I realized that your dreams were not disturbed by any ominous thoughts. After my letter to Nadiika, sending both of you name day greetings, I did not write any others. I lost the right to write another letter in September. Another related issue is that our meeting has been postponed by 34 days.

However, that's not all; starting October 11, I will be transferred to another regime [i.e., to the PKT –M. M.] for five months, as was the case earlier. Since this also postpones our meeting, now together with the April postponement, it looks like our following meeting will not happen until October 13, 1983. Furthermore, our two short-term meetings will not be scheduled until February 13, 1984. Unfortunately, as of yesterday, October 13, I have also been deprived of receiving any food parcels, so Mama's cookies are awaiting a trip back home. Now, as far as the other package you sent goes, I should receive it shortly, but if it is returned to you, do not worry, just send it back to me (as long as it does not contain any food items).

To this lengthy itemization, I must add that under this new regime (as in the past), I will be able to write to you only one letter every two months. No doubt, time will drag on for you, and you might not receive my next letter until New Year's, if it gets there on time. I have probably tired you out with all this, so now my dear ones, please relax. I am also pacing around my cell, trying to imagine what you might be doing at a given moment. I will reminisce a bit, and then I will sit down again to write another letter. (October 14, 1982)

The subsequent years are a blur in my mind. The KGB and the camp administration apparently managed to curtail outgoing information because the *Chronicle* shows significant gaps for those years. No doubt I had my stints in the ShIZO—but this is normal for a political prisoner, so it left no lasting impression. I do not remember any other long periods there, though.

National Life in the Camp

I have already made several mentions of the national aspects of life in camp. After all, the national element was one of the foundational ones there. As Alexei Smirnov has commented, "Unlike life in the free world, in prison nationality is respected."[39] The zone was like a little Tower of Babel, not only in an ideological sense but also in the national sense. Although in general, as is well known, Ukrainians predominated always and in every camp:

> The Soviet Union's nationalities policy is reflected in the national profile of political prisoners as well. In the Mordovian and Ural prison camps, Ukrainian prisoners make up thirty to forty percent, often even more; thirty percent are from the Baltics. Russians and other nationalities make up less than thirty percent. It was the Ukrainians who shouldered the bulk of the struggle against Stalin's terror. They continue to do so even now.[40]
>
> Approximately forty percent of the dissidents in camp, those boys who declared that the emperor had no clothes, were Ukrainians. They included linguists, historians and other free thinkers. There were no Belarusians, Uzbeks, or Kyrgyz among them. This attests that the ferment of opposition existed and still exists; therefore [former Ukrainian President] Yanukovych did not have enough time to even start wanting to become a dictator when he got the Maidan.[41]

This is perhaps why I never felt homesick in camp. I heard Ukrainian spoken on a daily basis by my fellow prisoners, I had a Ukrainian-speaking KGB captain available to me at all times, and I could see the ersatz Carpathians on the Ural horizon.

Obviously, when you first landed in camp, you gravitated toward your own countrymen. A note in the *Chronicle* dated March 9, 1982, records a solemn commemoration of Taras Shevchenko's birthday, with a reading of his poetry, the words of which had always provided solace and encouragement to persecuted Ukrainians—in this lies its deep kinship with the Gospel.[42]

If it was relatively easy for Ukrainians to communicate with their compatriots, it was much more difficult for inmates from the Baltics or Caucasus to do so. National trauma was experienced by many political prisoners in this valley of doom, but the predicament of the Armenian Ishkhan Mkrtchian can truly be considered extreme. He reminded me of a lonely bee that had been separated from its hive. I felt this particularly strongly in the fall of 1982

39 Smirnov, "Vybor."

40 "U Mordovii ta na Urali 30-40% politv'iazniv – tse Ukraintsi," *Svoboda*, September 28, 1979, 1.

41 Tat'iana Selezneva, "Pogranichnoe sostoianie. Psikhiatr i dissident Semen Gluzman o vyzdorovlenii Ukrainy i strakhe pered Putinym," *Fokus*, March 19, 2015, http://focus.ua/society/326571/.

42 *Chronicle,* 64:89.

when we were held together in the PKT. How emotionally alien this seclusion in Soviet "wonderland" was for him! He exemplified the harsh treatment that the quasi-Russian authorities inflicted on those of non-Russian cultures.

Norair Grigorian recalls that Ishkhan's "crime" had been organizing a youth group that went around Armenia posting patriotic flyers. For this he was sentenced to five years in camp, with five additional years of internal exile. After his trial, while in a transit camp in southwest Russia en route to a Ural prison, a criminal prisoner pried open seven separate doors with a nail, and all the prisoners managed to escape. They were all caught a few days later. And after the severe beatings that ensued, Ishkhan had blood coming out of his ears and was urinating blood. They were informed that one of the escapees died and another one went crazy as a result of the tortures.

So that Ishkhan could hear his native tongue, I asked him to teach me some Armenian. He gladly complied, and I gradually began to learn the unique characters of the Armenian alphabet and to write down simple everyday phrases, which I later used to converse with him. I also learned and later sang him a popular Armenian song, "Tsitsernak" (The swallow). It was only later that I learned that in 1985, on the black day of April 24, Armenian Genocide Remembrance Day, Ishkhan hanged himself in his cell, no longer able to tolerate the national persecution and torment. (I was already in internal exile by that time.)

During my first few months in camp, I learned from some Ukrainian prisoners, specifically from Anatoly Zdorovy and Yevhen Proniuk, about their idea of a national consortium, which they hoped to put forward for general consideration. The gist of the idea was that any plan to wage a collective protest would first have to be discussed and approved at a general meeting for a given national grouping before it could be proposed to the whole camp population. It would be a sort of "multi-ethnic parliament." I remember that when Yevhen Sverstiuk and I heard of this idea, independently of each other, we each rejected it in turn. It struck me as too cumbersome and impractical. Most of all, it seemed to deprive a person of individual freedom. If you wanted to initiate a project without the support of the general group, you'd have to concede. Since your deeds had already been paid for dearly, not only by your own health and future but also by that of your family, it would have been unthinkable to yield to someone else's will instead of to your own conscience.

Often the camp created complicated situations. Within the same enclosed space there were Ukrainian nationalists who declared the need for Ukraine to separate itself from Russia, as well as Russian monarchists such as Igor

Ogurtsov, who considered Ukraine the crown jewel of Russia's empire. Committed anti-Communists and people like the fervent Bolshevik Grigory Isaev, who demanded that the "holy" Communist ideology be purged of all extraneous contaminations, rubbed shoulders on a daily basis. Jews lived alongside former Nazi policemen; Armenians and Azerbaijanis had to avoid any mention of Nagorno-Karabakh.[43] The camp put all of them on the same platform: all of them had been persecuted, tormented, and incarcerated. No one had a higher social status than anyone else; everyone's head had been shaved, and we wore the same garments. This common camp camaraderie required a certain level of tolerance and the ability to respect your opponent's convictions, as he had paid a similar price for them as you.

Everyone, regardless of nationality, shared a collective status and a common enemy, and we all felt it. This is how Are Vudka, a Jewish political prisoner, expressed it:

> We all had a common enemy and a similar goal, and we had to support each other. We were well aware that the authorities were trying to create animosity between people of different nationalities, and in camp we felt that we all were in the same situation and all had the same enemy. Thus, we resolved to overcome the animosity that the authorities were sowing among us, to stand by each other and work together, not only on a personal level, but among the [national] communities.[44]

Once in a while, the Russians in camp actually stood up for Ukrainian issues. I already mentioned that once while walking around camp, I witnessed Sergei Kovalev, in the presence of many others, arguing with a KGB representative who was trying to convince everyone that UPA was a criminal gang. Kovalev meanwhile argued that they were simply freedom fighters. One can only imagine how shocked the KGB man must have been when he heard arguments in favor of Ukrainian military efforts against the Communist regime coming not from a Ukrainian but from a native Russian from Moscow.

---

43 Nagorno-Karabakh: territory disputed between Armenia and Azerbaijan. Following a 2020 war between the two countries, Armenia withdrew from most of the areas it had occupied since 1994. Azerbaijan now controls all but the unrecognized breakaway state of Artsakh, which is closely linked with Armenia.

44 Izabella Khruslins'ka [Chruślińska] and Petro Tyma, *Dialohy porozuminnia: Ukrains'ko-ievreis'ki vzaiemyny* (Kyiv: Dukh i Litera, 2011), 154.

What's more, the administration could not understand what Semen Gluzman, a Jew who had been raised in a family loyal to the Soviet regime, had in common with the UPA veterans and Bandera loyalists who were now in camp with him. This is how Gluzman himself remembers it:

> The completely natural and friendly relations between the three of us [Yevhen Pryshliak, Vasyl Pidhorodetsky and Semen Gluzman] quickly became the target of rather emotional "operational developments." The authorities could not accept a close friendship between two aging Bandera devotees and a Russian-speaking Jew. One internal spy or another—members of the former Nazi police—tried to warn his "Jewish sympathizers". The astute Pryshliak sarcastically related their efforts to me.[45]

These words are worth juxtaposing with the account of Yevhen Sverstiuk, an ethnic Ukrainian:

> I was very surprised to see that veteran Banderites and other people who were finishing up their twenty-five-year terms had not been infected with any degree of antisemitism. This is a very important indicator. The tolerance seen in the camps had never managed to be instilled in overall Soviet life. Even if there might have been some traces of xenophobia in the camps, you could always have a talk with that person. In contrast, in the normal circumstances of our life, non-freedom had been imposed on us.[46]

The camp environment made it possible for diverse groups that had originally been antagonistic toward each other to listen to one another's arguments. For example, for the first time, Ukrainians began listening to Jews, and vice versa. They not only learned to listen but tried to delve into the opposing side's arguments and find common ground and respect for each other's pain. The same happened between Ukrainians and Russians, as well as other nationalities that had long-standing issues to grapple with. Their common status and standing made it possible for all of them to open their eyes and ears and made their souls more receptive to the plight of others.

Zenovy Krasivsky's behavior was significant in this regard. Taking the typical Soviet mindset as a starting point, this committed nationalist would have been presumed to be an ardent anti-Semite. In reality, however, he was the

45 Pryshliak and Pidhorodetsky were prominent UPA leaders; Pryshliak had been in the Soviet penal system since 1952, Pidhorodetsky since 1954. Gluzman, *Risunki po pamiati,* 204.

46 Khruslins'ka and Tyma, *Dialohy porozuminnia*, 97.

very model of courtesy and amicability. He always had a smile on his face and was friendly with all the Jews in camp. It was remarkable how much this stereotype was shattered. All this was possible because his feelings for Ukraine came from his love for the country and not from hatred for its enemies.

In one of my conversations with Semen Gluzman, when considering the attitude of many Ukrainians toward Jews, I remember mentioning that many Ukrainians believed that Jews were responsible for supporting the spread of Bolshevism and for many KGB crimes. Gluzman listened to me patiently and then said: "Even if we were involved in the formation of this system, we will certainly destroy it." And indeed, by demanding the right to emigrate from the Soviet Union, Jews created the basis for the dissident movement in the USSR.[47] I therefore consider it only fair to acknowledge their contribution to our efforts to defend human rights, rejecting the Black Hundreds' anti-Semitic interpretation thereof.[48]

In camp we not only learned to listen to each other; we also learned to act in concert, respecting each other's unique viewpoints. Are Vudka put it very well:

> Two camp resistance factions were clearly defined: Ukrainians and Jews. When those two groups said "yes," then a given action was guaranteed. You could actually feel the KGB authorities' trepidation that the two subjugated nations might find common ground in the "big zone."[49]

Bohdan Rebryk went even further, boldly asserting that "the Jews did more for the independence of Ukraine than all the Banderites put together."[50] It was actually this camp experience of interethnic cooperation that provided

---

47 In the 1960s and 1970s, responding in part to personal and professional discrimination, a growing number of Soviet Jews sought permission to leave the Soviet Union; the vast majority were denied. An activist movement developed among so-called refuseniks, who worked to raise the international community's awareness of this Soviet policy.

48 Black Hundreds: anti-Semitic ultra-nationalist movement in the Russian Empire at the turn of the twentieth century. Here the allusion is to the conspiratorial notion that the Soviet human rights movement was a Jewish plot.

49 Ar'e Vudka, *Moskovshchina* (S.p.: Izd-vo Moriia, 1984), 35.

50 Bohdan Rebryk, "Ievreis'ki dysydenty zrobyly bil'she dlia nezalezhnosti Ukraiiny, nizh banderivtsi," interview by Andrii Meva, *Firtka*, March 3, 2011, http://firtka.if.ua/?action=show&id=4088.

the inspiration for the initial Ukrainian-Jewish academic conferences that were so widespread in the early 1990s.

As I mentioned earlier, the first mass protest initiative that I was involved in, between July 23 and August 1, 1978, was focused on the nationalities issue. Some twenty individuals from Zone 36 marked a *dekada* (ten-day period) of national solidarity against Russo-Soviet imperialism and colonialism, with hunger strikes and letters of protest and petitions. Anatoly Zdorovy dispatched a letter to numerous high officials of the USSR and the Ukrainian SSR, analyzing the frequent "violations of the declared Soviet law on the national equality of citizens perpetrated by the MVD (Ministry of Internal Affairs) of the USSR," as the *Chronicle* reported:

> Zdorovy cites a number of instances of discrimination against prisoners on grounds of nationality: obstacles to taking out subscriptions to national publications (the author himself, for example, was unable to take out a subscription in 1978, despite all his efforts); the absence from many libraries in places of imprisonment of books in the languages of Soviet minorities (they are not prohibited, but are not "provided for" in the recommendations of the political administration of the Main Administration for Corrective Labour Institutions); the lack of opportunity to listen to radio broadcasts in Ukrainian in camp (on week days the radio is switched on for only an hour, at a time when there are no Ukrainian broadcasts); the numerous occasions when it is forbidden to use one's native language during visits from one's family; the delays over letters written in languages other than Russian (in 1976 the Head of Vladimir Prison, V. F. Zavialkin, told the author: 'Write in a human language and we won't make a fuss'); the groundless confiscation and numerous 'losses' of letters; the refusals to examine complaints not written in Russian; and the forcible shaving of mustaches."[51]

Speaking of mustaches, the *Chronicle* mentions that on December 20, 1978, I was "warned" about my mustache.[52] But interestingly enough, for some reason, unlike the earlier incident in the army, I do not remember anything like this in camp; I don't remember wearing a mustache nor having it shaved off. I only know that my mustache must have been shaved off because on December 9, 1980, I wrote to my family, "The only new thing is that the mustachioed Uncle Myroslav is no more. It all happened against my will, but even this I consider just one more challenge I have to endure." Recently I learned that Oleksa Tykhy underwent a similar ordeal. In one of his letters

51 *Chronicle*, 52:53.

52 *Chronicle*, 52:42.

from camp he mentions, "My mustache has been shaved off—and not just once, but four times already."[53]

During the aforementioned *dekada* of national solidarity, the Russian Vladimir Balakhonov's deep concern over the nationality issue was particularly noteworthy. He didn't simply support the "nationalist" demands but also dispatched numerous appeals to the parliaments of the Soviet Union and the RSFSR (the Russian republic within the Soviet Union), stridently giving voice to thoughts which the Russian conscience should indeed have expressed:

> V. Balakhonov, "To the Presidium of the RSFSR Supreme Soviet" (23 July 1978): The author registers his protest against all forms of deportations of persons of non-Russian nationality, including the widely accepted practice of keeping prisoners and internal exiles outside the borders of their national republics.[54]

> V. Balakhonov, "To the Presidium of the USSR Supreme Soviet" (1 August 1978): Behind the Soviet Union's trampling on this most important principle of international law (the right of nations to self-determination—*Chronicle*) lies the unyielding, constant and never weakening ambition of the Russo-Soviet colonial empire, an ambition determined by the internal laws of its existence and posing a mortal threat to mankind—at all costs to preserve, strengthen and expand itself, eventually to the limits of the earth itself, thus bringing about the death or complete degradation of civilization in conditions of ideologically regimented, collective slavery on the Soviet model.[55]

According to Yosef Mendelevich, after Balakhonov ended up in the Chistopol prison, he developed these theories into a formula of "saving the world from the Russian threat":

> As a Russian, I must warn the world of the threat that Russia presents to the rest of the world. The only chance of salvation for us and for the whole world is to dismember the Russian Empire, leaving the Russians only those lands upon which they came together as a nation (*natsiia*) in the 15th century.[56]

---

53 *Oleksa Tykhyi,* 122.

54 *Chronicle,* 52:55.

55 *Chronicle*, 52:56–57.

56 Mendelevich, "Operatsia 'Svad'ba.'"

How resonant these words are today, with the threat that Putin's Russia poses to the world.

Other Russians, such as Sergei Kovalev, Viktor Nekipelov, and Aleksei Smirnov, were also part of this supportive environment in camp. Still, I do not want to present a totally cohesive picture in this respect. For example, Sergei Kovalev told me openly that he "did not comprehend the nationality issue." But his very keen appreciation of human rights issues helped him to acknowledge that depriving a nation of its right to national and cultural self-determination was a crime that violated all basic principles of our civilization.

The poet Viktor Nekipelov and his wife Nina had spent some time in the city of Uman in central Ukraine, where they often crossed paths with the prominent Ukrainian writer Nadiia Surovtseva. Nekipelov was therefore familiar with Ukrainian issues. I suspect that he was more concerned with issues of totalitarianism rather than Soviet imperialism. Nevertheless, in his own way he was able to come to the defense of aggrieved sentiment, while also warning against any excesses of "the murky and fickle feelings of the voice of blood":

> Ukraine, I am your stepmother's son . . .
> I didn't like that Grand Lady,
> For all her hidden boasting . . .
> But here you stand—strange and proud
> Our common pain forgotten
> And you are heaping eternal insults
> Upon my bowed head . . .
> Yes, we are of different blood, that's true,
> But is this where your righteous vindictiveness
> Should be directed today, oh my Ukraine?[57]

This poem was written in 1966—eight years before Viktor's first arrest and thirteen years before his second incarceration, when he and I first met. Being in camp changed many things for the Russian inmates, opening up an understanding of nationality issues that many Russians in the "free" world

57 *Ukraina! Ia – syn tvoei machekhi. / [. . .] / Ia ee ne liubil, etu Baryniu, / Za ee neprobudnoe chvanstvo. / [. . .] / No stoish' ty – chuzhaia i gordaia, / Nashi obshchie boli – zabyty, / Na moiu, na sklonennuiu golovu, / Gromozdish' vekovye obidy . . . / Da, my raznykh krovei, eto pravil'no, / No tuda li, dla mshchem'ia sozrev, / Ukraina moia, ty napravila / Svoi segodniashnii, pravednyi gnev?* Viktor Nekipelov, "Ukraine," https://proza.ru/2009/06/20/1.

had never suspected existed. In this respect, Aleksei Smirnov's experience was quite representative. He was a Moscow human rights defender who discovered the nationalities issue through his contact with the Ukrainian prisoner Zorian Popadiuk and the Armenian Vardan Arutiunian:

> The life of the inmates of Camp 36 became more orderly with the arrival of Zorian Popadiuk and Vardan Arutiunian. Both were quite self-sufficient, determined, with a strong will, sharp mind, and a good soul, possessing a rare ability to differentiate good from evil, and find the most precise solutions. You cannot classify people on the basis of their theories, discussions or ideas, but on their everyday behavior and reactions.[58]

An honest soul, Aleksei was also hotheaded. He didn't watch his words, and this often resulted in many animosities that persist to this day. Aleksei wholeheartedly reached out to the spiritual source concentrated in these people and understood issues that many Russians in the zone never managed to grasp. He mentions some of the things he heard from several Russian prisoners:

> Russian patriots are harbingers of the new Fascists, with Ogorodnikov at their head. "Why are you with them? Come join us, after all, you are a Russian!" More than once the criminal prisoners were set against me, and I had to put up quite a resistance. Thank you, old-timers and nationalist fighters, you set my mind straight: are you looking to get stabbed? Stay away from them![59]

The requirement that we speak only Russian with the camp administration often resulted in spontaneous protests. I learned from Valery Marchenko that in the early months of Mykola Matusevych's incarceration at Camp 35, he gave up trying to adjust to Russian and switched completely to Ukrainian. Once, in our camp, the Estonian Viktor Niitsoo also blew his cool:

> 1 April [1982]. For being late for supper, replying in Estonian at a roll-call and an altercation with the detachment during a search in the corridor, Niitsoo was deprived of access to the camp shop. In protest, Niitsoo stated that during April he would speak only in Estonian with administration officials of officer rank.[60]

58 Smirnov, "Vybor."

59 Smirnov, "Vybor."

60 *Chronicle*, 64:90.

If someone switched to speaking exclusively in his own native language—not just with the administration but in general—this national assertiveness was not viewed very positively by the other prisoners. After all, a Georgian, an Armenian, or an Estonian was not at fault for not understanding everything in Ukrainian.

I was not the first to notice that there were no Belarusian political dissidents; there were those in jail for "wartime activities" (i.e., partisan resistance to the Soviets or collaboration with the Germans), but there were no dissidents. We chalked this up to the absence of the sort of historic resistance to national subjugation that Ukrainians could boast about. There were only a few political prisoners from Muslim countries of the Soviet Union, like the Azerbaijani Aliev, who was in Zone 36. However, even he ended up in the political zone by chance because of some politically charged things he had said while in the criminal zone. Apparently, some officer in the criminal zone overhead his allegedly political statements and tried to win brownie points by reporting Aliev as an "enemy of the people." This young lad was not prepared for a political struggle, and he virtually reeked of his experiences in the criminal zone. Still, he did not collaborate with the administration and was often subjected to the same punishments as the rest of us.

I had one moral dilemma where Aliev was concerned. During one of our conversations he mentioned that he considered vulgar language to be a national insult. I found this appealing because, generally speaking, most of us in the political zone did not use vulgarities (although a word or two might have slipped out occasionally). At one point, Aliev reverted to his criminal ways and overstepped his bounds, and we all took issue with what he had done. I felt particularly insulted because I had been trying to arbitrate a conflict. I lost my cool and, for the first and only time during my prison term, lashed out at him with some vulgarities. Aliev was stunned, and before he had time to take umbrage, I apologized immediately, being shocked at my behavior. To me, this was a warning for the rest of my life.

We Ukrainians constantly discussed the eternal unhappy issues: the nation's lack of cultural self-awareness, its never-ending Little Russianness, the betrayal of the elites, and the need for dialogue among Ukrainians.[61] I remember when Mykola Rudenko, who himself hailed from the Donbas,

61 Little Russianness (*malorosiistvo*): that is, political and cultural subservience to Russia. "Little Russia" was a common term for the Ukrainian lands within the Russian Empire.

suggested that in the Ukraine of the future, there would be a need for patriotic radio and press in Russian. He alleged that the Russian-speaking majority in the Donbas would not listen to Ukrainian media and would thus remain beyond the Ukrainian sphere of influence. Obviously, this opinion did not get much support from the rest of the Ukrainians in the camp.

At some point while speaking with Yevhen Sverstiuk, I raised the question of Ivan Dziuba's repentance after the publication of *Internationalism or Russification?* I did not hear any bitterness or ideological reproach in Sverstiuk's reply, just sincere sorrow for his friend, as he simply said, "It certainly would have been better if he could have just served out his term."

Once in a while, to tick the boxes, the authorities would bring in a delegation of writers from Ukraine. In keeping with the bureaucratic agenda, these writers were supposed to convince us how fortunate we Ukrainians were to be part of this "family of brotherly nations" (*sim'ia bratnykh narodiv*) and reminded us we could truly enjoy this privilege if we would just repent. I remember Vitaly Donchyk, a member of one of these delegations that visited us in 1978. At that time, he was an associate scholar at the Taras Shevchenko Institute of Literature. Our conversation then was rather trite and uninteresting compared to one we had thirty years later in 2008, at that same institute during Oles Obertas's dissertation defense. Everything about this occasion was symbolic. Obertas's dissertation was about samizdat during the dissident period, and his thesis defense was conducted in the very institute that had been notorious for its diligent and persistent persecution of any alternative viewpoints—in other words, of those samizdat authors themselves. This defense was held in the same room where, decades before, Ivan Dziuba's samizdat sensation *Internationalism or Russification?* had been raked over the coals. This was also where Mykhailyna Kotsiubynska had been ousted as one of the institute's rank-and-file staff members. Now she sat in this room again as one of Oles Obertas's advisers. What's more, the candidate's supervisor was none other than Vitaly Donchyk, now an academician. I was asked to speak about the samizdat phenomenon, and this short circuit of Ukrainian history practically made my mind explode. That day, I had to leave the room early, and when I did, Donchyk caught up with me in the hall and said: "I can't remember where we met before." "We met over there!" I said, gesturing toward the vast distant space. When it dawned on him, he just blanched.

Religious Life in the Zone

The Camp and "Cult Services"

In Brezhnev's concentration camps, religious life did not officially exist. Conducting services of any kind was strictly forbidden. Thus, Soviet prisoners were diligently protected from becoming dependent on the "opium of the masses." Nevertheless, many of the prisoners maintained an intense religious life. Contrary to all the guards' efforts, the Holy Ghost did not comply with their camp guidelines and managed to show up anywhere and anytime it wanted. In this respect, the words that I wrote to my family should not be considered at all bizarre:

> I was a bit upset to see Nadiika use the word "devastation," because on a practically daily basis I am almost brought to tears as I experience the depth of spirituality, when during moments of lesser or greater enlightenment, I am seized by the feeling that I have come face-to-face with the holiest of holies. (November 25, 1980)

Many prisoners who had been indifferent to religion prior to their incarceration turned to faith while in camp. The complete absence of normal religious observances often just bolstered one's receptiveness to a profound sense of God, as the loss of sight usually strengthens the other four senses. The inability to pray in a physical church transformed one's tortured soul into a virtual sanctuary. Instead of singing the standard psalms, their aching souls would write their own hymns.

Most of the prisoners of my era were Christians, although only a few individuals came to camp with fully established religious convictions. Most of the time, their first step toward piety was the total rejection of Communist ideology—a psychological denunciation of all its postulates. Since atheism was one of its principal tenets, it was one of the first ones to be shed. Once the basic principles of atheism were removed, religious values stepped in to fill the void. A few prisoners experienced God's grace in a sudden and unexpected burst of energy—nothing short of divine enlightenment. The reader might remember that I myself also underwent such enlightenment.

The "born-again" Christians faced immediate challenges: how could they "turn the other cheek" and "love thy enemy" when that enemy was the cynical and merciless camp guards? There was surely no better opportunity to test one's Christian devotion than in camp! There was nowhere to hide behind the backs of other parishioners from the Almighty's all-seeing eye. In camp, you had no helpful guidance from a priest. You had to face God all by yourself, just like a timorous little ant that finds itself in a human palm, as described in one of Svitlana Zholob's poems:

> Oh, little ant with a torn whisker,
> perched on my palm, do not shiver
> I am afraid of the rain, and of deep loneliness,
> just like you . . .
> In the terrifying motion of the universe,
> I whisper: "Oh Mother Earth,
> Do not abandon me, protect me![62]

There is nowhere to hide from this test. But how blessed was the prisoner who was able to pass it successfully!

Some of the Jewish prisoners also embraced their religion, even though camp offered no opportunities to do so for two reasons: first, in the Soviet penitentiary system there were no facilities for religious observances of any kind, and second, since the one free day had been designated as Sunday, and since keeping the Jewish Sabbath was considered "illegal" by the camp administration, violating this was severely punished.

Yosef Mendelevich, a Jew originally from Riga and today an Israeli citizen, has spoken at length about the difficulties a Jewish person encountered when he wanted to celebrate the Sabbath or any other Jewish holidays. He was one of the most devout Jews in the zone. He and Yevhen Sverstiuk were the pillars of morality in camp. The pressure Israel put on the Soviet Union to liberate Mendelevich was so strong that they were compelled to free him ahead of his term, and he was expelled from the Soviet Union. His memoirs were written in Israel, and I would recommend that everyone read them, to walk with this suffering Jew through all the circles of his prison hell. [63]

As I remember, in Zone 36 it was Mendelevich who took it upon himself to try to informally convert other nonpracticing Jews back to Judaism.

---

62 *Murashynko z odirvanym vusom, / na doloni moii ne tremty – / ia zh tak samo doshchu boiusia / i velykoi samoty . . . / U strashnomu vselens'komu rusi / shepochu: "O, pryrodo, matuse, / ne pokyn' mene, zakhysty . . .* I am quoting here from memory. –M. M.

63 Mendelevich, "Operatsiia 'Svad'ba.'" I should note that Yosef mistakenly states here that I was incarcerated in the Chistopol prison because of my protests. That is not correct—I remained in Zone 36. –M. M.

He would conduct lengthy discussions with every newly arrived Jew, such as Vadim Arenberg, a young Jew from Leningrad, who arrived in Kuchino in 1979. The twenty-five-year old lad, who had been completely indifferent to religious life while in Leningrad, suddenly embraced Yosef's teachings wholeheartedly, changed his name to Dan, began to learn Hebrew, and started to observe Jewish rituals. His worldview also changed, and as Norair Grigorian remembers, Dan liked to humorously adapt a popular saying from the Russian poet Vladimir Mayakovsky: "I would avoid learning Russian for the sole reason that Lenin spoke it."[64]

The issue of conversion prompted an unfortunate clash between Mendelevich and myself. My relationship with Arenberg had been cordial and friendly, and we kept no secrets from each other; I was then surprised when he began to withdraw from me. When I questioned him directly about it, he told me after some hesitation that it was because he had heard from Mendelevich that I had allegedly made some negative comments about him. This was such an obvious falsehood that Arenberg and I went immediately to Mendelevich and asked for an explanation. Yosef grew red in the face and told me: "You know, Myroslav, for us Jews there is nothing more important than to try to convert other Jews back to their faith." I could not accept this alienation of Jews from Christians. Mendelevich's explanation was obviously ideological, but he made his ethical position clear by turning red. Luckily for humankind, the human heart is endowed with a conscience that does not respond to national or religious motivations. This was the only case in which our ethical systems did not converge; in all other instances, Mendelevich's behavior was nothing but morally exemplary.

Other inmates were punished for observing religious rituals. In the *Chronicle*, dated February 2, 1982, there is a short mention that "Kalinin was installed in the [ShIZO] for five days for wearing a beard—a regular occurrence."[65] Kalinin was an Old Believer, and this was part of his struggle against the Soviet disciplinary machine. His religious principles required him to wear a beard, whereas a prisoner was not allowed to do so.[66] The punish-

64 Mayakovsky's expression was the exact opposite: "I would learn Russian just because Lenin spoke it" (*ia russkii by vyuchil tol'ko za to, chto im razgovarival Lenin*). From Vladimir Maiakovskii, "Nashemu iunoshestvu," 1927.

65 *Chronicle*, 64:88.

66 Old Believers, a sect of Russian Orthodoxy that emerged in resistance to widespread ecclesiastical reforms in the seventeenth century, hold that shaving is prohibited by the Old Testament. The issue of beards is a long-standing source

ments were meted out as quickly as his beard grew back, and this constant torture completely devastated this man, although he never gave in.

There was also a Jehovah's Witness in camp who suffered. It would have been unthinkable to suspect him of collaborating with the prison authorities. For his convictions and for rejecting Soviet ideology, he had been incarcerated numerous times; nevertheless, his stamina and spiritual strength evoked only the highest respect. He and I had a cordial relationship, though we did not speak very often. I had a difficult time accepting the extreme convictions of his faith. For example, he often told me that the only book worth reading was the Bible because reading any other books would sooner or later lead you to sin. I recently had the chance to compare my impressions with those of Patriarch Josyf Slipyj, and amazingly enough, they were almost identical:

> A member of the Jehovah's Witnesses had also been unjustly subjected to prison, but he did not break down, saying, "I know that I am suffering for God." He was well versed in Jehovist literature, but he was very stubborn, and there was no use arguing with him.[67]

Prisoners were forbidden to have a Bible in their cells. A legend prevailed that there was only one time during the Stalin era when a Bible and a Koran made it into the cells: when Eleanor Roosevelt came to visit and asked to see the prison conditions. Immediately after her visit, those books quickly disappeared. In the 1970s, however, Jewish prisoners were permitted to have religious literature, although it had to be in Hebrew. Anyone who did not know Hebrew had to settle for reading the Russian translation of Léo Taxil's stridently atheistic *La Bible amusante*, available in the camp library.[68] Fortunately, even in this literature one came across a phrase from the real Bible once in a while, and often I borrowed those phrases for my own use.

This was far from enough for me, and so I found another solution early on in my camp experience. When Ihor Kalynets was about to be released from prison in August 1979, we agreed that once in internal exile, he would

---

of conflict with the Russian state: in the early eighteenth century, Peter I levied high taxes on those who refused to shave for religious reasons.

67 Slipyi, *Spomyny*, 189.

68 *La Bible amusante pour les grands et les enfants*: originally published in 1882, this anti-Catholic work used humorous illustrations to point out what Taxil saw as the inconsistencies and absurdities of Christianity and the institution of the church. The Russian translation, *Zabavnoe Ievangelie*, was widespread in the Soviet Union.

copy the Sermon on the Mount and send it to me in letter form. Ihor did not forget his promise, something I learned when I ran into KGB Captain Surovtsev, who chided me: "Oh, Marynovych, your plan did not work out! You agreed with Kalynets that he would send you the Sermon on the Mount, and you thought I would not find out about it, but we did, and the letter has been confiscated!" This only made me laugh because he sincerely believed he had unmasked a potential crime and eradicated it in time. A note in the *Chronicle*:

> Nekipelov was informed that on July 13, 1982, some "suspect" materials had been confiscated from him. This included the Lord's Prayer, the Creed, and the Hail Mary. Nikomarov, the Task Force Commander, confirmed that the Lord's Prayer was a "suspicious text."[69]

Every so often, protests would flare up because prisoners objected to the ban on reading the Bible. These protests took the form of written appeals or hunger strikes. Thus, between October 26 and December 29, 1981, the Russian Aleksandr Ogorodnikov went on a hunger strike, "demanding the right of prisoners to possess a Bible, the right to confession, communion and service with a priest, the right to subscribe to religious publications issued in the USSR, the right to receive religious literature from close friends and relatives and the right to study by correspondence in ecclesiastical colleges of higher education."[70] On Human Rights Day that year, in a sign of solidarity with him, a group of prisoners, including me, also declared a one-day hunger strike. In support of Ogorodnikov's demands, Viktor Nekipelov appealed to Pimen, the Patriarch of Moscow and All Russia, writing that he had received an explanation from the Perm procurator as to why prisoners were not allowed to have a Bible.[71] The procurator rationalized that prisoners were only allowed to receive literature that was published in the Soviet Union, and, as was well known, the Bible had never been published or distributed there.

---

69 "Permskie lageria," *Khronika tekushchikh sobytii* 65, http://old.memo.ru/history/diss/chr/index.htm.

70 *Chronicle*, 64:91.

71 Pimen: head of the Russian Orthodox Church from 1970 to 1990. In keeping with the church's role within the Soviet Union, Pimen was "widely regarded as a compliant supporter of the Kremlin line." Obituary of Patriarch Pimen, *New York Times*, May 4, 1990.

As I previously mentioned, the *Chronicle* did not record the fact that in 1980 (I think it was) I also waged a lengthy hunger strike for the right to have a Bible. Prior to that, I had written numerous appeals, warning that I would be compelled go on a strike—but to no avail. Eventually, I did refuse to eat, and after the fifth or seventh day they started intermittently force-feeding me to keep me alive. At some point, I realized that I was on the verge of death, and I understood that I didn't have to read the Bible to know that committing suicide was a mortal sin. I acknowledged the paradox that in order to know God better, I was willing to violate one of His basic commandments. I don't know if it was pure religious convictions or the instinctive demands of a hungry body that predominated, but eventually common sense took over, and I terminated my hunger strike.

Nevertheless, immediately after that, I received a great gift, not from the camp administration, but from the Almighty himself. As soon as I dared to stop my hunger strike, the KGB decided to teach me a lesson for the future by bouncing me around in a series of transfers. This punishment turned out to be elaborate: first of all, after a hunger strike, the body is significantly weakened, making those camp transfers twice as difficult. Secondly, having received permission to eat from my brain, my body craved satiation. During transfers, however, that is next to impossible because all you got was half a loaf of bread and some rotten herring.[72] This was certainly not enough to fill up a hungry body. Furthermore, this is not the kind of food your body needs after a long deprivation. Nevertheless, my young organism managed to digest even that and wanted more. Finally, I was brought to a transit prison and placed in a cell with three criminal offenders. I greeted them and sat quietly in the corner. All three of them glanced at each other, took out their bread rations and placed them all in front of me.

It is difficult to describe how this simple act of human kindness affected me. With tears in my eyes, I thanked them for that bread, which at that point had even taken on liturgical significance for me. I had no idea what criminal act these unexpected benefactors had perpetrated, but I ardently prayed to God to forgive them their transgressions, no matter how grave. It was then that I realized unequivocally that even the worst criminals have a spark of God in their souls, and woe to any society that cannot recognize that spark and nurture it in a timely fashion. Eventually, during my internal exile in Kazakhstan, I remembered this incident and vowed that I would

72 This was a long-standing Gulag tradition. Oksana Meshko mentioned it while describing her transfer in 1949; see *Ne vidstupliusia!*, 37. –M. M.

always find some food for the destitute people who worked in my village. Quite often they did indeed benefit from this.

Religious Holidays and Camp Ecumenism

The camp taught us to experience the depth of Christian unity, and a camp ecumenism of sorts developed. This was facilitated by certain pragmatic preconditions: it was much easier to persecute people when they were splintered; when they were spiritually united, they were a formidable force. Our common status as "political prisoners and anti-Soviets" rendered interconfessional differences rather insignificant. Therefore, in our camp, all the Christians celebrated Christmas and Easter twice, according to both calendars.[73] In the face of an all-powerful antireligious machine, Christians of various denominations all banded together and supported each other.

At different times, the camp administration took different stances toward prisoners celebrating religious holidays; sometimes, it would punish them for "violating the regime"; other times it would just ignore it. Soon after arriving at the zone, I heard stories about the punishment prisoners received for celebrating Christmas in January 1978. As a sign of protest, on January 11, ten prisoners declared a hunger strike and lodged objections with the Council for Religious Affairs at the Council of Ministers of the USSR. A week later, the number of prisoners on hunger strike had risen to sixteen in protest of increased restrictions on their right to perform religious rites. In response, the camp commander, Colonel Mikov, threatened them with reprisals not only in camp but also after their release.

My first Christmas (or rather Christmas Eve) in the zone was unforgettable for me, thanks to a funny event. Yevhen Sverstiuk had been taken from camp and placed in the ShIZO before his transfer to internal exile. This was both a pragmatic and a retaliatory gesture: it deprived Sverstiuk of any opportunity to gather any secret materials to take out with him, while also providing the guards with additional means of humiliating the soon-to-be-released prisoner by shaving his head (as he mentioned in his open letter to Major Fedorov).

73 Eastern rite Christianity celebrates Christmas and Easter according to the Julian calendar, Western rite Christianity according to the Gregorian calendar. Christmas was therefore celebrated on both December 25 and January 7; the dates for Easter varied.

The ShIZO cells were in another building nearby but separated from our barracks by barbed wire. I was wandering about the camp, reminiscing about home, Christmas Eve dinner, and *kutia*, when I noticed that since it was not very cold, the cell window where Sverstiuk was being held was open. I immediately decided to bring him some Christmas cheer by caroling for him as loudly as I could. I came as close to the ShIZO as the barbed wire allowed and belted out "*Nova radist' stala*" ("New Joy Has Come," a traditional Ukrainian Christmas carol). About halfway through, the doors to the ShIZO opened and a guard (who must have heard my singing) appeared, shaking his fist at me. I cut the carol short, not wanting to turn this into a political demonstration. Still, I was overjoyed, knowing that if the guard had heard me, my friend must have heard me as well.

The next day, the task force commander, Rozhkov, called me in and, with a certain hesitation in his voice, read out a report reprimanding me for violating the regime. This report detailed everything that had happened near the isolation ward, making particular mention that "Marynovych sang a monarchist song." The commander looked at me suspiciously, wondering if I had changed my pro-national orientation. At first, I was also taken back. Then suddenly it dawned on me, and I just burst out laughing. I had indeed referred to a tsar in my song. The guard came out just at the moment when I sang the line, "Oh our Tsar, our Heavenly Sovereign." The word might have been the same, but it referred to a totally different spiritual code. And thus, for a short moment, I became a Ukrainian bourgeois monarchist!

Over the course of my incarceration, several holidays passed peacefully and uneventfully, as fragments of my letters to my family demonstrate:

> My birthday was great. Since it was a Sunday, I was able to sleep in for my good health, and then managed to fix some little sandwiches—some with fried onions, and others with whipped cream. I tried to fry up all my tears [for the year] along with the onions, although obviously a symbol is a symbol, and [I know that] not everything will be sweetened with whipped cream in my 32nd year. Christmas Eve was celebrated almost the same way, and I called out to Ukraine by singing carols quietly. We now have a new accordion, and the keys no longer stick, creating full-fledged sounds and emotional harmonies. (January 18, 1981)

> I don't know about you, but I had a particularly wonderful Easter. To be quite honest, I didn't expect this. The atmosphere was very cordial, and the holiday table was laden with half a simple colored Easter egg for each person (we ran out of time to paint the eggs in full traditional *pysanka* style); we each got a

> small slice of sausage, some ham, cookies, and nuts—a virtual feast for the eyes! Early in the morning, as it should be, the sun danced with its golden rays, although in the afternoon it snowed. I was urged to give a "concert," and I sang for about two hours, becoming quite exultant as a result. (April 29, 1981)

> Generally speaking, Christmas was fun, if a bit uneven. All it took was a single moment of forgetting myself and allowing memories, dreams, and emotions to enter my heart, and everything holding me up flew out from under me, plunging me into an abyss of despair. In fact, I became rather capricious and unbearable, and when I recognized this, I grew even more despondent. I did not have my dear ones to relieve the burden of guilt and soothe me. At the same time, there were moments of joy, when I got to bring joy to others through caroling. It is possible that the reason for [my changeable mood] is the periodic sun and contrasts in temperature, because one day it might be forty-five degrees below zero, and minus twenty with a snowstorm the next. Such conditions would make even a dog howl, never mind a thirty-three-year-old who hates the cold. (January 10, 1982)

> Easter was peaceful, sunny, and even sweet, because on May 5, I received your packet and our dinner spread was splendid. (May 22,1983)

> My birthday was unexpectedly festive: I hadn't imagined that everyone would congratulate me so warmly, even with homemade cakes. Christmas Eve, on the other hand, was a bit nostalgic and somber, because honestly speaking, I am at my wits' end; I had only enough energy to quietly sing some Christmas carols in a secluded corner, together with another man from Galicia. (January 22, 1984)

But our holidays were not always this peaceful; the Easter of 1982 has been permanently carved in my memory. Our relationship with the administration had taken a turn for the worse, and the authorities signaled that we would be punished if we decided to celebrate Easter. We had no illusions regarding those threats, understanding that they were deadly serious, but we ignored them. We gathered for a common prayer and then started our simple camp repast, which we never finished because a number of guards tore into our barrack, and practically all of us "violators of the regime" were punished. The chief organizers, Mykola Rudenko, Viktor Nekipelov, and I, were placed in the *kartser* for fifteen days. Still, for a Christian, it is always a special blessing to suffer for Christ, so we took our punishment with a clear soul. In a letter to my family I later wrote:

> Easter passed rather mystically for me, because just after praying about love and forgiveness, fate decided to test the strength and sincerity of my prayer. (May 5, 1982)

For me, this sense of blessing was even stronger because being placed into a cell together with two renowned poets was far from punishment—indeed, it was an inspiration. For the whole fifteen-day term, we did not have to go to work, and our food rations were diminished. Instead, we had the most interesting and intense literary discussions. We were hungry but elated because no one interrupted our discussions and poetry readings (although it was mostly Nekipelov who recited his poems because Rudenko didn't know his poems by heart).

This Easter punishment kicked off two distinct tracks of my camp life, and later I reaped truly unique rewards.

While still in the cell, we felt that the whole Christian world should know about the punishment we received for our communal prayer. His Holiness Pope John Paul II was at the top of our list because the respect for him in camp was extremely high, and he was considered everyone's Pope regardless of their confession. I still remember the general burst of enthusiasm when Karol Wojtyła was elected Pope on October 16, 1978. All the political prisoners were elated, regardless of their attitudes toward religion or their religious convictions. It was obvious to us that with a pope who was a Pole, and who had experienced all the atrocities of Communist dictatorship firsthand, the Communists would be faced with a worthy opponent. Many of us had joyously predicted that this would certainly be the end of Communism. But on a personal level, I had no idea at that time how my own life story would cross paths with that of this eminent Pole. I couldn't even have imagined that I would have an audience with him in his summer residence in Castel Gandolfo in 1993; and, later, in September–October 2001 I would spend a whole month watching him preside over the Catholic Bishops' Synod in the Vatican Palace. On one occasion, I would even be present at a dinner in his Vatican apartments. But we should return to the story of our Easter letter.

Pope John Paul II was the first and most important person we addressed this letter to. As for most of the religious leaders in the Soviet Union, we held no particular respect for them because each one in his own way paid fealty to the godless Soviet regime. To some extent, Vazgen I, the Catholicos of the

Figure 7.6. An audience with Pope John Paul II during the Catholic Bishops' Synod, Vatican, autumn 2001.

Armenian Church at that time, stood apart from the rest. And since there were several Armenians among us, we decided to include him in our mailing list.[74]

I was asked to write this letter, so I spent a few days drafting it in my mind, trying to spur my soul to a high spiritual level—in other words, trying to lift my heart to this high task. I had never written letters like this before, so it was inevitable that it would be somewhat flawed. Nevertheless, this letter contained one important thing: sincere honesty and real truth. The text of the letter has been painstakingly preserved by the Russian NGO Memorial:

> Your Holiness,
>
> In our weary world there are too many people who need your prayers and your help for us to dare to write to you about our difficulties. But the time has come when all our hesitations have vanished. So please hear us out, Your Holiness!

74 Vazgen I: head of the Armenian Apostolic Church, an Oriental Orthodox church, from 1955 to 1994.

On the Day of the Holy Resurrection of our Lord Jesus Christ [i.e. Easter], which we celebrated on April 18th, according to the Orthodox calendar, some fourteen prisoners, Orthodox as well as other denominations, gathered around our humble prison table, wanting to congratulate each other on the holiday. Among us were devout Christians as well as those who hesitate to identify the voice of their conscience as the voice of God. One of us, Myroslav Marynovych, was reciting a prayer, and before he could utter words on the resurrection of Love and Forgiveness, fate decided to test the sincerity of our convictions. A team of guards broke up the gathering, and political prisoners Myroslav Marynovych, Viktor Nekipelov, and Mykola Rudenko were accused of organizing a prayer meeting, which is considered contrary to the rules of the regime. They were all thrown into the *kartser* for fifteen days. Some of the others who had gathered were also detained, notably Leonid Lubman, a Jew who had come to congratulate his Eastern-rite friends.

Alas, the days when Eleanor Roosevelt was shown model prisoners reading the Bible and the Koran are long gone. Nowadays, even after many months of hunger strike (by Ogorodnikov, 1980/1981), the prisoners cannot even obtain a Bible. Going to confession is unheard of; in the internal prisons, crosses are being ripped off prisoners' chests, and all religious rituals and even prayers are totally forbidden.

Your Holiness, for people who have dared to stand up to apocalyptic evil in its stronghold, it is difficult to comprehend the essence of Christian humility. We cannot, nor do we want to, render unto Caesar that which by right belongs to the Lord. Most of us envision the essence of our existence in disclosing to the world the true nature of the vociferous Soviet "dove" bearing a nuclear cudgel. Are people who take part in Easter processions for peace in the West, so actively supported by Soviet propaganda, aware of the fact that on those same April days, prisoners in the Soviet concentration camps who call on the Holy Ghost are being thrown in disciplinary segregation by those same Soviet Communist authorities?[75] We beg You, Your Holiness, to apprise them of this. We would like Patriarch of Moscow and All Russia Pimen, and the Exarch of Ukraine and Metropolitan of Kyiv and Galicia Filaret, who so blindly attest that there is freedom of religion in the USSR, to know about this, as well as the Catholicos of Armenia Vazgen I, because any appeals we might send to them would be confiscated immediately.

We wish for all Christians and all humankind to live in peace, well-being and truth, but not at the expense of sacrificing the highest of blessings—that of our God-given souls.

---

75 Easter processions for peace: a reference to the so-called Ostermärsche, held in both East and West Germany beginning in the late 1950s, calling for nuclear disarmament.

May the Almighty grant You, Your Holiness, a long life in the glory of God!

Bowing our heads before the Holy Altar, we ask for Your blessing.

Glory to Jesus Christ!

Signed, Prisoners of Camp 36, Kuchino: Genrikh Altunian, Vladimir Balakhonov, Norair Grigorian, Valentin Zasimov, Leonid Lubman, Myroslav Marynovych, Viktor Nekipelov, Viktor Niitsoo, Aleksandr Ogorodnikov, Mykola Rudenko, Antanas Terlackas, Oles Shevchenko[76]

Having familiarized ourselves with the finished text, those of us who took part in this initiative hid it, and soon thereafter the meticulously written sheet of paper with the letter to both religious leaders (the pope and Vazgen I), was secretly dispatched to the free world. Days passed, and the tension of the Easter episode slowly receded. Then a coded message reached our camp: "The Pope has received your letter and prayed for you during his Vatican Mass." Our joy had no end. We were grateful to the Almighty that our voice had been heard and equally grateful to His Holiness the Pope for broadcasting our voice to the whole world and for praying for us. We were experiencing a well-known evangelical principle: when "the least of these my brothers" (Matthew 25:40) appealed to the pope from prison, he came to them.

The second gift my fifteen-day Easter incarceration brought was the inspiration to write my first philosophical essay. Both Rudenko and Nekipelov started urging me to finally put pen to paper. "How long can you just write appeals to procurators?" After having left the internal prison, I kept their words in mind. Oles Shevchenko was also helpful in this respect when he gathered us one day in the courtyard to read us his new poem. In it, as if in a psychotherapeutic session, he tried to purge his soul of a very painful traumatic incident he had once experienced in Kyiv. Sometime before his arrest, his mother had a heart attack, and, being concerned, he called the emergency services, speaking of course in Ukrainian, only to be told in Russian: "Speak in a human language (*govorite na chelevecheskom iazyke*)!" For a long time, they refused to send an ambulance, insisting that he should speak to them in Russian.

Understandably, Oles's poem was riddled with hatred for Russia, which he called "the Big Bitch" (*velikaia suka*), and every so often, in great pain, he raised his voice to a high pitch. I could totally understand my friend's anger, and I wholeheartedly commiserated with my friend. At the same time,

76 Myroslav Marynovych, *Vybrane*, vol. 1: *Avtobiohrafichni ta ranni tvori. Lysty.* (Lviv: Vyd-vo UKU, 2010), 66-67.

I wanted to cover my ears, run and hide, and my whole being was internally crying out and objecting to this hatred. My heart could not accept this approach, and I felt that I had to respond to Oles with a logical counterargument. The title of my resulting essay, "The Gospel According to a Holy Fool," emerged naturally. After all, only a feeble-minded person can talk about forgiveness in a situation when anger is so completely justifiable. The title itself provided the tone, the rhythm of the words, and everything else relating to the essay. This is when the aforementioned *Bible amusante* came in handy because the first lines of this work contained a quotation from the Gospel of John, and they became the basis for the opening of my essay (see appendix).

I had heard from Lithuanian Catholics about the miracle at Fatima and about the Mother of God's appeal to pray for Russia, and this story was crucial for my essay.[77] It was an eye-opener for me, and it naturally evolved into my own prayer for the country. Today, as Russia continues to plunge itself ever more deeply into satanic darkness, this prayer is ever more relevant for humankind.

At that time, as I mentioned previously, my mind remained unencumbered; my hands were occupied with mechanically combining various elements for the electric irons that I was assembling, while my mind searched for suitable words and organized them into appropriate phrases. Once I got back to the barracks, I would write those phrases down on little scraps of paper and hide them in various crevices where they might not be confiscated. It was not that I was afraid of being punished for these "anti-Soviet" writings; more importantly, I didn't want my most sacred innermost thoughts to be used as a source of humiliation. Thus, this essay was assembled sentence by sentence, initially on paper and eventually stored in my memory.

Finally, the day arrived when I finished writing my essay, and I decided to read it to my friends. I assembled all the trustworthy inmates who understood Ukrainian: Mykola Rudenko and Oles Shevchenko, plus Genrikh Altunian and Viktor Nekipelov. I recited my essay from memory, which provided a good opportunity to observe my listeners. I had a difficult time hiding my fear: "Will the idea of forgiveness, the core of my thesis, be acceptable to

77 Fatima: 1917 Marian apparition in Portugal. One of the pronouncements attributed to the apparition called for Russia be consecrated to the Immaculate Heart of Mary. If not, Russia "will spread her errors throughout the world, causing wars and persecutions of the Church." See "The Message of Fatima," Congregation for the Doctrine of the Faith, http://www.vatican.va/roman_curia/congregations/cfaith/documents/rc_con_cfaith_doc_20000626_message-fatima_en.html

them?" This, after all, was a prison camp, and forgiveness did not come easy here. But the men before me were people of a lofty spirit forged out of suffering. It was an astounding success. Rudenko was captivated and said that "this essay will be bedside reading for Ukrainians for generations to come" and that I was simply obligated to continue writing. Nekipelov volunteered to translate "A Holy Fool" into Russian and said that he would someday like to present his reply in Russia's name. Perhaps the most significant reaction for me was that of Oles Shevchenko: "This work makes a person want to be better." This meant that for the time being, at least, I had attained my goal.

This story had an important sequel: Mykola Rudenko insisted that I transmit "The Gospel According to a Holy Fool" via our secret prisoner dispatches to the West. I was a bit hesitant because that meant that the whole essay would have to be written in miniscule handwriting on small thin strips of cigarette paper as soon as possible. This would take many hours, and it would have been virtually impossible to be isolated without being "supervised" by a guard or spy. Rudenko tried to convince me that everything would be all right. "You will see that an essay with such important ideas will certainly make its way to the West. Just remember how Campanella's book *The City of the Sun* was written. He was incarcerated in a medieval dungeon and had no paper upon which to record his thoughts. Nevertheless, when it became crucial, a miracle happened, and a little girl started to appear by his prison window, bringing him all the necessary materials and taking away his entire work page by page. This is how *The City of the Sun* was secured for posterity."[78]

Eventually I worked up the courage, and one Sunday morning I began to write. The day was sunny and beautiful, and all the prisoners had left the barrack to go outside, so I was alone in the room. A calm tranquility filled the air; the guards were not making their rounds, the spies were idling in the sun, and I wrote. Several hours went by, and conscious of the miracle that no one was coming into the barrack, I managed to finish my work. I went out into the sun and, delirious with emotion, reported to Rudenko. "Well, it's just as I expected," he replied with equal passion.

The text made it successfully to Moscow, and from there to the West. Then, through various channels, it ended up in the hands of Nadiia Svitlychna, the former political dissident who by then had been exiled to the United States

78 *The City of the Sun* (*La città del Sole*): 1602 utopian work by Italian Dominican philosopher Tommaso Campanella, written while Campanella was imprisoned for heresy.

and lived and worked in New York. Eventually, "The Gospel According to a Holy Fool" was published in *Suchasnist'* (Modern times), a current events magazine for the Ukrainian diaspora, with the disclaimer "published without the author's knowledge or approval."[79]

Searching for Religion in the Camp

Generally speaking, life in camp had religious undertones, even when there were no specific religious issues at stake. Every challenge or punishment could become a part of your spiritual (and therefore essentially religious) experience, providing that you actually wanted it to. In this respect, even simple interpersonal relations were revealing.

As I mentioned previously, there was no lack of conflicts among the inmates, and it took me a while to get used to this psychologically. I considered everyone languishing unjustly behind bars to be practically a saint—and therefore faultless. In reality, they were all just regular people—good, dedicated, and honest—but nonetheless fallible and flawed. Even though he was not even aware of it, Yevhen Sverstiuk was the one who helped me sort this out. He was transferred from Zone 35 to Zone 36 in July 1978, and from then on, my relationship with him was a source of great inspiration for me. At that time, there was an ongoing conflict in the camp that we were all having a difficult time resolving. Once, as Sverstiuk and I were strolling through the camp, Aleksei Safronov, an inmate from Crimea, walked up to us and mentioned this conflict to Sverstiuk, asking him what he thought should be done about it. Sverstiuk answered succinctly and straightforwardly: "That's simple, just act according to the Gospel." Both Aleksei and I were stunned. Aleksei, who was totally emotionally consumed by this conflict, was dumbfounded. He considered Sverstiuk's suggestion of the Bible to be unrealistic and impractical. I was amazed by the simplicity and aptness of Sverstiuk's formula. I was startled by the sheer thought that the Bible was not just for Sunday sermons but that its "recipes" could be applied to concrete worldly situations. My worldview short circuited.

Toward the end of his life, Yevhen Sverstiuk explained the secret of his influence on people: "My fate is to try to remind people of some basic axioms. They are very difficult to prove—they are simply universal truths that are self-evident,

---

79 Myroslav Marynovych, "Ievanheliie vid iurodyvoho," *Suchasnist'* 331, no. 11 (1988): 13–17.

without any proof. I turn them into axioms—some basic truths, namely that people are happy only when they are good and love one another."[80]

Equally important for my religious experience was my first experience in the ShIZO, which I mentioned earlier. At that time, I was held alone in a separate cell. One evening, I experienced a major episode of spiritual humility. I no longer remember what it was that I needed from the guard, but I began to pound on the metal doors to get his attention. He ignored me, and I proceeded to pound even harder with my fists but to no avail. Then, like a wild animal, I became infuriated and started yelling. Suddenly, I heard strange noises in my head and saw red. At that moment, I visualized myself as if from the side, and I was appalled: "Is it possible that this enraged man, face contorted with anger, could really be me?" The shock was so strong that my rage vanished instantly. I walked around my cell, begging God to protect me from such devastating rage and to bring back my Christian likeness.

That night was an important lesson in humility for me. In the morning, I quietly summoned the guard and told him: "Yesterday I was trying to call you, but you ignored me. That's not good because I am locked up in this cell and cannot take care of things for myself. But I behaved badly because anger never solves anything, and I want to ask for your forgiveness." Obviously taken aback, the guard said, "That's OK," and just walked away.

No man-made miracle followed: the guard did not open the cell door for us to embrace, à la *Don Quixote*. The miracle was not external but rather within me, and I spent the rest of my time in the isolation cell spiritually renewed. It was then that I realized how Heaven can reward a person when he lives in harmony with it. Nevertheless, it is also important to add that this episode did not transform me into a righteous and virtuous individual. There were numerous other times during my prison life when I got angry and started ranting and raving. But that incident remained in my soul as an important element of my spiritual growth and served as a lasso to curb my future bouts of anger.

As time went by, my spiritual endeavors became known to our camp KGB agent, Surovtsev. As I was told, his reaction was rather interesting: at first, he allegedly just groaned and then said angrily, "He should have thought of it earlier and joined the seminary instead of the dissidents."

In contrast to the outside world, in camp various religious matters were frequently discussed; God was a legitimate topic for discussion. After all, all too often the zone became a valley of moaning and anguish. In the zone, as

80 Pavlenko, "'Khochu sydity v tiurmi za Ukrainu.'"

in a sort of hellish cauldron, anger bubbled and repentance swirled, sin simmered and hope smoldered, evil multiplied and goodness crystallized. Here, behind several layers of barbed wire, was the real purgatory. It was a virtual collection and distribution center: some of the inmates were perpetually drawn into the lower depths of a black hole of ever greater sin, while others, by the grace of God, purged their souls and reached out for greater good. It was not easy to grasp the mystery of such transformations. Sergei Kovalev's assessment of this situation is revealing. In camp, he avoided labeling himself as a devout Christian and was inclined toward agnosticism:

> We considered the ideal in its final form, not attempting to perfect or supplement it, except in one respect: we were profoundly aware of the uniqueness of the ideal, its imperative sense and global scale, which provides the world community with an opportunity for a stable life within a just and secure environment. Therefore, we were acting within the global bounds of this "political idealism," which had not yet been properly named. Individual motives made it crucial for the dissident environment, which mostly comprised non-believers and agnostics, to live by the principles of religious morality: Do what is necessary and let the chips fall as they may.[81]

At one point, Father Alfonsas Svarinskas, a Lithuanian priest, was also in the zone with us. Being incarcerated, he obviously didn't even try to conduct any clandestine religious services— in the zone, every inmate was very visible, and therefore such a grandiose violation would have certainly been intercepted immediately. And yet, in the memoirs of Russian Orthodox believer Viacheslav Dolinin, I found an unexpected testimony:

> Father Alfonsas secretly provided support not only for Catholics, but also for Uniates [i.e. Ukrainian Greek Catholics], including Stepan [Khmara], as well as some Orthodox, particularly if he trusted them unconditionally. I myself took communion from him. Not everyone knows this, but in exceptional circumstances such practice is permitted by our churches, and in Zones 35 and 37, Father Gleb Yakunin was also able to secretly provide communion to the Catholics.[82]

---

81 Sergei Kovalev, "Za ideal otvetish'?," *Novaia Gazeta*, June 15, 2009, https://novayagazeta.ru/articles/2009/07/15/42095-za-ideal-otvetish.

82 Viacheslav Dolinin, "O pravde i vran'e," in *Ne stol' otdalennaia kochegarka* (St. Petersburg: Izd. im. N. I. Novikova, 2005), http://solidarizm.ru/txt/kochegar.shtml.

I suspect this might have happened when Stepan Khmara was in our zone during my absence. Be that as it may, Father Alfonsas and I often had spiritual discussions, during which I shared some of my spiritual questions with him. For me, these discussions were priceless. Unfortunately, he rarely talked about himself, and it was only recently that I learned of his personal acquaintance with Patriarch Josyf Slipyj during their mutual Siberian incarceration. In an addendum to the Patriarch's memoirs, the following information is included: "Learning of Fr. Svarinskas's imprisonment in 1983, Patriarch Josyf immediately wrote a letter of solidarity to our Lithuanian brothers, calling Svarinskas the pride of the Lithuanian Catholic Church and nation, comparing his loyalty to his nation while he was in prison to that of Titus to the Apostle Paul."[83]

In the zone, where I was moved as if standing before the altar of the holy of holies, another prisoner, Bohdan Klymchak, rebelled at just one mention of God. Fate had indeed been cruel to Bohdan. Sensing his innate incompatibility with Soviet reality, this Galician native found himself in 1978 in the far reaches of Turkmenistan, where he carefully crafted a plan to cross the Soviet border; he successfully crossed over to Iran, where Shah Reza Pahlavi was still ruling at the time. Klymchak trustingly communicated with the authorities (particularly with the American CIA), explaining the substance of the literary works he had brought with him. Eventually, at the request of the Soviet authorities, who had found out about him from their Iranian spies, Iran handed him back to the USSR as a criminal and a terrorist. At the last moment, fully aware of his impending fate, Klymchak begged the Iranians to at least safeguard his literary works. But that request was not granted either, and all his materials were handed over to the Soviet authorities. That is how Bohdan, who had hoped to escape Soviet "paradise," was subjected instead to Soviet "justice." He was charged with treason and was sentenced to a fifteen-year prison term and five years of internal exile. Such cruelty by the Iranian authorities and American intelligence, who obviously found no particular pragmatic use for this fugitive, resulted in a tremendous trauma for him, which he found incompatible with belief in God. One time, while sharing a prison cell with him, I struck up a conversation about God, and he responded with a volcanic eruption of pain: "Don't talk to me about God! It's better for him not to exist! Otherwise how can he explain the injustice he has heaped upon me?"

83 Slipyi, *Spomyny*, 378–79.

Aleksandr Ogorodnikov's arrival at the zone was cause for yet another challenge for me. He was an activist working for spiritual rebirth in Russia and the coeditor of *Obshchina* (Commons), a samizdat Orthodox journal.[84] On the one hand, I respected his dedication to his faith and supported him in his legal efforts to override the absurd laws governing the prohibition of all religious cults. But on the other hand, the forms of spirituality that each of us nurtured were in stark contrast. For example, many of us objected to the way he observed Lent: he didn't differentiate it from a regular political hunger strike. Every time Lent was approaching, everyone in the Zone knew that Aleksandr would announce a hunger strike along with some political demands. Our administration learned to recognize this as well. One time, I witnessed Surovtsev humiliating him on the eve of Lent: "Well, Ogorodnikov, I guess you will be starting your hunger strike tomorrow?" Just as soon as Lent was almost over, Aleksandr would announce with contrition: "Tomorrow the Christians will end Lent, so I guess I should end my hunger strike as well." I considered this a violation of both the sanctity of Lent and the concept of a political strike.

In the dining hall, before starting his meals, he would demonstratively stand up and pray (at that time, I was not yet spiritually ready to do that myself). At the same time, he would not make space for anyone else in the shower room, and oftentimes this would cause some conflicts. When I once tried to appeal to him, citing the Christian axiom "love thy neighbor," he shot back, "Myroslav, I can fully appreciate the phrase 'love thy God,' but I have difficulty understanding 'love thy neighbor'." Today, I am fully aware that Ogorodnikov practiced a very ideologized version of Christianity. In my view, in such an environment the true evangelical faith withers, giving rise to religious fanaticism.

In our political camp there was a Russian man who ended up there completely inadvertently. His name was Vladimir Osipov, and he had grown up in an orphanage. He was far removed from politics and lived rather passively. Most likely he wound up in the political camp because some KGB agent wanted to earn himself some extra points by "uncovering" yet another "political case." Passive prisoners like Osipov were used by the administration as ideal bait to spy on us. I tried not to push him away and even drank

84 *Obshchina* was published by Ogorodnikov and colleagues, collecting materials discussed at a seminar on Russian religious revival that was held monthly in Moscow beginning in 1974. Seven people involved with the journal were arrested in 1979. See *Chronicle*, 55:14–15.

tea with him, which in camp was akin to Native Americans smoking a peace pipe, but it became all too obvious that you could not apply any standard measures to him.

One time, his uniqueness put me into a rather unusual situation. Vladimir invited me to have tea with him. I gladly accepted, and as we were chatting and drinking the camp brew, he suddenly smiled and said to me, "Do you know what kind of tea you are drinking?" Upon seeing my surprised look, he continued, "My supply of tea had just run out, and I was thinking how I might replenish my stock, so I decided to go to Surovtsev and told him that I saw you hiding a *ksiva* in the wall behind the barrack.[85] For that he gave me this packet of tea, and I decided to treat you to it, since you were certainly instrumental in my procuring it. I knew that I would not harm you in any way because in reality I never saw you putting anything into the wall." This multilayered moral dilemma made my head spin. For a while, I didn't know what to say. Then I decided that I did not want to read him the riot act, nor did I want to happily just finish drinking the tea as if nothing had happened. So, I analyzed my options from different perspectives and ultimately just quietly finished my "well-earned" tea.

At this point I would like to return to the story I described in chapter 4 of my episode of enlightenment in the Kyiv interrogation cell in 1977. This event had a vivid sequel in camp. Generally speaking, in terms of the development of my civic awareness, camp life forced my psyche to split in half. One half was involved in the normal physical survival of a political prisoner, carving out my living space in daily resistance to the camp administration. My other half continued to hover in metaphysical space, accumulating more "bumps" while experimenting and perfecting my religious mindfulness. But the intensity of my Kyiv catharsis had by now abated, and once in a while I was aware of some doubts creeping into my soul. I wondered if what had happened to me had simply been a hallucinatory experience.

Then around 1980 another big day in my life occurred. It happened on the second day of a hunger strike, which I had declared because they had torn off the cross that I was wearing around my neck while transferring me to the isolation cells. That day, I was alone in my cell, and the first day of my hunger strike passed uneventfully. Then, on the second day, the task force commander called me in and told me that he was in contact with the

---

85 *Ksiva*: Russian criminal slang for a slip of paper or letter intended for other prisoners or the outside world. Derived from Hebrew *katiba* via Yiddish *ksive*, "writing."

procurator, who informed him that after my release from isolation, the cross would be returned to me. Anyone who has ever been in camp knows full well that it's next to impossible to achieve anything with the administration. I therefore almost felt victorious and terminated my hunger strike, and by the end of the day I was elated.

In my excitement I paced around my cell, floating above the universe in my thoughts. I returned to moments of enlightenment, searching for the answers that still eluded me. In other words, I had completely detached myself from the prison environment and was totally immersed in my thoughts. Among all those thoughts, one imperceptibly separated itself from the others and seemed to emerge as the most intriguing. I began to apply this newfound model to the most diverse situations in the world—in Ukraine, or in my family—and in each case, it seemed that not only could I easily explain the past, but I could actually predict the future. At first it all seemed intriguing, and I began to take more risks and manipulate this model. Then I became frightened, sensing that I might be venturing into something forbidden. People should not know about their future. But it was no longer possible to stop. With my inner sight, I was able to look into my most secret depths, as my newly discovered formula revealed the future. This made me feel frightened but also delirious.

I didn't even notice when nightfall arrived, and the guards lowered the bunk beds that were locked and bolted to the wall during the day. It was just in time because I couldn't make my brain stop its wandering, and this brought it all to a halt. My mind went blank, and I blindly made it to my cot. As I lay down, I heard a loud command: "Pray!" Then, almost deliriously, too weak to physically lift my hand, I crossed myself in my mind, and the dark shroud was suddenly lifted from my eyes. My strength immediately returned to me, and I bounded off my cot. Still a bit disoriented, I looked around: "What was that?" I recall that I was conscious of a formula that gave me some understanding of the future. I was trying to remember it but couldn't. It was erased, blocked out. For a while I still tried to bring it to mind, but eventually I gave up. Even more, I understood that I had just been saved from insanity.

Obviously, my nature was not prepared for omniscience. The formula itself had been erased but not the memory of the effect it was capable of creating. I only remember that the formula itself was simple and that it revealed that life in general was rather simple as well. Its complexity lies in the variety of combinations that this simple formula is capable of generating. You can compare it to a child's kaleidoscope. Just a few random fragments of glass within a tube rotated between a system of mirrors are capable of producing an infinite number of images that are virtually unlimited and unrepeatable. In the same manner, the formula for the world is composed of just a few primary elements. There is one (and only one!) system of interconnectedness between them—a primary dynamic model of coactivity. The complexity of the world, its multipliable hierarchal construction, stems from this dynamic model that continuously creates new entities (subelements), which replicate the dynamics of the primary model on their own hierarchical level and plane. This is how the non-Euclidean geometry of space is generated, within which myriad submodels of various sizes break up and cross each other's paths.

The complexity is magnified by the fact that as the submodels multiply, the original elements of the gigantic supermodel begin to develop imperceptibly, and they encompass our whole universe. For us, this supermodel seems gigantic, even though on its hierarchal level, when it finally matures, it might be microscopic. Therefore, the development of our world is simultaneously in the embryonic stage of the formation of this supermodel. When the embryonic stage is concluded and a new supermodel has been formed, this is when the end of this world occurs, and the entire developed multipliable entity is transferred as a single unit onto another plane.

More time went by, and doubt started creeping into my soul. What if this was just hallucinations again? Could it be the result of a day of fasting? Perhaps it wasn't having uncovered that formula that had caused a preinsanity episode. Maybe the formula itself was the result of a bout of insanity? These doubts tormented me, until one day I was granted some proof. In a letter that I received from Nadiika, she told me about a personal incident that had happened to one of her friends. A flash of memory brought back the fact that this was precisely the event that I had envisioned during my visionary experience. Answering my sister on October 22, 1980, I wrote: "There was another incident, when half-intuitively and partially due to a 'magical' premonition that came to me in meditative contemplation, I could envision the future, and this really gives me the goose-bumps."

Even though the information in Nadiika's letter did not bring the formula itself back to me, it did, however, confirm its existence. Since then, I have never forced myself to try to remember it. Primarily because total omniscience requires a person's complete transformation, and an imperfect, sinful individual should not take it upon himself to handle such a fine and delicate instrument. Such a person might turn it against other people, and most importantly, even against himself. Therefore, I trustingly and indeed gratefully accepted this memory block. Furthermore, I am totally convinced that, should it become necessary, this blockage will be released automatically. On the other hand, I cannot deny that I feel a certain sense of loss. As the mathematician John Nash aptly notes, "Rationality of thought imposes a limit on a person's concept of his relation to the cosmos," and thus it is "not entirely a matter of joy."[86]

There is no doubt that all my religious enlightenment and experiences in the SIZO and in the zone have radically changed my worldview. I became more religious and more Christian; nevertheless, my worldview only partially coincides with a purely ecclesiastical paradigm of the world. I will not attempt to go into any details because some elements of my worldview are too nontraditional and "insane" for me to put them out in the open. They did, however, provide me with the particular vantage point from which I regard God's Earth. What's more, I have learned through experience that positions taken by the church that seem unacceptable today might be looked upon as perfectly logical in the future.

Another thing that my moments of enlightenment have left with me is a firm sense of an impending miracle and the anticipation of that miracle.

The camp taught me to see the well-known benedictions of the Sermon on the Mount in a completely new light, such as "Blessed are those who are persecuted for righteousness's sake," and "Blessed are you when people revile you and persecute you and utter all kinds of evil against you falsely on my account" (Matthew 5:10–11). Now I understand how precise and true these words are! The awareness that you are not guilty of any criminal offense, and that you are simply being punished for speaking the truth, sanctifies every day of your camp life, renders it justifiable, and fills it with meaning, even if you did nothing of particular significance that day. This feeling makes your spirit soar and becomes a bulwark for you, the meaning of which you begin to understand only after you leave prison and have to earn your daily bread and to justify your existence through good deeds. It is only then that you can appreciate how blessed and meaningful all those years in camp were.

As I realize that these words might seem like vain exaggerations, I will quote three of my friends on this subject:

> Semen Gluzman: "Here, in the concentration camp, I have a fulfilling spiritual life, happy in spite of everything I have to endure."[87]

86 John F. Nash Jr., "Autobiographical," *Les Prix Nobel 1994*, https://www.nobelprize.org/prizes/economic-sciences/1994/nash/biographical/.

87 Gluzman, *Risunki po pamiati*, 25.

Oleksa Tykhy: "Please let my mother know that I am fine. There are many magazines, books and people here, whose works will be read for many years to come, and monuments will be erected to them. Thus, here, behind bars and barbed wire, I am a hundred times happier than she or Zina [Tykhy's relative] are, without barbed wire, but nevertheless still in prison. There are, and there still will be many torments, but a person needs them to understand what's what."[88]

Yevhen Sverstiuk: "Now, regarding me, am I fine? I actually should not be fine. It should be very difficult for me—it's the measure of my soul. My cup should be filled to the brim. That's what makes sense."[89]

88 *Oleksa Tykhyi*, 119.

89 *Ne vidstupliusia!*, 84.

Chapter Eight

When the Soul Snagged on Barbed Wire

This chapter could have easily been incorporated into the previous one, which deals mostly with religion. In my case, all aspects of my camp life were clearly rooted in my religious experiences. I am turning this into a separate chapter only because I suspect many of my readers will find some of my conclusions more acceptable without any references to religion. The reader should also be aware that this chapter has the greatest number of quotes from my letters. There is no point paraphrasing some of the thoughts I expressed at the time because I doubt I will be able to express them any better. Furthermore, those quotes are valuable because of their authenticity. After more than thirty years, they are not just quotations: they are also testimonies.

Formation of My Worldview

In camp, one's worldview develops the same way as it does in the free world: through the tension of an intense spiritual field that emerges between two diametrically opposing poles. These poles create a field of coordinates within which a person calibrates his own position, taking into consideration his doubts, revelations, torments, and exultations. The only difference is that in camp, the intensity of those torments and exultations is stronger.

From practically the first days of my incarceration—and to be honest, until today—I have grappled with the same dilemma I described in great detail in a letter sent to my family on May 16, 1982, referencing a poem that had been sent to me by one of my cousins, Olenka Tashuta. The gist of it is simple:

> You cannot go through two doors at once. The first door represents one of my principles, "do not cause any hostility." I am trying to make sense of the idea of

> all-forgiving Love. The second door is the desire not to be a naïve utopian in the real world; it can be quite aptly described by the proverb, "Don't be too sweet, because you might get licked away." . . . It is quite easy to predict what would happen should you try to enter both doors at the same time: you would just smash your nose against the frame. That is the reason why I am plastered in the middle of a dead wall, and that is also why I am disappointed in the futile results of all my explorations. And there is nowhere to hide from this choice.

I am convinced that the main result of my "post-graduate studies" in camp was not any concrete answers to specific tangible aspects of this dilemma but rather my general conceptualization and visualization of it. After all, concrete solutions will always err when one perilously distances him or herself from one pole or the other. Nevertheless, this dichotomy is perhaps the essence of human life.

An equally important problem in camp was the tension that arose when the admirable dedication to one's convictions (particularly when being brutally punished for them) conflicted with one's right to alter those convictions once they ceased to reflect one's conscience. Thankfully, this problem interested me less in the sense of wondering if I did the right thing by becoming a human rights defender, than in terms of my right to choose between the "rebellious" and the "evangelical" models in defending my truth.

This problem particularly resonated for me in the 1980s when I read the short story "The Quarantine" by Aleksandr Grin, written during his younger years when he was enamored of the Russian Socialist Revolutionary Party.[1] The plot is simple: a young socialist revolutionary decides to commit a terrorist act, and afterward his friends "quarantine" him for a few weeks in a nearby village so he can evade police. But his life philosophy is radically altered by idyllic village life, lush nature, and the unspoiled beauty of a young village woman. Against the backdrop of a sunlit meadow, his terrorist values seem contrived, if not extreme, so the young man abandons his terrorist aspirations and resigns from the organization. I suspect that a lot of this was autobiographical, but I was obviously more interested in the eternal moral dilemma posed by the story: What does it mean to reject your convictions when you no longer subscribe to them? Should this be considered an act of treason, or, on the contrary, should it be looked at as a justifiable act dictated by your

1 Aleksandr Grin (1880–1932): Russian novelist and writer of short fiction whose works mostly take place in a fantasy world known by readers as Grinlandia. Grin joined the Socialist Revolutionary Party, a democratic socialist party that particularly appealed to the peasantry, in the early twentieth century.

conscience? After all, continuing to support values that are no longer congruent with your convictions can also be considered dishonest and coercive.

I polled many prisoners on this issue, recommending that they read Grin's story first. Most of them concluded that the hero of the story did indeed commit a traitorous act. Only a few individuals, after some contemplation, endeavored to accept the possibility of approving of someone changing convictions—but only if this change would not cause any direct harm to any of their former colleagues. Generally speaking, I consider this an acceptable resolution of this dilemma. But even today I have some doubts whether it could actually have an unequivocal and undisputable resolution.

Another major theme of my life in camp was the organic uniformity of life as a whole. In my personal archive I have several notebooks full of quotations from scientific and popular magazines and books. After my epiphanies in the SIZO in Kyiv, my brain was saturated with the conviction that there was no insurmountable rift between the physical world and the spiritual realm. It was obvious that having probed the particulars of one sphere of existence made it possible to understand the essential phenomena of a variety of other spheres. In other words, one could do exactly what is contradicted by positivist science.

To illustrate other similar comparisons with which I used to exercise my brain, I would like to cite just one comment I made in a letter to my family:

> A while back, I read a review of a study done by some American scientists who had surveyed individuals who had experienced clinical death. The critics particularly ridiculed the accounts of those who claimed they had seen a dark tunnel lined by people they had known during their lifetime. The dying persons remembered approaching the end of the tunnel, reaching the light. Then, in the journal *Tekhnika–molodezhi* (Technology for the Youth), someone who has the gift of making lightning-fast calculations explained that he never does arithmetic in the normal sense of the term. Instead, he envisions himself in a long tunnel, with various numbers blinking along the sides. He walks through this tunnel to the end, into the light, and there he sees the answer; he just reads it out. I was so impressed by the similarity of those two processes that I was compelled to make a deduction that was perhaps not scientific but poetic: at the moment of death, when one has reached the end of the tunnel, one sees the result of one's earthly journey and the sum total of all his or her good or bad deeds. (June 21, 1981)

Most of my other findings remain hidden in my subconscious. Certain things should not be prematurely put into the realm of evidential logic because they might be torn apart by the distrusting critical brain. In other words, every thought has an embryonic phase and has to go through the appropriate gestation period. This period of gestation was evident to me in camp:

> Lately I have become rather apathetic, and I just aimlessly saunter around camp without any goal, wherever our little stream will lead me. I don't worry about this at all because I know from past experience that some sort of internal work is going on inside me, and employing logic can be detrimental to this process. Inevitably the result will be a new enlightenment of some kind. (July 24, 1983)

Even though these enlightenments were the "invisible mass" of my universe, they themselves—or their forbidden analogies—had a strong gravitational pull, and they provided, as they do even now, a significant internal motivation for my actions. My internal self often speaks to me through those visions that upended my soul in the Kyiv SIZO.

The new version of the world that arose from these epiphanies had a clearly eschatological character. My whole being was directed toward the future, toward some moment "X" when the screaming dissonances of today's epoch would find resolution in the promised harmony of Heaven. The camp, with all its torment and pain, only increased my eschatological expectations and rendered them psychologically desirable and redemptive. Here, the effects of my religious discoveries on my worldview were layered over humanly comprehensible aspirations for freedom. My letters were riddled with the seeds of this new world attitude.

> Just a few years ago I would not even have taken note of your words, "I will raise my hands to the distant heaven." . . . To me, heaven is not remote, and we are capable not only of reaching it, but also of peeking into its mystical essence. For where does heaven actually begin, if not at your feet? Perhaps this is a sinful understanding, but I cannot abandon my conviction that blindness is an even greater sin. (To Nadiika, April 23, 1980)

> How the world has changed since it started doubting the idea of an everlasting soul! Death, which had previously been considered a liberation and an unburdening, is now considered the worst tragedy, and people are willing to sacrifice everything that is sacred, even their soul, for just one fleeting moment of a life that has lost its meaning. (May 17, 1981)

> I read very little; I listen to the radio more, because there is something worthwhile to listen to. More and more, I regard the world as a frightened woman in labor. (June 21, 1981)

But everyone who is *waiting* cannot avoid experiencing the disappointment that comes from knowing that his impatience has tricked him. That is the reason why the image of Sisyphus appears so often in my correspondence from camp.

My time in camp also provided me the opportunity to work out and confirm new life maxims and "categorical imperatives." They appeared particularly frequently in my letters to my sister Nadiika. Because of her terrible scoliosis, she had to pay a double price for things that other women took for granted. I therefore felt that it was my duty to somehow cheer her up and help her with the many challenges she had to deal with. The true essence of my dialogue with Nadiika was the "eleventh commandment," which I had formulated for her in camp: "Do not envy someone else's fate." With this, I hoped to help her come to terms with her irreversible illnesses and the merciless challenges that had traumatized her whole life. I cannot claim authorship for this commandment, however, because it is paraphrased in a well-known aphorism: "Do not desire to exchange your God-given cross for that of another because for you this cross is the best one." In the zone, I was often convinced of the validity of this sentiment.

The Raw Nerve of the Soul

I experienced many paradoxes in camp, but one of them was truly unique. On the one hand, due to the never-ending and mostly unexpected blows fate brought me, I had developed a thick skin—my protective psychological shield. I was always ready for yet another surprise and for new suffering. And, as I have previously mentioned, some of my friends claimed that this readiness was even reflected in the strong glint of determination in my eyes. I was not the only one who noticed this otherness. Igor Guberman's poem is indicative of this condition:

> Those who know the air of prison
> are filled with inexplicable nostalgia,
> we are different for the rest of our lives,
> not better and not worse, but different.[2]

---

2 *Izvedavshie vozdukha tiur'my / polny neob"iasnimoi nostal'gii, / pozhiznenno uzhe drugie my, / ne luchshe i ne khuzhe, no drugie.* Igor Guberman, "Izvedavshie vozdukha tiur'my," *Gariki iz Atlantidy*, http://guberman.lib.ru/gariki/6GA/ga003.htm.

On the other hand, my soul resembled an exposed nerve. It was extremely sensitive to music, words, and beauty. I was filled with a sense of trepidation and reverence, and all this had to be reconciled in one essence:

> It is difficult for me to describe my current state of mind with any accuracy. I am either elevated to the highest pinnacles of exultation, with tears of joy streaming down my face, or those same tears appear when I plunge into despair, unable to retain my equilibrium. Then the road again leads upward, and your clumsy Sisyphus climbs upward, because there at the top are the two people dear to me, and the Almighty above them. They are the ones who taught me how to love and forgive—such extremely difficult tasks in human life. (October 14, 1982)

> I'm in a relatively good mood, although it's rather unpredictable. One moment nothing can please me, and then an hour later I'm laughing and radiating such joy as you never thought was possible. (December 11, 1983)

> The very first sounds yanked me out of my environment. I never thought that a key change from major to minor could be so merciless. The unbearably long minor segment contorted my whole body into one exposed nerve, and I no longer saw the white screen, but from two dark corners I saw both of you stretching out your hands towards me. Now I am afraid to listen to music, and I doubt that I would be able to listen to organ music in a cathedral for even a few minutes. (December 25, 1978: on the soundtrack to the Italian film *We All Loved Each Other So Much*)

In camp it was our Ukrainian poet Shevchenko who spoke to me the most. My own copy of *Kobzar* (his famous poetry collection) was with me in all the prisons and camps I inhabited throughout my ten-year term. I can confirm that when you read Shevchenko's words in the zone, all the barbed wire suddenly dissolves, and even space and time seem to vanish. You experience a sort of "short circuit" with the poet's soul. The guiltless person who is being humiliated recognizes the truth and blessings in the seemingly paradoxical axiom, "Blessed are those who are persecuted for righteousness's sake" (Matthew 5:10).

The Song of the Heart

I would like for this portion of my book to serve as an anthem to the two persons closest to my heart—my mother and my sister Nadiika. As I write these words, they are both already in the afterlife, so they will not be able to read this book: the Almighty is turning the pages of our Book of Life for them. Nevertheless, I would like my readers to know that these two individuals were indeed the pillars of my universe. My mother is not just the person who brought me into God's world, and my sister was not just my first teacher, who laid the foundation for my world awareness: they were both part of the undivided "family trinity" without which, until just recently, my existence would have been unimaginable.

Atena Pashko once wrote that she did not exist in the singular. At that turbulent time in my life, I also claimed that "I exist only as part of a unit of three. Otherwise, the stars will dim, and the world will cease to exist." In his early youth, a young lad normally tries to pull himself out of his family's magnetic field, not fully appreciating it. To some extent, I only became fully aware of this magnetism while in camp, when I had already been so brutally deprived of it.

In order to illustrate this, no further explanations are needed; I will give the word to the prisoner himself:

> Nadiika, do you really believe that we become less romantic and naïve with age? On the contrary, I believe that neither people nor events can beat anything out of us. They can only teach us to better hide our raw wounds. I will not swap our bright attitude toward people for any treasure in the world, nor will I sell the purity and joy of trusting people for any tarnished "maturity" or "stalwartness." Because no matter what you call that immunity to life, it always was and will always remain simple indifference. (April 25, 1979)

> Another mother and another Nadiika simply do not exist. There are three pterodactyls from the land of naiveté and sentimentality that still live among the population. (June 21, 1981)

> My dear Mama, I don't remember when I had such a hearty laugh as when I read what you wrote: "Take care of yourself! (Do not overlook the one and only wish I have for you!)" The crux of the matter was that I did indeed skim over your message and got caught on the spot. Good for you, Mama! (February 1, 1983)

My incarceration lasted seven years; including internal exile it was ten in total. I was arrested when I was twenty-eight and released at the age of thirty-eight. During the last year of my internal exile, Liuba Kheina and I got married, and she joined me in Kazakhstan to share that final year. In other words, most of those years a grown man spent alone, without a mate. It was therefore inevitable that this topic was to some extent reflected in our correspondence. There is no need for any comments on the following quotes:

> As I expected, my words about "family bliss" upset you quite a bit. Nadiika, please understand that those were not just maudlin grievances, they were thoughts that help me find my way in the darkness. I would like both of you to remember that I will accept anything that fate has in store for me. One time, Modest [Mentsinsky, one of my relatives —M. M.] told me that I should have been born in a previous century. That must be where I got my readiness to abstain from things, which for me is deprived of any of the negative meaning that people of the twentieth century inevitably ascribe to it. This is perhaps the only quality that the two of you are not able to understand about me. I have been endowed with a characteristic typical of a Ukrainian farmer: tranquility laced with hope and blessed self-assurance that God does not deprive you of everything, but by withholding just a certain portion provides you with those things that others do not have. This ensures the balance between good and evil, so that justice is not tipped over to one side. In the past, people did believe in God's justice. (August 11, 1979)

> My soul has split in half. One half is soaring so high above the earth that it is no longer visible, while the other half is wallowing in the dirt of sin and is stuck in it up to its ears, giggling that a large plus and a large minus together amount to zero. (August 23, 1983)

Reviewing my old letters from camp, I am amazed time and time again that so many of them were written in a humorous key. I therefore want to reemphasize: It's not because I was so happy, but because many of my addressees were curious about how I lived. Equally important to them was to learn what my state of mind and mood was. I was aware of this, and in the letters to my family I tried to incorporate as much humor and warmth as I could:

> My head is practically glowing with all the wisdom I am gaining every day. It looks like soon there will be "white nights."[3] (April 1978)

> Now I would like to paint a picture of one scene from my life for my mother. I was trying to mend my socks. I was bragging that even as a small boy, I used to mend my great grandmother's stockings. I was therefore quite disappointed when I did not get an even patch, but instead wound up with a bunched-up lump that not so much covered the hole, as rubbed the toe of its creator. So much for my bragging! (December 17, 1979)

3 That is, his glowing head will create a similar effect to the lack of darkness at night in the weeks around the summer solstice at northerly latitudes.

Finally, greeting cards and postcards constitute a separate genre in my correspondence with my family. In them, I would pour out my whole soul—they were to be an anthem for my love:

> May Christmas Eve begin with serenity and peace. May the New Year come to you as a peaceful little caroler, and may you wait with him for the appearance of the Son of God, because only with peace and love can you greet His arrival. Love is the best gift that you can bring to His humble manger, and it can create a miracle, making us closer in our separation than had we been together but apart. I kiss your hands, my dear ones. Christ is born! (Christmas 1978)

> May you be sent the ability to understand the language of birds, so that perhaps one of them might chirp and convey to you my quiet gentleness. (to my mother on March 8, 1979, International Women's Day)

> All-in-all, our best letters are composed in our thoughts: letters and prayers. (April 5, 1983)

I opened part two of this book with an excerpt from one of my letters: "There was a spot in the Ural Mountains where the most fortunate people in the world lived in comfort and love." I would like to close this chapter with a wonderful quote from my camp colleague Semen Gluzman's memoir:

> There weren't many of us, really, but by loving and protecting each other we considered ourselves a complete, diverse, interesting, and self-sufficient world. We were indeed a complete world, with its discoveries, difficulties, and goals. We all had our own specific griefs and simple joys, like everyone else. We just lived. Our world was complicated, and it could take a few months to enter that world, but once you became part of it, you became as strong, free and confident as never before, even in the free world. Ukrainians, Estonians, Jews, Armenians, and Russians; old and young; writers, engineers, and farmers; we created our own world, and we were free.[4]

This is why I have called my book *The Universe behind Barbed Wire*. This name refers not just to the "small zone" of the camp; to a certain degree, it also encompasses the whole "big zone" of the totalitarian USSR—surrounded by barbed wire.

---

4 Gluzman, *Risunki po pamiati*, 15.

Intermezzo 2

Transfer to Internal Exile

On December 10, 1982, while I was either in the ShIZO or the PKT, we suddenly heard some excerpts from *Swan Lake* and other somber classical music over the guard's radio. It was obvious that important news would follow. When the announcer declared in a tragic voice that Leonid Brezhnev had died, most of the inmates in the ShIZO building burst out in unbridled joy: the hateful epoch had ended. Logically, I understood why people rejoice when tyrants die; honestly speaking, however, at that time I was simply not in the mood to cheer the death of anyone. To be sure, I shared the sentiments of others that the old era had ended and a new one was about to begin, but I wondered what it would bring us.

Obviously, this issue became the main topic of our discussions. Later, I was amazed how accurately I predicted what was to come. I remember that my fellow inmate Grigory Isaev and I strolled around the camp, and I shared the formula of my political vision with him: "I have no idea how many more Secretary Generals will follow Brezhnev, but eventually there will be one who, in his attempt to salvage the Communist system, will bring it down." This was still a number of years before Gorbachev appeared on the scene.

In earlier years, the KGB warned me and all the other unruly Ukrainian prisoners, "You think that you will return to Ukraine someday? Not with that sort of behavior!" This threat was not an empty one because many a Ukrainian prisoner had received additional time and was forced to languish in camps for more years. At the same time, the KGB continued to offer a way out: repent and "choose the correct path." Their efforts to turn us grew even more fervent around 1983–1984, when it became known that Oles Berdnyk, one of the ten founding members of the Ukrainian Helsinki Group, had "repented." The KGB approached Ukrainian prisoners throughout the camps, showing them a copy of Berdnyk's declaration of repentance, urging them to do the same and citing this as a good example for them to follow. This agitation became even more ardent when on March 15, 1984, the Presidium of the Supreme Soviet of the USSR issued a proclamation pardoning Berdnyk. All this was very painful to hear. I wasn't sure whether he was just paying the price of his pardon and parroting what was imposed on him or if he had really undergone a transformation. Much of this became clearer later in internal exile, as I will discuss later.

My camp term came to an end in April 1984, but as my letters seem to indicate, starting in January of that year I began to experience a certain amount of travel anxiety:

> I'm fine, if such a thing is possible a few months before my release. On the other hand, every so often I become nostalgic for those days just a few years ago, when my brain pulsated with new thoughts, and new worlds emerged before me. All this is gone now, and I am just functioning on token energy, just taking a rest. (January 22, 1984)

> After some good tea and some nice discussions, I was in an excellent mood, and unexpectedly even to myself, I started dreaming about the future. The dreams floated up so effortlessly, and the details were so vivid, that I was quite shocked. (February 4, 1984)

> For some reason people complain that time seems to drag on before being released, but for me, January and now also February have just flown by. Perhaps it is typical for people to try to drag out the time when they are facing such an unknown future. (February 18, 1984)

> My mustache has sprouted once again, because just before your release, the rules permit you to let your hair grow out. And so, barring any last-minute surprises, I will leave this place with a mustache and bushy hair. (March 8, 1984)

I was taken from Camp 36 on March 23, 1984. I don't remember any special farewells. Perhaps the guards yanked me out of the zone before anyone noticed. Major Zhuravkov, the camp commander, came to the exit gate, and we exchanged a few words. Zhuravkov spoke guardedly, choosing his words carefully because during my time spent in Zone 36 we had been on opposing sides of the barricades. He wished me a good journey and a life free of any new challenges. Basically, all of it could be interpreted as skillful manipulation. Even today, however, I think that he was trying to be sincere in his own way. He had been loyal to the Soviet system and considered any confrontation with that system to be futile and self-defeating.

When I finally walked out of the gate, something unthinkable happened to me: I felt sad and had tears in my eyes. I was leaving behind friends I had forged a close bond with, and I was facing nothing but the unknown. I was surprised by my sorrow; is it possible for a person to become attached to a place that had caused him so much suffering? Somewhat later, I read about the similar feelings experienced by Semen Gluzman:

> Love was the only thing that remained. Love for the dead and living friends who shared freedom and suffering, bread and rotten fish with you. Love for the place where you experienced torment and suffered lies and hatred over those seven long years, and where, in spite of it all, you left behind a portion of your soul.[1]

At that time, the entire camp, complete with its sanctioned terror and lawlessness, seemed eternal. It would have felt utopian to imagine that a time would come when Kuchino would house a museum run by the Perm branch of the NGO Memorial and that former prisoners such as Vasyl Ovsiienko and Yevhen Sverstiuk would come to visit. Unlike my colleagues, I never went there.[2] That's why I was so emotional when I heard Yevhen Sverstiuk's words after he had visited the camp in 1998 at the invitation of Perm Memorial:

> I was amazed. On the spot where my barrack once stood, there were now just weeds, and the seven layers of barbed wire had disappeared like a mirage. That barbed wire had been untouchable! The penal isolation cell, where I knew every window, every brick, and every crack in the floor, has all but disappeared. I asked my friend Sergei Kovalev to stand by the birch tree where we used to have our tea, and when he stood there, he was just drowned by the weeds that reached over his head. So we didn't manage to get a photograph.
>
> The only thing that remains are the objects that I still see in my dreams; the barrack with its two-tiered bunk beds is still there. The gangway along which Major Fedorov used to walk along and then suddenly surface to pin us down

1 Gluzman, *Risunki po pamiati*, 185.

2 For a while, museum activists were trying to actively resist pressure from the Putin regime, but they were not able to win their showdown with the government. In 2015 the museum changed its exhibition to an ideologically correct topic: "Contributions to the Victory," http://www.rferl.org/content/russia-perm-gulag-museum-takeover-contribution-to-victory/27152188.html. Thus, step by step, yet another rare exhibition dealing with Gulag atrocities, already barely surviving, will be wiped off the face of the earth.–M. M.

with his tiny piercing tormentor's eyes. The birches which we were not allowed to approach in the spring with our cups in an attempt to draw some sap.

Out of all the well-trained guards, only Kukushkin is still there (although without his KGB insignia), and he roams around the museum like an abandoned soccer ball left behind by the players.[3]

Once I was taken out of Camp 36, I was brought to a camp hospital in the town of Vsekhsviatskaia, where I was placed in a quarantine ward for several days in preparation for my transfer to Kazakhstan. Somehow, I found out that Mykola Matusevych was also being held in quarantine at the same hospital. After some difficulties, we did manage to have a short conversation, although I was not a particularly good communicator at that time, mainly because I wanted to collect my thoughts, get in touch with my feelings, and prepare myself psychologically for the transfer.

At one point, when I was in the exercise area, I suddenly saw an emaciated face and heard a quiet whisper: "I'm Tykhy." Even though Oleksa Tykhy and I had been among the ten original founding members of the Ukrainian Helsinki Group, I was not personally acquainted with him. We now got to know each other, exchanged a few words, and then fell silent, communicating only with our eyes. We did not want our sudden pleasure to be cut short by the guards. That day, my allotted exercise time seemed really short.

What follows are some excerpts from letters to my family, where I talk about getting ready to be transferred:

As you can see from my address, I am now in a different zone, waiting for my transfer. I am not working any longer; I'm just eating and sleeping. My head is in chaos, and I'm depressed because of my departure (yes, one can even get used to the camp) and because my future is so uncertain. This chaos is fused with apathy and self-loathing. But this is just prosody, which I had hoped to avoid. (. . .) I mention only one letter from you, my sister. They handed it to me just before my deployment. I read it quickly, and thus wrapped in the warm fur coat of your love, I got into the car. As is typical, I still don't know where I'm being taken; therefore, you will also have to wait patiently (I repeat, patiently) for my telegram. (March 29, 1984)

This region has already turned to spring. The snows are melting, the willows are swelling up with buds, and the forest, which I can see only 20 meters away during our outings, is rustling, every tree hungrily reaching out to the sun.

3 Sverstiuk, *Na khvyliakh "Svobody"*, 206–7.

> What a forest; I have not heard its wise message for seven long years. (April 4, 1984)

Finally, the day came when I sent my final letter from camp:

> My dearest ones, I am getting this mini-letter ready for the moment when I will actually be departing. That's when I will date it and turn it in. I want to do this so that you don't have to wait for my telegram after April 24—the official date of my release—and from the date on the letter you will know when I left. The journey will be quite long, and if I am sent to Magadan, it could take up to two months. Therefore, please be patient. . . . Everything is fine and quiet. I listened to all those reports on astronauts' return to earth and thought about how I was also getting ready to return to a hostile world from a long and difficult voyage. Pretty soon, I will take my place in a "landing capsule" and will no doubt also experience a certain degree of landing decompression. Then, in some remote desolate area, I will finally land. Well, farewell for now! (April 13, 1984)

But all this was just a false start. They took me to the train, but they did not put me on board. So, I was returned to the hospital and didn't depart until April 15.

It was almost like having a premonition: the landing "decompression" did indeed turn out to be awful. First, I was taken to Perm and placed in an interim prison. When the metal doors of the cell were thrown open, among the other three prisoners I saw Oleksa Tykhy. We hugged, and five minutes later we were chatting as if we had known each other since childhood. Oleksa had ended his hunger strike, but his stomach was still not able to hold any food, and every half hour, everything that had not been digested would come back up. His body had been completely devastated.

Realizing who was standing before me, I got a bit nervous. Since my search for how to implement evangelical principles into my own life had advanced, I wondered how he, such an uncompromising fighter, might perceive me and how he might react to my spiritual journey. I did not want to deceive him, so I just told him about my spiritual insights as well as doubts. I talked about Christ's Sermon on the Mount and how I reconciled my spiritual path with it. I no longer remember the details of our three-day conversation, but I do remember that our views of the world, people, and their relationships were in complete harmony. It turned out that Oleksa Tykhy had also been on a spiritual quest.

He was certainly a fighter—but not one that struggled for the sake of the battle itself, or because of internal aggressiveness. Not at all. I was amazed because before me was the personification of the spirit, although his body was already totally wasted. I saw only his huge eyes, and in them I saw tremendous love and spirituality. After the guards summoned him to leave and we said our goodbyes, for a long time I felt nothing but complete emptiness.

At that time, I did not yet know that I was one of the last people to see him alive. He was taken for surgery for a gastrectomy of his atrophied stomach, caused by his numerous hunger strikes. He was left to take his final journey alone, without any guards. Somewhat later, I found out from Vasyl Ovsiienko, that

> on April 19, 1984, in the Perm camp, Oleksa was granted a short 40-minute visit with his first wife, Olha, and Volodymyr, his son from his second marriage, who lived in Kyiv. Tykhy, who was fairly tall, was extremely emaciated, and even back in 1981 he had weighed only 40 kilograms. His stomach no longer accepted any food. He was supported under his arms, and all his nails were gone. Nevertheless, he was calm and smiling, imbued with the spirit. He said that he forgave everyone—even his tormentors. "Remember the Sermon on the Mount!" he pleaded at the end. Then, on May 5, during surgery, he returned his tortured soul back to God.[4]

My onward journey took me to Kazan, Syzran, and Kuibyshev (today Samara). Out of all these transfers, I remember one particular cell in the Syzran transfer prison. It was incredibly filthy, and you could not bear to touch the mattresses because they had several generations of prisoner filth covering them. A thick tobacco stench permeated the cell, as did the thick atmosphere of the inmates' profanity. But it was a special day—April 22, Easter. At one point I couldn't take it any longer and reminded them, "Hey guys, it's Easter!" For a moment they fell silent, as if considering this, then muttered "Oh" and immediately dove back into their verbal filth, which apparently they could not survive without.

A day later, on April 23, at the same prison, I celebrated my "liberation" with another inmate by putting some sugar in water and drinking a toast. According to the rules, every day in prison beyond your term length counted as three days toward your internal exile. At the time, however, this did not bring me any joy at all. The tally was to be made five years hence, and you still had to live up to that date, whereas every day of my freedom was being taken from me now.

---

4 Vasyl' Ovsiienko, "Oleksa Tykhy. Spravzhnyi donets'kyi ukrainets'," *Istorychna Pravda*, February 3, 2012, http://www.istpravda.com.ua/articles/2012/02/3/70406/.

It was only on April 27, when I finally wound up in a transit prison in Aktiubinsk (today Aktobe, Kazakhstan), that it became obvious to me that I was being taken to the prairies of Kazakhstan. In Aktiubinsk I was held for fifteen days in a cell together with some juvenile criminals, and that was perhaps the most difficult period of all my time in prison. They behaved like small wild animals that still did not understand the nature of human interaction and were trying to find a rightful place for themselves through force and aggression. The fact that these juveniles and I had experienced different camp regimens reflected on the whole range of our behavior: from the way we approached the administration to how we used the *parasha*. This resulted in many conflicts. At the beginning, I was able to appease them with some classic tales, such as Alexandre Dumas's *The Count of Monte Cristo*. Had I been kept with them a few days longer, however, the outcome would have been tragic for me because the psychological danger became unbearable. I still think of that time with particular dread, and having read Patriarch Josyf Slipyj's account of a similar situation, I am left in total agreement with him: "One could find countless young transgressors in camp, and they are the most dangerous element. . . . The teenagers are among the most vicious ones."[5]

Psychologically, the situation was exacerbated by the fact that every day they kept telling me that I would be sent on my way, so I lived in that false hope. Instead, as every evening came, I was forced to abandon hope. This lasted until May 12, when they loaded me into a car and dispatched me into the Kazakh interior. After a two-hour ride, my guards stopped the van and let me out of my cage to stretch my legs. It was May, and we were surrounded by abundant fresh greenery, and after such a long time I once again got to breathe the fresh air and marvel at the beautiful vistas of God's earth. My Kazakh guards were simple, cordial people. They offered me cigarettes and something to drink. After the humiliation that I had experienced in Aktiubinsk, their simple gestures seemed positively magnanimous. I remembered this moment when I recently read the account of yet another innocent convicted person: the Ukrainian accordionist Ihor Zavadsky:

> Both lady medics treated me very kindly, and I couldn't help myself when tears started streaming down my face. It is amazing that even now the mere hint of some simple kindness can move me so deeply.[6]

5 Slipyi, *Spomyny*, 176, 188.

6 Igor Zavadskii, *Tiuremnye dnevniki* (Kharkiv: Prava liudyny, 2015), 52.

Eventually, we got back into the van, which brought me to the regional center of Uil, around 250 kilometers southwest of Aktiubinsk, where I stayed for two more days. I thanked the chief commander for the kindness his guards had shown me. The director was a Kazakh, and he was eager to talk with me, particularly about religion. He was proud of the fact that unlike Jesus (who for him was a totally mythical individual), Muhammad was a "real, historical person."

Another surprise awaited me in the Uil police courtyard: there was an apple tree in full bloom. I had not seen one in so many years!

On Monday, May 14, 1984, I was officially released from guard and briefed about the rules of engagement and my current status. Then they placed me on a milk cart that was heading for Saralzhin, Uil District, Aktiubinsk Region, where my "landing module" was to touch down, to start my new life: five years of internal exile.

Part Three

Exile

Chapter Nine

Among the Kazakhs

Forging a Place for Myself under the Kazakh Sun

Saralzhin, the village where I was sent to spend my internal exile, is a Kazakh word for a type of small, thorny bush that miraculously survives in the sandy soil. These bushes are sturdy: you can't just yank them out of the ground. No wonder the whole village was also named after this bush: the village had also entrenched itself firmly in the sand, barely peeking out above it. When I finally jumped off the milk wagon, wearing a jacket and a small backpack, I got the sense that I had landed on a beach.

Bathing (or, rather, splashing myself with water) in a small stream called the Uil, which flowed near the village, truly saved my life that first unbearably hot summer. Saralzhin was fortunate to have this little stream, which doesn't flow into any other river, it just dries up. I was surrounded by the endless desert, which made one of the rules of my internal exile absurd: I was permitted to wander off only in a radius of thirty kilometers from the village. But where could I go? Except for some scattered farms, the nearest town was the regional center, Uil, around fifty kilometers away. Obviously, I needed the permission of the authorities to go there.

The distance from the village to the nearest city, Aktiubinsk, was about two hundred kilometers, but the transport connections were adequate. You could get there by taking two or three regularly scheduled buses, but the route was a dirt road that was frequently washed out during big rainstorms. These transport connections would also frequently be disrupted by summer sandstorms and winter blizzards, which were common in this area.

The time difference with Moscow was the same two hours that I had gotten used to in the Ural region. The only difference was that now I was south of that mountain range. The village of Saralzhin was rather small, anchored

Figure 9.1. Among the sands, under the Saralzhin sign.

by a state-owned animal farm that mainly raised cattle.[1] In addition to the village administration building, there was also a school, a post office, a building materials depot, a grocery and hardware store, a bakery, a cinema, and a small library with mostly Kazakh literature (it only had a few dozen Russian-language books in its collection). The public baths were open on weekends. Several sheep farms surrounded the village.

All the residents of Saralzhin were Kazakhs. They spoke their native Kazakh tongue, and only a few knew Russian. I was the only Slavic person among them, and I soon became known as "Slapka."[2] From the very beginning, I tried to get my hands on a Kazakh language textbook so I might at least understand what was being said around me. I managed to get a

1 State-owned animal farm (Ukr. *tvarynnyts'kyi radhosp*): state-owned farms, often known by their Russian abbreviation *sovkhoz*, were distinct from the better-known collective farms (*kolkhozy*). State-owned farms tended to be significantly larger, and employees were paid fixed wages rather than a share of proceeds; they were concentrated in Central Asia.

2 Slapka: a distorted version of the nickname "Slavik" (Russian derivative from "Myroslav").

textbook only after my backbreaking hard labor had deprived me of any ability to retain the difficult Turkic grammatical forms in my head.

Most Kazakhs are Sunni Muslims, but the village did not observe any religious traditions, of which only vestiges remained in certain everyday customs. Nevertheless, they were steadfastly dedicated to their Muslim heritage and proud of it. Saralzhin did not have its own mullah, and during the one funeral I attended, it was one of the elders who read a passage from the Koran.

At first, "Slapka" was received only guardedly. By then, Saralzhin had already made its mark in the KGB records. Prior to me, Valery Marchenko had "warmed a spot" there from July 1979 until May 1981, followed by our fellow dissident Zorian Popadiuk from June 1981 until September 2, 1982. Marchenko was rearrested after his release in Kyiv, and Popadiuk was also rearrested during his internal exile while still in Saralzhin. The KGB had conducted inquiries about both of them in town, and by the time I arrived, none of the Kazakhs wanted the KGB's eye on their village again. Additionally, the KGB had diligently prepared the local regional authorities for the arrival of some "exceptionally dangerous" individuals. This made the first few months of my stay in Saralzhin somewhat difficult.

On the other hand, the locals knew that while political exiles should be avoided on ideological grounds, they posed no threat on the day-to-day level. Both my predecessors were remembered respectfully and courteously in the village. They had never insulted anyone or stood in their way. All the same, there were also those who thought that saying a good word about those internal exiles might be considered unpatriotic.

This cautiousness collided with a purely pragmatic issue. The political prisoners' relatives used to send food and other items that were not available locally. Good tea was one of those deficit products, and it served as virtual currency. All three of us would order tea from Ukraine and give it away as gifts to the Kazakhs or trade it for other household products.

Obviously, the KGB had their trusty informants here as well. They also relied on the fact that our contacts with the locals would be rather limited. But they were wrong. The Kazakhs of Saralzhin were truly children of the steppes. As Yevhen Sverstiuk had written me, they were distant from politics but closely connected to nature. They were not concerned with our ideological position; their only concern was how we treated them. If you respected their customs and traditions, they respected you as well.

Since the room where Valery and then Zorian had lived was not available, I was temporarily placed in an old shack near the building materials depot.

It was a small adobe hut, where an older Kazakh woman known as Apai Sysenova worked ("Apai" is a term of respect in Kazakh). She was both an accountant and the deputy director of the depot. Her desk and telephone were there, and that's where they also placed my bed. I had access to it only after Apai Sysenova had finished her work and gone home. Obviously, this room was not equipped to be used as a dwelling, and I had to walk some three hundred meters just to get water.

After a few days, when trying to combine the functions of an office and a residence became unbearable for both sides, the office furniture was moved to another location, and the room was turned over to me. They constructed a table and a chair for me, but the stove that stood in the middle took up a lot of space.

I was assigned to work as a carpenter in the same facility. The head of the state farm asked me if I knew how to ride horses, but when I answered in the negative, there were no other duties that could be given to me other than that of St. Joseph and his blessed Student.[3] My salary was contingent on my production, which was also not without its problems. During one of the first months, my colleagues and I worked in the lumber yard, so we made a bit more—all of 186 rubles. My supervisor, Ural Turemuratov, who was particularly unfriendly toward me at the beginning, responded immediately, "Why did you receive such a high payment?"

That first day after my arrival, I received twenty rubles in advance, which vanished in the blink of an eye. The first thing I did was to send a seven-ruble telegram to my mother to give her my new address, but unfortunately she never received it. I also bought myself a hat because the scorching heat made it impossible to walk around with an uncovered head. So as not to perish from hunger, I also bought myself some bread, marmalade, and tea, and just like that, the money was gone. The only hope was that I might get some money from my family. The good people of the village did not let me perish, however. The following day the Kazakhs gave me some milk, and Apai Sysenova brought me a jar of sour cream from home, which was a real luxury for me. I ate some of it, and the rest I saved for the next day, storing the jar in the cold stream next to my hut—my makeshift refrigerator. But the next day my sour cream had disappeared. I was very bitter, though in those days I tried not to show my emotions. I was composed and as taut as a wire. In those days, there was only one joke that made its way into my letters:

3 Joseph trained Jesus to work as a carpenter.

It's no time for emotions or lyricism. Once I just burst out laughing when the rooster crowed with a pure Ukrainian accent. Silly me, I thought that here he would sing in the Kazakh dialect! (May 16, 1984)

Eventually, not having received any telegrams from my mother, I borrowed some money and sent an urgent telegram to Nadiika. This time it worked, and the next day I received two hundred rubles from my family. What's more, I came to an agreement with the administration that the state farm would give me some milk and meat, and the appropriate amount would be deducted from my pay. For me this was a great help because even if you had the money, liquor was the only thing you could buy in the state-run store. Everything else could only be procured from the farm itself.

The conditions of my internal exile required me to report twice weekly to my local commanding police officer, Nurtanov, to confirm that I was still around. This requirement had its own complications: in the depths of Kazakhstan, the officer was often absent from the village for long stretches of time. But generally speaking, I saw him so frequently that it seemed redundant to formally register with him. At the very least, I do not remember any psychological stress on account of this obligation. At some point, my official KGB minder also came from Aktiubinsk to meet with me. I don't remember his name, but he was Russian, not Kazakh. He treated me courteously and correctly, so there was no cause for conflict. We understood that we were both just doing what was expected of us.

My biggest source of stress at that time was looking for a place to live. Even though the hut was at my disposal, living there wasn't easy. Kazakhs would come in all the time, still seeing it as an office. I did not have any peace even on Sundays because even though I refused to work on that day, everyone would hang around the warehouse where my teammates worked, which meant near me as well. It was tough to extricate myself from all this, and I was also worried about where I would receive my mother and sister when they came to visit. I never stopped looking for a more suitable dwelling, and the history of these efforts reflects all the challenges of my early internal exile.

The regional authorities considered my efforts to find a new dwelling to be the gripes of a typical complainer. Once, my supervisor Ural even explained to me, "You have a place to sleep, so what else do you want? We don't actually need you as a workhand, no one asked us. Why don't you wait another fifteen days, or even until the fall?" Ural's unfriendliness got on my nerves. At some point I just asked him, "Why are you so negatively disposed towards me? I have never treated you or the farm badly." He became a bit intimidated by this, although his animosity toward this "enemy of the people" did not diminish right away. That's why I wrote to my family at the beginning of June: "I hate to pick a fight with the authorities because I had been dreaming of a quiet and peaceful life, but I can see now that all this was just wishful thinking."

My KGB minder from Aktiubinsk promised to help me, but I suspect that what eventually changed things was that the building materials depot needed to reclaim my hut as an office. That's why, by mid-July 1984, two months after I arrived in Saralzhin, I was temporarily moved into a little train car that was placed near my old hut. Later, on the orders of my KGB minder, it was moved closer to the village houses, which meant closer to the well and to the outhouse. This little train car was a typical Finnish model, designed for four people. It was equipped with a little "kitchen," another room, various cupboards for clothing, two beds, and a table. There was little cause for rejoicing, however, because they warned me from the start that I would live there only until September, and then it would be handed over to the herders.

At some point I went to see the village's head physician, who was in charge of the room that had been promised to me. (This was the room that had been previously occupied by Valery Marchenko and Zorian Popadiuk.) She was reading a book, and as I spoke, she barely looked up. But when I finished, she asked me coldly:

"So, who told you that you would be living here?"

"The commander," I replied.

"So, go tell the commander that he should find you another dwelling; you will not be living here. I am having a difficult time evicting those who live here now."

I obviously went back quite upset. And my subsequent efforts just further angered the authorities. At that time, my unfriendly supervisor Ural was overheard telling someone, "He should be living in a toilet, and here he is requesting a room."[4] I therefore braced for even worse things to come.

4 The irony of fate is that toward the end of my stay in Saralzhin, Ural practically became my friend and treated me respectfully. Then, in 1991, he unexpectedly came to visit me in Drohobych, arriving just in time for the presentation of my book *Ukraina na poliakh Sviatoho Pis'ma* (Ukraine on the margins of Holy Scripture), which was being held at the Prosvita Hall. He sent me a little note up to the stage, and when I spotted him in the crowd, I enthusiastically introduced him to the audience. –M. M.

On August 13, Ural told me that the regional authorities needed my little rail car and that I had to vacate it. When I asked him where I should move to, he replied, "Into the barn." I then told him exactly what I thought about that and refused to move. I told him that I would move only under the condition that this was authorized by my KGB commander. This worked, as the next day the commander telephoned and requested that I be given one of the rooms in a nearby adobe building, where the seasonal workers were living. They were expected to go back to Dagestan in a few days. Thus, a few minutes later, having gathered my belongings, I left the little rail car, finally able to procure some decent housing only three months after arriving at Saralzhin.

This was not the end of my adventures where my living arrangements were concerned. Not long after my arrival in Saralzhin, I got the police's blessing to go to Uil, the regional center, to get some photos taken for a residency permit that was to serve me instead of a passport for the next five years.[5] I arrived around noon and took care of all my errands, but since there was no return transport available back to Saralzhin, I had to stay overnight in a hotel. The police had called the hotel ahead of my arrival and given them my passport number. Still, my arrival caused a commotion. The Kazakh hotel administrator was aghast, since it had been the chief of criminal investigations who had called on my behalf, and she proceeded to lecture me on how I should behave myself in a hotel. Not anticipating any difficulties, I took it in stride.

When I showed up in the morning to return my key, however, this woman—this shining example of Soviet lawfulness—told me that I needed written police authorization to check out. Without it she would not let me. Even though our conversation got rather heated this time, I still had to go and wake up the police chief, and once out of bed, he did write me the required authorization for that Cerberus in a skirt. I was ready to curse that blasted Uil, had it not been for the kind-hearted Kazakhs who treated me to some fresh milk, as all the grocery stores were still closed.

At some point I heard that there was a piano at the Saralzhin school. My fingers were itching to play, so I went to the school director and asked him when I might be able to come and do so. He told me that the piano was out of tune because no one ever played on it. Then he told me that I could come every day at 10 a.m., except on Sundays. When I told him that I had to be

5 During internal exile, convicts' passports were confiscated to hinder their mobility.

at work at 10 a.m., he just shrugged, and I got nowhere. This was the same director who had rudely refused to give me a Kazakh language textbook.

In those early weeks, people still avoided me. On my way to the post office one day, I fainted, as I used to do in camp. As I lay there, people just walked around me and went on their way. After coming to, I could still see people walking by, and no one would help me get to my feet; I was still too weak to get up by myself. Why would no one help me? In my feelings of isolation, and hoping to at least hear some music, I decided to purchase a Spidola radio with the money I had saved from my initial wages.[6] I did not get to enjoy it for long, however, because a few days later someone stole it. I reported this to the regional authorities, but as expected, the perpetrator was never found.

I will relate another incident of human inconsideration that occurred after I got my room. That episode devastated me so much that I poured all my emotions into verse. This poem is totally self-explanatory:

It's cold – very cold
I never hurt anyone around me,
And they broke my window pane.
The broken slivers of glass, covered by snow,
Fell into the hot *plov*[7]
I had cooked Kazakh-style.

When I ran outside,
I was greeted by the neighbor's dog.
He sits by my door every evening,
Waiting for some warmth
And a piece of meat I might throw him.
He didn't bark—it was someone local.

It's cold to be an outsider
As cold as the crucifix
Bolted to these Muslim walls.
I will not plant any plum trees
outside my windows.
They might be trampled
When they come to break my window,

6 Spidola radio: popular transistor radio manufactured in Latvia; named after a character in the nineteenth-century Latvian epic poem *Lāčplēsis*.

7 *Plov*: Central Asian rice dish.

As they once did to Roxolana.[8]

(On the other hand, perhaps I should.
After all, the crucifix does hang above my head.)
They broke my window
    When I delved into the games of childhood,
        Looking for a compassionate soul
            That might be hiding nearby.
They did warn me:
"It's cold—very cold."[9]

In all fairness to the Kazakhs, however, this was the last incident when I was treated as a stranger. By the end of July, my letters already referred to some positive changes, which improved even further as time went on:

> My life here is changing as we speak. People are slowly getting used to me and showing me real consideration. I have *plov* for dinner, and oftentimes I have to turn down invitations because I have food waiting for me at home. This morning, the vegetable vendor stopped by my house. I am very happy. I get nice letters, everything is going well at work, so my mood is excellent—I just hope it doesn't get jinxed. (July 31, 1984)

I was happy with my work, and my two workmates, Zhaken (I don't remember his last name) and Bukenbai Arenov, did not tease me for being inexperienced. I compensated for my lack of experience by stepping in to help

8 Roxolana (c. 1502–1558): wife of Suleiman the Magnificent. Born in modern-day western Ukraine, she was captured by Crimean Tatars during a slave trade and taken to the Ottoman capital to be part of the Imperial Harem. Having found favor with Suleiman, she became his wife and consort, gaining political power within the empire.

9 *Kholodno . . . kholodno . . . / Ia nikoho dovkola ne skryvdyv, / A meni rozbyly shybku. / Zasnizheni shkel'tsia / vpaly v hariachyi plov, / Iakyi ia zvaryv po-kazakhs'ky. / Koly ia vybih, / Do mene lashchyvsia susids'kyi sobaka. / Vin shchovechora chatuie / pid moimi dveryma, / Shchob ia kynuv iomu / shmatok tepla i m'iasa. / Vin todi ne zahavkav – / tse buv khtos' zi svoikh. / Kholodno buty chuzhym. / Tak kholodno Rozp'iattiu, / prybytomu do moikh musul'mans'kykh stin./ Ne budu sadyty slyvy / pid viknamy khaty: / Ikh zatopchut', / koly rozbyvatymut' shybku, / Iak zatoptaly kolys' Roksolani. / (A mozhe, taky posadyty? / Nad holovoiu zh u mene – Rozp'iattia!) / Rozbyly shybku, koly ia porynuv / u zabavu dytynstva, / shukav nelukavoho sertsia, / skhovanoho des' nedalechko. / Meni pidkazaly: / "Kholodno . . . kholodno."*

Figure 9.2. Our carpentry team.

and did not try to pass work off on them. We made tables, doors, siding, floorboards, outhouses, and other household items. We worked in harmony, and the boys treated me with respect: not because I was a political prisoner but because I tried to help them and because I was older. The Kazakhs in Saralzhin lived under a patriarchal system, and its most remarkable feature was their respect for elders.

Rereading some of my letters to my mother recently, I came upon a characteristic phrase: "Work is going well and it's fun, because with Zhaken it cannot be any other way." Equally cordial were my dealings with Bukenbai and with the aforementioned Apai Sysenova, as well as with Kuliash, one of the warehouse workers. Other Kazakhs, such as Atapkel, who was a bit older, and the young boys Yermek Seitmagulov and Apai Sysenova's son (whose name I no longer remember) worked with us in years to come. Eventually, Alibek Taubatyrov also became part of my close circle.

Years later, my coworker Zhaken told me an interesting story dating back to the early years of our acquaintance. He was getting married in August

1984 and wanted to invite me and some of his other coworkers to his wedding. Just to be on the safe side, he went to the local Kazakh policeman and asked him if it was OK for him to invite me. A bit surprised, the policeman asked him, "Did he do anything bad to you?" "No," he answered. "So why are you asking me?" This set a precedent, and after that I was often invited to various village festivities. At that wedding, by the way, I was one of the first ones to be asked to give a toast. At first, I got a bit flustered, but then I found my footing and was eventually rewarded with good applause.

My relationship with the Saralzhin post office was a separate saga all its own. I think that all three of us political exiles had caused the young Kazakh women who worked at the post office quite a headache and vice versa. For us, the post office was perhaps the most important nerve center of our lives. All essential communications were performed through the post office: telegrams, telephone messages, intercity telephone conversations, all kinds of packages, and a torrent of letters. In my letters to my family, the post office comes up many times.

People who have never been deprived of their freedom for any extended period of time have a difficult time imagining the information hunger someone in internal exile experiences. This hunger can best be illustrated by a portion of a letter to my mother thanking her for a food parcel. The products had been wrapped in pages from *Radians'ke Slovo* (Soviet word), the newspaper issued by the Drohobych city council. This had evoked a storm of emotion on my part, and I wrote: "This evening I will study it. I doubt that the editors of this little newspaper could have envisaged that there would be someone who would consider it almost a treasure." (I could not have even imagined that some six years later, I would become a journalist for this very same newspaper.)

Today, it is equally difficult to imagine the embryonic state of communication services at that time. To start with, post office clerks would transmit telegrams to Uil by telephone— if there was a connection at all, that is. There was no difference between regular and urgent telegrams; it was lucky if they got there at all. The clerks' proficiency in Russian can be demonstrated by one telegram I had sent to Nadiika: my message "I am glad you got back OK" (*rad schastlivomu vozvrashcheniiu*) was received as: "Brother of a happy return" (*brat schastlivogo vozvrashcheniia*). A telegram from Mykola Matusevych, which he had written in Ukrainian, had been transliterated by the girls, who rendered it in Russian into an atrociously mystical abracadabra: "Greetings to a Kazakh from a Mongol" (*servus kazakhovi vid mongola*). (Mykola had been exiled to Buryatia, so he lived among the Mongols.)

Telephone communications could drive one mad. Our first six (!) attempts to connect did not work. Eventually, the girls told us that it was better to reserve a phone connection for late in the evening. But who knew that? Just imagine how my family saw these failures. When they could not make the connection between Saralzhin and Uil, they would report to my family on the other end that "the caller did not show up." Why did he not show up? Did he get arrested again? Is he ill? All us Marynovyches were gifted with a rich imagination.

The poor connections go without saying. I might be screaming into the phone, only to be told, "Speak a little louder!" Eventually I found out that the communications were better at the regular telephone station, so I started going there. I should explain to younger readers who are used to cell phones: there was a special ritual in making an intercity phone call. First, at least a day ahead, you had to notify the other party by telegram to expect a telephone call. Then you had to advise the telephone operators at both ends as to where the phone call would be made from. When it came to connecting with the wild provincial interior of the country, these procedures were truly something out of Dante's inferno.

Regular mail service was a bit easier, but when the roads were washed away by excessive rainfall or snowdrifts, even this service was disrupted. Often, the postal vehicles would break down. Once, not having gotten any letters from me for about two weeks, my mother managed to contact the head of the state farm in a panic, and she shocked him with her blunt question: "What have you done with my son?" Delays in parcel delivery also caused problems. By the time a parcel of fruit sent to me by some of my new friends from Dagestan arrived, 90 percent of it was rotten, and it's hard to describe how heartbroken I was when I had to trash it.

Life was slowly settling into a rhythm. Mykola Matusevych wrote that he had not lost the ability to live freely; it felt like those seven years in camp had never happened. For me, on the other hand, it was just the opposite: it was as if I had to learn how to walk on two feet again. Other than the very first day I was there, it took me a while to experience any joy at being "free." The initial shock of finally being out of the camp was slowly passing. I became familiar with the local lifestyle, which in itself was fairly complicated, so I didn't perceive all the difficulties I faced as deliberate personal cruelties. My courteous attitude toward the Kazakhs was also bringing some positive results. But this was not what brought about radical changes in my life in Saralzhin.

Assistance from My Family and Settling In

My first guest in Saralzhin was Mykola Matusevych's nephew, Vadym Slobodianiuk—Tamila's son. I found out about his impending visit during my phone conversation with Mykola, and I was aghast. At that time, in early June 1984, I was still living in the little hut in precarious circumstances, and the idea of receiving a guest was absurd. A bit upset, I told Mykola this, and he took offense. As I walked out of the post office after our phone conversation, I spotted Vadym himself, who had already made it to Saralzhin, so I had no other choice but to host him. To Vadym's credit, it must be said that he did not cause me any problems. On the contrary, he settled himself on his mattress on the floor and helped me deal with some of the problems facing me. Vadym stayed with me for a few days, awaiting word from Mykola about visiting him in the Chita Region, but I don't remember how that turned out.

Around the same time, I met a group of Chechens who had formed a seasonal construction team to build various farm structures. I first met their team leader, Said Zhanaraliev, and his right-hand man, Adam Bashirov. They were both exceptionally jovial and friendly. They immediately declared to me that they were not interested in politics and that "Chechens are a nation that no one will ever be able to drag into politics." I suspect that if anyone had told them that in some dozen years Chechnya would be known across the world for its efforts to fight for independence from the Russian Federation, they would not have believed it.

Even though they rejected politics, they did not reject me, a political prisoner. On the contrary, having visited me, and having heard my stories about the camps, they sincerely commiserated with my fate. Our friendship blossomed very quickly because it brought us mutual benefit: they enriched my life with their friendship and helped me resolve some of my daily challenges, while I opened my doors to them, and they were always welcome to spend the night or have something to eat. After just a few days of acquaintance, I had visited them on the farm, and most of them and their wives had visited me in my home. Thus, they took me under their wing, and to a certain extent, I did the same for them.

I also made friends with a few young Kazakh families. Nadia and Sirpai Kystaubaev were my closest neighbors, and they often invited me over to their house. I helped Sirpai with his domestic chores, and they provided me with milk, butter, and other products. Eventually a young couple, Umirzhan and Ania Kaliev, moved in nearby, and we also became good friends. I grew closer with my colleague Bukenbai and his friends. I will talk about them a bit later.

Through these families I became familiar with some everyday Kazakh customs that I had not known about before. For example, I was not aware of the fact that you addressed men and women differently. This is how I jokingly described this to my future wife, Liuba:

> Assalamu alaikum, dear Liuba! Or rather, "Salam berk!" This is how Kazakhs address women, immediately letting them know that "render unto Caesar what is Caesar's, and what is women's unto men." I like this rule so much that I'm wracking my brain trying to figure out how to implement it in Ukraine. I have no doubt, however, that in three and a half years I will manage to come up with something. (September 15, 1985)

All these friendships, however, paled in the presence of my family—my mother and my sister, Nadiika. My mother came to visit for the first time in June 1984 and stayed for a whole month. She came alone; Nadiika was supposed to come as well, but she came down with a persistent fever, and it would have been unwise for her to risk her health by traveling such a distance into unknown circumstances. That's why only my mother arrived at my hut, and with typical motherly dedication, she went about setting up my household.

That year, the scorching heat was unbearable, and we received a warning from the regional radio station that the temperature was expected to rise to fifty degrees Celsius the following week. I can still see my mother's flushed face as she diligently carted buckets of water from a well that was some three hundred meters away, or as she chased away the mosquitoes from her sleeping son as he lay sprawled on his bed after a long, tiring day at work, having enjoyed a wonderful meal prior to that. We awaited Nadiika's arrival, and I kept jokingly enticing her in my letters:

> We are not the only ones who are waiting for you. Half of Saralzhin already knows that Slavik is waiting for his sister. The geese look around in all directions to see if their favorite person has arrived. The sheared sheep show up every evening to check if they might spot your fur coat, and then they bleat dejectedly and just settle down and devour all the vegetable peelings Mother has accumulated for them during the day. The mosquitoes sing their sad song of being parted from their tasty companion, but Mama deftly conducts them with her little fly swatter and their song ends with my mother's resounding "that's for you, you bastards!" In other words, both people and all of nature await you! (July 9, 1984)

The day after her arrival, my mother had a chance to see how the Chechens had taken me under their wing. One of the Chechens, Sultan Sakiev, introduced himself to her and, sporting a large dagger stuck in his belt, told her: "Do not worry, Mama, we will not allow anyone to insult your son; otherwise they will have to answer to us!" That day, she greeted me after work in sheer panic. No sooner had her son gotten rid of his political oppressors than he had fallen into the hands of some bandits brandishing daggers. It took her some time to overcome her fear, but eventually she came to appreciate and love those kind people.

My mother got to know some local Kazakh women, with whom she bonded much faster than I did. She also visited Kalynivka, a neighboring (though by no means nearby) village that was mostly Ukrainian speaking, to purchase essential household items, and then she assisted me in moving into the little train car and helped me get settled there.[10] The month went by in a flash, and soon it was time for her to return to Ukraine, as Nadiika was still unwell and also needed her mother's love and care.

That was when I got my own room and enthusiastically proceeded to set it up. I was assisted by the Kazakhs and Chechens, as well as several Dagestanis. I was thirty-five years old at that time, and this was the first home I had to myself, my own nest. This is how I described it in my letter to Liuba:

> The room is about twenty square meters, with a high ceiling. The ceiling is the typical Kazakh style, not caulked. The earthen floor is covered with roofing felt. The stove spans the whole wall, and they say it's quite warm there in the winter. The single window is rather small and could probably be enlarged, but I will not bother, because it's not like the view overlooks the mighty Dnipro River—just sand. But if I had such a room in Kyiv, I would be mighty happy. And indeed, I am quite happy here, because I have my own private dwelling, unlike several of my friends who have to languish in dormitories. (August 15, 1984)

I slept on a wooden cot I made myself, with a mattress and bedding of course. I also procured two cots for my guests. Household items were placed on a homemade shelf. This is what I wrote to my family about my wardrobe:

10 Mostly Ukrainian speaking: due to forced resettlement of western Ukrainians to Kazakhstan during and after the Second World War, as well as former prisoners in labor camps near Karaganda, in central Kazakhstan, who opted to remain in the region.

> I have not written the last few days because I was busy making a wardrobe. Now I am proud to inform you that it stands tall in the corner, very tall and narrow, and quite heavy, and its creator is most likely the only one who really likes it. But it holds everything I needed it to. (February 25, 1985)

Since the ceiling constantly kept shedding straw, I procured some clear plastic and, with the help of my new friends, tacked it onto the ceiling. The effect was fantastic; word got out throughout the village, and groups of people would come to look to see how it was done. One of the impressed Kazakh visitors told me: "This looks like a restaurant."

In the beginning, my dwelling consisted of just this one room, but as time went on, I managed to acquire more space. If you flash forward, as in a film, this is how it progressed:

> October 1984: Added a kitchen, with a stove (fueled by gas canisters), a table, and shelves for dishes. Constructed double frames for both windows, and installed bars.
>
> November 1984: Installed a TV antenna and purchased a TV.
>
> April 1985: Blocked off part of the shared entryway to create a separate hallway, with shelves for food and household items. Installed my own private entry door—much sturdier and without any cracks. Purchased a refrigerator.
>
> September 1985: Moved the toilet to a new location.
>
> November 1985: Finished building a veranda with a slate roof and plasterboard walls, which helped retain heat.
>
> May 1986: Together with some neighbors, blocked off part of the road with a fence, creating a cozy little yard in front of the house. Hauled in some soil and created a flower garden in front of my kitchen window. (One of the Kazakhs asked me: "What for?")
>
> June 1986: For relaxation, constructed a table and two benches near the flower garden in the yard. Constructed a shower cabin next to the house, with a solar-heated water tank.
>
> September 1986: Created a storage area in an abandoned barn near the house. When Adam, one of my Chechen friends, saw all this, he joked: "It's time for

you to de-kulakize (*raskulachivat'*) back to Ukraine."[11] It's as if he had a premonition, because within six months I was dispatched homeward.

Both my mother and Nadiika had shared in the joy of setting up my home, helping me whenever they could. Nadiika helped me financially, and Mama served as a ferry between Ukraine and Saralzhin. She had brought a hand-embroidered rug, all essential household and kitchen items, an artificial Christmas tree, my accordion, and then toward the end of my internal exile she also brought a camera and some photographic equipment. The most important thing that they both did for me was to sanctify my home with their presence.

The first time they came together was in September 1984. Nadiika's temperature was still elevated, but she ventured out because she really wanted to see me. Over the following two years, they visited me frequently during the summer school vacations. They also managed to dispel the aloofness and detachment that the Kazakhs initially felt toward me. The first few weeks, as I mentioned, my fellow villagers regarded me as an "exceptionally dangerous political criminal" that the police had foisted on them at their peril. After my mother and Nadiika arrived, I was regarded as someone whom these two delightful Ukrainian women adored. If this man was supported so selflessly by such a mother and sister, he couldn't possibly be some sort of ruffian without family or heritage. Thus, through their love and dedication, my family gave me a human face within the Saralzhin community.

Starting with their first visit, our room buzzed with numerous festivities, and the three of us were often invited to the homes of many Kazakhs and Chechens. To convey the spirit of those parties, I want to relate two rather humorous incidents in which my sister was the heroine. At that time, she was at the height of her beauty, and her candor and sincerity in dealing with people, together with her professional skills as a teacher, placed her at the epicenter of every gathering and celebration.

At one point, we were invited to dinner by a prominent Kazakh family whose children already knew and adored Nadiika the teacher. The main dish served at a Kazakh table was usually *bishbarmak*—lamb with noodles. Before the feast, ritual called for one of the honored guests to eat a Kazakh culinary delicacy: the tip of the lamb's nose. In our case, Nadiika was selected as the

11 De-kulakize: the implication is that his accommodations had become ostentatiously well outfitted. Many of the victims of de-kulakization in the 1930s had been sent to Kazakhstan; the joke lies in reversing the direction.

Figure 9.3. Our trio in Uil, Kazakhstan (1984).

Figure 9.4. My mother and Nadiika with Aiza, Said, and a Kazakh tyke at a dastarkhan.

honored guest, and you should have seen the range of emotions that flashed across her face when she realized her honorary obligation and how she proceeded to fulfill it.

A few days later, we were invited to a Chechen home, where after a sumptuous feast the traditional *lezginka* (a traditional Chechen dance) got underway. This dance is performed with great gusto and temperament, although the women's part is just to gracefully glide around the circle, waving a little scarf, while the men put all they've got into their dancing. My friend Sultan picked up his accordion, which he played magnificently, while Sibirbek asked my sister to dance with him. At first, she was a bit unsure of herself, but after a while she got the hang of it and proceeded to glide around, gently waving her little scarf. The dance went on for five and then ten minutes, and Nadiika blissfully danced around in circles, while poor Sibirbek started turning blue. Finally, one of the Chechen women went up to Nadiika and whispered something into her ear. Tradition calls for the woman to put an end the dance, not the man. Nadiika let out a yelp and stopped dancing, while Sibirbek gasped for air. He was happy, though, that he managed to survive and vindicate his masculine honor.

No matter how happy we were together, eventually the time came for them to leave—a time of deep sorrow. My mother's face grew long, and Nadiika's smile became more and more tense. It seemed that there was nothing that could alleviate our parting grief. We left my house with all their things and headed toward the Aktiubinsk bus stop. We walked along, deep in sorrow and silence, not daring to speak, so that our quivering voices would not give away our grief and sadness. As we trudged along in the sand, suddenly, out of nowhere, three sheep appeared just in front of us, going in the same direction, gyrating their round butts right in front of us. The parallel was so obvious that we literally rolled with laughter. Our profound sadness yielded to the Almighty's lightheartedness.

After my family left, someone would always drop by for just a few minutes to ask how I was doing. "Don't be sad! You have no right to be!" This would make me emotional: I realized that I had finally become part of the Saralzhin "circle." Life became more enjoyable; serenity had entered my soul, and this is reflected in my letter to Liuba:

> I am doing well, Liuba, because I have my own apartment, which I take care of by myself; I have a good job; and I am surrounded by good people. As you can see, I'm in a good mood, and for this I am grateful to my mother and Nadiika. They have the magic touch, and after they left, I have not been irritable even one day—if you ignore the sadness on the day of their departure. (October 7, 1984)

Generally speaking, life in this remote Kazakh village, with its patriarchal traditions, was pleasant and comfortable. Fate was generous to me when compared to the conditions my other political prisoner friends encountered. Their situations were much worse. Mykola Matusevych, for example, had a difficult time among the destitute Russians in the Chita Region, on the border with China and Mongolia; Vasyl Stus found himself among drunken criminals in a workers' dorm in Magadan. They really got on his nerves. Also revealing is Oksana Meshko's later account of her experience of internal exile:

> After a long journey, they finally brought me to Khabarovsk region, to the town of Aian, and placed me in a small hut that had previously been occupied by some Yakut people. The house was some five hundred meters from the Sea of Okhotsk. All the winds blew directly at me, and the blizzards would sometimes last for weeks. Then the electrical wires would be blown down, and I would be without any lights for weeks on end and couldn't leave my house. It was quite a feat to make it to the road. At first this was very difficult for me, but then I figured out a method to save myself. During blizzards, I would bundle up and go outside to stomp down the snow. Taking periodic short breaks, I would repeat this until I managed to create a tunnel all the way to the gate, and then to the road, some 35–40 meters away.[12]

That same year of 1984 I received a postcard from Mykola Matusevych that was both mysterious and frightening: "I am alive, and that is a grounded assertion, although it might have been groundless. This is not a lame joke, unfortunately, and I'll tell you about it some other time. Everything is just too raw right now. I am amazed at the tenacity . . . when you've got a gun pointed at you." Even today, I cannot say what happened there, but I received similar notes from various other internal exiles, and they gave me a strange feeling. Perhaps a phrase taken from one of my letters might explain it: "Well, another day of stolen happiness and tranquility has gone by; and who knows what tomorrow might bring."

The new year of 1985 was approaching, and my mother kept shuttling back and forth between Drohobych and Saralzhin to help her son get settled in. The third time she came was for a week in November, and she brought the aforementioned embroidered rug, as well as some miscellaneous household items. She came unexpectedly, without giving me any advance notice. I was amazed by her maternal dedication and also thrilled that she had

12 *Ne vidstupliusia!*, 275.

come to celebrate her birthday with me on November 22. This is what I wrote to Nadiika at that time:

> I have become aware that you and Mother are better people than me. You are kinder and more dedicated. Perhaps the fact that I did not purchase any gifts for her has induced these feelings, but there is nothing to buy here. Everywhere I look in the house, whatever I pick up or consume, everywhere I see both of your kind eyes, and that's when my guilty conscience begins to kick in. (November 13, 1984)

By the end of December I was expecting her again because she could not even imagine abandoning me to celebrate my first Christmas in internal exile all by myself. What's more, she even brought an artificial Christmas tree: although it had no real aroma, it was still a Christmas tree. I still have this tree, and I decorate it every year for New Year's and Christmas, along with the *didukh*.[13] I described the moment of her arrival in a letter to Nadiika:

> Mama arrived on Monday at 3pm. I took the day off, and some children notified me that she had arrived. Her bus stopped not too far from my house, so just a few minutes later Mama was sitting in my little kitchen, still all decked out in her furs, surrounded by her bags. It turns out that on the way, she had already met up with the Chechens, because Sibirbek and Sultan, who were traveling in another bus going in the opposite direction, stopped both buses and burst into Mama's bus to greet her. I can only imagine the commotion on the bus. (January 2, 1985)

The two of us celebrated New Year's in front of my newly purchased TV set, on top of which stood my mother's Christmas tree, sporting the decorations that she had brought with her.

My birthday on January 4 turned out to be a unique occasion. Said arrived and asked me for a favor. Their team included a few derelict non-Chechens, who got drunk during the holidays and then caused all kinds of mischief. During the New Year holidays, they got into big fights and knifed a Belarusian guy to death. The Chechen team members got into a lot of trouble with the police. Another problem was trying to organize his funeral. The dead man's mother, whom they had notified, had already arrived. However, the Chechens didn't think it appropriate to bury him without some prayers. That's why they turned to me: as the only Christian in the

---

13 *Didukh*: traditional Ukrainian Christmas decoration made from a sheaf of wheat.

region, they thought that I might be able to read some appropriate prayers in order to bury him "properly."

It would have been unthinkable to turn them down, even though I had never assisted in a funeral ceremony. I glanced through my Bible (given to me by Yevhen Sverstiuk), and then I joined the Chechens at a remote farmers' cemetery. There we collectively dug a grave, and then, for the first and possibly last time in my life, I conducted funeral rites, reading several prayers and singing some appropriate hymns. Then I asked the Lord to accept this sinner's soul and also forgive me for conducting this unprofessional ritual. The Belarusian's mother thanked me for seeing to it that her son was not buried without a prayer, and I returned home amazed at the mysterious paths that the Lord was guiding me along.

Then, on January 6, Christmas Eve kicked off a series of sacred days, when for the first time in seven years my mother and I could sing those beautiful Ukrainian Christmas carols and enjoy the traditional Ukrainian Christmas Eve dinner of *borshch* with *vushka* (mushroom dumplings), *varenyky*, and *kutia*. Our time together had been calm and happy, and I gushed about it in a letter to Nadiika. I will cite just two segments; perhaps it might resonate with some sensitive person who appreciates the magic of love:

> Mama has taken charge in her typical manner: she puts things in the wrong place, she neglects to bring the tea or a spoon in time, and for this she gets rightfully reprimanded by her son. Then this: how can I not get angry when she enters my room wearing the same slippers she wears on the dirty kitchen floor, when there are separate felt slippers for walking around on the carpet in my room? This is outrageous! . . . In other words, our daily routine has started, and the only thing that is lacking is the bird (i.e. Nadiika) for the Marynovych chattering to be at perfect full volume. (November 16, 1984)

> Nadiika, help! Mom is making me eat a pomegranate – she wants me to explode! I have already ballooned to such an extent that I no longer fit into the mirror when I shave. But wait! Why am I complaining to you? You, my dear sister, are the one who actually sent me that pomegranate. Woe is me! (January 15, 1985)

I was overjoyed that my mother was with me and that I had good colleagues at work and wonderful friends to speak to, so much so that I temporarily forgot where I was; but then I would wake up:

> Do I have any new wishes? I think not. At least not any clearly defined ones. But I have sobered up and become aware of the realities that I had forgotten about

for a time. It would be awful if I started wishing for a different fate than the one I have. I am totally happy with my fate, and *pas de problèmes*. (February 1, 1985)

At the same time, fate was preparing new surprises and challenges for all of us. God did not forsake us, but evil remembered us as well.

The Kaleidoscope of Triumphs and Losses

The autumn of 1984 has remained in my memory as an endless period of loss due to the deaths of several of my close friends.[14] Soon after my arrival in Saralzhin, I got word that a few days after we had met during my transit to Kazakhstan, Oleksa Tykhy had died in a Perm prison. I also learned that Borys Antonenko-Davydovych had passed away, and this is what I wrote to Liuba:

> Losing Borys Dmytrovych is very painful to me. I would have loved to spend even a single day just listening to him. He died while I was suffering in the Aktiubinsk transit prison for those awful fifteen days. Now all we can do is cherish our wonderful memories of him. (August 15, 1984)

Then, on October 25, I learned in a letter from Yevhen Sverstiuk that our friend from Zone 36, Valery Marchenko, had also died. This is what I wrote to my family:

> I almost cried when I read the letters. This is what Yevhen wrote: "On *Pokrova* (the Christian holiday of Our Lady the Protectress) in the Pokrova Church, we sang the funeral service over Valery's zinc casket, and now the autumn flowers give me allergies. It has been a year since my release, and how many nails have been driven in?" Valery—he can only mean Valery Marchenko. My spirits just sank. I abandoned all my household chores and started writing letters because my soul was howling. You took away a wonderful person, oh Lord, such grief! (October 25, 1984)

I started writing not only letters but also a poem. A martyr's death required some special words:

---

14 Oleksa Tykhy died on May 5, 1984; Yury Lytvyn on May 9, 1984; and Valery Marchenko on July 10, 1984. Vasyl Stus also died in the spring, on April 9, 1985.–M. M.

For departed prison friends

Death has donned an embroidered shirt.
It is designed with crosses
From the homes of St. Bartholomew's Day.
It is embellished with deep precipices
Where the true Word once stood
With tall graves.

Among the colors of ripe wheat and sky,
There is a black mound of reaped lives.
It mourns the field of cut stalks
With an epilogue
Of the living,
While the dead wrote the prologue.

Death carries a scythe
Like the one a farmer has.
Both look like the number 7.
You, my friends,
Have merged with the Universe.
Your flame has died,
So that someone's soul might ignite.

Each year, the land becomes
More cherished with the graves.
You are an outsider on your own soil.
The field goddess protects the stalks:
"Do not kill! Do not cut!"
And take off the embroidered shirt,
Oh Death!
Just take it off![15]

---

15 *Polehlym tabirnym druziam. Vdiahnula smert' vyshyvanku. / Vzierets' ii—khresty z domivok / Varfolomiivs'koi nochi. / A pomerezhana hlybokymy prirvamy, / de stoialo pravdyve Slovo, / I vysokymy mohylamy. / Pomizh kol'oriv / styhloho zhyta i neba / prolih chornyi valok / skoshenoho zhyttia. / Zhalobyt' sternia epilohom / zhyvykh,/ A pokiini dopysaly prolog. / U smerti kosa taka zh, / iak selians'ka. / Obydvi – spravhnisin'ka tsyfra "sim". / Vy, druzi, / zlylysia z pul'som Vsesvitu. / Vy zhasly, / shchob khtos' tam u dushi spalakhnuv. / Shcho ne rik, to zemlia / vid mohyl ridnishaie. / Na zemli zh miz liud'my— chuzhyi. / Mavkoiu sertse kolosky zatuliaie: / "Ne ubyi! Ne kosy! / I znimy vyshyvanku, / Smerton'ko, / Nu znimy!"*

That autumn, fate had another surprise in store for me: someone knocked on my door one evening, and when I opened the door, a woman asked for Myroslav Marynovych. She turned out to be a Lithuanian named Monika, one of Father Alfonsas Svarinskas's parishioners, from the town of Viduklė. She came to find out how he was doing because she had heard that he was in Camp 36 with me.

I was amazed that this young woman had the courage to travel to a totally remote Kazakh province to visit a completely strange person, confident that the dissident status of the exiled individual would be sufficient guarantee of his moral standing. She was totally convinced that the Lord would not abandon her in her need. Obviously, I received her, fed her, and told her everything I knew about her beloved vicar. As a memento of this visit, she gave me a wooden crucifix, which I immediately hung above my bed. Since then, this crucifix has always hung above my bed, wherever my home might be. Later, Monika sent me parcels from Lithuania, and I have very warm and grateful memories of her.

After a while, the autumn rains washed away all the roads, even the bridge over the Uil River, which was the only way to get to the regional center. For me this had amusing consequences. Not being able to cross the river to get to Uil, the delivery trucks from Aktiubinsk had to unload their deliveries—mountains of Pepsi-Cola bottles—at the Saralzhin grocery store. Pepsi-Cola had just become available in the USSR. Previously I had only heard about this drink, and here—what luck!—it came to me, and I was able to actually taste it. With great joy I supplied myself with it, and I got so used to this refreshing drink that I would keep glancing into the store to make sure that the supply did not run out. This was my first immersion into Western civilization.

In October they placed Igor Ruvinov, an internal exile from Azerbaijan, in a room next to mine in the same house. He had been arrested for currency manipulation, but I never asked him for the details. In Saralzhin he was assigned to work as a welder, and it was thanks to Igor that my windows sported new bars.

The lofty list of all my domestic accomplishments would in reality have been much more modest had it not been for my friends. So in all fairness, I have to include another list of both Chechens and Kazakhs: Vakha fitted the doors to my stove; Sibirbek installed my gas stove; Abdul-Kadir procured my antenna, and Sibirbek and Said helped mount it; Adam often provided me with extra helpers from his team; Zhaken and Hussein helped put down the wooden floor and then covered it with felt; Adam helped me paint the walls. And this list of helpers is far from complete.

Figure 9.5. My self-made bed with a crucifix on the wall.

My home, which the Chechens jokingly called the "Chechen base," was always lively with guests. Some Chechens had to stay overnight in Saralzhin—sometimes with their whole families— because it was rather difficult to get back to their remote farms. I would like to describe one of those occasions.

One time, four men and two women were staying in my room. I offered my wide wooden cot to the two women, and I was getting ready to settle down next to the men on the floor, which by then was already covered with felt. Suddenly, I noticed that the women were whispering something among themselves but were reluctant to talk to me about it. I thought for a while, and then it came to me: it was the crucifix above my bed! Generally speaking, the Chechens regarded the religious symbols in my room with tolerance and equanimity, but this was a bit much: by lying in my bed under the crucifix, it was like they were yielding to its influence. That was the reason why the women hesitated and didn't know what to do. Not wasting any time, I removed the crucifix and assured the women, "I understand. Do not be concerned, I am not trying to push my religious convictions on you." This time, they were the ones to be amazed, and Aiza, Adam's wife, told me, "Now I can see that you are a true Christian!"

I had acted spontaneously, and rationality set in a bit later. I was concerned that in doing this I might have rejected Christ. It does say in the Bible, "Whoever denies me before others will be denied before the angels of God" (Luke 12:9). But even today I am convinced that I did not deny Christ; I only chose not to forcibly impose Him on others. I therefore confirmed Him in the highest sense: I confirmed His nonforceful witness. This is what that simple Muslim woman sensed. I am not fabricating some sort of contrived explanation thirty years later; I was thoroughly convinced of this at that time, as a fragment of my letter to Liuba confirms:

> Missionary coercion is not to my liking. I can certainly interfere with anyone taking a wrong step, but I consider pressuring or compelling people to think the way I do to be complete foolishness. (June 8, 1986)

Speaking of Aiza, I recall a conversation I had with her that was an important step in my understanding of Islamic culture. Generally speaking, the Chechens were more devout in maintaining their religious traditions than the Kazakhs. I often saw them walking to the toilet carrying a jug for their ritual ablutions. Having visited their farms, I noticed that women never attempted to sit at the table while the men were still eating. When the Chechens first appeared in my house, however, I told them right away, "I follow Christian tradition, and everyone eats together. I will not be feeding your women separately." The Chechens accepted this, and we had no problems in this regard.

One time, Aiza and I were at the house all by ourselves, and our conversation turned to women's issues. I knew that she was aware of the existence of other women in her husband Adam's life; she even knew their names. In the Muslim fashion, she accepted this stoically and would sometimes even send them small gifts. Without going into any details, I expressed my commiseration with the Muslim women for their difficult fate. With a certain spark of benign irony in her eyes, Aiza retorted, "Don't worry, our women have a variety of ways to exert influence on their men. It's not as tragic as it seems. I, for instance, feel sorry for your women, who have to strain carrying huge shopping bags from the bazaars. With us, the responsibility for getting food always belongs to the men." Certainly, such things can be debated endlessly, but at that time I realized that both the Christian and Muslim civilizations have their unique basic philosophies and their own fundamental codes. It is therefore impossible to comprehend one culture through the logic of a different one.

I was so impressed with the Chechen Sultan's accordion playing that my own fingers started to itch. This is where my family again came to the rescue. In September, my mother brought me a brand-new accordion, which she had purchased for me. From then on, with such an excellent teacher, I learned Chechen songs from Sultan. I became so infatuated with them that I even learned the Chechen words. At some point, I even noticed that my mother was a bit taken aback because I was not playing enough Ukrainian songs. In reality, I was not rejecting Ukrainian songs, but rather embracing the Chechen tunes that I had newly discovered. The same thing happened with Kazakh songs, which I also mastered, including the words.

I should mention one other concern that my mother had: my drinking. After my father's alcohol abuse, this was a very touchy subject for her. Here, suddenly, she started noticing that all our Chechen festivities were accompanied by alcohol, and she certainly had a right to be concerned. Ahead of time, I agreed with my guests that I would have a small dose of alcohol and that I would not exceed it. If someone attempted to force me, I would resist. Far more perfidious was when no one forced me, but my own conviviality enticed me to increase that dosage. During those moments I felt I understood Taras Shevchenko, who also hoped to thaw out his soul with good company after his liberation. I became so much closer to him, finding myself in the same Kazakh steppes he had once inhabited.

I wasn't concerned about myself; I didn't like to get drunk—mostly for aesthetic reasons. I also painfully remembered how my father's inability to control his drinking had affected the family. But I was no less sociable than my father, and I would totally abandon myself to any given festive occasion. When the Chechens did drink, they never lost their human face; that's why their parties were truly joyous events, not just blind drinking brawls.

Since I have already touched on this theme, I would like to relate two other stories—this time about the Kazakhs. Klshpai, one of my supervisors, told me one day that he and a few of his friends would like to come and have tea with me, to see how I had settled into my new dwelling. I immediately sent a telegram to my family, asking them to send me some decent tea. When my guests finally arrived, I had some choice teas displayed on the table: Indian, Ceylonese, and Chinese. I proudly asked them which one of those they might like me to brew for them. They just stared at me and asked: "So where is the vodka?" It turned out that the phrase "to come for tea" was a euphemism for rowdy drinking. Everyone knew that except me. I became despondent because I didn't have any liquor, and all the stores had already closed. I was totally humiliated, and from then on, I made sure that I always had some alcohol on hand in the house.

For the second story, we have to jump forward to March 1986, the height of Gorbachev's antialcohol campaign.[16] All the liquor had disappeared from Saralzhin's stores. No bottles of alcohol were allowed to be displayed at any of the Kazakh weddings. Then a directive came out instructing all village residents to write official letters pledging to never use alcohol again. All the adults wrote those letters except for one: I refused. I had had my fill of these stupid games with the government. Luckily, my status as a political prisoner placed me outside the jurisdiction of the local authorities, and they paid no attention to my refusal. In any case, a while later, I noticed that at various weddings or other festivities, it had become popular to serve a variety of kefirs and assorted fruit drinks. No one bothered to divulge the secret that all those drinks were heavily laced with alcohol.

My life at that time was filled with numerous unexpected adventures. Often the Chechens would just show up at my house without warning, often arriving late in the evening, intending to sleep over. I always tried to stock up on basic staples and cook enough food to be ready for such eventualities. One time, the Chechens arrived on a truck and handed me a live sheep. This was one of their ways of compensating me for all the food they ate at my house. I held it in my arms, wondering what I would do with it. The idea of slaughtering it was totally out of the question. Eventually, the Chechens took the sheep back and later just brought me the meat.

Another time, we almost had a catastrophe. I was sitting in front of my house when Adam and several of his Chechen friends arrived in a car. As he got closer, he started to speed up just to scare me. I, of course, remained seated, and then suddenly I saw through the windshield that Adam's face had become deathly white, and his eyes were filled with terror. When the car finally screeched to a halt just a few centimeters away from me, I realized that I had been a few seconds away from death. Terrified and pale from fear, Adam staggered out of the car and explained that, for a second, his brakes had failed.

---

16 Gorbachev's antialcohol campaign: from 1985 to 1987, partial prohibition was implemented in the Soviet Union. Prices on alcohol were raised and restrictions were placed on amounts and times of day alcohol could be sold. The campaign mostly led to a boom in black market alcohol production and sales.

Daily Life and Festivities, 1985

My mother departed Saralzhin in January 1985, and after that, my days became gray and uneventful: work, household chores and extensive correspondence. Every year I used to send at least fifty or sixty cards for Christmas alone. February of the new year was dedicated above all to Liuba Kheina. First, I greeted her on her birthday, infusing the text of her card with particular emotion:

> Dear carrier doves, lift the birthday girl on your wings and bring her closer to her happiness!
>
> Dear apple tree, bend your branches so she might sample your harvest!
>
> Oh water well, my sister, sprinkle some cool sparkling water to quench her thirst and to salute the birthday girl!
>
> And you, Baba Yaga, stay away from her path and her fate, may there be no sign of you!
>
> And you, Myroslav, wash your face, put on a clean shirt, and lean forward to kiss her cheek.
>
> Happy Birthday! (February 10, 1985)

When I sent that card, I had not yet heard that her father, who had been a village schoolmaster and was much respected by everyone, had died on the eve of her birthday. When I did find out, I wrote again, this time a sympathy card.

> Hang in there! Do not beat yourself up with any regrets, because it's typical for everyone to have regrets about their attitude towards their parents when it's already too late. This is one of life's rules, and it hits us with equal force when we ourselves become parents. So just hang in there and be strong! (March 8, 1985)

In March 1985, the saga of Oles Berdnyk developed further. I first heard that he had "repented" in March 1984, when the newspaper *Literaturna Ukraina* (Literary Ukraine) published his statement of contrition entitled "Returning Home," which renounced his involvement in the UHG and stated that "the establishment of the Helsinki movement was a CIA creation." He went on to say that if Mykola Rudenko and Levko Lukianenko had any fortitude, they would have abandoned their antipatriotic stance and deliberate isolationism a long time ago.[17] All this was very difficult to bear

17 Oles' Berdnyk, "Vertaiuchys' dodomu," *Literaturna Ukraina*, May 17, 1984.

because this was the first (and thankfully the only) time a Helsinki Group member had double-crossed the rest of the group. But it was a bedeviled time that sometimes broke even the most valiant of men.

Then, in March 1985, by chance I saw a TV program showing Berdnyk and someone named Lytvyn, a bandura player.[18] They were seen sitting on the Dnipro bluffs, and with the bandura playing in the background, Oles reiterated his words from the article, asserting that the Helsinki movement was a CIA creation and that the West was tricking and provoking us. This was more than I could bear, so I wrote the poem *Mezha* (Boundary) because I felt that Berdnyk had certainly crossed the line. Later, I sent the poem to my sister, Nadiika.

In the world there are many paths,
But there is only one border line.
You consider your life to be a feast,
You glance around with guilt,
And your sin has been consumed in full.

> To know your fate in stone,
> Choose what you like:
> Going to the right will take you behind bars,
> Going left will lead you to difficulties,
> Going straight will not get you to heaven either.

No one can tell you where the border line is.
Don't ask people where the border line is.
Will they hail you as "Prince"?
Or call you "Enemy",
Or point at you: "Judas".

> You might think that a moment before your execution
> You could be saved by lies.
> Don't bring sin upon your head.
> Search for Atlantis, my brother.
> That's where your conscience is, and your border line.[19]

---

18 Bandura: Ukrainian folk instrument similar to a zither or lute, played by plucking the strings.

19 *Na sviti dorih bahato, / I til'ky mezha – odna. / Zhyttia spryimaiesh, iak sviato, / Ohlianeshsia vynuvato, / A vypyto hrikh do dna. / Shchob z kamenia doliu vznaty, / Shcho khochesh, te i vybyrai: / Pravoruch pidesh—za graty, / Livoruch—u*

That TV program had a similar effect on other political prisoners, such as Mykola Horbal:

> Later, while [I am] locked up in a particularly strict regime cell in the Urals, they will show this film [to us], brought from Ukraine by the KGB. In it, Berdnyk will appear as a prophet, wearing an embroidered Ukrainian shirt, walking above the Dnipro River, with the wind blowing his thick prophet's beard. Freedom! "And here you are, fools, sitting locked up!" Obviously, this was to serve as an admonition to us all, conceived by the KGB. Berdnyk must surely have been aware of this. He knowingly betrayed both his friends as well as the idea. Yes, this was treason![20]

Today, even though I do condemn his behavior because it was painful for us all, I nonetheless do not want to blame him more than the system that broke him down. It seems that Oles Berdnyk experienced numerous powerful religious episodes of enlightenment throughout his life, and he came to believe that he was destined to be a prophet. In the cramped cell of a special regime camp, every political prisoner became convinced that he was a general, not just an infantryman in someone's army. Each of them considered himself to be a tribune and did want to simply listen to someone else's sermons. In prison, Berdnyk was painfully reduced to a prophet without any listeners: a missionary without a flock.

The punitive wringer of this giant system was not only oppressive—it was also diabolically treacherous. Berdnyk, who back home had painted portraits of numerous imaginary prophets that he had seen in his visions, was allowed to work as a painter. This had created yet another barrier between him and his cellmates because the authorities expected him to paint politically charged images in support of the Soviet regime. Furthermore, Oles had a family, and his family wanted him home; they were unconvinced by the example of other families' steadfastness. Semen Gluzman's comments are relevant here:

> Later, with time, in another life, I would ask myself: does a reasonable person have the right to beat his head against the wall, turning his own family into

---

tarapaty, / A priamo—tak tezh ne v rai. / Mezhu nikhto ne pidkazhe. / Mezhu ne pytai v liudei. / Chy skazhut' do tebe: "Kniazhe", / Chy obzyvatymut': "Vrazhe", / Chy pal'tsem tyknut': "Iudei". / Zdaiet'sia, i za myt' do straty / Vriatuie tebe olzha. / Ne tre' hrikh na dushu braty. / Shukai Atlantydu, brate, / Tam sovist' tvoia. I mezha.

20 Horbal, *Prezentatsiia zhyttia*, 128.

> hostages—as Vasyl Stus, Ivan Svitlychny, Yevhen Sverstiuk, and many others had done? There is no answer to this; it's a matter of moral philosophy. Therefore, let's build a country where individual weaknesses do not have to be put to the test. After all, those who succumbed to KGB pressures did commit a sin by betraying their cause—but they were not born that way, and everyone's disposition is unique.[21]

So, let the Lord judge the extent of the evil or good that every individual has done. After all, those who perished behind bars—those who refused to willingly reject the Truth—were not the only victims of this system. Its victims also included those who broke down and were forced to yield to the system. For me, therefore, it is more important to testify to the good that was done; perhaps this is even more important for those who succumbed. And evil tends to be rather boisterous, anyway, and will not allow itself to be forgotten.

To me, the punishment the Lord levied against Berdnyk during his lifetime is also highly significant. Having appeared to Berdnyk in his religious visions, the Lord did indeed grant him the gift of prophecy. But when Oles sinned, and he began uttering words of deception toward the end of his life, the Lord deprived him of the power of speech. For several years before his death, Oles could not speak at all and could only convey his thoughts in writing. How eloquent fate can be!

At some point, I started receiving postcards from all over the world from members of Amnesty International. That organization took me, along with other prisoners of conscience, under its protective wing and actively demanded our release. Some of the Amnesty groups, such as in the French city of Avignon, declared me to be their "adopted son." In camp, however, I knew nothing of this. In internal exile, on the other hand, when Amnesty members learned my Saralzhin address, I started receiving letters from them. Today it is difficult to convey the emotions those cards, which came from all over Europe, America, and even Japan, evoked in me. By encouraging their members to write letters to Soviet prisoners of conscience, Amnesty International was doing a great humanitarian deed. A few simple words of friendship were capable of evoking a storm of emotions in the recipient—and even some fantasies. A woman named Agnès Erkens from Avignon was particularly diligent in writing. Later, after my release from internal exile, she even invited me and my wife to visit her in France, and this was Liuba's and my first trip abroad.

---

21 Selezneva, "Pogranichnoe sostoianie."

Figure 9.6. A postcard from an Amnesty International member in Japan.

Figure 9.7. Liuba and I meeting Agnès Erkens (first on the right) with her husband Pierre and her daughter, Nîmes, France, March 1990.

Once, there was a funny story associated with one of those letters from Amnesty International. In Saralzhin, all the letters addressed in Latin script were automatically given to me. The girls who worked at the post office would make a pile of all the letters that were not written in "our tongue" for me, without any particular scrutiny. I would likewise automatically open them all. So, once I opened a letter from Amnesty addressed to the secretary of the regional office of the Communist Party, asking them to "support Myroslav Marynovych and facilitate his immediate release." I immediately returned this letter to the post office so it could be delivered to its rightful recipient, but I am sure that the girls just discarded it because it would have been too dangerous for them to acknowledge such gross ideologically tinged negligence.

The new year brought some health problems with it. Back in Drohobych, my mother broke her arm, and it was out of the question for her to visit me anytime soon. I also had some medical issues, so the year 1985 passed under the sign of Asclepius, the Greek god of medicine and healing. It all started with an innocent itch, and later the head physician (the same one who had been so rude to me and refused to give me a room) made a rather serious diagnosis: psoriasis. I started using various ointments and had to stay in both the Saralzhin and Uil hospitals for a while; even a blood transfusion was of no help. Nadiika sent me some miracle herbal ointments created by an herbalist from Rivne in northwestern Ukraine, but this created some additional problems: all my clothing, including my bedding, had to be laundered daily, and my hands were scrubbed raw from all the washing (automatic washing machines did not exist yet). So, after a week I gave this up; there were no visible results. The pustules would disappear in one place, only to appear somewhere else. My bout of what had been diagnosed as psoriasis lasted from March until November of that year, at which time I visited a dermatologist in Aktiubinsk. He determined that the diagnosis, as well as the treatment, had been all wrong. In reality, all I had was an allergy—and "the allergen was Kazakhstan." The problem disappeared immediately with simple allergy medications.

The head physician's fondness for bombastic, mind-boggling diagnoses turned out to be a weak spot for the Saralzhin hospital. In May, I came down with a high temperature, and several times I even fainted at the Saralzhin hospital. Once again, the head physician made an outlandish diagnosis: malaria. So, I was taken by ambulance under a strict precautionary epidemiological regime to the Uil hospital. There, they just rolled their eyes at this diagnosis, and after a few days, my temperature did go down.

That spring brought another drawn-out bureaucratic saga: trying to get permission to visit Ukraine. Beginning with that first year in internal exile, my official discussions with the Uil authorities, in the presence of my family, indicated that I should not expect any trips to Ukraine in the next five years. I realized that this, no doubt, had been a KGB decision, and therefore I did not harbor any real hopes.

At the beginning of April 1985, however, there were some insinuations that the trip was feasible—around a fifty-fifty probability. The bait had been cast and, honestly, I partially swallowed it. But final authorization was dragged out so demonstratively that I finally realized that this was simply a game and gave up. Thus, when I was told in mid-May by the Uil militia that because of my previous "sins" my permission to visit Ukraine had been denied, I received this with a certain equanimity:

> I walked out of there in a good mood, because finally the uncertainly had been settled. I had never placed any big hopes on this. . . . It's amazing that other people took this much more to heart than I did. (May 14, 1985)

That same day, I was introduced to a new commander. It turned out that going forward, I would have two "heads." Direct supervision, including all my evaluations, would be handled by the new policeman, while the previous one, Nurtanov (who would now reside in Uil), would be responsible for general oversight and would handle special problems. Such dual jurisdiction was not much to my liking, but alas, no one bothered to ask me about this. It turned out, however, that this change was not too bad for me. The new commander was on good terms with the Chechens, so he became friendly with me as well. He was a pleasant and nonmalicious Kazakh, who often visited me together with the Chechens. He did not shun me, knowing that I would not compromise him.

In April 1985 there was another memorable event that should be mentioned. At that time, I was on sick leave, but I found out that my workmate, Atapkel, had become very ill and could no longer recognize people. Going to the post office one day, I noticed a crowd of people in front of Atapkel's house. I realized that this was the end, so I went in and said goodbye; then on Sunday, for the first and only time in my life, I attended a Muslim funeral. My presence shocked everyone, but later I found out that all the Kazakhs were grateful to me. I was amazed that Atapkel's death had actually "elevated my reputation."

At that time, I had several opportunities to symbolically reciprocate the kindness that I had experienced in the transit prison, when inmates had offered me some bread after my hunger strike. As I have already mentioned, there were some vagabonds who worked with our Chechen team, and that summer they often had to spend the night in Saralzhin. The Kazakhs were not too fond of them, so remembering the kindness those prison inmates had shown me, I would always receive them in my house. This was not dangerous: although they were vagabonds, they were not without dignity. I could leave them in my house, with money or alcohol left visible on a shelf, but they would never touch it. They did always warn me that I should never leave any cologne lying around. This was their weakness: they could not resist drinking it.

When my mother and Nadiika came to visit me that summer, at my insistence they fed them as well. They still remained cautious, however, especially my mother: with a son like this, life is never boring. Eventually, after their departure, I told Nadiika a story one of those vagabonds had told me:

> One of them made me laugh when he described meeting you. Once, he said, he came and asked Mom if Slavik was in, and "suddenly your sister came out—how beautiful she is! And as you know, I was shabby and dirty, so I just closed my eyes and backed out of the room." (April 3, 1985)

Having lost all hope that I might be able to visit Ukraine, Nadiika decided to spend her whole summer vacation with me. My mother spoiled us endlessly, taking all domestic and cooking chores upon herself. Only the most loving mother, after working endlessly for two months in the scorching heat, could have said: "This was a summer when I could finally rest up properly!"

That autumn brought us new challenges: a dark shadow fell on Nadiika's marriage, and this is what I wrote her:

> Nadiika, I know how hard it must be to bear your cross, but you have to bear it as valiantly as our mother has. Any rebellion she might have shown would certainly have been provoked by *our* defiance. In other words, Nadiika, be brave, and if you encounter difficult moments, recall all your happy moments. Remember the light that has been sent only to you. It will illuminate the darkest pain and bless you. (September 26, 1985)

Then, some three days later, I faced my own calamity. This is how I described it in my letter to Liuba:

Figure 9.8. In the carpentry shop.

I was well rested and alert when I came to work that day. An hour later, the board that I was working on jumped out of my hands and my left hand slipped over the saw. I jumped into a car with my bleeding hand, and a half hour later I was on my way to the regional hospital in Uil. In the car, I looked over the doctor's referral, and suddenly I saw a heart-stopping word: "amputation." But do not reach for a tranquilizer; the Uil physicians turned out to be a bit more prudent, and they did not amputate my hand or even my fingers. They just sutured everything that was sticking out every which-way and bandaged my hand. For a few days I was moaning both in Kazakh and in our own language, and then after I inspected my hand, I was thrilled. The third and fourth fingers of my left hand might be a bit shorter, but only by about half a nail. They might look a bit weird, but the girls will no doubt be impressed when I tell them how I fought a wild beast all by myself in the middle of the African jungle. What's more, the surgeon assured me that I should be able to play the accordion with as much expertise as I played before. . . . So as you can see, I'm truly a hero. Please do not try to console or cheer up my mother or Nadiika, dear Liuba, because they still don't know anything about this. My heroism is insignificant compared to theirs. (September, 29, 1985)

On October 14, my Chechen friends Alkhazur and Adam, along with the local policeman, took me to the Aktiubinsk hospital, where my KGB minder placed me in the surgical wing, and I stayed there for the duration. They attended to the wounds on my fingers, removed the sutures, and then everything healed. It was while I was in the hospital that I received dermatological consultations regarding my abovementioned episode with "psoriasis."

Jumping forward some three months, I was amazed to learn that my former prison mate Oles Shevchenko, who was also internally exiled to Kazakhstan and worked as a carpenter, had injured the same two fingers of his left hand on the same equipment on January 30, 1986. He was not as lucky, however, because the last knuckle of his fourth finger had to be amputated. It seemed that just as there had earlier been a "parade" of deaths, now we had a procession of injuries.

Unexpectedly, my incident elicited even more sympathy from my co-workers:

> This morning Apai surprised me by reprimanding me, "Why are you not coming to get some milk?" I replied, "It's winter and you probably don't have enough for yourselves." She insisted that I come and get some and handed me a jar of fresh milk. I felt warm, in spite of the blizzard outside. (October 10, 1985)

I still have a photo from those years in internal exile, in which I am making some *varenyky*. They look more like patties than my mother's elegantly shaped dumplings, but you cannot see their deformity in the photo. Besides, to me and to the guests who took this photo, they tasted wonderful. This, however, did not stop me from anticipating my mother's next visit:

> My mother is still in Drohobych, but my eyes keep gazing at the bus stop. My soups grow less tasty, the broom gets much heavier, and the dishes become downright grimy. (November 29, 1985)

Her journey this time was filled with some adventures, which she later described to Nadiika:

> The trip was very difficult—there was a lot of snow, and then after we passed Kalynivka, the driver suddenly cranked the wheel, and we wound up in a ditch. I was sitting in the back seat and didn't notice much because I was suspended in the air. But both the driver and the bus were excellent, and we soon managed to climb out of there. Luckily, it was not very deep.
>
> Myros had already given up hope of my arrival, so he was overjoyed when he finally saw me. There were no cars available, so we left everything in the

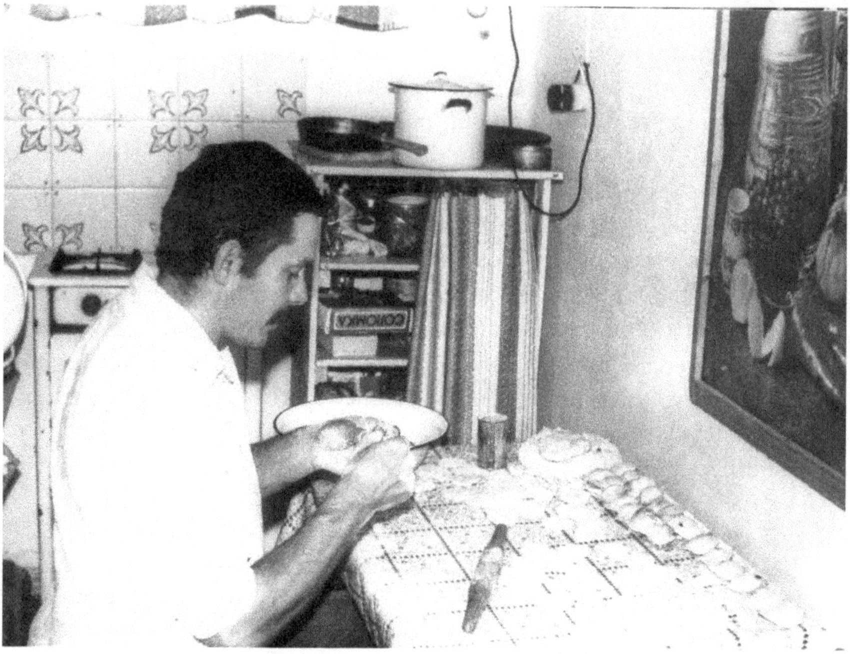

Figure 9.9. Making varenyky in my kitchen.

> store and just walked home. Later Myros and Igor Ruvinov got a sleigh and brought everything home. Now I'm in his cozy house enjoying his warm embrace, and the difficult journey is forgotten. (December 8, 1985)

Mom's arrival had an immediate effect on my appearance. Apai Sysenova said it best when she noted that "when Mom comes, 'Slapka' immediately begins to round out." My mother stayed to celebrate the New Year. That evening we went to the school gymnasium, where they had a joyful New Year's carnival. I did not see much of it, truth be told because I brought my camera with me and spent at least half an hour sweating, trying to keep up as everyone badgered me to take their photo.

Daily Life and Festivities, 1986

It is not said in vain that how you greet the New Year is how your whole year will turn out. My photography, which was just a hobby, grew into a monster that consumed all my free time. At that time there were still no photo studios in Saralzhin; for that, people had to travel to Uil, the regional center. Starting with the new year, therefore, everyone in Saralzhin would come to my house asking me to take their photos. I could not refuse them, and all I asked for was for them to compensate me for the cost of the materials.

Pretty soon my police supervisor from Uil started to consider this "unlawful enrichment."[22] I remember that, in order to eliminate this risk, I even tried to get official permission to "photograph the population," but alas, nothing came of it. We found a suitable compromise: I continued to photograph whomever I wanted, but, citing "legal considerations" I rejected all mass requests that were bound to consume a lot of my time.

Starting with the new year, I noticed a certain cooling off in my relations with the Chechens. As I remember, it all began with some trivial gossip, which they took to be true. I was also starting to get a certain feeling about them, which I described in one of my letters: "The Chechens seem to be losing their sense of 'enough is enough.'" This probably stemmed from specific cultural differences in the way they communicated, as well as some of our incompatible everyday cultural traditions.

On April 20, 1986, my good friend Liuba Kheina came to visit me in Saralzhin. We didn't yet suspect that she would later become my wife. Her arrival was associated with a funny story that even today brings a smile to my face. Her visit had been planned in advance, and I diligently prepared for it by cooking an impressive banquet for her. But when the last bus from Aktiubinsk arrived, she was not on it. Something must have changed, I thought, as I sadly trudged back home, wondering what I would do with all that food that was laid out on my table. I didn't think that I could consume all of it by myself, so when I ran into two Kazakh women that I knew, I invited them to join me. As the three of us were sitting at the table and talking, we heard a knock on the door. When I opened it, there, in the semidarkness, was Liuba! Apparently, she had forgotten about the difference in time zones and missed her bus in Aktiubinsk, so she resorted to hitching a ride, and some of the local boys brought her to my house. The situation was rather grotesque: this poor exiled man, instead of worrying about his lost visitor, is just having a banquet with two Kazakh women! The women, of course, scattered, without even any proper introductions, while I invited Liuba to finish the leftovers.

22 Private entrepreneurial activity—per Article 153 of the Criminal Code of the RSFSR, "activity . . . with a view to acquiring riches"—was illegal.

Liuba stayed with me for six days, which were filled with a truly luxurious abundance of communication. I obviously unceremoniously delegated all culinary chores to my guest, but I quickly realized that my culinary demands were driving her to complete exhaustion. I then assumed some of the chores myself and destroyed her completely; in total despair, she asked me: "So why do you think you need a wife?"

The April air was magical, the prairie was blooming with tulips, and Liuba dragged me out three times to explore Saralzhin. I did not pay much attention to nature, however, because I dedicated every minute I had after work to telling her about the camps, about my spiritual quest, and about the mystical enlightenments I had experienced. We usually stayed up late because I would pick up my accordion and play all my favorite songs for her.

Liuba's visit to Saralzhin was an extraordinary situation for the village, and of course they immediately "married me off." My workmates, Adam and Alkhazur, would sometimes stop by after work, and even though the number of visitors was much less than in the past, Liuba would just shake her head. "I don't have this many visitors in Kyiv, and here we were thinking that poor Myroslav is lonely!" No wonder that the days went by so quickly, and soon enough I was getting her settled, all in tears, in the back of the bus on her way back to Kyiv. This is what I wrote to her in my first letter after her departure:

> My darling Liuba, was I just imagining it or did the back window of the bus really get all fogged up [from your tears]? Let's say I was imagining it. . . .
>
> After I returned to my room, totally consumed by emotion, I noticed your earrings on the table. On the one hand, they seemed like a token of remembrance, a kindly greeting; on the other hand, should I go chase down the bus?
>
> I didn't even get a chance to contradict you: it was really you who gave me everything, while I gave you nothing! If I did give you anything, it would most likely be future problems because of your visit to me. Liuba, no matter what happens, please do not regret coming to see me! I wish I could convey to you my faith and the sense that the time will come when you might be able to consider your life happy, and just the thought that it might have been different would appall you. I realize that this might be difficult to do, but when you are down, please remember these words, and I hope they might help you.
>
> Christ Is Risen! Have faith that this miracle will shine upon your home!"
>
> P.S. Regarding my mood: it is only thanks to you that my spirits have finally been lifted. (April 27–28, 1986)

Liuba left on April 26, 1986, a very dark day for Ukraine—the Chernobyl disaster, which at that time we still knew nothing about.

My stream of guests did not end here. One of Adam's friends came to visit him on the weekend. She and I had also become friends when I met her at the Aktiubinsk clinic, and so Adam asked me to host her. Since the weather was very pleasant, we went to the river, and for those two days we had a wonderful time. Adam treated us to some wonderful shish kebab, and I also managed to get some rest. She left on May 3, and I started getting ready for Easter.

I had more guests for the holiday than I had anticipated, but I managed just fine. I am still proud of the fact that I was able to prepare more food than any other person could, except for my mother. I had only five hours to make everything, but I managed to make a salad, a cake made out of wafers and sweetened condensed milk, a ton of fried potatoes, and six fried fish. I also managed to tidy up the room, remove the two beds, wash the floors, make a batch of compote, prepare some appetizers, and pile them up on serving dishes, etc. The only thing I had ready in advance were some Easter eggs, the condensed milk, and peeled potatoes. I couldn't believe that I managed to get everything ready. All my guests were amazed, and after tasting the salad and the cake, Zhaken told me that he would dispatch his wife to me for a month to be trained.

But my life at that time was not consumed with festivities alone. There were periods of loneliness, when things that had been hidden deep in my soul would come to the surface. That spring I wrote a literary miniature that I still like now:

The Little Cloud

The little cloud was very sad because she never saw people being happy.

When people laughed and rejoiced, there was no cloud on their faces. It would appear only when people's hearts were wrenched with pain and despair.

The little cloud was envious of the flower because it enjoyed the tenderness and soft whispers of lovers. Even when she died, the flower could still see the smile of the one to whom the flower had been given. No one ever gave a cloud as a gift. All she would ever hear was the humiliating sentiment, "I wish the sky were cloudless."

The little cloud was jealous of the flower because she knew the gentleness of human touch. No one ever hugged a cloud. The only thing she ever knew since her birth was being hurled by the angry wind. People never noticed her; all they did was yell at her for blocking the sun or allowing it to scorch the earth.

Nevertheless, the little cloud adored people and wanted to finally see them happy. Then the day came when, filled with life-giving love, the little cloud violated the rules of the sky and, with maternal fervor, lowered herself more and more, so that she could embrace the people and see how joy might flow from their smiling eyes.

But people did not believe her and continued to hide themselves under their umbrellas and beneath the roofs of their homes.

Then, when a little boy on a deserted street took refuge under the dense crown of a tree, the little cloud's heart just couldn't take it any longer. A sharp beam of grief broke it in half, and the little cloud fell to the ground with cold torrential rain. She touched the earth that still harbored the warmth of human steps, and the flower that had just been caressed by someone's hand.

When the sun came out again, the little boy's face gazed up from under the tree, and it shone with joy, but the little cloud could no longer see it.

I will let the readers draw their own conclusions about the emotional state of mind of someone in internal exile who would settle himself on his couch, rest a writing pad on his knees, and fill it with cramped handwriting. That year, this particular attitude toward life was reflected in my Easter card:

There once was a little egg, who thought that life was wonderful. His destiny got him thrown into boiling water and cooked. Then some molten wax was applied to his shell, causing painful scars, and the poor little egg decided that his fate was nothing but an evil step-mother. He was in agony in the hot onion-peel brine, until someone's blessed hand wiped off all the wax scars, and the egg became a lovely Easter egg, its former scars turned into beautiful designs. The little egg no longer wished for a different fate, because this one became like a wise mother to him, and the little egg proclaimed: "Christ Is Risen!" (Easter 1986)

Summer was approaching, and that meant that I would be reunited with my dear ones. Prior to my mother and Nadiika's visit, I decided to renovate my dwelling once again. This is how I described it to Liuba:

Two days ago, I made a gate for our fence, and yesterday I carted in some soil and made a flower bed in front of the kitchen window. I even planted a sunflower. It looks very nice because those little Saralzhin bushes my mother planted fit very well. It all turned out so well that some stray cow came and trampled over all my work, and to further show its appreciation left behind a large patty. Darn it! I leveled everything again, and by evening I had planted some flowers. In a word, I've got a new torment. (May 22, 1986)

After lunch and until the evening, or rather until my complete exhaustion, I was doing yard work. Now I have a garden, and I planted some flowers, dill, onions,

> and then once I had watered everything, I sat down and said: "This is nice!" (May 25, 1986)

After my family arrived, my subsequent letters were filled with joyous remarks:

> I am relaxing at the table in my garden and my "army," made up of my mother and sister, is executing my highest commands. (July 30, 1986)

> My sunflower has blossomed, the purslane has not wilted yet, and the night violets are so fragrant that when the doors are open, you can smell them inside. (August 13–14, 1986)

Time was passing in peace and grace, and the photos from that summer certainly confirm this.

Around that time, a KGB agent came to see me from Alma-Ata, the capital of the Kazakh SSR (today Almaty). Lively discussions about Mikhail Gorbachev's perestroika were spreading throughout the country, so the KGB

Figure 9.10. My favorite photo with my sister during my exile.

was attempting to get a read on my sentiments about it. I remember that I told him the following: "I am very pleased about *perestroika* because I am certain that this will lead to what you call 'separatism,' which I consider fulfilling the right of subjugated nations to self-determination." My guest just laughed and self-assuredly told me, "No, that's what YOUR perestroika would lead to, but OUR perestroika will never permit that." I wonder if my Kazakh debater remembered this conversation a few years later.

During our conversation, the same KGB agent from Alma-Ata commented on the possibility of my visiting Ukraine, saying that because of my unwavering position, it was not very likely. Remembering the previous year's foot dragging, I told him directly, "I am not hassling you about this, so please, do not get on my nerves and the nerves of my family!" Eventually I did receive permission to visit Ukraine. I remember arriving at the Lviv airport and looking for the bus to Truskavets, which would pass through my hometown of Drohobych. This is when I first heard the Galician Ukrainian dialect being spoken in a long time, and having always been very vigilant about the purity of the language, I suddenly felt a great warmth in my heart: "I'm home!"

I remember that trip as an endless series of visits with friends and family who came to see me at my mother's apartment in Drohobych. I remember some fragments of discussions between a relative of mine from Lviv, Nusia Mentsinska, and Yevhen Sverstiuk. The discussions with Atena Pashko from Lviv, Halyna Didkivska from Kyiv, and my sister Nadiika were truly feasts of good humor and mutual amiability. I also remember Liuba Kheina and Olia Heiko coming from Kyiv.

Then it was back to Zhuliany airport, which was to take me from Kyiv to Kharkiv and then on to Aktiubinsk. Around a dozen of my friends met me at 2 a.m. at the Kyiv train station and joined me on my way to the airport. I got to spend some time separately with each of them, talking about everything that we had suffered, all that we had endured. This is when, while strolling with Liuba, I asked her to marry me and to unite her life with the rather uncertain fate of a political exile. I had been thinking about this continuously after her visit to Saralzhin. She agreed without any hesitation, and I was grateful to her and respected her for her bravery, which followed the Decembrist tradition and was typical of the wives of many Ukrainian political prisoners.[23] We agreed that soon she would come to join me in Saralzhin, and then I left.

---

23 Decembrist tradition: Participants in the 1825 Decembrist uprising were internally exiled to Siberia; many of their wives followed them.

The time between a marriage proposal and the wedding is always complex for a man. In this case, there was also my sense that I was taking another person hostage in my turbulent life. My letters to her at that time fully reflect this:

> Saralzhin welcomed me with fine weather, and I am hoping that December will bring you to me. I remember our conversation every day, and I am planning and trying to chase away all my fears. . . . If you only knew how I dread the thought of making you unhappy. I am only sorry that I did not tell you that you should buy some patience—be it wholesale or retail, in cash or on credit. (November 2, 1986)

> It is easy not to believe in your own personal happiness. But realizing that you might make someone else miserable, and not for the first time in your life . . . makes it very difficult. When you know yourself and you can see the pitfalls you might fall into and then drag another person with you, it makes it even tougher. (November 10, 1986)

Since I knew that Liuba was allergic to cigarette smoke, I decided to quit smoking. The stimulus was so strong that unlike the three previous times I had attempted to do this unsuccessfully in camp, this time I succeeded in getting rid of this bad habit, and I still don't smoke.

In December, Liuba managed to get away and came to join me. She arrived on Western Christmas Eve, on December 24. The following day, I invited all the village elders and all the respected women of Saralzhin whom I knew and officially introduced Liuba to them, explaining that due to my internal exile status, I was not permitted to register her as my wife, but I asked them to regard her as such. All my Saralzhin friends were happy for us, and from then on, they accepted Liuba as one of them, particularly since, under the watchful eyes of the older women, Liuba managed to master the tea ceremony. Eventually, they even reported this to my mother: "she can even serve tea the Kazakh way." It was at that time we were given our Kazakh names. Liuba became "Makhabbat," which means "love" in Kazakh (Liuba means the same thing in Ukrainian), and I became "Zhasasynbek," meaning "worthy warrior." We consider the lovely party at which I introduced Liuba to be our Kazakh wedding.

We greeted 1987 with love and peace, and the traditional Saralzhin New Year masquerade stands out because I unexpectedly won a prize. In general, the Kazakhs were good at organizing these masquerades. Practically the whole village gathered at the school gymnasium, and according to tradition,

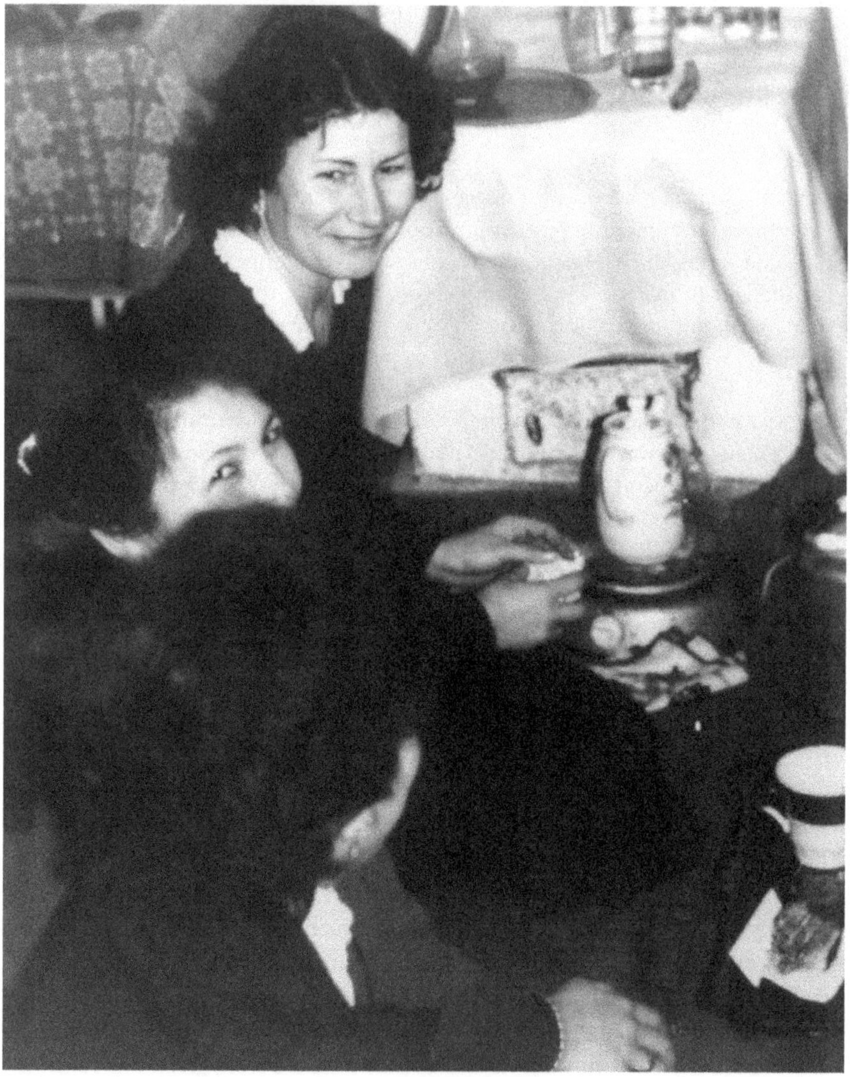

Figure 9.11. Liuba at a tea ceremony during our Kazakh "wedding," December 25, 1986.

they divided themselves into groups by generation. They had prepared diligently for the festivities, and the program, although amateurish, was interesting. My neighbor Umirzhan and I decided to present a surprise. By that time, I had already mastered many Kazakh songs, so I decided to don their

Figure 9.12. Liuba and I celebrating the new year, 1987.

national costume and sing one of their folk songs about their native language, "Ananyn-Tele." We altered Umirzhan's folk costume to fit me, and I was transformed "from a Cossack into a Turk." I let Umirzhan wear my embroidered Ukrainian shirt and taught him to sing a Ukrainian folk song, "How bright and starry is the night" (*Nich iaka misiachna, zoriana, iasnaia*). I transliterated the words into Russian so he could understand.

I was the first to sing, accompanying myself on my accordion. Then it was Umirzhan's turn, and I accompanied him on my accordion as well. I was touched when I heard him sing this lovely song, and at some point it got funny when he mixed up some lyrics, swapping the word "tea" for "meadow."[24] We were a great hit, and I won either second or third prize.

24 The original line is "Come, my work-weary love, to the meadow, if just for one minute" (*Vyidy, kokhanaia, pratseiu zmorena, khoch na khvylynochku v hai*). Here the word *hai*, "meadow," was replaced by *chai*, "tea."

Imagine: a prize going to a political exile! This was only possible among the Kazakhs, "removed from politics, but close to nature."[25]

At some point, Liuba had to return to Kyiv to resign from her job and somehow keep the rights to her apartment. In her stead, my mother made her way to visit me during a blizzard. Once again, my home became a cozy haven. At that time, another creature came to live with us, and I jokingly wrote about this to Liuba:

> We have another creature living in our little house, and she has immediately become the central character, living up to her patrician name: "Lutecia." Neither my mother nor I can hold our tails up as straight as our kitty. (February 11, 1987)

The year 1987 began with a sense that my life was finally well ordered. I was accustomed to my simple life as a carpenter, and my relations with the authorities and my colleagues were stable. Thanks to the generosity of my family and the kindness of my friends, my daily routine was firmly established. I had found a mate for myself, and we began to establish our life as a family. From then on, it was Liuba who made the *varenyky*, cooked *borshch*, and made the pancakes. Subsequent events seemed to be turning out the way my friend Adam had anticipated, paving the way for my "dekulakization" back to Ukraine.

25 Quote attributed to Yevhen Sverstiuk.

Intermezzo 3

Once Again on the Threshold of a New Life

It was during my mother's stay in Saralzhin in February 1987 that a whole delegation came to visit me: a Kazakh procurator from Aktiubinsk, another procurator from Lviv, and two KGB agents, also from Lviv. They told me that things were moving in the direction of democratization in Ukraine, and they needed to settle the issue of political dissidents. Additionally, they had gotten very positive evaluations about me from my workplace and from the local police, as well as from the Aktiubinsk, Kyiv, and Lviv KGB. "We are authorized to tell you that if you write a letter of repentance for everything that happened, you will be free within a month." They were insistent that I do this, coming up with new arguments against each of my objections. My position was unchanging: "Listen here, good people, you are being totally irrational. I spent seven years in prison camps and three years in internal exile, and now, practically at the end of my term, you want me to repent, something that I refused to do from the very beginning. Since I did not do it then and have served practically my whole term, I certainly will not do it now." At that time, I had not yet read Yevhen Sverstiuk's words, which would have been apropos, but their essence was certainly on my mind: "Political prisoners do not beg for forgiveness—that is the whole point of their resistance in the first place."[1]

Finally, after a long debate, they asked me if I would be willing to write a statement saying that I refused to ask for forgiveness. I agreed and wrote on a piece of paper that I do not consider myself guilty and will never repent because I acted appropriately. Eventually, I learned that this KGB meeting was not a new or unique tactic. This is how Patriarch Josyf Slipyj recounted it: "The Commander told me to write something asking for my release. They

1 Sverstiuk, *Na khvyliakh "Svobody,"* 197.

Figure I3.1. My Australian family nicknamed this photo "The Warrior."

were convinced that because I was in such a hopeless and desperate situation, I might write God knows what. Instead, I wrote about all the abuse and violations that I had endured. Most likely, they were planning to stage my release, based on my appeals."[2]

2 Slipyi, *Spomyny*, 227.

The procurators received my rejection calmly, but the KGB agents were angry. As they were leaving, standing at the door, one of them shouted, "Well, I guess you can't outrun yourself!"

After they left, my mother and I were alone in my room, and she was confused and upset. She had not gotten involved in this conversation or pressured me in any way, but I could see in her face that it was difficult for her to give up even such a fleeting moment of false hope. In my soul, on the other hand, I was battling two feelings: I regretted causing her more pain, but I also felt pride for my mother—that in spite of her pain she did not try to make me feel guilty for my decision.

Soon thereafter, my mother returned home, and in her stead, having settled all her practical affairs in Kyiv, Liuba came back. We had to accept the fact that we would be staying here for two more years. Because of *perestroika*, however, there was already a new feeling in the air, and what had previously seemed impossible was becoming attainable. Nevertheless, my former camp experience kept me on guard and did not allow any excessively optimistic feelings to take hold in my soul.

Then, on March 23, 1987, my local Kazakh policeman called me in and in a rather confused voice said, "I'm quite surprised, but I have the authorization to release you." Apparently, he had received a document stating that this pardon was "in conjunction with a decision by the Supreme Soviet of the USSR." Later I learned that some two hundred other political prisoners were also released at that time. That's when I realized why it had been important for the KGB to receive a "written statement" from me rejecting my appeal for pardon. For them what mattered was simply having a record of a statement of any kind, no matter what it said.

What happened next was best described in a letter that Liuba wrote to my mother:

> Mama, are you by any chance feeling something special this minute? I was just crying, nestled in Myros's arms, because a historic moment has arrived: he was released! He went to work this morning, not suspecting anything, but then he suddenly came home. He didn't tell me anything until he had changed his clothes, and then, standing in the door, told me with guarded strength: "You can congratulate me on my release!"
>
> This was a moment beyond space and time. We celebrated with some tea, and then, as usual, our Kazakh brother Alibek came in, and became a bit confused when he learned of the news. He almost cried as well, and we had to comfort him. He told us that in the future, when he goes for a walk in the

evenings, he will always stop by our little house, even when we are no longer there. (March 24, 1987)

Now we had to quickly gather our belongings and plan our return to Ukraine. I did not hesitate in choosing Drohobych as the city I wanted to return to. Even though Liuba had an apartment in Kyiv, I had no desire to go there. I wanted to go to my mother's home, to the dearest person in my life, who had so faithfully waited for me and supported me with such dedication throughout my entire incarceration.

The local Kazakhs were happy for us. But at the same time, like Alibek, they were saddened by our inevitable separation. For the next few days everyone invited us over for a meal to say goodbye. Since all of our lunches and dinners were already spoken for, some people even invited us for breakfast. The state farm helped organize our transportation to Aktiubinsk, and to commemorate our departure, we took a photo in front of the truck, surrounded by all our friends.

I left Saralzhin with a feeling of sadness, as I had done when leaving camp because I was leaving behind my friends and the little house that had become my home.

Figure I3.2. Our farewell to Saralzhin, March 1987.

Finding myself with some free time in Aktiubinsk, I decided to visit my KGB minder. I harbored no ill will toward him and understood that he had just been doing his job; I saw that he was not an evil person. When I came to the KGB office and asked to meet with him, everyone got nervous. When he finally did receive me, my minder looked baffled. It is hard to imagine what he was expecting from me, and during our entire conversation he never really understood why I had come. Eventually he did calm down, but then he went to the other extreme: he started talking to me almost intimately, wishing me a happy life. For me, it was interesting to just watch his reaction.

On the train from Aktiubinsk to Moscow, I struck up a conversation with a young Uzbek, and I candidly related my life and experiences to him. He was honestly moved by my story and told Liuba that she should take good care of me. I still remember Liuba's face and how intensely she reacted to his words. His was a typical Eastern style of thinking: it didn't enter his mind that it was my obligation, in turn, to take care of Liuba as well.

On April 2, 1987, Liuba and I entered my mother's apartment. This is where I was to once again drop anchor, find an apartment, find a job, and seek my place in a politically charged atmosphere. As we will later see, with God's help, slowly everything fell into place. I was amazed by Nadiika's prophetic words that she had uttered back in camp, at a time when I was so pessimistic. "Everything just *has* to be fine!" she had said, and her intuition seldom let her down.

Living in my mother's one-room apartment was a bit too tight for the three of us, so Liuba decided to try to trade in her Kyiv apartment for an apartment in Drohobych. At some point, Liuba and I went to Kyiv, where we had the chance to see Liuba's mother, Nina, and Myshko, the son of Liuba's brother Valery, who had both come to Kyiv to meet us. Our meeting with Mama Nina was warm, and her trust in me was instantaneous. She was a village teacher, and not only was she not afraid to give her daughter in marriage to a recent political prisoner, but because of the challenges that I had lived through, she was actually proud of it.

A while later, in May, we visited Liuba's brother Valery, his then-wife Alla, and their older son Andrii in the village of Pidlisne in Mykolaiv oblast in southern Ukraine. We also met some of her other relatives and friends. I remember one rather embarrassing incident from that visit. I was always very eager to help my mother-in-law, though as a city boy (except for my time in Saralzhin), I was not very adept at farm work. At some point, Mama Nina asked me to churn some butter. I eagerly set to my task, but a mere five minutes later the muscles of my right hand had become numb. I switched to my left hand, but there the numbness set in even sooner. When Mama Nina came out of the house, she found me just staring at the churn in quiet desperation. She understood immediately and took away the source of her son-in-law's humiliation. Later, I tried to save face in the fields, as Liuba and I harvested beets along with her whole family.

While in Kyiv, I tried to visit all my friends, though Mykola Matusevych was not there because he was still finishing up his term in Buryatia, near Lake Baikal. Eventually he explained this himself:

> When my "pardon" came in 1988, I refused to end my internal exile and told the KGB that I had not yet paid my debt to the Motherland. They were furious! Then, on December 7, Gorbachev announced at the General Assembly of the UN that there were no political prisoners in the USSR. I did this deliberately, as a sign of protest, because instead of rehabilitating us they "forgave" us. That's why I chose to serve out my term and didn't return home until the beginning of February 1989.[3]

It was bittersweet seeing my Kyiv friends, but I no longer had any desire to stay in the city. I realized that it would have been impossible to restore my old life. While in Kyiv, I decided to fulfill the old promise I had made to my case officer, Oleksandr Bereza. Exactly ten years had passed since my arrest, and I wanted to keep my promise to meet with him and "take him out for coffee." My arrival at the KGB headquarters created a similar reaction as in Aktiubinsk, except without the same cordial ending. Bereza was totally flabbergasted and looked frightened. I jokingly reminded him of the promise I had made back in pretrial detention, but he was barely able to eke out a few words. This was understandable: it was 1987, and no one knew which way things would turn. They were all totally frightened. After some ten minutes, I understood that there would be no conversation, so I got bored. I thought to myself, "Good man, you were so cheerful and relaxed then, sitting in your office, when I was the defendant, but I was still able to joke with you, inviting you to coffee in ten years! So why are you so threatened now? Surely you must realize what you did then!" I finally ended the meeting by saying, "Well, I will not disturb you any further. Goodbye."

In order to get the proper documents to swap Liuba's apartment, Liuba and I had to register our wedding immediately, rather than waiting for a

---

3 Matusevych, "Ia vyhrav dvobii."

Figure 13.3. Wedding photo.

church wedding.[4] On July 2, we did so in Drohobych, with Olia Heiko and Zorian Popadiuk as our witnesses. At that time Zorian lived in Sambir, and soon thereafter, he and his girlfriend Oksana also got married.

Eventually we did find a satisfactory deal to exchange Liuba's one-room apartment in Kyiv for a three-room apartment in Drohobych. We got a truck to move all her furniture from Kyiv; my sister Nadiika purchased the items that were still lacking, like the bedroom furniture. Then we started settling in.

Soon thereafter, a small incident illuminated our little dwelling with providential light. I ran into a former school friend in Drohobych and invited him and his wife for a visit. After seeing our apartment, my friend's wife admonished him quietly. I didn't realize what was up, but later I figured it

4 Legally, marriages had to be registered at the ZAGS (vital records office); religious ceremonies could also be held but were ceremonial rather than legally binding.

out. A year prior to my arrest, when I last saw him, he had told me about some semilegal deal he was contemplating that would help him get an apartment. Now it turned out that, a decade later, he still did not have an apartment. In that amount of time, I had served out my term in camp and in internal exile and now, with God's help, I also managed to get a three-room apartment. How can one not cite the passage?

> Therefore I tell you, do not worry about your life, what you will eat or what you will drink, or about your body, what you will wear. Is not life more than food, and the body more than clothing? Look at the birds of the air; they neither sow nor reap nor gather into barns, and yet your heavenly Father feeds them. Are you not of more value than they? . . . Therefore do not worry, saying, 'What will we eat?' or 'What will we drink?' or 'What will we wear?' For it is the Gentiles who strive for all these things; and indeed your heavenly Father knows that you need all these things. But strive first for the kingdom of God and his righteousness, and all these things will be given to you as well. (Matthew 6:25–26, 31–33)

Our early days in Drohobych were blessed by Zenovy Krasivsky's diligent care for us. He would often visit us in his car and tried to help us with everything he could. I eventually learned that he had taken on the mission of serving his former camp mates in all their daily needs. The key word here was "serve." One moment that comes to mind was Liuba's and my church wedding on October 16, 1987: Zenovy took it upon himself to create a photo album of this special event. He drove us to church in my grandfather's village of Stebnyk, where we had decided to get married. Later at home, when a small group of friends was about to dig into the feast without first saying grace, he timidly began a prayer, thus setting a valuable example for all of us. At that time, he was still grieving the tragic death of his beloved wife Olena, who had died in his presence a year and a half previously. He still missed her very much, but at the same time he managed to demonstrate to us how to accept God's will.

It is a remarkable story of how his recommendation helped me find employment. At that time, I still didn't know that Krasivsky was one of the leaders of the Organization of Ukrainian Nationalists. I was not a member of that organization, so given the secrecy of this group, there was no need for me to know this. I did know that he was a loyal representative of the nationalist movement and that he had close contacts with the Ukrainian diaspora. I was therefore not surprised when he told me that he had the necessary funds to start a new sociopolitical magazine, *Ukrainski problemy* (Ukrainian issues), and proposed that I, being unemployed at that time, become its literary editor.

I was not convinced that this was a good idea, but I had no grounds to reject him. Once I consented, Krasivsky immediately brought me a typewriter from his home in Morshyn and some articles for me to review. They were to be included in the first issue. I ran into problems as soon as I began to read an article by Dmytro Dontsov that Krasivsky wanted to reprint: I realized that it differed radically from my own viewpoint.[5] My heart started racing from this internal dissonance. I glanced at some of the other manuscripts and my feeling of disagreement continued to grow, and I realized that I would not be able to work for this magazine. There was nothing else to do but to call Krasivsky and tell him that we had to talk. Our conversation took place in his car, and I candidly and frankly told him how I felt and apologized for inadvertently disappointing him. He listened to me carefully and then, with some pain in his voice said, "Good God, why is it that those I want to engage in this project reject my proposal, and those who are eager to get started would be better not doing it?"

Pan Zenko had been schooled by the camps and had a lot of experience in life. Not only did he react to my rejection with understanding, he remained a good friend, always helping me in all my everyday needs. Eventually he also supported my decision to opt against a political career and all the get-rich-quick schemes that went along with it. He placed more emphasis on this than I did because for me, my lack of interest in practical politics was long held, constant, and innate.

In any case, the problem of finding a job resurfaced and not because of any direct intervention from the KGB. At that time, the local Drohobych KGB chief was a man named Viktor Husiev. He cordially received me, and even during our first meeting he assured me that my past would not influence my current situation. In other words, the KGB would not try to hamper my life here. He did keep his word: my difficulties in finding a job had nothing to do with the KGB, but with the heads of the local Drohobych enterprises' basic fear and reluctance to hire a former political prisoner, lest this bring them some difficulties with the KGB. It took a few months for me to finally find a job.

That summer I became acquainted with another Drohobych resident, Oleh Pelekhovych. Moved by my life history, he was eager to help me. He spoke with Ihor Saranevych, then the head of the Second Drohobych Oil Refinery, who turned out to be a brave and optimistic person. Soon thereafter, I began working as an operator of a catalytic reforming unit that

5 Dmytro Dontsov (1883–1973): leading theorist of Ukrainian integral nationalism whose views provided the ideological underpinnings for OUN.

converted crude oil into high octane gas. Obviously, I started from scratch, but my workmates treated me courteously, sharing their professional skills with me.

Thus, with God's grace, my new life was becoming stable: I had returned to Ukraine; I lived near my mother; I could visit my sister Nadiika, who lived not too far away in the city of Rivne, where she still worked as a teacher; I was setting up a household with my wife Liuba; and I had found a job—though it wasn't my favorite work, I had friendly colleagues, and it gave me at least some minimal means of survival. This was the beginning of a twenty-year stretch that Nadiika later called the happiest years of our lives.

To be sure, it was not devoid of challenges, but there were also some blessings as well, like my job as a journalist for the Drohobych regional newspaper *Halyts'ka zoria* (Galician Star), and later my hallowed haven at Ukrainian Catholic University in Lviv, where I began working in 1997. In 2000 Liuba and I moved into our comfortable Lviv apartment, where

Figure I3.4. With my mother.

Figure I3.5. With my colleagues from the daily newspaper *Halyts'ka zoria* (Galician Star), 1990.

Figure I3.6. During the inauguration of Ukrainian Catholic University, 2002.

Figure I3.7. The "Marynovych Trio."

Figure I3.8. With my mother-in-law Nina.

my grandfather's pump organ and the "Marynovych Trio," blessed in my memory, could be heard once again.

While my private life with family and friends settled into place nicely, the dilemma of what civic path I should take still remained unresolved. One day in the summer of 1988, driving with Zenovy Krasivsky from Stryi to Lviv, we had a noteworthy conversation. Yevhen Sverstiuk was also in the car with us. It is not difficult to imagine what happens when three former Ukrainian political prisoners find themselves together: they immediately embark on a conversation about the future of Ukraine and the world, and all that Providence has to do is to stop and listen.

Our conversation was weighty indeed: society was transforming itself, new possibilities were emerging, and you needed to decide what your position and future direction would be. On the one hand, each of us saw the enormous civic task that lay in front of him, and none of us intended to hide in his own shell. Most former political prisoners saw themselves as civic missionaries, called to transform society, and my fellow travelers were no exception: they were a perfect example of this. For politically oriented individuals, the late 1980s were a golden opportunity because society was ripe for change. But what were those who did not see themselves in politics to do? The question was a simple one: should all former dissidents automatically follow charismatic leaders like Viacheslav Chornovil or Mykhailo Horyn and fully immerse themselves in politics, or was there another niche for them?[6]

Of the three of us, Yevhen Sverstiuk's path seemed to be the most straightforward. His renowned name and accomplishments automatically positioned him as a noteworthy figure in Ukraine's cultural rebirth. People would gather to hear him speak, and his graying head never stood alone in any Kyiv gathering. Sverstiuk became the key figure in the rebirth of the Ukrainian Autocephalous Orthodox Church, and just a year after our car ride, it declared its autocephaly.[7] Patriarch Mstyslav, the head of the Ukrainian Autocephalous Orthodox Church, often sought Sverstiuk's opinion.

---

6 Chornovil was one of the leaders of Rukh, a pioneering non-Communist political movement in the late 1980s. Chornovil was a key figure in Ukrainian political life in the lead-up to and immediately after independence, serving in the Verkhovna Rada and garnering 23 percent of votes in the 1991 presidential election. Horyn also served in the Verkhovna Rada.

7 The Ukrainian Autocephalous Orthodox Church (UAOC) was initially created in the interwar period; it was revived in Ukraine in the late 1980s, having been kept alive in the diaspora. On December 15, 2019, the UAOC became

During this conversation, Krasivsky didn't say much, but the path that lay before him at that time was obvious. He became one of the organizers who helped get the Ukrainian Greek Catholic Church legalized and helped organize the political movement State Independence of Ukraine (*Derzhavna samostiinist' Ukrainy*).[8] He worked diligently for the restoration of the historic memory of renowned Ukrainians. In memory of his wife Olena he got involved in charitable activities to help former political prisoners who had no means of survival. He was tireless in helping people and did not hesitate to pick up a sack of potatoes from one friend just to take it to the Carpathian Mountains to help another friend. This humble man's tireless work, however, remained unheralded. He did not shun the behind-the-scenes dirty work, only to later relegate the leadership to another person while remaining on the sidelines.

Therefore, I was faced with more questions than the others. From that conversation, I remember several deductions that I offered to my companions. First of all, having been deprived of my freedom, I had not been part of my community for the last ten years. This was a substantial amount of time, and I felt that it was crucial for me to get reacquainted with the populace. I felt that I had to learn to understand their attitudes and their inner aspirations for the future. I was not ready to "lead the people" without really knowing what they thought and felt.

Second, I was skeptical of any attempts to successfully build a new nation in Ukraine as long as we still bore the blueprints of the old governing systems in our heads. I considered the nation's mental and spiritual state to be the most important thing, not politics. Gorbachev had initiated a transformation of the political and economic systems, but people still maintained a Soviet mentality, attitude, and lifestyle. Thus Ukraine, like all other post-Soviet countries, still had to undergo a spiritual transformation—a reverse mutation of sorts. Only then would real reforms be possible: the economy could be regenerated, corruption might cease, and respect for the dignity of each individual might be achievable. At that time, it was this spiritual and moral transformation that I was interested in facilitating.

Today, I am not embarrassed to have taken this position, and both Maidans (the Orange Revolution of 2004 and the Revolution of Dignity

---

part of a united Orthodox Church of Ukraine that received a Tomos of autocephaly from the Ecumenical Patriarch of Constantinople.

8 State Independence of Ukraine: political party from 1990 to 2003 with a staunchly nationalist platform. Promoted an exclusively ethnic conception of the Ukrainian nation, adhering to the ideology of the OUN.

in 2013–2014) only confirm this. But this position did relegate me to dissonance with the revolutionary mainstream of that time. As a rule, I was not an avid participant in any mass political movements or demonstrations. All those slogans, the black-and-white verdicts, and shouts of "disgrace!" were not for me. Most political activists in Drohobych could not understand this because they felt that given my prison experience, I certainly could have been the "Chornovil" of Drohobych. They were disappointed when I refused to take a seat at the head tables and did not rush to take to the podium. Then in 1990, on the eve of the first democratic elections, they urged me to run for a parliamentary seat, and when I refused, they called me a "coward."

I myself did not feel like a Chornovil but rather like a Cassandra.[9] I did not rejoice during the enthusiastic demonstrations because I did not trust the loud dramatic froth of the crowds. I saw in them a lack of readiness to immerse themselves in the constructive and serious work of governance. Communist stereotypes cast their influence on the populace, and they weren't even aware of it. They were convinced that all you had to do was change the flags or adopt nationalistic rhetoric, and those former Communist methods would lose their menace and become totally acceptable. Furthermore, politics had completely consumed their minds, while spirituality, the biblical cornerstone, was relegated to the "future." People rejoiced that power had been captured, proud to have hauled giant Trojan horses into our revolutionary squares, but they failed to see the danger hiding within. This was the tragedy of my situation: I saw impending doom on a day of rejoicing and general celebration.

All my fears eventually came to pass when revolutionary Galicia had won, when in the coming years and decades the activists who had been leading the demonstrations fell victim, one by one, to the temptations of career, money, and political power. Back then, however, at the end of the 1980s, my Cassandra-like "sadness in the midst of joy" seemed a bit odd, if not suspicious, and I was fully aware of this. In the afterword to my first book, *Ukraina na poliakh Sviatoho Pys'ma* (Ukraine on the margins of the Holy Scriptures), I told the reader:

> I am talking to you from a philosophical "house on the outskirts," not from a political rally. I am fully aware that most people regard my position skeptically, being convinced that the only way forward for a member of the Ukrainian Helsinki Group, clad in a dissident's robe, is as a political leader and a fighter. In

9 Cassandra: A Trojan priestess of Apollo. Her name is employed as a rhetorical device to indicate someone whose accurate prophecies are not believed.

> my own defense, I will only say that I never joined the enemy ranks and did not pass the flag to anyone else. In reality, I never ceased being a fighter; the only thing that changed is the arena for my fight. Unfortunately, some people do not see this.[10]

Every so often, my unforgettable Saralzhin would resurface in Liuba's and my memory. We invited our Kazakh friends to our wedding, designing the wedding invitation in the same manner they did, using the Kazakh language. Of course we called ourselves Makhabbat and Zhasasynbek, as they called us. We received very warm responses. Later, Bukenbai and Alibek did come from Saralzhin to visit; our meeting was very joyous, and the parting was equally sad.

A year after my release, for my first vacation, I embarked on a nostalgic tour, visiting Antanas Terlackas in Vilnius, Yury Būmeisters in Riga, Genrikh Altunian in Kharkiv, Grigory Isaev in Kuibyshev, and then also to Kazakhstan, to visit my dear Saralzhin. The Kazakhs were profoundly moved and told me, "The first time you came, it was because you were brought here. But since you came a second time, by your own will, then you are truly our friend."

It was just too bad that my Chechen friends were no longer in Saralzhin. At some point, Adam came looking for me in Drohobych, but unfortunately, I was not in town at that time. Eventually my contacts with them were severed, and then after the Chechen war, I lost all hope of ever seeing them again. Still, every time I pick up my accordion and start playing Chechen songs, I become engulfed in a wild hope: what if one of them might be walking by my window at this very moment? Hearing Chechen songs, they might just knock on my door.

Today, the massive participation of Chechen mercenaries in terrorist groupings in the current war Russia is waging in the East of Ukraine consumes my heart with profound sorrow.[11] Over the past few decades, the Chechen nation has experienced two massive tragedies: their quest for independence made them the targets of astounding terror from the Kremlin, especially during the Chechen wars of 1994–1996 and 1996–1999; and then some of them became enamored with their oppressors and started serving

---

10 Myroslav Marynovych, *Ukraina na poliakh Sviatoho Pys'ma* (Drohobych: Vidrodzhennia, 1991), 106–7.

11 Several hundred Chechen mercenaries have fought on the side of the Russian-backed separatists against the Ukrainian army.

them by joining a number of terrorist organizations, under the leadership of the criminal Ramzan Kadyrov, today the head of the Chechen Republic.

As I have previously mentioned, my former Kazakh supervisor Ural also came to pay us a visit. He was vacationing in Ukraine and came to see us in Drohobych. He came to my book presentation. Eventually, in spite of all my letters, my connections with Saralzhin were severed. Perhaps this had something to do with a moment during my last visit to Saralzhin, when I was relaxing at a tea ceremony while visiting Apai Sysenova and talking with her husband. This was in 1988, and Gorbachev's *perestroika* brought with it not only certain elements of freedom but also a lot of disruptions. At that time, my host proclaimed, "It is wrong for so many people to talk. It is essential for only one person to talk, and for others to just listen to him." This was the voice of another civilization, for whom the democratic process was considered a misguided and erroneous degradation of the vertical power structure. Eventually, under President Nursultan Nazarbayev, this vertical structure was reestablished in Kazakhstan and, under this new "order," maintaining contacts with a former political prisoner once again became too dangerous.

Conclusion

The Price of Growing Up in Freedom

Well into her seventies, my mother still liked to tell a funny story about the time when, as a young student, I came home from my Lviv dorm and handed her a bundle of my dirty laundry. To get out of an uncomfortable situation, as I handed her this lovely "gift," I sang the first few lines from the popular song "Two Colors" (*Dva kol'ory*):

> My life has bounced me around the world
> And the only thing I am bringing home
> Is a bundle of timeworn cloth
> With my life clearly etched upon it.[1]

Today, as I finish my memoirs, I am reminded of those words. My life has indeed bounced me around the dissident paths of distant camps, and what did I bring back home? What kind of life is embroidered on that timeworn cloth?

As I look back, all I see is the unending crescendo of my incompatibility with the Soviet system. For me, Moscow's "enforced love" resulted only in a series of punishments because I refused to become a stool pigeon: difficulties in finding employment, then losing my job; having trouble obtaining housing; secret and overt surveillance; and provocations and persecutions from the KGB. Then came my arrest on April 23, 1977, followed by interrogations, an unlawful trial, continuous transfers by armored trains between various prisons, an extended deprivation of freedom in a strict regime labor camp in the Ural Mountains, hunger strikes and labor strikes, extreme cold and food deprivation in numerous isolation cells, searches, and confiscations, and then, starting in April 1984, a three-year internal exile in Kazakhstan.

---

1 *Meni viinula v ochi syvyna, / Ta ia nichoho ne vezu dodomu, / Lysh zhortochok staroho polotna / I vyshyte moe zhyttia na niomu.*

Even if you don't count the extrajudicial persecution before my arrest, it spanned a full ten years. I was arrested when I was twenty-eight and returned to Ukraine as a thirty-eight-year-old.

At that time, many people considered this to be a disproportionate price to pay in the struggle for human rights. Some of my friends, however, paid far more: they lost their lives in the struggle. Even then, I opposed the idea that I had sacrificed too much, and I haven't changed my mind. I remember Mephistopheles's allegation in Goethe's monumental *Faust*: "I am part of that power which eternally wills evil and eternally works good." The miracle of my experiences as a dissident and in prison hinges on the fact that the Good Lord used all the evil I endured from the KGB, and indeed from the whole Soviet regime, to help me turn into something worthy. True, in the pinnacle of my flowering youth, they did deprive me of a whole decade of freedom, but in reality, I was given a lot more.

First of all, the suffering that I endured provided me with the spiritual strength that gave my life its true meaning. For this reason, I was able to leave prison a new person, as if born again. The camps reforged me, and from then on, I had my own worldview, my own backbone. As subsequent years have confirmed, that backbone has not always been an asset: often people think it is too soft or warped, and my opinions are sometimes deemed to be rather bizarre. But I am grateful to God for it. None of today's oligarchs could purchase this gift at any cost—it is granted only to those who endure undeserved punishment.

Furthermore, by joining the dissidents and becoming a part of the movement of nonviolent resistance to totalitarian terror, I had the honor of being one of the last witnesses to Communist atrocities, witnesses against whom all the KGB's cruelties were powerless. Here I should make a clarification: had it not been for strong international reaction and support, we Brezhnev-era dissidents would no doubt have been silenced in the Siberian wilderness just like the millions of victims of the Stalin era. It is important not to overestimate the effectiveness of the dissident movement in challenging the Soviet system. At the same time, I do not want to undervalue the sacrifices that my colleagues made, placing everything they treasured on the line.

Third, my experience helped me to recognize my own shortcomings, and in the years that followed I have always kept them in mind whenever I receive recognition for my accomplishments. Fighting the totally invasive, all-encompassing, and depraved system of Communism cannot be as regimented and enthusiastic as marching in a parade. A struggle is inconceivable without fear. Your self-preservation instinct cries out at the top of its voice when you are staring down the barrel of a machine gun, surrounded by vicious trained dogs, suffocating in overcrowded vehicles, so exhausted by malnutrition that your body swells up, threatened with additional time added to your term, or warned that you will never be permitted to return to Ukraine. But just as heroism is not eternal, neither is fear. Eventually you grow weary of it, and out of nowhere, your strength is renewed. This is when you realize that no sin or false step is final, that the human spirit is capable of leading you out of any chasm. Yes, I also had moments of hesitation and weakness, which made me susceptible to KGB provocations. But I often remembered Rudyard Kipling's words: "And lose, and start again at your beginnings / And never breathe a word about your loss."[2]

This brings me to the main source of human strength: the human spirit. It is this spirit alone that can convince an innocent person that it is better to sit behind bars than to condone injustice. It is this spirit that helps a prisoner to turn down a slice of bread during a hunger strike, even though this bread is all he dreams of. If a person's conscience is clear, there is no limit to this spirit. Not every prisoner identifies this spirit as the grace of God. To me this was obvious because it was in camp that I realized how immense the spiritual dimension of a human being is.

Faith and sacrifice are inseparable because they provide natural support to each other. Without faith, sacrifice becomes torture, and then the torturer becomes the central figure. The Stockholm syndrome speaks to this: the victim begins to love his torturer, who becomes the dominant figure in their relationship. If there is faith, however, the victim becomes a witness; the central character is the one who willingly suffers for the truth. Faith is also confirmed when a person sacrifices himself or herself in one way or another. Perhaps this is the reason that until the 2013–2014 Revolution of Dignity, Ukrainians were floundering in an ever-growing moral quagmire, where sacrifice was considered foolish and faith was looked upon as a respectable demonstration of showy piety.

To have a strong spirit, a person must be convinced of the validity of his or her cause. I was totally convinced that the reign of Communist deceit would come to an end sooner or later. I believed that striving for truth and justice could not be a crime. I was confirmed in this because as soon as I began to hesitate over the appropriateness of my actions, my energy would immediately diminish.

---

2 Rudyard Kipling, "If—," *Poetry Foundation*, https://www.poetryfoundation.org/poems/46473/if.

Another thing that gives us strength, which we often forget about, is the love of our family and friends. Only an extremely loyal and dedicated mother and sister could come to visit me in a remote camp, drowning in the mud of the Ural wilderness, exposing themselves to humiliating searches and the threat of subsequent persecution. Only a truly devoted wife could abandon the comforts of the Ukrainian capital and come to live with me in the snowbound and sand-blown wilderness of Kazakhstan. All this, together with the unwavering friendship of those around you, create the Archimedean fulcrum that makes it possible for you to believe that you can overturn the entire world.

I am truly grateful to God for the day that I met Mykola Matusevych. The pain that accompanied particular moments in our friendship will never surpass the gratitude I have for him. Without his strong gravitational field, I would have never entered that civic orbit that was so pivotal in my life.

Even if monks don't study theology professionally, they still come to know it perfectly because they read liturgical books daily. This metaphor comes to mind when I think of my own social development. Every member of my family, all my childhood friends, my dissident colleagues, and later my camp and internal exile associates: together they served as an open "liturgical" book from which I absorbed all the wise maxims that guide my life. May God reward them a hundredfold!

In some sense I was extremely fortunate because in those turbulent years there were moral highs and lows; there was an epicenter of goodness, which one could strive for. There was a clear picture of right and wrong. The truth was on our side and evil on the side of our opponents. This simple bipolarity fostered a certain degree of stability and the intellectual assurance that our beliefs were correct. Eventually this bipolarity was gone with the wind, and the epicenter of truth was lost. What remained was a variety of shades of gray; everything merged and was considered relative—and therefore acceptable. Consequently, truth fused with evil in a sort of pseudo-alliance, and thus evil partially took on the noble outlines of truth. During such periods, one's moral compass starts to falter, as a geodesic compass would on the North or South Pole.

It is this kind of confusion that Vladimir Putin, a former KGB agent, seeks to instill in people's souls. How many confused and zombified people have become a shield for his devilish provocations? Many of them are good illustrations of Yevhen Sverstiuk's thesis: "A society without faith and love loses its ability to differentiate between good and evil."[3] The only salvation

3 Pavlenko, "Khochu sydity v tiurmi za Ukrainu."

lies in relying on one's own intuition, just as during a blizzard a rider relies on his horse's instincts to bring him home. Harmony and order can only be brought into the world if people keep a place for God in their souls. The only hope lies in a maxim from the Greek Catholic Metropolitan Andrei Sheptytsky: "Remember that if you go contrary to God's rules, you will never be able to accomplish anything good for your country."[4]

Spiritual growth is far from just a pleasant stroll down the Champs-Élysées; along the way you might hit some painful bumps, and some sacrifices might be required. But it is this experience, lived through by many people, that can serve as fertile soil for a just social order to take root. In other words, in a free society growth is only possible in sporadic spurts. Only the impatient jumped from "feudalism" to "socialism," inevitably finding themselves mired in a quagmire of barbarism.[5]

The Genesis of the Ukrainian Dissident Movement

The regulatory mechanism of the Soviet system was not money but ideology. The ideological regime was based on one canonized version of truth, which included myriad versions of itself, each devised to fit a variety of concrete spheres of life. People joked that one could diverge from the party line only together with the party. Those who dared to outstrip the party, without its sanction, put themselves outside the bounds of the law, thereby becoming prime targets for persecution.

The Khrushchev thaw of the 1950s and 1960s shattered the façade of the unilateral perfection of official doctrine because the dismantling of the Stalin cult after his death in 1953 revealed that the party line was capable of being wrong. The *shistdesiatnyky* were the product of this ideological transformation. It also gave rise to the hope that the system could be modified and humanized. Sometimes, this was one of the criticisms that was levied against it. Yevhen Sverstiuk, one of the leading *shistdesiatnyky*, analyzed this insightfully:

> Some say that all they [the *shistdesiatnyky*] wanted was to improve on Socialism, while others claim that they wanted to alter the regime. Yet the "competent

4 *Mytropolyt Andrei Sheptyts'kyi: Dokumenty i materialy 1899–1944*, vol. 3, *Pastyrs'ki poslannia 1939–1944* (Lviv: ARTOS, 2010), 304.

5 Feudalism to socialism: that is, according to the Marxist scheme, skipping over the capitalist phase, as the Soviet Union was said to have done.

> [Soviet] organs" wrote that "beginning in 1965, on the grounds of anti-Soviet nationalist convictions, they systematically produced, safeguarded and disseminated libelous anti-Soviet documents, aiming to weaken and discredit the Soviet system." In other words, the KGB thought that the dissidents wanted to undermine and destroy the regime.[6]

The *shistdesiatnyk* movement was the forerunner of the human rights movement, which elevated the concept of spiritual and cultural freedoms to the international legal sphere. The emphasis shifted from appeals to the Soviet leadership asking them to change their governing methods to exerting civic pressure, albeit still weak at the time.

The dissidents' attempt to organize an open and legal movement that was critical of Soviet rule focused on dispelling the fear that had been institutionalized by Stalin and the KGB. The inertia of fear persisted, and respectable functionaries still "denounced" things that they had not even read, but the fear was no longer all-encompassing. There were some who openly ridiculed the system and publicly claimed that the emperor had no clothes. Such audacity seemed a complete folly, like banging your head against the wall. I remember the annoyance of those straitlaced patriots who had convinced themselves that it would be impossible to bring down the Communist system within their lifetimes. This psychological breakthrough had a crucial impact on the future resistance movement.

The genesis of the Ukrainian dissident movement was twofold, arising from the duality of the Soviet system: it was simultaneously a totalitarian country and a re-creation of the Russian Empire under the guise of the Communist Soviet Union. On the one hand, the dissident movement was an attempt to offer serious resistance to a lawless totalitarian empire, but at the same time it was also aimed at democratizing the nation. In this respect, the Ukrainian dissidents occupied the same platform as all other Soviet dissidents. During the early stages, there were some committed Communists who also joined the dissident ranks. They hoped to achieve "socialism with a human face." On the other hand, the Ukrainian dissident movement drew its inspiration from the Ukrainian struggle for national independence in the early twentieth century; it was essentially a continuation of that movement, while employing different political strategies. This differentiated the Ukrainian dissidents from their Russian counterparts,

6 Sverstiuk, *Na khvyliakh "Svobody"*, 200.

who considered the Ukrainian movement not "truly democratic" but "polluted" by national or nationalistic demands.

The Ukrainian dissident movement developed in several stages: a period of romantic hopes, prior to the first arrests in 1965; a period of sobering up and public demonstrations, before the second wave of arrests in 1972; and a period of radicalization and human rights defense efforts, between 1972 and the end of the 1980s. During the third phase, the single label "Ukrainian dissident movement" encompassed a variety of dissenters: moderate intellectuals who wanted intellectual and creative freedoms first and foremost, human rights defenders who were responding to the international movement for human rights, and political fighters who focused their efforts on struggles with the Soviet empire and striving for Ukrainian independence.

It turned out that within the resistance movement, the open, legal groups were seen by Soviet authorities as more dangerous than the underground ones. After three months of hesitation, the government systematically arrested eight of the original ten Ukrainian Helsinki Group members and exiled the other two. This only further mobilized the dissenters among the Ukrainian populace, and during the 1980s two more waves of "kamikaze" members joined the group. Among them were those who were already in prison or in internal exile, and who were thus inevitably exposed to new persecutions. Today it is known that some forty-one individuals joined the Ukrainian Helsinki Group during that decade. During its entire existence, there was only one abdication (Oles Berdnyk) and one suicide (Mykhailo Melnyk).

The Ukrainian Helsinki Group never officially announced its dissolution and continued to exist either in prison or abroad. This was true until July 7, 1988, when a declaration was made by the Ukrainian Helsinki Union (UHU) that "the Declaration of Principles of the Ukrainian Helsinki Union, as well as its auxiliary statute, was drafted by the current Ukrainian Helsinki Group (established in 1976), which hereby terminates its mandate and joins in full complement the Ukrainian Helsinki Union."[7] "Full complement" is somewhat inaccurate, however: I, for example, did not join the UHU because I considered myself a defender of human rights and wanted nothing to do with their political activities. I even said this to Viacheslav Chornovil, one of the coauthors of the declaration, with whom I had numerous discussions about this. At the same time, I did not want to be pedantic, nor did

7 "Ukrains'ka Helsins'ka Spilka. Deklaratsiia pryntsypiv," *Suchasnist* 12, no. 332 (1988): 99.

I want to block the aspirations of the majority of UHG members because I sensed they were on the brink of a new era.

Still, I am convinced that the UHG's conversion into the UHU was a product of the political situation of the day. A year later, in 1989, appearing at the founding of the Ukrainian Republican Party, Viacheslav Chornovil asserted that they were not the inheritors of the Ukrainian Helsinki Group, but that they inherited the entire national liberation movement that had existed previously, above all the *shistdesiatnyky*.

It has to be emphasized that the dissidents were not the first intrepid individuals who rose up against the lawlessness of Communist rule. The Ukrainian liberation underground had existed prior to them, people of irrefutable courage. For the average Soviet citizen, however, who was already infused with Soviet ideological propaganda, underground organizations were not convincing: "They must be enemies—otherwise why would they be in hiding?" Thus, the unconcealed public existence and activities of the Ukrainian Helsinki Group were fundamentally significant in this regard.

When Ukraine became independent in 1991, the broader Ukrainian resistance movement of the 1960s–1980s fragmented into a number of sociopolitical orientations. Those who were focused on changing the governmental system led the political opposition, thereby creating careers for themselves. A smaller segment of the former dissidents chose not to participate in any political activities, deciding instead to continue defending human rights or working in the cultural and religious sphere. Yet another group of former dissidents and prisoners, due to their age or health, abandoned active participation in civic life, only occasionally joining some selected events.

The variety of orientations chosen by the former dissidents clearly illustrates the fact that though they all opposed the imperialist, totalitarian Communist system, they differed in their vision of how Ukraine should evolve. Eventually it became obvious that this was a handicap for the former dissident movement because it splintered its potential political strength and resulted in many internal conflicts.

The dissident movement led to the destruction of another important myth. Like the Polish Solidarity movement, which broke the supposed myth that the working classes supported the peasant and worker unions, the dissident movement (in Ukraine in particular) shattered the myth that the Soviet system was the "most democratic system in the world." It put the Soviet government in a very difficult position: the documents of the Ukrainian Helsinki Group did not advocate regime change but instead insisted that the principles laid out in a document signed by the Soviet leader must be adhered to.

Not arresting the members of the UHG would have signified that the "virus of disobedience" was being allowed to infect the rest of the population. On the other hand, arresting them meant acknowledging the antidemocratic nature of the system and the authorities' persecution of dissent and freedom of speech. The government chose the second option, further tightening the screws, although their traditional claims that UHG members disseminated libelous fictions to compromise the social stability of the Soviet Union were no longer believed by anyone.

The dissidents' activities underscored and sped up the demise of the ideologically based propaganda construct that turned out to be the only thing holding the Communist system together. The whole Communist empire was essentially a politically incarnated falsehood, and therefore the word of truth, even if not formulated in strictly political parameters, had an enormous impact on the political life of the country. I personally consider Russian dissident Andrei Amalrik's explanation of what dissent is to be perfect: "[The dissidents] accomplished a remarkably simple thing: living in an enslaved nation, they started acting as free people. In so doing, they managed to alter the moral atmosphere as well as the predominant tradition within the country."[8]

This was why the dissident movement was a notable phenomenon from a spiritual perspective as well. Even though it had not been a strictly religious movement (the opinions of many UHG members differed quite a bit when it came to attitudes toward religion), it supported the religious dimension of life as a whole and defended specific religious communities who were demanding their rights. More importantly, dissidents throughout the Soviet Union were finally able to awaken people's consciousness, leading to mass protests against the regime in cities across the Soviet Union during the Gorbachev era. The Communist empire was an empire of evil and deceit, aggression, and violence, and thus the dissidents formed the front lines of spiritual opposition to the government. This connection was eventually confirmed when, having immersed themselves in political fervor, they began to slowly lose their moral capital. Only when the pedestals of these moral authorities began to be vacated did it become apparent who they previously had been.

I certainly do not expect the UHG (or dissidents in general) to receive exclusive recognition for their achievements. First of all, that would certainly

---

8 Quoted in Liudmila Alekseeva, *Dvizhenie za prava cheloveka*, http://www.memo.ru/history/diss/books/ALEXEEWA/Chapter16a.htm.

be unfair to all the others who also fought against the Communist regime. Second, tributes and final evaluations are always made by history and not individuals. Still, at least one of the dissidents' contributions is obvious even today: they fostered the understanding that there was a link between the social ills facing the population and their civic passivity. Society has to want to get healthy, and this process has to be generated from the bottom up, by people who finally snap out of their civic inertia. People with the mentality of slaves will always wait for a "good life" to be passed down to them from the top. People worthy of their civic mission change themselves individually and then transform society as a whole.

I am pleased that thanks to this contribution, the dissident movement has identified a certain spiritual genetic code that has been the hallmark of both Ukrainian Maidans, in 2004 and 2013–2014. The labels might change, but the essence remains the same: during such fleeting historic moments, people find their unique tonality, be it spontaneous or well conceived, and their language begins to strongly resonate with the fundamental principles of being.

The Values of the Dissident Movement Today

Today, the Ukrainian dissidents can be proud of their involvement in obvious national-democratic accomplishments, while also grieving the equally obvious moral losses.

Perhaps the most important value that the fighters of the resistance movement stood for was freedom: civic as well as national, creative and religious. By and large, their goals were achieved, although everything is relative. Today's level of personal freedom is certainly higher than it was during the Soviet period, but violations of human rights did not disappear altogether: they just changed their character. This is not the time to rest on the laurels of the former dissidents. I am convinced that the topic of civil liberties will no doubt resurface in full force after the current "hybrid" (or, more accurately, repugnant) Russian war against Ukraine is ended.

Another of the dissidents' goals did come to pass: national independence for Ukraine. But the umbilical cord that had tied Ukraine to Russia has not been properly severed, and therefore our de facto independence was substantially weakened, oftentimes seeming downright ornamental. But what the dissidents were not able to achieve is today being accomplished successfully by Putin. By shedding blood and sowing suffering in Ukraine, Putin's regime is both consolidating a consensus around the need for real independence and, amazingly enough, strengthening the Ukrainian nation and giving it the vigorous strength that had been lacking up to now.

This was made possible by another of the dissidents' accomplishments, namely their tireless efforts in fostering interethnic harmony and ethnic freedom for minorities. The Russian propaganda machine had to resort to grotesque lies and sow deceptive fears in order to play the separatist card in Crimea and in eastern Ukraine. Without the peaceful coexistence that thrived in independent Ukraine, and without the realization that the dignity of every citizen (regardless of ethnic origin) was protected in this country, the Revolution of Dignity would certainly not have been possible.

But perhaps the most obvious change is progress in the sphere of religious freedom, which the prisoners in the Brezhnevite camps demanded so forcefully. Because of the nearly equal strength of the various religious and confessional groups, any government attempt to favor one religion over another was met with strong resistance. In spite of ousted president Viktor Yanukovych's tireless attempts to introduce the Russian model of instrumentalizing the Orthodox Church, religious freedom managed to hold strong in Ukraine, and it is even showing signs of self-stabilization. Fortunately, it proved impossible to put the religious genie back into the bottle of the "Third Rome" and the "Russian World."[9]

Thus, the mission of the dissidents was mostly successful, although this accomplishment should not be thought to be irreversible because their achievements were never solidified through appropriate legislation or incorporated and guaranteed on a system-wide basis. And there are still two spheres where the dissident mission has failed to date: efforts to establish the rule of law and the reestablishment of personal and collective (societal) morality.

The lawlessness and amorality of the Communist period simply changed form, only to seemingly acquire even more power. The old forms of restraint failed, while new ones were never fully developed. Consequently, corruption blossomed. The Orange Revolution of 2004 temporarily gave hope for civic recovery, but it was short lived. In the ensuing years, civil society's weakness only furthered uncontrollable economic and administrative excesses and

9 Third Rome: commonly used nickname for Moscow, indicating that it was a third center of Christianity after Rome and Constantinople. Russian World (*russkii mir*): geopolitical concept that asserts a Russian civilizational space that extends beyond the bounds of the Russian Federation, embraced by the Kremlin.

abuses. The crisis of the judicial system exacerbated feelings of defenselessness. As a result, legal nihilism took hold across the country, and the national discourse quickly succumbed to clan loyalties and learned to tolerate lies and treachery.

All this brought about a predicament that is only too common in many weak democracies: those who came to power through democratic means now sought to put an end to democracy itself. During Yanukovych's rule, Ukraine degenerated to a Putinesque model of authoritarianism, and prior to the 2013–2014 Revolution of Dignity, only a very few individuals believed that the emergence of a fair and lawful system in Ukraine was ever possible.

The Revolution of Dignity was God's gift at the last possible moment. At the cost of many victims, Ukraine was able to free itself from the noose of the abhorrent "Russian World" that was tightening around its neck. The Maidan was able to demonstrate exactly what Ukraine did not want. Today, however, establishing a positive model is a bit more difficult. Putin's attack—that is, the annexation of Crimea and invasion of eastern Ukraine—stunted Ukraine at the moment of its highest ardent flight. Yet the Revolution of Dignity's potential has not been exhausted. Ukraine has realized that you have to fight for independence and the future well-being of society. In other words, it realized what during the Brezhnev era was seen as the dissidents' mute cries in the desert.

All those who opposed the Soviet system believed that the post-Communist system would certainly be wiser, more prudent, more knowledgeable, and more effective because the current Soviet system had reached rock bottom. Surely nothing could degrade further, right? But today this notion is also problematic. During the nearly three decades of Ukrainian independence, intellectuals have attempted to develop new, strategic modes of development. Yet these modes could never be implemented because of the authorities' ever-increasing insularity and unwillingness to listen. Intellect was needed by political elites, as well as the opposition, but only to serve their greedy and egotistical political goals. Thus, the lower bound of governmental degradation went even lower than had seemed imaginable.

The Maidan had the potential to improve the situation because, in principle, it could have served as a powerful social elevator, bringing in new cadres as decision-makers. It could have, but so far, that has not happened. Certainly, it would be a sin not to recognize that there have been some positive changes, but that is not enough to clean out the Augean stables of the current political elites.

It is equally difficult to trace how effective the voices of morally authoritative individuals like Yevhen Sverstiuk or any of the other dissidents have been. For the longest time, it seemed that their voices were crying hopelessly in the wilderness. Their weakness did not stem from society not accepting their assertion that the elites had become morally degraded: some polls from 2013 show that over 55 percent of respondents were convinced that moral degradation was the main reason for today's social ills in Ukraine. The real problem was that most people did not dare to follow those morally trustworthy voices. To oppose the legal and moral excesses of the ruling class when one is not convinced of basic social solidarity is akin to stepping out on a limb—going down a losing and self-destructive path.

Aleksandr Solzhenitsyn's old motto "live not by lies" also remained a dream.[10] In spite of all the accomplishments in the realm of freedom of expression, until just recently Ukraine still did not live in harmony with truth. Freedom of expression and freedom of the press were upheld by the existence of multiple political clans. Each clan presented the portion of the truth that benefited their individual interests, at the same time peppering it with a dose of falsehood. The simultaneous existence of semitruths only evoked total mistrust from the "plain folk," and it was all taken as one big lie.

When both Maidans, in 2004 and 2013–2014, had their say, their moral slogans were the million-voiced refrain of the same moral principles that had been expressed by the resistance movement, albeit on a smaller scale. This is totally normal because neither group invented any new moral dictums, instead basing them on long-established principles that formed the core of human civilization. The second Maidan prevented Ukraine from plunging over an authoritarian precipice of treachery and sent its enthusiastic participants on a path of spiritual reawakening. Still, it seems that the ultimate conversion, catharsis, and transfiguration of society as a whole still lies ahead.

In order to achieve this transformation, Ukraine needs a new, united, popular movement, one that would promote the rule of law and the moral restoration of society. One might have expected this transformation to happen as a result of the Maidan, but its impassioned participants were not able to withstand the tremendous opposition from groups they considered to be their supporters—the former opposition parties. After all, a new sociopolitical movement would jeopardize and destroy the long-standing party projects. For this reason, though the nation was practically boiling over with a

10 See, for instance, Aleksandr Solzhenitsyn, "Live Not by Lies," https://archive.org/details/LiveNotByLies/mode/2up.

desire for change, it was not capable of overcoming the twenty-three-year-old paradigm. We were therefore caught up in a vicious cycle: it was virtually impossible to enact successful reforms without actively engaging the current political elites, and they had essentially circled the wagons and overtly or covertly blocked any reforms; such reforms might land them in jail and would certainly destroy their political careers.

To sum things up, on the one hand, unlike their Polish and Czech counterparts, the Ukrainian dissidents failed to lead their country to a decisive democratic victory. Their accomplishments were temporary and unstable, and their enormous passionate energy was harnessed and taken advantage of by other political forces. On the other hand, it must be unequivocally acknowledged that the dissidents were among those who managed to firmly establish the concept of living in freedom, which will certainly be the cornerstone for any future transformations in Ukraine. Over the past decades, Ukraine has experienced a great lesson in democracy. Even if this experience is partially negative, it is still invaluable as people emerge from the totalitarian stigma and advance to the level of responsible citizens. Freedom is inconceivable without responsibility. Lacking the latter, people would only plunge back into lawlessness. Those Ukrainians who have attained this freedom without ever spiritually striving for it still have to be convinced of this; otherwise, in a drunken stupor of freedom, they will behave like children torturing a kitten without any accountability.

Thus, in spite of any shortcomings they might have, one should not lodge any accusations against the Ukrainian dissidents. It should be noted that all other "velvet" revolutions happened within a Western Roman Catholic or Protestant cultural platform. In Ukraine, on the other hand, the third wave of democratization (as per Samuel Huntington) encountered an invisible but very powerful wall, one that separates the Euro-Atlantic from the Euro-Asian cultural zones.[11] In their day, given the perceptions that were available to them at that time, the Ukrainian dissidents simply could not shatter that wall. In the future, to accomplish this, we might have to resort to new ideas and new approaches. This will not be a purely intellectual issue, but perhaps a spiritual one, as it was during the dissident movement as well. It seems we will have to finally make peace with the fact that the mills of God grind slowly.

11 See, for instance, Samuel Huntington, *The Third Wave: Democratization in the Late Twentieth Century* (Norman: University of Oklahoma Press, 1991).

The Bermuda Triangle of the Dissident Movement: Crime, Punishment, and Forgiveness

The Ukrainian political elite's inability to establish the necessary mechanisms for the rule of law in Ukraine raises an important question: after the fall of the USSR, were the dissidents right not to bring their tormentors to justice? The prevailing feeling at that time was, "We are not persecuting you, so why don't you just make a break with the past and proceed to build a democratic state?" Was this the right position?

Personally, after my liberation, I did not want to play the role of judge because I remember how I almost succumbed to the evil of Communism. In my case, therefore, positioning myself as a judge would have been morally inappropriate, and it would also have been inadequate: more than half the country would have had to be indicted. In the early 1990s, therefore, being spiritually ready to pardon, I was one of those dissidents who was not concerned with bringing our tormentors to justice.

In my 1993 essay "Repentance for Communism" (*Spokutuvannia komunizmu*) I even expressed my conclusion that "the crime of Communism" is akin to the crime of Cain, who raised his hand against his brother Abel. This crime is too great for ordinary people to judge. Indeed, the USSR was a tremendously evil country, which, like Babel, arrogantly imagined itself building a tower high enough to reach the Communist heaven, while in reality it was building bloody steps to hell. To torture and devastate, during peacetime, tens of millions of your own countrymen in the 1932–1933 Holodomor, and then to start a world war in collaboration with Hitler, obliterating Poland from the world map, going after Finland, raping the Baltic nations, sending half of Galicia to Siberia, and exiling the Crimean Tatars to Central Asia, is a horrendous betrayal, not just of the so-called Soviet nation but of humanity as a whole—on the level of Cain's crime, which can certainly never be atoned for.

For that reason, I remembered the biblical passage, "And the Lord put a mark on Cain, so that no one who came upon him would kill him." (Genesis 4:15) With this, the Lord does not remove Cain from the bounds of judgment and punishment. He merely keeps that task for himself alone. This taboo, placed on people who want to dole out punishment by themselves, is also clearly reflected in Paul's teachings: "Beloved, never avenge yourselves, but leave room for the wrath of God; for it is written, 'Vengeance is mine, I will repay, says the Lord.'" (Romans 12:19).

But have I interpreted the Bible appropriately?

In the early 1990s, having recovered from their fright, the unrepentant Communist elite managed to simply change their ideological flag without altering their core principles. This is why the lack of judgment and atonement for Communist crimes gave birth to the wrongdoings during the eras of Ukraine's first and second presidents Leonid Kravchuk (1991–1994) and Leonid Kuchma (1994–2005). The Orange Revolution of 2004 once again insisted that the rule of law be established. But President Viktor Yushchenko's lack of resolve elevated the same people who had flouted the election laws to legitimate political opponents. All this had a detrimental effect on people's ability to trust that justice would ever be restored. Eventually, the criminal elites became totally convinced that they would be able to shove anything down the people's throats, which brought Viktor Yanukovych and his outrageously criminal government to power in 2009. It seems that there is no end to this, as we seem unable to avoid the same pitfalls. It stands to reason that crime can only be relegated to the past if it is prosecuted and atoned for. Unrepented crime returns with ever new tragedies. Apparently, we dissidents did not factor this in.

To name another characteristic mistake: in 2005, Lviv residents objected to the fact that none of the criminals who had perpetrated the election fraud that led to the Orange Revolution had been convicted. President Yushchenko answered their frustration, saying, "I thought that all of you in Lviv were Christians!" His sentiment only seems to confirm that we don't know the basic principles of the rule of law, nor the logic of Christianity. Forgiveness is not a synonym for a lack of accountability. The lack of accountability makes crime more attractive and the perpetrator more impudent. Not only does he not respect a victim who fails to punish him, but he also looks down on him, regarding his forgiveness as weakness. Spineless all-forgiveness has nothing to do with Christian forgiveness. When Pope John Paul II visited Ali Ağca, the Turkish terrorist who attempted to assassinate him in 1981, in prison, he forgave him for his attempt on his life, but he did not seek to get him released from prison.[12] Christian forgiveness is a moral act first of all, and it does not overrule the rule of law, nor does it override its power. It purifies the soul, but it does not get you out of prison. Fair punishment for a crime is not retaliation, but rather the essential cleansing of society from toxins and other waste that is contaminated with violence. Without such cleansing, a society becomes nothing but one gigantic cancerous growth.

---

12 Ağca shot and wounded John Paul II on May 13, 1981, at the Vatican. The motives for the assassination attempt are still disputed.

The real beneficiary of forgiveness is not the recipient, but the one who grants it. By forgiving, a person liberates himself from the rule of vengeance. Punishing a criminal is necessary not just to placate the feeling of revenge but also to cut short the chain of evil, as an unpunished criminal might bring more suffering to other people.

South Africa has managed to almost perfectly merge both principles: the rule of law and Christian forgiveness. Apartheid was demolished not by any special deals made under the table (thereby absolving the chief perpetrators of any accountability) but by an open dialogue with the people, which resulted in their awareness that a total purification was essential. A Truth and Reconciliation Commission was formed, including the most trustworthy individuals of impeccable moral standing, and this commission heard testimonies and voluntary confessions and contrition from those whose conscience was burdened with crimes. The sheer fact of such heartfelt repentance liberated a person from any future punitive measures, whereas refusal to do so indicated that the person remained dangerous to society and therefore had to be subjected to prosecution and trial.

The success of the South African commission was based on the creation of an effective legal mechanism for purifying people's souls. By willingly acknowledging their crimes and receiving absolution from this authoritative body, individuals no longer had to worry about their safety but could now join the ranks of those who were on the side of good. It was no longer necessary for people to maintain the criminal system of apartheid in a panic and at any cost because their past no longer hung over them: now they had the moral right to start again with a clean slate. Anyone who has experienced the joy of clearing one's conscience understands the spiritual energy that is released at the same time.

Taking this into consideration, it is astonishing to consider how inadequate Ukraine has been in this regard. Even after the second Maidan in 2013–2014, many blatant criminals who had openly abused the nation and cynically mistreated the people did not repent; in fact, they are now making a renewed attempt to neutralize the cleansing effect of the Maidans so that they can continue their depraved abuses. A new system threatens them with the prospect of being uncovered and having their loot confiscated, so they are trying to hang on to the old system with all their might, finding new justifications to safeguard themselves and their families.

So, we find ourselves again at the edge of a precipice.

As a society, we need to revisit the question of accountability, not only for the big fish but also for the so-called little people who in turn abused others, mostly without even being aware of it, considering injustice as a regular part of life. Today, their conscience lies dormant, and they resort to the slave's refrain: "Well, we just did what the law said at that time!" In order to understand this mindset better, I will cite one moment from Valery Marchenko's life. When he returned to Kyiv in the early 1980s after his first stint in the camps, Valery had to get treatment for his kidney disease. Sandra Fappiano, an Italian Amnesty International activist who had become good friends with him through their correspondence, was eager to help. She did everything she could to get a permit for Valery to come to Italy for medical treatment. Valery filled out all the appropriate documents, all the while suspecting that he might not be able to see Italy after all. Talking with my relatives in Kyiv during the short time between his two arrests, he told them with some bitterness that his path would not take him to the West but most likely "out there," as he pointed nebulously toward the East.

This indeed was what the clerk in the visa office told him indignantly: "You should be put in jail and not try to go to the West!" She may well have been someone's loving mother and wife. She most likely has a clear conscience today because she did not violate any rules. After all, she was only following the generally accepted party policy toward this "vicious anti-Soviet criminal." Nonetheless, she was obviously a voluntary participant in this crime. There was certainly no law that required her to deprive a gravely ill person of the opportunity to get medical care and the chance to save his life. There were no laws that would compel the KGB agents who had Valery's life in their hands to steal the invitations for treatment that Valery had received from Italy or just to discard Sandra's harmless letters, which were truly compassionate spiritual treasures. They did this simply out of their own malicious will and their depraved sadism.

As a devout person, I am convinced that even though they never repented and skirted any responsibility here on earth, they will most certainly be judged appropriately in Heaven. But how can one convince the whole nation that these millions of "little people," focused on their own personal gain or security, just look the other way when confronted with obvious evil? They don't think twice about forging election ballots, bribing a judge, altering school records, knowingly selling dangerous medications, and so on. They are the malignant cells making up the "cancerous growth" that prevents society from healing. Their small crimes, which they don't even consider crimes, become a reliable prop for the powerful criminals who are proud of their ability to neutralize the cleansing effects of any Maidan.

Figure C.1. The cover of Valery and Sandra's book published in Ukraine.

Thus, returning to the question raised earlier, I am compelled to acknowledge that my attitude as an all-forgiving dissident was partially misguided. Yet I still think that my unwillingness to see my tormentors behind bars is morally justifiable. On its own, this does not contradict the rule of law. But there is a legitimate qualifying countermeasure to this position: first of all, the perpetrators' evil actions must be qualified as criminal, and then the perpetrators must be convicted by an unbiased court. Only then, with the will of the community, might they be pardoned without being punished, if their contrition is deemed sincere. In that case, I believe, neither the concept of the rule of law nor the Christian theory of forgiveness would be compromised.

Communism on Trial

Life compels me to add this concluding section, which also indirectly deals with the dissidents' resistance to the Communist regime. As I write this, our young men are perishing in eastern Ukraine so that I could write these lines in peace and quiet and ponder the conundrum of this cruel turn of our history: Putin's cynical aggression against Ukraine.

In the past few years, most Ukrainians have come to interpret Ukrainian history in a new light, starkly realizing that Kyiv and Moscow are somehow tied together in a fatal and mutually exclusive interdependence. The elevation of one seems to inevitably lower the other, and vice versa. Even Prince Andrei Bogoliubsky of the Vladimir-Suzdal principality instinctively felt this back in the twelfth century and cruelly devastated the princely Grand Duchy of Kyiv.[13] Then, in the ensuing centuries, it became Moscow's ongoing mission to impede Ukraine's independent development, making sure that it would never rise as a sovereign star to bask in its own glory. Hopefully, in the current geopolitical environment, this era is slowly coming to an end; unlike in the past, Ukraine might even have a fair chance to emerge as an independent player. Even if this were the only explanation for Russian aggression, Ukraine's sacrifices would be totally justifiable, and they certainly deserve countrywide recognition and appreciation.

Still, it would be an oversimplification to consider today's aggression against Ukraine only in the context of an abiding conflict between Kyiv and

13 By the twelfth century, the previously dominant Kyiv principality was challenged for supremacy within Rus' by the principality of Vladimir-Suzdal, under Bogoliubsky's leadership.

Moscow. Putin considers himself a world player, and Ukraine is not his main prize but rather a secondary foe that he has to crush before he can face off against his principal adversary in a duel. Following the classic rules of mimesis (imitating one's rival), Russia is constantly competing with the country that serves as its example and whose actions Russia tries shamelessly, though hopelessly, to ape: the United States of America.

Perhaps this is why all of Angela Merkel's current efforts are bound to fail.[14] It is virtually impossible to appease Putin as long as Ukraine is independent. He will most certainly violate any peaceful agreement because he sees conquering Ukraine as the stepping-stone to the bigger prize he is pursuing.

In any case, all of Putin's efforts are doomed because his strategic goal is to reestablish the former bipolar world, in which Russia played a major role in its opposition to the West. But Russia's role in this standoff is already slowly but surely being assumed by China. In contrast to the Kremlin, Chinese political elites understand patience very well, so time is on their side. Putin's current elevated visibility, which has thrown off the balance of the world's status quo and heightened its military vigilance, is akin to a school experiment of electro-magnetic polarity, where the light shines the brightest just before the electro-magnetic cycle is broken and the light finally goes out.

There is yet another sphere of analysis in which the Russian-Ukrainian conflict looks like a prism within a larger mosaic, where the future demise of Putin's Russia is not only inevitable but morally justified. This is the domain of values. Putin and his clique are the quintessence of the antispiritual metastasis that, it might seem, is triumphantly spreading across the whole world today. We in Ukraine have already encountered a whole cohort of these degenerates, who were delirious in their unchecked efforts to run circles around us "defenseless kittens." Putin's ambitions hinge on becoming the leader of this "successful new order," which aims to destroy the "totally rotten" world of Old Europe. Putin's principles, like those of his chosen elites, are based on deceit, imitation, falsifications, spiritual devastation, untrustworthiness, treachery, aggression, violence, annexation, gas and trade blackmail, theft, and assassinations. This list could go on forever, turning the basic principles of civilization inside out, but all of them without exception are self-evident indications of evil.

The West is afraid to demonize any government in this way because in the world of "ordinary" conflicts, excessive demonization by an adversary is

14 A reference to the German chancellor's desire to broker a peace deal that would resolve the war in eastern Ukraine.

usually the main barrier to reconciliation. This is the reason Western politicians, amazingly, continue to dogmatically apply the current politically correct templates, stubbornly refusing to acknowledge that they are dealing with representatives of incarnate and triumphant evil. They all lack President Reagan's unwavering courage to call the Soviet Union the "Evil Empire." Today, the world stands face to face with a criminal power that revels in its ability to fool all the dunces—a category that, according to their former criminal standards, includes everyone who lives according to the principles of civilized benevolence. This is where sheer evil serves as the main guarantee of its own inevitable success, and the greater that evil is, and the more surprising, the more certain will be its success.

In the mid-twentieth century, there were two frightful dinosaurs, two giant incarnations of evil, who both decided to try to alter God's earth in the "image and likeness of a tailor's dummy," as Bruno Schulz called it.[15] Then everything happened as in a child's riddle: "A" and "B" were sitting on a bench. "A" fell, then "B" disappeared, so what remained?

The Nazis fell, and their collaborator, the Stalinist regime—the regime Hitler started the Second World War with and that was ignominiously thrown out of the League of Nations—seemed to have "disappeared." What was left behind was "the conqueror of Nazism, savior of all mankind, the hope of the persecuted and the hungry, the peace-loving and life-giving Soviet Union."[16]

No wonder Putin has made victory in the Second World War a dominant event in the narrative of Russia's history, which no one has dared to scrutinize. Otherwise, one might analyze the joint Nazi and Soviet parades held in Brest-Litovsk, which they had conquered in 1939 in a criminal joint venture. Then one might ask the same question that Polish philosopher Leszek Kołakowski posed: "Should a prisoner languishing in the camps of Vorkuta [major Gulag site in far northern Russia] really have felt happy that he was able to avoid a similar fate in the camps of Dachau?"[17]

15 See, for instance, Bruno Schulz, "Manekiny," in *Sklepy cynamonowe* (Warsaw: Rój, 1933).

16 That is, the postwar, post-Stalin Soviet Union presented itself as a totally different entity with a new agenda. The quotation marks here are meant to exemplify the rhetoric employed, rather than a specific quote.

17 Leshek Kolakovskii [Leszek Kołakowski], "Otvet Alenu Bezansonu," *Novaia Pol'sha*, no. 3 (1999).

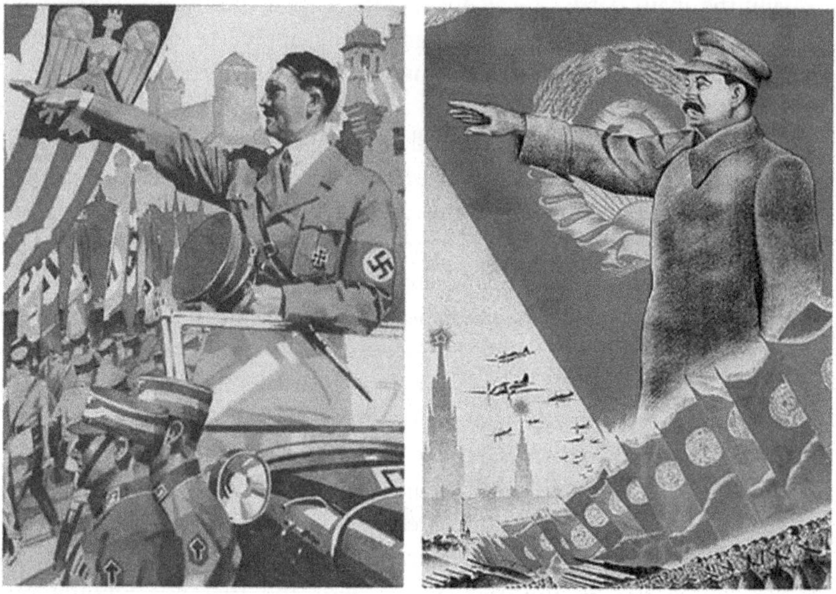

Figure C.2. Nazi and Communist posters.

Behind the fabrications of this truly great conquest lies the mystery of the greatest falsification of the twentieth century, which carries immense moral losses. The 1945 Yalta Conference led to a massive injustice: a double standard in evaluating the criminal behavior of two totalitarian regimes. The Nazi regime was publicly condemned, while Communist crimes were kept hidden for security reasons and were never brought to account, legally or morally. The official European narrative of history became one sided: the Nazi regime was considered the "ultimate evil," while Communist crimes were considered a Slavic aberration from a potentially ideal concept, that of communism. In other words, who cares that there might be some dark spots on an otherwise sparkling external façade? After all, they did help bring down the Nazi regime, and the enemy of my enemy is my friend.

As a result, the world heard of the suffering of the victims of the Gestapo, but it failed to pay any attention to all the pain inflicted by the KGB on millions of victims. The tragedies of Auschwitz, Treblinka, Buchenwald, and Guernica became classic examples of crimes against humanity, while Solovki, the Holodomor, the Siberian Gulag, and the crimes at Katyń were seen as regrettable events which are best not mentioned.[18] It was an irony of history: apocalyptic evil came to be seen as the savior of mankind.

But sooner or later that clandestine evil had to emerge as the seed for a new world conflict. The demonic evil power at the core of the Communist system had to sooner or later metastasize; the world had to reap what it had sown. Today, if a former Nazi were to become chancellor of Germany, the West would consider this a sign that the core of civilization was crumbling. But when a former KGB chief became president of the Russian Federation, the West, in all its political correctness, didn't even blink. As a matter of fact, has anyone in the West ever recognized the KGB as a criminal, terrorist organization? Eventually, the West did not pay any heed to the fact that Russia's wounded pride grew ever more reminiscent of the "ruffled feathers" of Nazi Germany, which felt itself downgraded by the Versailles Conference of 1919. The West was not at all concerned that the old Nazi doctrine of "defending our native speakers abroad" was beginning to acquire more and more power in Moscow.[19] The West did not properly evaluate the war in Georgia in 2008 and was not concerned by Russia's opposition to Ukraine joining NATO, as seen, for instance, in Putin's efforts to dissuade NATO from offering Ukraine membership at the 2008 Bucharest Summit.[20] Russia's attempts to control the entire post-Soviet space seemed legitimate and justified by the West. No wonder Putin considered the reestablishment of the Soviet Union to be totally justifiable and legitimate as well. The annexation of Crimea is on the conscience of those European politicians who chose to openly and categorically disregard the similarities between it and the annexation of

---

18 Solovki: early Soviet prison camp on the Solovetsky Islands in the White Sea, built on the site of a former monastery. Katyń: series of mass executions of Polish military officers carried out by the NKVD in the Katyń forest in April–May 1940.

19 Protecting the interests of Russian speakers in Ukraine was one of the justifications given for the 2014 annexation of Crimea and invasion of eastern Ukraine.

20 War in Georgia: While many countries condemned Russia's behavior in the 2008 Russo-Georgian war, there were no significant international consequences imposed on Russia. Bucharest Summit: Ukraine was under consideration for membership, but following Putin's visit to the summit to take part in bilateral NATO-Russia talks, NATO officially welcomed Ukraine's "Euro-Atlantic aspirations" but did not offer the country membership. See "Bucharest Summit Declaration," NATO, April 3, 2008, https://www.nato.int/cps/en/natolive/official_texts_8443.htm.

the Sudetenland before the Second World War. It is inevitable that a clash between politically correct European politicians and the newly regrouped KGB *Übermenschen* will happen sooner or later. The European culture of compromise and negotiation is fertile ground for the meticulously groomed and methodically trained KGB to bring about a crackdown and implement divisive tactics to achieve victory.

Thus, the long-forgotten Communist crimes are beginning to pulse through current European history, and today they have matured into new tragedies. As long as Communist crimes are not acknowledged, brought to justice, and finally repented for, as long as the still-looming legacy of the bloody KGB is not brought before a jury, any hopes for peace and reconciliation are futile. Perhaps "soft power" is indeed stronger than "hard power," but to this point all we have is "deceitful power."

Obviously, at this stage, any possibility of condemning Communism is, as a Polish proverb puts it, "the wishful thinking of a severed head" (*marzenie ściętej głowy*). The West will try to avoid the possibility of a Third World War at any cost, betraying their basic values and principles, but in so doing they are actually bringing this war that much closer to their doorstep. After all, Europe has its own favorite blind spots, and we are therefore doomed to witness many more fatal mistakes.

Nevertheless, the twenty-first century can be successful if it brings all the twentieth-century accounts to a close and does not allow them to poison our world today. This requires a total catharsis—that is, not only bringing all Communist crimes to justice but also seeing to it that they are atoned for. Repentance is not necessarily a political act but, above all, a spiritual one. Its rules are unique. This is how Russian writer Vladimir Sorokin described it with regard to his own country:

> Repentance is only possible after a total shake-up. It is not a medicine that can be administered. I personally think that in Russia, voluntary repentance is not possible. Before you can repent, you first have to get a good jolt. Only after you get a bump on the head and you rub it, asking yourself what you did wrong, will repentance be possible. In order to repent, you have to first see yourself from the side, without any embellishments. . . . We are not talking about a single person, but about a large country. The country has to see itself objectively from the side, then acknowledge its sins, and only then, after a major catastrophe, can it repent. Who will repent when everything is hunky-dory?[21]

21 Vladimir Sorokin, "Postsovetskii chelovek razocharoval bol'she, chem sovetskii," interview by Andrei Arkhangel'skii, *Kommersant*, August 17, 2015, http://kommersant.ru/doc/2786007.

I would like to have Martin Luther King's ability to foresee that a society that once wouldn't even allow a black person to enter a white café, would eventually open the doors of the White House to the first black president. I will therefore nurture my own version of his wonderful prophetic phrase: "I have a dream." I am convinced that the day will come when what is currently unattainable will happen:

1. Communist crimes against humanity will receive their day in court, and the nature of the Communist evil will be brought to light. The illusions and temptations that inevitably lead to the sin of Communism will be uncovered, as with the sin of Nazism in the past.
2. Putin and his clique, along with their satellites like Viktor Yanukovych, will be brought to justice by an international tribunal for their attempts to reinstate their previous Communist evil and for trying to destroy the foundations of Western civilization.
3. All former Communist countries, especially Russia, will experience their own catharsis and purge themselves of their Communist "demons," collectively acknowledging their mistake in supporting and celebrating the Communist beast. Western Europe will also have to go through a similar catharsis because of its own infatuation with Communism, which only supported and legitimized the apocalyptic beast that was raging in Eastern Europe.
4. After this shared repentance, the former Communist countries will cease to bear responsibility for their bloody past.
5. Only then will the blessed day arrive when spiritually cleansed nations will don the purified garments of Communist victims and achieve that which only victims have the right to do: to forgive.

It is only by collectively judging Communist crimes, jointly acknowledging their collective blame for celebrating this evil, and collectively pardoning each other for the evil that they perpetrated in a state of Communist delirium, that civilized nations can attain final victory over Communism and thus transform their formerly bloody lands into places of true reconciliation and benevolence.

Appendix

The Gospel According to a Holy Fool

I dedicate this to my Mama and my sister Nadiika,
for being the first ones to teach me the power of Love

In the beginning, there was the word, and the word was false, and the word itself became falsehood, dissolving in a black stain on the pure parchment of the human soul.

In the dwelling where Jehovah reigned, there settled betrayal and scorn, anger and deception.

And the word became flesh, and dwelled among us, filled with malevolence and contempt, and we saw its glory and we luxuriated in the exquisite fruits of this glory.

The word became a blade, which cuts up a heart sooner than Cain's knife, and it sprouted intoxicating weeds in sacred life, and became suspended in the air in a myriad of viruses, malignant and hostile.

And evil, begotten with the first foul word, became the Law of Life. And people began to curse with the word, no longer understanding that it is God.

I am a holy fool.

My lineage begins with Moses, and the rocks which the angered Hebrews hurled at him are my undeniable, bitter, exclusive heritage.

When my Lord rests, I—His most loyal guardian—go against the treacherous servants of God, for whom the seventh day is a time for blasphemy and ridicule.

I am he who wants to see those who are distant as my neighbors, though to my neighbors I am infinitely distant.

Not knowing with how many fingers I should cross myself, I paint the Crucifixion in my mind and try it on myself.

I am the Knight of the Absurd, because in every monster I see Goliath. Encased in prison like the brain in a skull, I hover over the pain-racked world with unfettered thoughts.

I see the stigma of death on the face of my planet and I beg God that even when the worst happens, He will send Earth the fate of the resurrected Lazarus.

I am the clown at the fair. I insult people with my noisy insolence, while in my heart I create the Gospel of Forgiveness.

In the moldy prison walls I feel the current of universal pain, and so I laugh like a buffoon, so that the prison guard does not see that I hurt, too.

Forced behind bars so that I might not lay an anti-government mine, I am preparing such a charge of Love, against which even Satan himself is helpless.

❧

My life is an uninterrupted Last Judgment over me. In every person with whom fate unites me are personified my virtue and my sin. I shall give praise to a good person—and good shall be given unto me. I shall not disdainfully push away the spiritual cripple, but shall forgive his sins with an exceedingly kind word—and my sin will be forgiven me. There is no judgment more frightening than when it is unnoticeable: after that, there may be time left only for repentance.

You, oh God, sent me into the very stronghold of universal Evil, where it is hardest to forgive, where anger and desire for revenge are the moral law of human justice. So then, make me the most foolish among fools, so that my chest does not burn from shame when I forgive harm inflicted on a weaker person.

❧

Truth cannot be wielded like a sword. As long as there is a sword, it will continue to be thrust upon new incrusted shields of deception. Truth, when it is a sword, cannot conquer a twelve-headed Dragon: its heads will grow back, and the Dragon, like a tree in spring whose dead branches are cut off, will become even stronger.

Christ's scourge, with which he chased the merchants from the temple, more than any kind of relics, attests to His real earthly existence.

The world has sharpened thousands of steel truths, yet it is dying from the demographic explosion of lies. The earth is seething with dragon heads, decapitated as well as fresh—cunning and insatiable.

And one shall never conquer the power of the Serpent, unless one becomes a holy fool.

Wipe off your face, or better yet, from your heart, the Satanic mask of hatred and contempt, for your truth will only become God's truth when it is cultivated with Love.

❧

Kyiv and Jerusalem.

Two rocks on which stands the altar of my faith.

Two acupunctural points on the ailing body of the Earth.

Two eyes with which my planet gazes at God.

The more zealously unrepentant Jerusalem prays to its God, the more clearly stand out its fatal stigmata—the crucifixion of Jesus.

The deeper the sinful stamp of the Antichrist gnaws into the flesh of my Kyiv, the more luminously the pure image of the coming Christ forms below it.

I stand on the shore of the Slavic sea and I see off on their long journey the sons of Israel, who rush at the call of Rachel, in order to fulfill their eternal destiny. Good luck to you—and I apologize that the tempestuous swaying of my cradle produced in your heart such an unwise *pogrom* pain. I shall sing sad Ukrainian songs for you—maybe, on the way, one of you will remember my blood-drained Ukraine.

Live according to your law, but never let the temptation overcome you to avenge your enemy by taking out his eye for the Old-Testament tooth knocked out in battle. Farewell, I shall not go with you, for I am the son of this land, which could not help but offer its right-bank cheek, when its left turned red from the diabolical slap.

❧

Russia! When you created your fairy tale "The Frog Princess," were you aware that you were incorporating your own history into it? How were you able to decipher the verdict of Providence, according to which you were destined to become like this creature which is repugnant to mankind, seeking love in vain, sometimes demanding it with hatred, and finally finding that insane prince who would love and free you?

I am not a prince, O Russia, I am only a holy fool. Not having found my spouse yet, I now choose you, bewitched by the evil witches of your forests and bogs, and condemned to forever wear the cancerous skin of contempt and arrogance. Let it not be your shroud, frog princess! Give me your hand, slimy from the encrusted filth of sins, and we shall walk into the church below the miraculous Fatima sky, where the Lord Himself will marry us.

—Our Father! In the name of Love, which you bequeathed us, deviate from the established canon and do not ask those present whether they know of anything that would bar this marriage. I know everything they will say. I even know what at this moment millions of my innocently martyred compatriots would say. But I implore You, strengthen my belief that beneath these rotting sores beats a pure and good heart; send the gift of wisdom when anger flares up; let my hand never jerk away with disgust.

A small part of Your own Self, O Lord, which you placed into this people, is now in the dungeon—I want to come unto it.

—My servant, O a Holy Fool, do you take my servant Russia to be your wedded wife, of your own free will?

—Yes.

—My servant, Russia, do you take my servant, a Holy Fool, as your wedded husband, of your own free will?

— . . .

❧

At the very moment that the croaking police wagon was taking me from the Kyiv isolation cell to court, I glimpsed the gold cross of St. Sophia through a small chink in the metal armor. It sailed by in a few seconds against a background of indifferent playful clouds, but I understood that I was seeing it for the first time: imprisoned, so that I would crawl forever, I finally learned to look upward.

Thank You, my Ukrainian Infinite Wisdom! You understood better than all of vain and stupefied Kyiv how much I needed Your Christ's blessing in the time of the reveling of injustice.

Send me once again a minute of this sweet aching, and give me your blessing to preach to my friends behind bars.

❧

And a large circle gathers, and it is joined by the wronged and injured, by the angry and the thirsty for revenge, in order to judge the one who stands in the middle—to judge the Antichrist himself.

In everyone's hand there is a stone: for so it is written in the law of human justice.

Only there is no one to say, "Let him among you who is without sin be the first to throw a stone at him."

I know that none of you will avenge your enemy when he lies vanquished before you. But what anger sears your souls when a rapacious mocking smile plays on the face of the Beast! I am convinced that only through forgiveness can the eternal chain of reincarnations of Evil be broken. Cast the stone from your hand: it is from the Evil One, Satan's coat of arms is carved on it.

Do not kill the Devil, for you will not be worthy of your own salvation. Our younger brothers view us like the Beast who stands inside the circle. Have you not read this in the eyes of the humble creatures which you carelessly take to the slaughter? Have you not seen in the zoo's jail cells, created for our pleasure, the torment of the free animal, who desires the same thing as yourselves—freedom? In the constant search for truth, have we not forgotten how to see nature, except through the researcher's scalpel? Every one of us has the ignominious stamp of three sixes on our forehead.

Do not kill Lucifer, the carrier of light, in whose moonlight rays we cried and loved, do not extinguish the lantern with which we recognized and contemplated the world.

Do not lift your hand against the teenager who rebelled against his father: the first male seed will remove his rebellion and insolence.

Do not curse the Devil for the sufferings you have endured. To him you owe the blessing of catharsis, for he weeded the sown field, so that Goodness could blossom with abundance.

Do not kill the Antichrist, do not cut the sinful womb: only in it can be fulfilled the promised Second Coming of Christ!

❧

Silence in the cell. The peephole blinked sleepily: the guard did not hear me. The sun plummeted to the ground and broke into tragic squares. The little spider on the wall—the prisoner's only consolation, an eternal promise of joyous changes.

It is sad in this world. Everyone is constructing his own Tower of Babel: even my native language coming from my lips is perceived as the ridiculous prattle of a foreigner and does not reach their hearts.

The Word is dead. Long live the Word!

I become the miraculous seed of chlorophyll in order to speak in the language of Light – the language of sunny Esperanto.

The universe is geocentric—you were mistaken, Copernicus! In the tiny diamond granule, bordered by heavenly giants, grows the might of David—Earth will be king!

At a certain time, all the worlds, all the spiritual fields will close in on the soul of one person—who of us can say for certain "It will not be me?"

We so did not want to be called servants of God. Why then is servitude to Satan so sweet?

A battle won in the soul is a stellar moment for the Universe, the center of crystallization of Goodness.

Without forgiveness, humankind does not have a future.

A scatter-brained mind will not fertilize far-away worlds.

Synthesized in the heart, it will shed the impotent armor.

And it will itself become God.

For ever and ever.

Amen.

August 1982, Kuchino Village

Translated by Tatianna Gajecky-Wynar

Index

Page numbers in italics indicate illustrations; those with a t *indicate tables.*